KIRGH

Tashkent

Ferghana Valley

Marǧelan

STAN

Kašgar

CHINA

TAJIKISTAN

SOCIALIST REPUBLICS

Vanč R.

Dushanbe

PAMIR MTS.

Surxandarya R.

Faizabad

Waxan

Panj R.

Badaxšan

Mazar-i Šarif

Katağan

Kokča R.

stan

HINDU KUSH MTS.

PAKISTAN

Salang Pass

KOH-I BABA MTS.

Kohistan

Bamian

Lağman

Khyber Pass

Istalif

Kabul

Jalalabad

Peshawar

NORTH

Mašreqi

Logar Valley

Northern Afghanistan
and Surrounding Areas

0   200   400 km

Music
in the Culture of
Northern
Afghanistan

VIKING FUND PUBLICATIONS IN ANTHROPOLOGY

Number Fifty-four   Colin M. Turnbull, *Editor*

Music in the Culture of Northern Afghanistan

MARK SLOBIN

Published for The Wenner-Gren Foundation for Anthropological Research Inc.

The University of Arizona Press   Tucson, Arizona

About the Author . . .

MARK SLOBIN'S interest in the ethnomusicology of Central Asia led him to analyze Soviet source material *(Kirgdiz Instrumental Music)* and to edit and translate (with Greta Slobin) the basic Soviet text on the subject *(Central Asian Music),* before undertaking fieldwork among the Central Asian peoples of northern Afghanistan. His initial musicological interest moved toward ethnography with consideration of the question of music as part of ethnic boundary maintenance. He has begun research in another area of interest, the folk music of Eastern European Jews. In 1974 Slobin was a member of the Board of Directors and chairman of the Ethics Committee of the Society for Ethnomusicology.

Photographs by author, except where otherwise noted

THE UNIVERSITY OF ARIZONA PRESS

I.S.B.N. 0-8165-0498-9
L.C. No. 74-31998

For Greta, Bibijan

Contents

ILLUSTRATIONS

Contents

MAPS

TABLES

Acknowledgments

The present study is the outgrowth of three trips to Afghanistan: a fifteen-month stay in 1967-68 on a Foreign Area Fellowship of the American Council of Learned Societies and Social Science Research Council; a three-week visit in 1971 under a grant from the Wenner-Gren Foundation for Anthropological Research and the Lloyd Postdoctoral Fellowship of the University of Michigan; and a one-month sojourn in 1972 under a Summer Faculty Research Grant of Wesleyan University.

I am extremely grateful to a large number of kind and sensitive people who furthered my research. In Afghanistan, I would like to single out Rawan Farhadi, patron saint to visiting scholars, Ġulam Saxi Taymuree and family. Saduddin Shpoon and family, Šukria and Azim Road, the Alizo family, Abdul Wahab Madadi, Faizullah Aimaq and Allah Berdi Surxi of Radio Afghanistan, Zia Xoja, Badruddin Šarafi, and Šah Mansur Elhami. In the Soviet Union, I would like to thank Faizullah Karomatov for extraordinary help, along with Messrs. Rakhimov, Pulatov, Jaffarov, and Petrosian, all of Tashkent, Nizam Nurjanov in Dushanbe, and numerous other helpful people in Ashkhabad, Frunze, Moscow, and Leningrad, especially Viktor Sergeevich Vinogradov. Among Western friends, Micheline and Pierre Centlivres, Nancy and Richard Tapper, the Leon Poullada family, and Lorraine and Tom Sakata deserve special gratitude. A particular type of thanks goes to William P. Malm, my graduate advisor, without whom I would never have become an ethnomusicologist.

It is, of course, the musicians of northern Afghanistan to whom I owe the greatest debt; they were almost unfailingly kind, hospitable, and patient.

Note on Transliteration and Translation

Transliteration of all Russian words and of cyrillicized minority-group proper names follows the Library of Congress system, with *j* used instead of *dzh*. All translations from Russian are mine.

In the transliteration of Persian, *a* stands for the English sound in *a*lms, *ā* for that in *a*wful; this distinction is noted only at the first occurrence of a term, except in transcriptions of song texts. For Persian, colloquial pronunciations are generally given rather than standard literary forms.

As I am not a speaker of Uzbek or Turkmen, the transliteration employed is an ad hoc system based mostly on the individual singer's pronunciations. In the case of Turkmen I am grateful to William G. Irons for advice.

Some ethnic and geographic terms are given in forms long accepted in English — e.g., Kazakh, Afghanistan.

Introduction: Aims and Scope
of the Inquiry

The point of departure for the present inquiry into the role of music in the culture of northern Afghanistan is a statement of Fredrik Barth's:

Ethnic categories provide an organizational vessel that may be given varying amounts and forms of content in different socio-cultural systems. They may be of great relevance to behaviour, but they need not be; they may pervade all social life, or they may be relevant only in limited sectors of activity. There is thus an obvious scope for ethnographic and comparative descriptions of different forms of ethnic organization. (Barth 1969:14)

The Afghan North, as delineated in the ethnographic outline below, is a multiethnic society many centuries old. Groups representing various branches of Iranian and Turco-Mongol languages and cultures coexist in an area that has also been a major crossroads of Asia for several thousand years. In Afghan Turkestan the steppe allows for broad interrelation of ethnic groups within roughly the same ecological niche, while the Pamirs to the east preserve vest-pocket populations speaking highly archaic languages and living in considerable isolation even today.

The aim of the present study is to focus on a single cultural trait — music — as it illuminates the patterns of interethnic contact in the North. A dictum of Barth's, that ". . . ethnic boundaries are maintained in each case by a limited set of cultural features" (1969:38), points to the possibility that music may be one of those features of social interrelationship that reflect underlying patterns of ethnic boundary maintenance. Izikowitz (1969:141) has defined three categories of social and cultural differences that go into the making of ethnic boundaries: "(1) differences in technique of expression, whether it be in language, ritual action, gestures, etiquette or customs . . . (2) value systems . . . intimately connected with techniques of expression; (3)

self-identification." Music, as a technique of cultural expression, easily
fits Izikowitz's first two categories, and by implication is included in
the third one as well, since groups may use music as one means of
self-identification.

In following the approach outlined above, this study presents two
kinds of data: (1) descriptive information about the music of the
North, including a comprehensive listing of musical instruments and
an analytical presentation of genres and styles, and (2) an examination
both of the musical traits (attitudes, repertoires, instruments) that are
shared by two or more ethnic groups, and of those discrete elements
that occur in the music of only one ethnic group and thus mark off
music subcultures. The major peoples of the area share in a joint
pattern of musical behavior to a greater or lesser extent, yet each
displays characteristic individual features of musical life. In presenting
the resulting mosaic of practices in northern Afghanistan I shall draw
on data from two crucial adjacent areas: (1) Soviet Central Asia to
the north, where nearly all the same ethnic groups (and in some cases
the same families) live, and (2) the rest of Afghanistan to the south
and west, as well as neighboring Iranian Xorasan, where there is a
good deal of cultural overlap.

Areas such as the Afghan North are not rare in the Near East;
many regions are occupied by a multiplicity of ethnic groups operating
with a high degree of multilingualism and common religious (if not
sectarian) affiliation within a relatively undifferentiated ecological niche.
To cite Barth once again:

. . . nomad, peasant and city dweller can belong to the same ethnic
group in the Middle East; where ethnic boundaries persist they depend
on more subtle and specific mechanisms mainly connected with the
unfeasibility of certain status and role combinations. (1969:26)

The anthropologists Richard and Nancy Tapper have succinctly summarized the way in which such "subtle mechanisms" work in northern
Afghanistan: "criteria actually used for maintaining ethnic boundaries
vary with the boundary and the group" (1973:p.c.*). It is my hope
that the survey of musical attitudes, repertoires, and instruments presented in the following chapters may illuminate some of those criteria,
as observed in the period 1967–1972.

---

*P.c.: personal communication.

THE GEOGRAPHIC AND ETHNIC SETTING

The great mountain ranges of Afghanistan — Paropamisus, Koh-i Bābā, Hindu Kush — form one giant system defining the backbone of the country (front endsheet). By its presence or absence, this mountain system defines the basic areas of the country. To the north, south, and west lie large tracts of desert plateau nearly indistinguishable from similar lands in adjacent Iran, Soviet Central Asia, and Pakistan. To the east, the mountain barrier links up with a yet greater system, the knot of the Pamirs, which eventually meets the wide belt of the Himalayas far beyond the borders of Afghanistan. The Afghan mountains themselves, with innumerable folds and valleys, enclose central Afghanistan (the Hazarajāt, Ğorāt, and Badğisāt) and, in the northeast, Badaxšān.

The focus of the present study is northern Afghanistan, which comprises three sectors: Turkestan (the provinces of Fariāb, Jozjān, Balx, and Samangān); Katağan (Bağlān, Kunduz, and Taxor provinces); and Badaxšan (a single province). To make the succeeding presentation of the role of music in northern Afghan culture more meaningful, it is necessary to define the integral ethnic and geographic components of these areas. Though we can read numerous discussions of the ethnic groups of Afghanistan, a comprehensive ethnography of the peoples in the North had not been undertaken as of 1973; moreover, the data that are available have often been presented with bias to make a certain case, and even estimates of absolute numbers vary wildly (200,000 to 2,000,000 for the Turkmens, for instance). These problems acknowledged, I shall proceed with the necessary attempt to survey the available ethnographic information, first describing the basic ethnic groups and then indicating how they fit into the three zones mentioned above.

The ethnographic map given here (Map II) is based on the Soviet map (as published in Bruk 1955: facing 72), which is still the most thorough and reliable source available. It is clear that members of two great Eurasian linguistic families, Turks and Iranians, form the chief components of the population. The former group includes Uzbeks, Turkmens, Kazakhs, Kirghiz, and perhaps some Karakalpaks, while the latter consists of various Iranian speakers labeled Tajiks and Paštuns. We shall begin our survey with the oldest resident inhabitants, the Tajiks, and continue with the other peoples in order of their population strength, from major to minor groups.

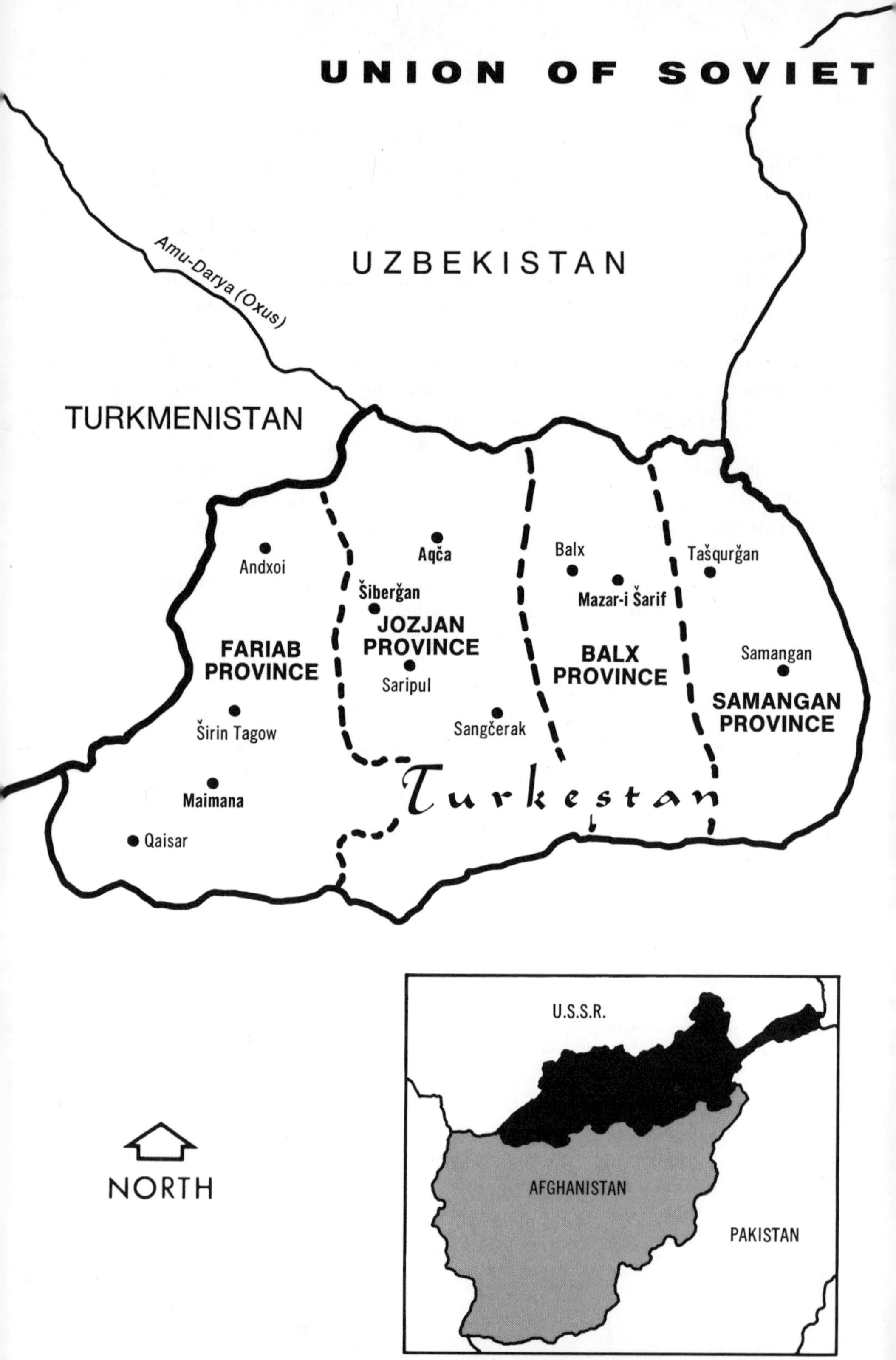

UNION OF SOVIET
UZBEKISTAN
Amu-Darya (Oxus)
TURKMENISTAN
Andxoi
Aqča
Šiberğan
JOZJAN PROVINCE
Saripul
FARIAB PROVINCE
Širin Tagow
Maimana
Qaisar
Sangčerak
Balx
Mazar-i Šarif
BALX PROVINCE
Tašqurğan
Samangan
SAMANGAN PROVINCE
Turkestan
NORTH
U.S.S.R.
AFGHANISTAN
PAKISTAN

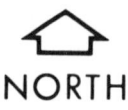

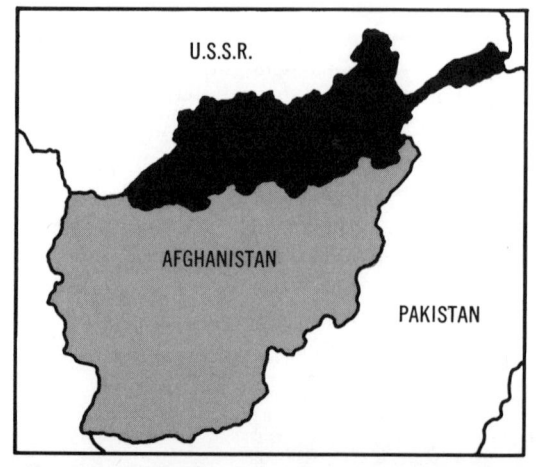

Map I. Provinces of Northern Afghanistan

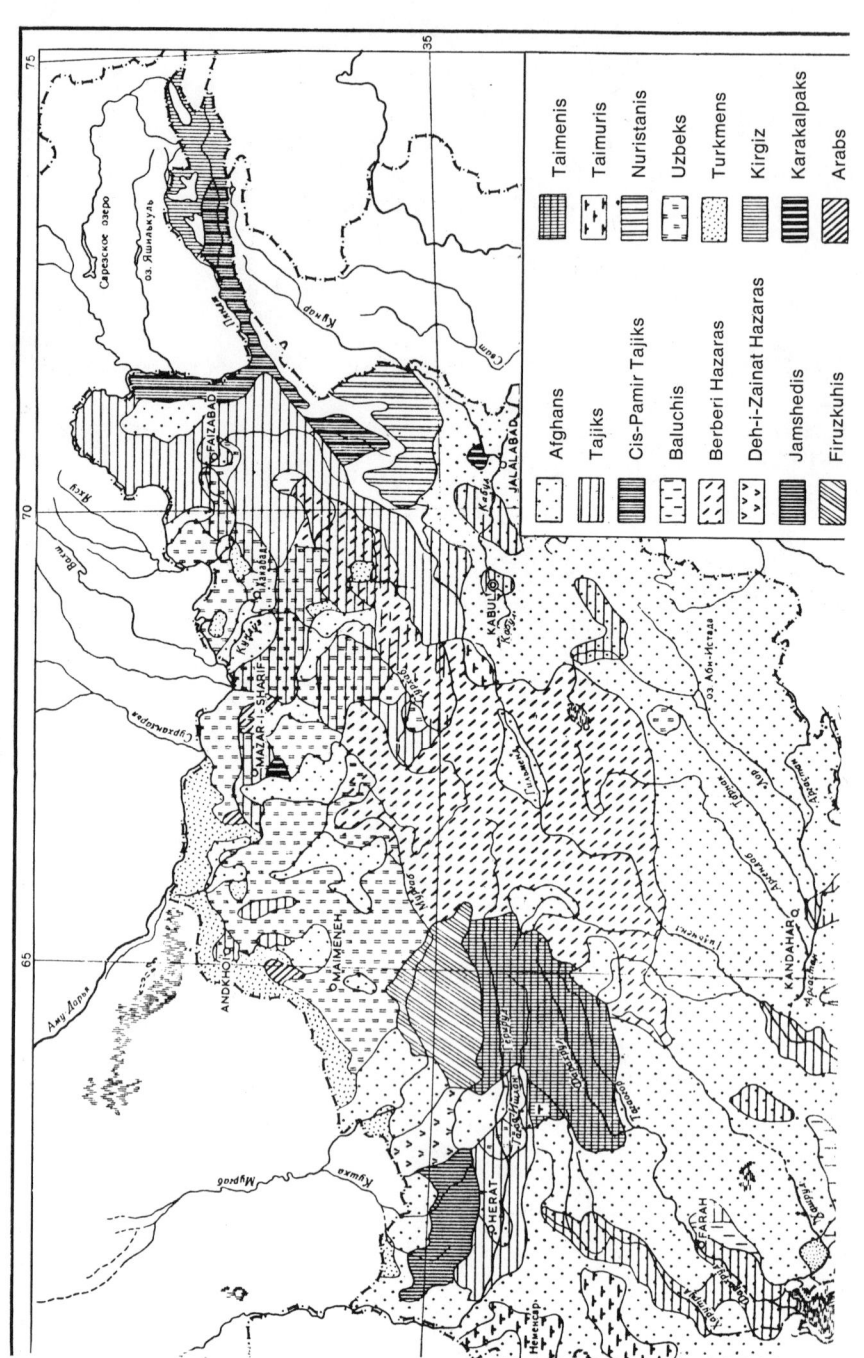

Map. II. Ethnographic Map of Afghanistan

THE TAJIKS

Like many other factors in the great ethnic mix of Afghanistan, the term Tājik itself is ambiguous and somewhat contradictory in origin and application. Browne, in his *Literary History of Persa* (1951:468), gives the standard etymology of the word concisely: *"Tajik,* a term originally applied to the Arabs (Tazik, Tazi) who garrisoned the towns of Khurasan and Transoxania, was later and is still applied to the Persian settled population as opposed to the nomads of Turkish stock." Perhaps typical of this vague usage is the fact that the famed Afghan hound is known in Persian as *tazi* to this day.

Bellew and Elphinstone, writing at different times in the nineteenth century, gave excellent summaries of the use of the term Tajik and of the habits of the Afghan Tajiks. Most of what they said holds true even today. Here is Bellew, writing in 1880 (110):

Tajik [must] be held to be merely the ancient name for the Persian cultivator or peasant. The word, in fact, being a Persian one, is restricted to the territories which formerly owned the Persian sovereignty. Hence its absence from India, and its presence in Turkistan. The Tajiks extend all over the plain country of Afghanistan, from Herat to the Khybar and from Kandahar to the Oxus, and even into Kashgar. The name is applied nowadays in a very loose way, and is made to include all the Persian-speaking people of the country who are not either Hazarah, Afghan or Sayyid. The term is also applied to the representatives of the ancient Persian inhabitants of Badakhshan and its inaccessible mountain glens.

Elphinstone, writing more than forty years earlier, came to much the same conclusion (1839:403-408):

. . . [The Tajiks] are mixed with the Uzbeks through the greater part of their dominions. In Persia, the plains of Afghanistan and the Uzbek country, they appear to have been settled before the arrival of the nations which are now predominant in those countries.

The name of Taujik is rather loosely used. It is sometimes applied to all persons mixed with the Toorks or Afghauns who are not sprung from those stocks . . . but it is with more propriety confined to those inhabitants of countries where Toorkee and Pushtoo are spoken, whose vernacular language is Persian. The names of Taujik and Parseewaun are indeed used indiscriminately both in Afghaunistan and Toorkistaun.

The Taujiks are everywhere remarkable for their use of fixed habitations, and their disposition to agriculture and other settled employments.

The Taujiks are most numerous about towns. They compose the principal part of the population round Caubul, Candahar, Ghuznee, Heraut and Bulkh, while in wild parts of the country . . . there is scarcely a Taujik to be found.

It is remarkable how closely these old descriptions of the place of Tajiks in Afghanistan fit the present-day picture. The only major change since Elphinstone's time is the apparent decrease of Tajiks in Kandahar and Ghazni, where they are hardly as numerous today as they seem to have been in 1839. Both Bellew and Elphinstone showed considerable sensitivity in defining the practical meaning of the term Tajik as it applies throughout Afghanistan today and in much of Soviet Uzbekistan and Tajikistan in the recent past.

However, when moving beyond these general descriptions to the more precise questions of identifying Tajiks in a given setting, one realizes the full complexity of the "Tajik problem." Many native speakers of Persian are not Tajiks, nor are all Tajiks alike in such basic matters as adherence to the Sunni or Shi'a branches of Islam or use of the same dialect of Persian. Moving around Afghanistan, one encounters a surprising variety of peoples all calling themselves Tajiks. In the Hazarajat, a large body of Shi'a Tajiks lives alongside the allegedly Mongolian Hazaras, their coreligionists. In the Panjšir, north of Kabul, the so-called Kohistāni Tajiks seem to have sprung from somewhat different stock. The Tajiks of Turkestan are greatly mixed with Uzbeks and have many Turkic words in their speech, and are Sunni. Those of Badaxšan are largely Shi'a, many of them belonging to the Ismaili sect, and are much less mixed with surrounding populations than are the previously mentioned groups of Tajiks.

Farther to the east, the so-called Pamir Tajiks inhabit the "inaccessible mountain glens" referred to by Bellew; they speak very archaic Iranian languages (Yaǧnobi, Sangliči, Suǧni, etc.) unintelligible to the other Tajiks of Afghanistan. The town Tajiks of Kabul have a different background; many of them are called Qizilbāš and are supposed to have descended from Turkic colonists settled by the Persian conqueror Nadir Shah in the early eighteenth century. The Tajiks of Herat form part of the population of old Xorasan, a part of the Persian Empire from the days of Cyrus the Great. Finally, across the border in the USSR live a large body of Tajiks settled in their own republic, the Tajik SSR; they speak a type of eastern Persian they call Tajik, while their Afghan neighbors speak Fārsi, now called Dari by the Afghan government.

It is clear that all of these varied groups of Tajiks do not spring from a single source in time or place, and that they represent various strata of settlement within the Iranian world. For the most part, Elphinstone's view that the Tajiks were the first to settle in areas that were later overrun by other Iranian and Turco-Mongol peoples seems sound enough, and it is supported by the presence of small pockets of

Tajiks, often speaking archaic dialects, in mountain refuge areas such as the Pamirs. Considerable field work undertaken by Soviet scholars in areas of Uzbekistan and Tajikistan reinforces the view of Tajiks as the old Iranian population of the entire area under discussion in this book, and the present-day differences in beliefs and practices among their various groups must be ascribed to the workings of two or three thousand years of continual flux and turmoil in an area that it often referred to as a major crossroads of Asia.

Turning to the Tajiks of Afghan Turkestan, it is very difficult to estimate their proportion in the total population of the area, but an educated guess of perhaps 25–30 percent might not be far from wrong; there are no reliable official figures bearing on this point. For the Saripul region of Turkestan, not an area of Tajik concentration, the Tappers (1973:p.c.) set the Tajik component at 20 percent. Thus the Tajiks form a minority in Turkestan, as they do in many other regions of the country, but they are a sizable and influential minority in an area where there is no majority group.

Sufficient reason for the cultural importance of the Tajiks could be found in the early descriptions of their life quoted above — they formed the backbone of the old peasant population of much of Afghanistan, including Turkestan, and as such they served as models of settled life for the pastoral nomads, principally Uzbeks and Turkmens, who arrived on the scene in recent centuries. However, trade was also traditionally in the hands of the Tajiks, and the position of their language, Persian, as the lingua franca of Turkestan's commerce gave added impetus to Tajik cultural predominance. Even in the city of Buxara (now in Uzbekistan), which was for centuries the capital of a great Uzbek kingdom, the majority of the population, regardless of ethnic affiliation, spoke Persian, and today, according to Soviet researchers, most Buxaran children still choose to study Tajik (Persian) rather than Uzbek in the public schools (Suxareva 1966:124).

Tajik primacy manifests itself in many ways. Pierre Centlivres notes that in the town of Tašqurǧan in Afghan Turkestan, many Uzbeks call themselves Tajiks and prefer to intermarry into Tajik families (1968:p.c.). It is also significant that a great many Uzbeks of northern Afghanistan refer to all of Soviet Central Asia simply as "Tajikistan."

Thus to a great extent Tajiks and Uzbeks have formed a kind of joint culture under Tajik influence in Afghan Turkestan (as well as in Transoxania). Influence does not run only one way, of course: Tajiks have picked up a good many Turkic words and customs as well. We shall discuss Uzbek-Tajik symbiosis at greater length below.

Schurmann (1961:73ff.) divides the Tajiks into four basic types:

Herati, Afghan Turkestani, seminomadic (north of Bamian), and mountain Tajiks (including Badaxšan and Pamirs); this classification is one with which I tend to agree. The main problem Schurmann runs into is one at which every investigator balks: defining Tajiks between Badaxšan and the region north of Bamian. Schurmann tends to call all of these mountain Tajiks:

> The region of Mountain Tadjik settlement extends from the Western Paropamisus to the Soviet-Chinese Pamirs. The Tadjik settlement of Sar-i Muskan (. . . in the Ghorat) probably forms the southwestern-most extension of Mountain Tadjik settlement . . . there are indications that prior to the incursions of Mongoloid nomadic groups, the principal population of both the Badghisat and the Hazarajat was Mountain Tadjik (or some form of Iranian population). (1961:77)

In the final parenthetical remark Schurmann begs the question; clearly "some form of Iranian population" is involved, but we remain in the dark as to the history of and links between various types of so-called Tajiks.

THE UZBEKS

As can be seen in Map II, the Uzbek population tends to cluster near the major northern urban centers. To the north, Uzbeks trail off beyond the edges of the steppe zone; to the east, a certain number can be found in Badaxšan alongside mountain Tajiks (Kushkeki 1926); to the south, they extend into the foothill zone stretching from below Maimana to Samangan, and in Saripul the Tappers assess the Uzbek component at 40 percent of the population (1974:p.c.); in the west, Uzbeks dwindle out between Qaisar and Bala Murġab in the Paropamisus zone.

Estimates of the number of Uzbeks in Afghanistan vary widely. Perhaps the figure of one million given in the Soviet survey of Afghanistan is most acceptable (Aslanov 1969:72); at any rate, it is clear that a fairly large population is involved for a country so sparsely settled as Afghanistan.

The Uzbeks, like the Tajiks, have no common place of origin or time of appearance on the Turkestani scene. Soviet scholars, particularly B. Kh. Karmysheva (1964), have inquired deeply into the ethnic composition of the southern areas of Tajikistan and Uzbekistan, and their findings probably hold good for northern Afghanistan. According to Karmysheva (1964:98), there are basically two major groups of Uzbeks in the area: (1) the vast majority (about 75 percent), consisting of Uzbeks whose origin can be traced to the Dašt-i Kipčak (in the present Kazakh steppe) and who arrived in the sixteenth and seventeenth centuries, mostly during the large-scale Uzbek invasion led by Šeibani Xan in the early sixteenth century; and (2) a smaller group of Uzbeks called Türk (10 percent), whose arrival considerably predates that of the Dašt-i Kipčak Uzbeks and who were already cultivators when the latter appeared on the scene. To these two groups can be added other minor components, principally the rather mysterious group called the Čagatai Uzbeks (2.6 percent), corresponding roughly to the Čagatai Tajiks (the origin of both is obscure, and a full discussion of the term Čagatai, though fascinating, lies beyond the scope of the present study). Karmysheva is able to supply a clear picture of the settlement pattern of these groups, placing the Türk in hills above the Čagatai and Dašt-i Kipčak Uzbeks, but below the mountain Tajiks (1964:98). She also points out the presence of tiny splinter groups of Uzbeks whose background is shrouded in historical confusion.

This interesting information notwithstanding, we are still in the dark as to the exact relationship existing between the Uzbeks (and for that matter, the Tajiks) of Afghanistan and their relatives in Transoxania. The general breakdown given by Karmysheva may well be valid in both areas, but recent history has provided a considerable barrier to the continued sharing of culture by these groups, in the form of a political frontier. G. F. Debets, a Soviet anthropologist, recently spent considerable time surveying the peoples of Afghanistan, and he offers this caveat: "Notwithstanding the common origin of the Uzbeks living to the north and south of the Amu-Darya, it is completely obvious that the political boundary introduced along this river as early as the eighteenth century has played a definite ethnographic role" (1967:88). Thus the common cultural heritage of the Uzbeks has been broken, and we shall see in later chapters how this is reflected in differences between the music culture of northern Afghanistan and that of Soviet Central Asia. Debets also notes that the Afghan Uzbeks are quite vague about their tribal identity, though some of them identify themselves as Čagatai Uzbeks (1967:88). This indicates that they have been cut off from the bulk of Uzbeks in southern Uzbekistan, who have strong tribal orientations. It seems likely, however, that the underlying distinctions made by Karmysheva probably held true for Afghan Turkestan in the past. Thus, for example, Vambery (1970:268) observed ". . . 200 tents of the Uzbeks, from the tribes of Kungrat and Nayman" near the Afghan border at Kerki in 1863, indicating that tent residence, mobility, and easy identification of constituent tribes were standard parts of Uzbek life a century ago.

Most of the Uzbeks of Afghan Turkestan are settled and live in towns or villages, but up until quite recently — the late nineteenth century — there was a considerable body of seminomadic Uzbeks in Turkestan. It was largely because of the pressure of incoming Paštun nomads (see below), who preempted much of the favorable grazing land, that the Uzbeks turned to agriculture and town life.

Karmysheva does not mention, for obvious reasons, one important group of Afghan Uzbeks: the émigrés of the early twentieth century who crossed the border during the Basmači rebellion against Soviet power in the 1920s and 1930s. Considerable numbers of these *mohajerin* ("refugees"), as they are called, live in Katağan, but some of them can be found in Turkestani towns such as Andxoi and Mazar-i Šarif. They tend to have urban rather than peasant or seminomadic origins, and they are still sharply defined within the Afghan Uzbek community.

THE TURKMENS

The Turkmens are the only people of the North who also live in the two adjoining countries, the USSR and Iran. Estimates of the number of Turkmens in Afghanistan vary as widely as those for Uzbeks. Schurmann (1961:86) has collected the Russian guesses as follows: Aristov at 50,000; Reisner at 200,000; Reiser at 4 percent of the population of Afghanistan; and Bochkarev at 380,000, or 3 percent. Schurmann himself gives "a minimum Turkmen population in Afghanistan of 200,000 or more." The most recent Soviet figure, 400,000 (Aslanov 1969:75), is probably as accurate as any.

The Turkmens are concentrated in a thin strip of territory extending no more than about fifty kilometers south of the Soviet border, except in the Herat area in the extreme west. This strip runs nearly the entire length of northern Afghanistan, from Herat to eastern Katağan. Outside of this zone of settlement, some Turkmens can be found in Kabul, where they are prominent in the carpet industry. There seem to be few, if any, Turkmens in Badaxšan.

The Turkmens of Turkestan and Katağan are largely of the Ersari and Alieli tribes. There are some Salor and Teke Turkmens in the Herat area, along with scattered representatives of other tribes. Though the vast majority of Afghan Turkmens are recent immigrants, who came across the Soviet border in the years roughly from 1915 to 1940, chronicles of the eighteenth and even seventeenth centuries indicate the presence of large groups of Turkmens in the Andxoi-Aqča sector of Afghan Turkestan, according to the Soviet scholar Yu. E. Bregel, who has compiled a valuable ethnic map of southern Turkmenistan for both the seventeenth and eighteenth centuries (1959:14). His chart shows first Imreli and then both Afšar and Jalair Turkmens in the area mentioned. Nineteenth-century travelers often remarked on the presence of Turkmens in the general area of Balx, which for them included land as far west as Andxoi. Vambery, for example, spoke of the Ersari as occupying the territory between Čarjau, now in the Turkmen SSR, and Balx, while he located the Alieli between Andxoi and Merv (1970:274). His judgment of the Turkmens is rather interesting, contrasting as it does with the common nineteenth-century view of the Turkmens as unscrupulous marauders and slave traders: "Turkmens, though predatory and anarchic in structure, have fewer thieves, murderers and breaches of justice and morals than all the other Islamic peoples" (1873:274).

Afghan Turkmens concede that there were relatively few of their people in Afghanistan before the first quarter of the twentieth century. Observation will bear out the impression that the most prominent and prosperous Turkmens are those who came during that time. The powerful leading family of the village of Qizilayāq, for example, which exercises great influence on Afghan Turkmens through religious authority, crossed the border in 1916, because of the growing troubles in their homeland.

Turkmens live in *qišlāqs* (villages) surrounding a local market center that serves as the major point of contact with the outside world. Apparently, Turkmens also resided outside city walls a century ago; Ferrier (1860), in his survey of northern towns, mentioned only a majority Uzbek and minority Tajik population in Maimana, Andxoi, Šibergan, and Aqča. Most Turkmen houses are built with the *gumbat,* or domed roof, construction that is found in various areas of the Near East and is particularly popular in Northern Afghanistan. There do not seem to be any purely nomadic Turkmens in Afghanistan and few, if any, seminomads.

The Turkmens do not make good ethnic mixers. They tend to remain aloof from their neighbors, even from fellow Turks like the Uzbeks, though Schurmann notes "much more intermingling between Turkmens and Uzbeks" at the Turkestani end of Turkmen habitation than between Turkmens and Aimaqs towards the Badǧisat end (1961: 95). One can indeed witness a certain amount of adaptation by Turkmens to Uzbek life-styles in the North, and this in turn is related to the Uzbeks' acculturation to Tajik norms mentioned earlier. This role of Uzbeks as cultural middlemen for other Turks has been documented for various areas of Central Asia, and as long ago as 1865 Vambery observed that in the Ferghana Valley area Kirghiz, Kipchak, and Kalmucks assimilated to Uzbeks "due to a certain prestige of breeding and *bon ton* of the Uzbeks, longer established in Turkestan" (1970:432).

For the most part, the Turkmens are economically well established in Afghanistan, thanks to the enormous importance to the Afghan economy of the carpets (of the "Afghan" and "Boxara" varieties) woven by Turkmen women and of the karakul sheep, which the Turkmens brought to Afghanistan by the millions. Rugs and skins form the two largest export items in Afghanistan. Much of the prosperity resulting from this trade falls into the hands of a small upper class of Turkmens, but Turkmens in general are fairly well off by Afghan standards. This judgment, of course, depends greatly on two principal factors: favorable sale abroad for Turkmen skins and carpets and favorable weather for livestock breeding. The disastrous drought and subsequent severe winter and flooding of 1970–72 had calamitous effects on Turkmen livestock holdings. Estimates of losses for karakul sheep herds tended to run at about 75 to 80 percent, with some villagers facing starvation.

Settled now in villages and adjusting somewhat to the Uzbek-Tajik model of village life, the Turkmens today are beginning to forget their old tribal ways and are participating in Afghan social and political life. G. F. Debets, who noted the differences between Afghan and Uzbekistani Uzbeks mentioned above, has this comment on the Turkmens: "The Afghan Turkmens find themselves in approximately the same position vis-à-vis the Turkmens of Turkmenia as the Afghan Uzbeks to the Uzbeks of Uzbekistan" (1967:88).

Some of the difference Debets notes, however, may well be ascribed to tribal variations among the Turkmens. The Ersari, for instance, who form the bulk of northern Afghan Turkmens, have long been distinct from other Turkmen tribes, as noted by Vambery:

The Ersari Turkomans, who only migrated hither from Manghishlak 200 years ago, have retained very little of the national characteristics of the Turkomans. They may be styled only semi-nomads, the greater part cultivating the land, and the remainder, still exclusively pastoral, having lost with their savage character all the primitive virtues of their kindred tribe. (1970:272)

Vambery's value judgment regarding "primitive virtues" aside, his remarks are useful evidence for associating the Ersari with a semi-nomadic or totally agricultural way of life well before they arrived in Afghan Turkestan in large numbers after the October Revolution.

THE PAŠTUNS

The Paštuns (or Pathans, in the British literature) form approximately 50 percent of the total population of Afghanistan but are in the minority in the North. They are unequally distributed in the region, being much more heavily represented in Katağan, their most recent area of immigration, than in Turkestan or Badaxšan. The Paštuns have been moving up and infiltrating the North over the course of more than two centuries. Various Afghan rulers, in the hope of either breaking up some dissident confederation of Paštun tribesmen or achieving domination over Turkestan, have sent groups of settlers to the North from traditional southern Paštun regions. One of the early waves of Paštuns arrived in the course of the Afghan (Paštun-led) invasion of Iran in the early eighteenth century; however, it was in the middle of late nineteenth century when more sizable bodies of Paštun nomads turned up in the North under the prompting of the Amirs Dost Mohammed (1835–63) and Abdurrahman (1880–1901). In addition, a large number of Paštuns appear periodically in Turkestan each year as a result of seasonal nomadic migrations that start as far south as Kandahar and move across the Hazarajat (central Afghanistan) to the North.

Study of the northern Paštuns has barely begun; Richard and Nancy Tapper completed intensive fieldwork in 1971 and 1972, and we must look forward to their publications for the first serious work on Paštuns (both nomads and villagers) in Turkestan. While Paštuns maintain the considerable ethnic distinctiveness that characterizes them across the wide sweep of their areas of habitation (cf. Barth 1969a), they have also come to terms with the basic Uzbek-Tajik culture of the North; of this, more below. In demographic terms, sedentary northern Paštuns tend to form isolated encampments or villages (e.g., Paštunkot near Maimana), or even separate quarters of a village if they are in the minority. They make up only a very small percentage of the urban population. For the Saripul region (town and country-side), early estimates by the Tappers (1973:p.c.) set the Paštun population at 25 percent of the total.

SMALLER GROUPS

Like all of Afghanistan, the North shelters pockets of ethnic populations of highly diverse backgrounds and sometimes insignificant size. Among the larger of these small minorities are the Hazaras, who spill into the North from their homeland, the Hazarajat. Though the origin of the Hazaras remains unclear despite considerable theorizing (Hudson and Bacon 1941; Schurmann 1961), it is at least apparent that they have had a very complex past, at least partially formed by contact with Mongols. Perhaps Schurmann's judgment is useful here: "Just as we know that the term Tadjik covers a number of diverse ethnic and culture groups, so must we remember that the same thing applies to the term Hazara" (1961:119). They are easily singled out as a group today, however, by their distinctive appearance (heavily Mongoloid) and their special dialect of Persian (Hazaragi), and they usually end up at the bottom of whatever community they live in.

Hazaras have occasionally been imported in large numbers to the North for specific purposes. Under Murad Beg, the Uzbek ruler of the short-lived Kunduz empire of the early nineteenth century, an English observer was able to meet "a Hazara of the Deh Kundi tribe, bringing part of the yearly slave tribute to Kunduz" (Wood 1872:132). Such importations perhaps account for the considerable Hazara populations in parts of Katagan today. For the most part, however, Hazaras are found in the southern foothill region close to the Hazarajat — for example, near Saripul and Sangčerak, where the Tappers (1973:p.c.) estimate their numbers at 10 percent of the population.

Similar to the Hazaras in ethnic complexity and area of provenience are the members of various small groups lumped together under the term Aimaq in the North. To a great extent these peoples have fused with and adopted the language of either the Uzbeks (e.g., in Andxoi) or the Tajiks (e.g., in Saripul). Two other groups of rather obscure origin also deserve mention: the Arabs and the Moğols. Schurmann, who has devoted considerable effort to the study of these groups, writes of the Arabs that they are not related to modern Arabs but may be connected to Turkmen tribes claiming Arab descent, to Uzbek tribes such as those named Arab and Qurais, or to those Afghans who are called Sayyids. However, "it is still a question whether there are any basic relationships between these various groups, and what their relation to the main body of Arabs further west is" (Schurmann 1961:102). Arabs tend to be nomadic or seminomadic and to be looked down upon by other ethnic groups.

Turning to the Moğol, they are no less enigmatic a group than the others just outlined. Despite their name, which means "Mongol," they are less Mongoloid in appearance than the Hazaras, yet they retain enough of a vestige of Mongolian speech to keep the interest of linguists and ethnographers high. Their basic homeland is in central Afghanistan (the Ğorat). In the North, they have "very little contact with the people surrounding them . . . they never intermarry. The Uzbeks and Arabs despise the Moghols and have little to do with them" (Schurmann 1961:400).

Rounding out the list of ethnic groups, we must not forget the Jews, no longer represented in the North but once an important component of the population. Indeed, as Le Strange noted regarding Maimana,

In the earlier middle ages it was called Al-Yahudan, or Al-Yahudyah, the 'Jews' Town,' and was often counted as the capital of Juzjan . . . the name was changed to Maymanah, meaning 'the Auspicious Town,' for the sake of good augury, since 'Jew-town' to the Moslems was a term of reproach. . . . (1905:424)

Despite this snub to Jewish importance, there was apparently no tradition of persecution of the Jews; Vambery noted for the fifty families of Jews he observed that along with "'a few Hindoos, and Afghans" they "enjoy equal rights, and are not disturbed for reasons of religion or nationality" (1865:292). This era of goodwill, however, ended in the 1930s, when the king, Zahir Shah, instituted a policy of forced emigration of all Jews from the entire North to Kabul. As of 1968, only one Jew remained in Balx, where he was employed to write out Muslim amulets *(tawiz),* which are sometimes considered particularly efficacious when written by non-Muslims.

Finally, we must mention the other Turkic groups of Central Asian origin, the Kazakhs, Kirghiz, and Karakalpaks. The last-named are hard to find, but are rumored to live in the North (Jarring 1939:76). The Kirghiz are found only in the far Pamirs and thus only marginally in Afghanistan — in the Waxan corridor — and they extend naturally across the Soviet frontier from their homeland in Kirghizia. Jarring has estimated their numbers at 3,000 (1939:70). The Kirghiz are the only Central Asians who still travel freely across the Soviet Afghan border. The Kazakhs, on the other hand, are quite cut off from their homeland. They are located primarily in Kunduz and Mazar-i Šarif. Those in the latter city, for whom I have some data, number about 500, and all stem from the Alma-Ata area of Kazakhstan (shown on Map 1.1), having emigrated around 1932. They are involved in the manufacture and sale of the *čapan,* the ubiquitous Turkestani long cloak worn by nearly all ethnic groups. Considerable pockets of Kazakh population can also be found in Kabul and Herat.

DEFINITION OF AREAS

Having completed a basic survey of the peoples of the North, we can attempt a description of the three basic regions — Turkestan, Katağan, and Badaxšan — that is more meaningful than the list of their constituent provinces given at the beginning of this Introduction.

Turkestan

As we shall see below, Turkestan's neighboring region, Katağan, has a similarly large Turkic population and an analogous mixture of other ethnic groups. In addition, Herat has a Turkmen population,

perhaps qualifying it for membership in "Turk-i stan." A certain confusion about the identity of Turkestan can be detected among native
informants, some of whom group Turkestan together with Katağan
against Badaxšan, while others see Katağan and Badaxšan as a unit
distinguished from Turkestan.

The roots of this problem lie in the historical development of the
region. Turkestan is the area where numerous small Uzbek city-states
held sway for many centuries, until the final consolidation of power
by Amir Abdurrahman in the late nineteenth century did away once
and for all with the independence of Aqča, Šiberğan, Saripul, Andxoi,
and Maimana. Turkestan was the buffer zone between the Khan of
Buxara and the Amir of Kabul, much as all of Afghanistan was a
pawn in the great imperial game between Czarist Russia and the British
Empire. Khanikoff, writing in the mid-nineteenth century, observed:

Most of those who have written on Central Asia have complained of
the difficulties they have had to encounter in the attempt to determine
its limits. . . . We lament that on the present occasion, we are forced
to join in the general complaint, because the Khanate of Bokhara, like
the states which are its neighbors, has no fixed boundaries, sanctioned
by time, or circumscribed by international treaties. They expand or
contract according to the strength or weakness of its rulers. (1845:1-2)

A region of wavering boundaries and shifting petty warfare,
Turkestan was nevertheless a recognizable entity during brief periods
when parts of the region were consolidated into one or another short-
lived empire (such as Murad Beg's in the 1830s, to be discussed below).
It remained a zone of changeable influence, never the center and always
the target of imperial ambition. It is only today, with the sealing of
the Soviet border and the development of a strong Afghan state, that
the area is becoming just a provincial region with great local color
rather than an important arena of Central Asian politics.

Katağan

East of Turkestan lies Katağan. The difficulty of defining a
Turkestani-Katağani border has already been touched upon, and this is
part of the larger "Katağan question." Many informants consider
Katağan to be a separate region, but what is their reason for this belief?
Katağan exhibits a composition quite similar ethnically to that of
Turkestan, and geographically it features no significant boundaries.
Although I have been offered a variety of ingenious etymologies for
the term Katağan, the identification of the region with an Uzbek tribal
name strikes me as the most attractive explanation. The Katağan tribe
of Uzbeks was located in the area that now bears its name, as witnessed

by Capt. Wood in the early nineteenth century (1872:134), and it still occupies regions of southern Uzbekistan adjacent to Katağan, where it is considered one of the older groups in the population (Karmysheva 1964:51).

Katağan was, until recently, a single province of Afghanistan, comprising the present provinces of Bağlan, Kunduz, and Taxor. Clearly the Afghan government thought of the area as a unit, but this concept of Katağan, like that of Turkestan, probably relates more to historical vicissitudes than to ethnic or geographic demarcation. In the second quarter of the nineteenth century, a strong Uzbek chieftain named Murad Beg established his domain over a considerable sector of northern Afghanistan. Wood stated that Murad Beg's "plundering expeditions embrace the whole of the upper waters of the Oxus, from the frontier of China on the East to the river that runs through Balkh, the mother of cities, on the West" (1872:140). Murad Beg conquered Badaxšan in 1823, after which he "destroyed Fyzabad, and forcibly removed its inhabitants to Kunduz" (Wood 1872:160). Thus the Uzbek leader unified a large area of the North, bringing both Badaxšan and eastern Turkestan into a realm centered in Kunduz. This could be called a Katağani empire, which was solidified by the bringing of settlers from rebellious Badaxšan and slaves from the Hazarajat. If we assume that the realm of Murad Beg remained alive in terminology long after its collapse under pressure from Kabul and Buxara, we might have the basis for both the concept and the term Katağan.

We can take this historical background one step further, adding information relating to the living conditions in Katağan. Wood, along with many other older writers, quoted the saying, "If you wish to die, go to Kunduz" (1872: 258) — a proverb referring to the high incidence of malaria in the Kunduz area, indeed in all Katağan. This is the reason Kunduz always remained a neglected town, despite its being the nominal center of Murad Beg's domain. As Wood noted, "Kunduz, the capital of Murad Beg, is one of the most wretched in his dominions. Five or six hundred mud hovels contain its fixed population . . ." (1872:138). Thus Katağan was, in a sense, "unified," thanks to its insalubrious climate. However, a thorough antimalaria campaign was initiated by the Afghan government in the 1920s and 1930s, and it resulted in the opening up of considerable new land for cultivation and for the building of new towns (of this, more in Chapter 2). This "Katağan revolution" brought about sweeping changes in the Afghan North. The social effects of this change will occupy us later; suffice it for now to point out that the modern development of Katağan, coupled with its nineteenth-century role as the center of a large prin-

cipality, probably forms the underlying rationale for the popular definition of the area as a separate region of the North, its lack of ethnic
and geographic distinctiveness notwithstanding.

To the east, Katağan has a rather extensive border area with
Badaxšan, the easternmost sector of northern Afghanistan. From
Taluqān to Kešm extends a kind of regional "no-man's-land that is
neither quite Katağan nor Badaxšan, to judge by local residents' conflicting definitions. Here one encounters numerous old Uzbek settlers
(many of whom retain vestiges of their earlier seminomadic life), some
splinter groups such as the Baluch enclave near Kešm, and the first
sizable groups of mountain Tajiks of Badaxšani origin. No doubt
Murad Beg's forcible introduction of Badaxšanis into eastern Katağan
strengthened the area's role as a border zone. We shall see in Chapter 2
how this situation has influenced the town of Kešm in particular.

Thus Katağan, though it has an important Turkic population and
is not set off by strong topographical boundaries, has as a result of its
history come to be a recognizable segment of the North.

Badaxšan

Past Kešm to the east, one is never in doubt that a new region has
been reached. The river that guides one's journey all the way from
Kunduz joins the Kokča, a main tributary of the Oxus, and the trip
continues along the narrow defile of the Kokča valley upstream to
Faizabad, some five hours distant by jeep. The road is dangerous
ground, for it runs directly next to the river, often at the same level,
and is thus subject to the whims of the turbulent Kokča. Frequent
washouts, especially in the summer flood season, cut Badaxšan off
from the world, except for limited air traffic.

Of the three regions of the North, Badaxšan is by far the most
homogenous ethnically. Here the Turkmen populations phase out,
and the Uzbeks fall to a much lower proportion vis-à-vis the mountain
Tajiks. Travel in Badaxšan is accomplished mostly by horseback,
for east of Faizabad there is only a rudimentary road running to
Iškašim and some distance south to Munjan. Thus the inhabitants of
the valleys in this highly mountainous region keep mostly to themselves and have preserved many archaic habits and beliefs. What is
remarkable about Badaxšan, as we shall see in the case of music,
is its cultural unity, which transcends the basic difficulty of transport.

Badaxšan province extends all the way out the Waxan corridor
to the Afghan-Chinese border, where the Hindu Kush joins the Pamirs
at "the roof of the world." Out there, the celebrated Marco Polo sheep,
a spectacular mountain goat, is hunted by the idle rich of the West.

The existence of pocket communities of "Pamir Tajiks" has already been noted; these peoples are treasured by linguists and other fieldworkers for their archaic practices and speech, but they have hardly been seriously studied or discussed, except in a few important Soviet monographs dealing with populations on the other side of the Panj river (especially Andreev 1953). Thoroughgoing Badaxšan-Pamir studies should be a main task of ethnographic research in Afghanistan, for this mountain refuge region is more tenacious in maintaining traditions than any other area of the North.

Fig. 1.1. A šowqi *activity: partridge fighting in Tašqurḡan*

Fig. 1.2. A šowqi *activity: hunting with falcons in the Laḡman region*

Fig. 1.3. A šowqi *activity: snake handling in Xanabad*

CHAPTER 1

The Shared Music Culture

THE OCCURRENCE OF MUSIC

In delineating the shared music culture of northern Afghanistan, it will be useful first to determine what niche music occupies in the general cultural pattern of the area. We shall examine music as part of a broad range of activities defined by northerners as belonging to a single set, and then move on to outline the particular characteristics of musical activity within that larger category.

The most common term associated with musical activity is *šowq,* or *šowqi,* a Persian word. Steingass's definition of *šowq* (1970:766) is worth quoting in full, as it conveys some of the nuances implied in the term:

Filling with desire; desire, yearning, love; affection, inclination, predilection; fancy, pleasure; curiosity; sympathy.

And for *šowqi* he gives "Loving, amorous; cheerful" (1970:766). In Afghanistan as a whole, šowqi is used by Persian speakers to describe a great many activities practiced by individuals for their own pleasure, and it implies the state of mind that leads a person to involve himself in those pursuits. In Afghanistan the adjectival noun form *šowqi* is used for this state, and it may also be applied to musicians as part of a professional name, e.g., Karim Šowqi. Different Afghans may provide varying lists of activities that can be included under the rubric of šowqi, but there is underlying agreement as to the general scope and connotations of the term. Let us look at a partial list of šowqi pursuits gathered from a number of Afghans:

Gambling of all sorts (dice, cards, casting sheep bones)
Collecting any sort of object, but particularly such things as weapons
Raising, training, and fighting various animals (quails, partridges, roosters, dogs, camels)
Collecting snakes, lizards, and scorpions
Admiration and raising of flowers
Kite flying, wrestling, and other sports
Decorating objects lavishly (radios, musical instruments, cars, trucks, horsecarts, etc.)
Patronizing favorite dancing boys or female entertainers
Playing a musical instrument as an amateur

The thread running through these diverse activities is the inner state that leads the individual to indulge in them. This state is hard to define precisely but involves several of the terms listed by Steingass: pleasure, affection, and predilection seem nearest the mark. Afghans describe šowqi as a condition of the *dil,* or heart, and by and large give the term a positive value. If a person is šowqi for something, "dilaš zende ast" ("his heart is lively"), although, as we shall see, an excess of šowqi can be harmful.

To compare the phenomenon with its counterpart in, say, American culture, šowqi embraces the range of pursuits we might classify as pastime, hobby, or avocation, though these terms are a bit weaker than the affective field of šowqi. One can perhaps think of a šowqi person as falling somewhere between the American "buff" and "nut" (as in "rifle buff" or "car nut"); the former term seems a bit mild for šowqi, while the latter falls into the overzealous range. Thus, šowqi lies somewhere in the zone between a hobby and an obsession and can perhaps best be described as a preoccupation with certain objects or activities, but one that does not constitute the individual's principal job or determine his station in life. In the broadest sense, šowqi can be used as a general epithet to sum up someone's character, generally in an admiring way: "U besiār šowqist" ("He's very šowqi"). The evident implication is that an individual who shows signs of life — of yearning, fancy, and desire — is on the right track. We shall discuss in detail below the ramifications of the term šowqi as applied to the musician; for now it will suffice to understand šowqi as a broad category that includes music.

Music, then, is one of the activities that enlivens life. Yet if this pursuit is carried too far, the bounds of šowqi are overstepped and music becomes a potential source of social danger. Perhaps the clearest reflection of this attitude toward music lies in terms applied to certain musicians or used by them to describe their own situation. To call a man a *diwāna* ("madman"), for example, clearly rules him beyond the pale of normal social behavior; yet this term may be used for particular musicians, even as a form of address. *Majnun,* the name of the love-mad hero of the old Arabo-Persian tale of Leili and Majnun, is almost a synonym for diwana. Further, a musician may be said to be *mast* ("drunk") while playing, and the activity itself might be termed *masti kardan* ("whooping it up"), implying drunkenness. Even the relatively less loaded term *āšeq* (also used traditionally in Iran and Azerbaijan for minstrel) literally means "lover" and comes close to majnun in core meaning. All of these epithets connote šowqi beyond normal limits.

A further terminological reference to the musician's special state relates to the warmth or heat generated by his performance. The musician himself takes this as a natural part of his life. For example, during a private recording session with Axmad-baxši, an outstanding Turkmen performer, I asked for a certain song; he declined, saying that the song "takes a great deal of strength," and must come after several more relaxed selections. Midway through the session I offered him some melon to effect a break for interviewing. Axmad-baxši refused, saying, "Dil-i man garm šud" ("My heart [soul] has become hot"); melon, locally classified as a cool food, would have been unsuitable for him at the moment. Pointing to a friend seated next to him, the musician said that *he* could have some; the friend, himself a musician, had no objection to melon as long as he was not performing. Similarly, a lively performance may be termd *porjuš* ("boiling over"). Such a conception of the internal heat of performers strikes a familiar cultural bell when one recalls terms such as "hot" jazz and "fiery" rendition. For the layman in Afghanistan, as in the West, this special ardor of the musician carries vaguely dangerous overtones.

In Afghanistan, as elsewhere, the peril lies in disruption of the social balance through loosening of public morals. To understand this possibility fully, we must step back and examine the place of music in Islam, since religion is usually cited as the principal support of morality in Afghanistan. It is generally agreed that while the Qur'an takes no explicit stand against music, the *hadith* (traditions) surrounding Mohammad's life contain numerous examples of antimusical bias — e.g., calling musical instruments "the devil's muezzin, serving to call men to his worship" (Hitti 1963:274). As Farmer has noted, these hadith "were used with considerable effect by the legists *(fuqaha)* to forbid any kind of music save that which was known to have been tolerated by the Prophet" (1957:427). However, there was some disagreement among Muslim theorists: "Most Moslem legists and theologians frowned on music; some condemned it in all its aspects; a few looked upon it as religiously unpraiseworthy *(makruh),* though not actually sinful *(haram)* . . ." (Hitti 1963:274). Farmer notes that while "the four great legal schools of Islam . . . decided, more or less, against 'listening to music,' a most interesting controversial literature on its permissibility or otherwise grew up" (1957:427). Thus it is difficult to generalize about Islamic attitudes towards music; the individual time and locale must be considered, and even then conflicting views might be unearthed. Even the practitioners of Sufi mysticism in Afghanistan differ in their stands on the usefulness or harmfulness of music as a means toward enlightenment. While it is possible to ascertain for a certain group of Afghans, for example, the Hazaras of central Afghanistan, that they "have come to feel that music in all aspects is religiously unpraiseworthy" (Sakata 1968:20), it is necessary to try to get at the roots of this blanket disapproval so often expressed by the general public.

From the religious point of view, the most censurable aspect of music is perhaps its guilt by association with activities that are clearly offensive to public Islamic morals — specifically, loose sexual behavior, linked to music through the medium of the dance, itself viewed with ambivalence. To see how this one sector of musical performance has cast its shadow over all entertainment, we must turn to the various types of music and dance performance, noting which are considered innocent and which dangerous.

The basic term for music throughout Afghanistan is *sāz,* which Steingass (1970:640) defines as "a musical instrument; arms, apparatus. . . ." There is thus implied a close connection between the general phenomenon of music and the specific material object, or apparatus, of the musical instrument. This link is not accidental to the Afghan conception of music. Time and again it becomes clear through interviews that the layman, whose only word for music is saz (the learned term *musiqi* has highly specialized connotations and is not in general use), defines as music only those performances that include use of a musical instrument. The singing of the lone nomad in the steppe, or the unaccompanied woman crooning a lullaby, and of the religious balladeer of the streets is rarely if ever counted as saz by the man in the street. Similarly, the principal term for musician is *sāzanda,* by definition a player of musical instruments. *Xunanda,* "singer," may be used for musicians who are not also instrumentalists, but such performers usually refuse to sing without instrumental accompaniment. Furthermore, in the North the terms diwana, majnun, and mast, cited above as special epithets for musicians, are usually applied to instrumentalists rather than to singers.

This narrow definition of music excludes most of the "innocent" manifestations, such as those cited above, and tends to focus on the sphere in which music plays a potentially dangerous role — for music with instruments occurs principally at public or private festivites, where dance is also likely to appear or to be implied by the type of music performed. Dance is almost universally recognized as an activity that oversteps the bounds of šowqi and leads to vice. If a boy dances in public, it is felt that he is liable to be tempted to enter a career as a *bačabāzingar,* a dancing boy of dubious morals. Similarly, a woman who dances outside the most immediate family circle will find her social position suspect. The institution of the *zirxāna,* a cellar room in which handsome abducted boys were trained as dancers, is well documented for the North through 1939 (Jarring). According to residents of Andxoi, the town Jarring describes, the zirxana has only recently declined, because of police pressure.

Dance can, however, be innocent, as when the female members of the family dance for a wedding, or boys dance within the domestic circle for recreation. It is only the presence of outsiders that the family solidarity and reputation become threatened through dance, which is then seen as slightly wanton if not downright lascivious. It can be argued that this dark side of music and dance reflects a fear of crumbling social barriers as much as the sanctions of religion.

Anxiety about losing social status is the other primary factor militating against freedom in performance of music and dance. As we shall see in detail when discussing the musician's role, performers are divided into two basic types, the šowqi amateur and the *kespi,* or hereditary-professional, musican. Since the latter are recruited from the lowest ranks of society (principally from the barbers), it is not surprising that members of the middle and upper levels of the population shrink from engaging in an activity so clearly associated with inferior social standing. Even šowqi performers known in the community for their love of singing will hesitate to perform in a public or semipublic place for fear of being thought of as lowly barber-musicians.

To summarize the animus against music, it is hard to separate the religious and moral concept of music as dangerous because of its implications of sexual looseness from the notion of music as a degrading activity because of its identification with lower-class status. Since in Afghanistan religion often serves both as guardian of public morality and as preserver of the social hierarchy, it is not begging the question to state that a supposedly religious bias against music is in fact an affirmation of the status quo.

Let us return to the brighter side of music. Farmer notes for the classical Islamic period that ". . . between the cradle and the grave, music was ever present in Islam," and that "the truth was that in spite of all the condemnations of music by the puritans, ways and means were found, sometimes with the most delightful casuistry, to escape censure" (1957:434, 435). The reference to music in connection with important moments in life (cradle and grave) is not accidental; music in the sense of saz is primarily an occasional phenomenon. The interrelationship between the music and the occasion is often straightforward, but it may also be rather subtle. An example of the former tendency would be the music played in the *samowad* (teahouse) for market-day shoppers in a town; here the occasion creates the audience and the music serves to heighten the eventfulness of the day for the listeners. However, the relationship is less clear in the case of a village *meila* (a sort of picnic) during the harvest season. Here the occasion is less specific, and one almost imagines the music to be the excuse for the gathering. G. S. Taymuree, a native of the Ġorband region of central Afghanistan, just south of our main region of focus, says that he clearly felt that many ostensibly ceremonial occasions in his village were in fact pretexts for recreation and music making. In other words, music may create the occasion as much as the occasion necessitates the presence of music. According to Taymuree, music served as a means of protest on the part of women and teen-age boys (who were allowed to mix with women) against the domination of older males, who absented themselves from any music making they deemed unseemly. Thus, it may be possible to add the feature of age- and sex-linked disapproval of music to the factors of religious-moral stricture and consciousness of social status adduced earlier as components of the antimusical bias so often voiced by informants. It is of course no accident that most informants, as well as religious and community leaders and vocal members of the middle and upper classes, are likely to be mature males, who thus present a united front to the outside world on the subject of music.

The possibility that a hunger for music existed among large segments of the population seems borne out by the rapid rise in music consumption since the rise of Radio Afghanistan in the late 1950s. We shall examine in detail below the impact of the radio on the role and life-style of musicians; here we need only point out the dramatic and universal acceptance of radio music by the entire population of the North, and indeed by all Afghans. Whether in the plush westernized homes of the urban elite or under the trees in a village clearing, Afghans at dinner have to raise their voices to be heard over the omnipresent radio. It is the music, rather than the spoken programming, to which most attention is paid, and we shall see later how important this factor has been to maintenance and change of musical repertoires, instruments, and personnel. What is important for the present argument is that regardless of earlier misgivings about music in live performance, and particularly when it involved dancing, the anonymity and disembodied nature of radio broadcasting have allowed the repressed enthusiasm for music free rein without disturbing the status quo. It is an important reason for the success of the radio in Afghanistan. It is only since the 1960s that the guardians of public morality have begun to realize that the radio, detached as it is from local life, nevertheless has its impact on local mores relating to the role of music, and that it is too late to turn back the clock.

THE MUSICIAN: STATUS AND ACTIVITIES

For purposes of discussion we shall define musician as anyone in the culture who at some time engages in music making.

It may be useful to begin by dividing all music makers into two large groups: those whose musical status and activities are fairly well defined by tradition from birth ("ascribed" musicians), and those who attain musician's status through individual effort ("achieved" musicians). Here is the result in outline form:

I. ascribed musicians
    A. most women
    B. Gypsy musicians
    C. barber-musicians *(kespi)*
    D. *ustāds* (masters) of court and radio music
    E. *šowqi* (amateur) families with musical proclivity

II. achieved musicians
    A. most types of amateurs *(šowqi)*
        1. nomad and peasant musicians
        2. bourgeois and urban amateurs
        3. student amateurs
        4. *šowqis* of Uzbek classical music
    B. professional musicians (except those under IB, IC, ID)
        1. *šowqi* master musicians (full-time)
        2. *ğaribi-šowqi* musicians (part-time)
        3. radio musicians
    C. military, police, and municipal band musicians
    D. religious singers
        1. *šowqi* amateurs
        2. itinerant professionals *(madā)*

IA. Most Women

Women's musical roles are quite clearly defined. Except for women in category IIB, women are expected to restrict musical activity to the female sections of the house, which are still rigidly demarcated in the North. To this spatial compression is added considerable temporal limitation: women perform principally at domestic festivities, mainly weddings and circumcisions. A final stricture is that women are generally allowed only two instruments: the *doira*, a type of tambourine, and the *čang* (Persian) or *čangko'uz* (Uzbek and Turkmen; sometimes merely *ko'uz*), a small metal jew's harp. Both are of local manufacture.

The reasons for this general limitation of female musical activity, touched upon briefly above, relate to the inherent danger in careless indulgence in music. Especially in the case of women, the connection between music and dance is quite strong, and as we have noted, dance is seen as closely tied to the possibility of moral laxity. Afghans have told me that they have been excluded from seeing even close female relatives dance at home. While such restrictiveness in male-female contact may well stem from male interest in guarding the womenfolk, it is possible that women may take the initiative in closing off their recreation from men's eyes. Although it has not been feasible for me to interview women extensively on such intimate topics, I have a strong feeling (intensified by talks with men) that women make the most of their few occasions to legitimately indulge in music and dance and that they deliberately exclude males to make the time and space their own. Even at weddings of the urban bourgeoisie one senses the discomfiture of the men, who wander about feeling like supernumeraries at an event inspired and dominated by women. Various covert women's practices, such as consulting quasi-medical healers and engaging in collective spirit-possession rites, confirm the existence of a sector of female activities designed to circumvent male dominance, specifically in areas disapproved of by the male guardians of public morality (see Lewis 1971:100-113).

In this light, the proliferation of ceremony surrounding weddings and occasions such as the birth of a son can perhaps be seen as female pretexts for recreation. For example, in Taymuree's village in Ğorband, mentioned above, there are separate festivities on the third, sixth, tenth, and fortieth days after the birth of a son. Most of these are geared to the woman's role, rather than to celebration of the child's appearance. The *šab-i šaš* ("sixth evening") turns on congratulating the mother on her successful convalescence after childbirth, the *hamām-i dah* ("bath of the tenth") focuses on the mother's first postnatal bath, and the *čelagurei* ("fortieth day") festivities involve the mother's visiting the homes of various relatives. All of these ceremonials include singing and dancing by females alone. Thus women stretch the ground rules of their ascribed musical role by maximizing their opportunities in socially acceptable ways.

IB. Gypsy Musicians

In Afghanistan the activity of Gypsy musicians is far more limited than in such regions as Turkey and the Balkans. It is not quite clear to me why this should be so, since a traditional reason advanced for the prevalence of Gypsy musicians in the areas just mentioned is the

distaste of Muslims for musical performance and the resulting assignment of musical roles to the outcaste Gypsies. The same reasoning
ought to hold for so strongly Muslim a land as Afghanistan, yet such
is not the case. Gypsies are, however, sometimes hired as performers
for weddings, or they may perform in teahouses, particularly in the
Saripul-Sangčerak area (Tappers 1969:p.c.). It is the sedentary *jat*
Gypsies rather than the nomadic *juği* Gypsies who are involved.

One major musical role of Gypsies is to make the doira tambourine
that serves as women's principal accompaniment to song and dance.
I have seen doiras made by Gypsies in such widely removed areas as
Aqča in Turkestan, Xanabad in Katağan, and Istalif in Kohistan (just
north of Kabul). As performers, Gypsies also seem to be drawn to
the women's side of the house. A wealthy Uzbek merchant of Saripul
(south-central Turkestan) gleefully produced a tape recording he had
surreptitiously made of a Gypsy woman entertaining his wives in the
women's quarters. Hoping to find some bits of rare musical repertoire,
I copied the entire tape, only to discover that it consisted mainly of
renditions of popular Radio Afghanistan songs. We shall take up below,
as a special case, the possibility of a far-reaching involvement of
Gypsies in Afghan music culture in their roles as master-singers of
Radio Afghanistan.

IC. Barber-Musicians

Barber-musicians are a major category of ascribed musicians in
the North and one that will be central to our eventual understanding
of the musician's status. Barbering tends to be a hereditary craft and
is generally looked down upon. Pierre Centlivres has concisely summarized the particular postion of the barber in northern communities:

Agent indispensable de l'opération de la circoncision, craint pour le
pouvoir magique que lui confère la détention d'ongles et de cheveux,
méprisé à cause de sa manipulation de déchets humains, le barbier
occupe une position particulière, liée à l'ambivalence même du sacré.
Assimilé aux musiciens et aux cuisiniers avec lesquels il a du reste
souvent des relations profesionnelles ou parentales, il exerce l'un des
métiers les plus déconsidérés du bazar. (1970:90)

The somewhat feared, shadowy, magical power of the barber
indicated by Centlivres definitely rubs off on his musical activities and
tinges all of music with the vaguely evil nuance we noted earlier.
It seems that the ability of music to enliven men and provoke sexual
license accords well with the barber's somewhat nefarious capacities
as expressed in his censured surgical practices which, as Centlivres says,
"s'exercent à l'abri du silence et de la complicité de la clientèle . . ."

(1970:90). The linking of barbering and musicianship is so organically rooted in the North that I have found it difficult to obtain reasons from northerners for the conjunction of the two crafts in a single artisan — it is so natural in their eyes as to be beyond question. Those with an intellectual bent see both barbering and music as service professions and feel that any personal service rendered by an artisan lowers him in the eyes of his customers. This sort of ascriptive linking might perhaps explain why one can also find such combinations as musician–bathhouse operator (for example, Sekundar in Mazar-i Šarif). Such a generally negative attitude towards purveyors of services (including drivers of horsecarts and pullers of transport carts) is confirmed by the investigations of Centlivres:

> Les métiers qui entrent dans notre catégorie des services ont quelque chose d'équivoque, de peu considéré . . . c'est la nature même de service qui est en question, à laquelle s'attachent les préjugés touchant aux intermédiaires, à ceux dont le gagne-pain est de s'occuper du corps des autres. . . . (1970:91)

Barber-musicians must be considered as part of a shared music culture in the North, since barbering itself is distributed among various ethnic groups. Each community tends to have barbers of a certain ethnic affiliation, but it varies widely from town to town. Thus in Mazar-i Šarif they tend to be Paštuns, while in Kunduz they are Tajiks. It is of course possible for barbers to stem from more than one ethnic group in any given town.

With barbers, we arrive at the central question of defining musicians, which revolves around a pair of dichotomous terms: kespi and šowqi. We have already discussed the concept of šowqi as a phenomenon related to personal taste and involvement in leisure-time activities. Here we must examine the usage of these terms in the more concrete sense of amateur vs. professional and ascribed vs. achieved, two dichotomies that overlap only marginally. It is worthwhile beginning with the word *kespi* as it applies most generally to a category of employment in the bazaar; here is the careful definition given by Centlivres:

> Le terme général employé pour le travail est *kar,* qui signifie également métier, emploi, par example: *kar-e bafandagi,* tissage. Plus précisément on utilise *kesp* pour métier, surtout métier manuel (*kespet či ast:* quel est ton métier?) . . . L'artisan se dit *kaseb/kespi,* au pluriel *kespia.* . . . L'artisanat *kesp* se dit aussi *kar-e dasti,* travail manuel. (1970:41–42)

Thus kespi signifies manual labor of any sort; for this reason barbers automatically qualify as kespi, and the categorization extends to their musical activities, even though the practice of music per se does not qualify as manual labor. However, when music is involved, there seem to be at least two other ramifications to the term *kespi:* (1) kespi as paid musician vs. unpaid šowqi amateur; (2) kespi as hereditary or guild/craft (ascribed) musician vs. (achieved) šowqi performer. These are quite different concepts since the former involves the dichotomy paid-unpaid while the latter introduces that of ascribed-achieved status. As we shall see below in refining the term *šowqi,* the two dichotomies are neither totally overlapping nor mutually exclusive. Once one departs from the universally accepted meaning of kespi as occupational category, one encounters considerable ambiguity on the part of Afghans as to whether the ascribed or the paid aspects of the vocation serve as the root definition of kespi musicianship. Some will go so far as to say that paid achieved musicians are automatically kespi, while others feel that remuneration is an insignificant factor as compared to the kespi performer's hereditary proclivity for music.

My own feeling is that the factor of low status is the decisive element in defining kespi. The inherited bent for manual/musical labor, particularly in the case of barbers, is bound to be potent in categorizing a man as being kespi for music. On the other hand, an achieved musician, no matter how free his family has been from music in past generations, is tainted by association with kespi musicians. Once a musician has become established as a paid professional, the fine line between šowqi and kespi is sufficiently blurred for some observers to put the performer in the latter category; the man has joined the lower ranks of society.

ID. Ustads (Masters) of Court and Radio Music

Steingass gives the following glosses for the word *ustād:*

A master, teacher, tutor; an artificer, manufacturer, artisan; a barber; ingenious, excellent, celebrated, famed for any art or work of ingenuity; enters into the composition of proper names, as *ustad rahman,* Ostad Rahman, etc. (1970:49)

and for *ustādi:* "An art, trade, craft; workmanship; excellence, skill in any art or profession" (1970:49). Steingass's definitions pinpoint the ambivalence of the term, which can apply to any artisan whatsoever, specifically including barbers, as well as to those who are excellent, celebrated, and famed for art and ingenuity. This ambiguity carries over into the use of *ustad* (or *ustā*) in Afghan Persian (Dari). Truck-drivers are sometimes called *usta,* but the term is also used for the singers of Indian or quasi-Indian art music of Kabul. Master performers

of any repertoire may be termed *ustad;* thus Bābā Qerān, the venerable
player of the *dambura* (a widespread folk lute), is often referred to
as the *ustad* of the dambura, and the term here could be roughly
translated as "doyen." In Turkmen, the term *baxši* for master performer
has none of the ambivalence of the Persian *ustad* whereas the Persian
speaker automatically injects a note of denigration even while using
a term expressing considerable praise.

The ambivalence of the term *ustad* is not a matter of mere philo-
logical bandying. Let us look more closely at the men to whom the
epithet is most often applied: the specialized art singers of Kabul.
We are not straying far from the North when we shift our attention
to the capital, for the voices and influence of the Kabul ustads reach
a considerable nationwide audience over the radio. Furthermore, the
ustads appear personally in the North from time to time when invited
by wealthy patrons to make guest appearances for festivities (principally in Katağan). To understand the position of the ustads we must
backtrack into the history of Afghan urban music. According to Abdul
Wahab Madadi, performer and archivist of Radio Afghanistan, the
groundwork for the present system of ustadi was laid during the reign
of Amir Sher Ali Kahn (1869–79). At that time the principal urban
and court singers were of Persian origin, though longstanding artistic
contacts with India must certainly have been evident as well. Sher Ali
chose to import some half-dozen leading singers from India to introduce
a new variety of court music. They were named ustads. He settled
them and their families in a district of Kabul that was later termed
the *xarābāt* (from *xarab,* "ruined, debauched, indecent"; Steingass
1970:451). The xarabat became the center both of lower-class musicians' dwellings and of Sufi (mystic) gathering places, a situation that
prevails today. Madadi estimates the number of musicians' homes in
the xarabat at more than one hundred.

At some point in the development of the xarabat a number of
Gypsy families is supposed to have attained musical prominence.
Under King Amanullah (1919–29) court music reached a new flower-
ing, and the ustad families grew in fame. With the rise of the radio in
the late 1950s, these court musicians became the pillars of a new
musical establishment. Today the busts of Ustad Qāsem and Ustad
Ğolam Husain stand in the front lobby of the Radio Afghanistan
building. The children of that generation of ustads, Ustad Sarahang,
Ustad Rahimbaxš, and Ustad Mohamad Omar, have become major
figures in the musical world of Kabul and of Radio Afghanistan, and
the debut of Ustad Sarahang's son, singing in Indian *thumri* style with
his father, forecasts the continued flourishing of this musical dynasty.

The ustads are highly spoken of and are treated with deference; they command large fees for private performances. Yet their low origin has not been forgotten, nor has the hereditary nature of their trade. One radio singer who does not sing for private parties has told me that his demurral is due to familial pressure: he is not supposed to indulge in the same activities as "those sons of Jats [Gypsies], the ustads." Whether or not any of the ustads are actually Gypsy in origin, such remarks place them in an inferior social category.

Thus the ustads provide us with an interesting juncture of several aspects of ascribed musicianship discussed above. The possibility that at least putative Gypsies may rise to considerable artistic heights is demonstrated; hereditary musicians are shown to have a viable occupation outside the domain of barbering and other service trades; and high financial rewards for both groups turn out to be possible as well. Yet the social stigma remains, if only in muted form, and the ustads are fated to be considered kespi after all. Šarif, himself a professional musician of Mazar-i Šarif, has a rather extreme view of the ustads' position as kespi performers. He says, "Only the ustads of Kabul are really kespi," since barbers, though hereditary musicians, may only be part-time performers, while the ustads live wholly by their hereditary talent.

IE. Šowqi (Amateur) Families with Musical Proclivity

Certain šowqi families form a limited, marginal category, which I include to show how fine the distinction can be between ascribed and achieved musicianship. It appears to me that in various parts of Afghanistan there are "musical families" in the Western sense — that is, they tend to produce more than an average number of musically inclined individuals. Theirs is, of course, a far cry from the "hereditary" musicianship of the barbers, Gypsies, and ustads. Whether they actually become musicians or on what level they might function as performers is more related to general societal pressure than to family tendencies. I imagine the number of such families to be rather small, but some outstanding musicians have come from them. The most prominent one I know of is Bangeča Tašqurğani, one of the foremost musicians of the North. Bangeča has told me with pride that his father, brother, and uncle are all *damburačis* (dambura-players): "Everyone knows my *qaum* [here the term means extended family] are all damburačis." Yet Bangeča insists on the title šowqi and would be offended if referred to as a kespi musician: after all, he is no barber. Šarif, the musician quoted above, concurs with this viewpoint; despite Bangeča's family proclivity toward music, he cannot be considered kespi. Such delicate intricacies of status lead us to an examination of our second large grouping of musicians, those who have achieved their position through individual effort rather than assigned societal role.

IIA. Most Types of Amateurs (Šowqi)

Under this category I include those amateur musicians in the Western sense (unpaid lovers of the art) who are termed šowqi in the local classification, and I have divided them into four rather different groups, all of whom are casual musicians operating without remuneration. The first type, nomad and peasant amateurs, is quite a large body of music makers, spread across most of Afghanistan. A great many nomads and peasants take pleasure in unsophisticated and open performance of folk music. Whether out in the steppe in the traditional pose of watching the flocks, in the encampment at night, or during communal gatherings, nomads (virtually all of whom are Paštuns) enjoy singing and flute playing. Peasants likewise find occasions to make music, most often as a means of *sā'at-tiri* (passing the hours) during the winter slack agricultural season. When this pastime (in the literal sense of the word) becomes an increasing preoccupation of an individual, he will, as we have seen, be labeled šowqi by his fellows. This status may put him on the rocky road to becoming a professional musician, for it is from among this group of casual nomad and peasant performers (some 90 to 95 percent of the population) that the bulk of the professional musicians stem. Theoretically, the nascent musician undergoes the stages in acquiring and mastering the folk music tradition described by Lord (1960) for the Yugoslav epic singer: years of listening, followed by a period of quiet, almost surreptitious experimentation, culminating in an experimental performance before a highly critical audience. Under this scheme, the changeover to professional would occur on the day that the performer first received wages for his work.

Unfortunately, the development of an amateur into a professional has not as yet been studied, so one must rely on descriptions of a performer's early years. As far as I can gather, there is indeed almost a total lack of formal training involved in becoming a musician — the trade is picked up by ear. Vital to the continuing progress of a fledgling šowqi is positive reinforcement from the local audience, and thus I doubt that the line between sub-rosa experimentation and full-fledged performance is as neat, at least for Afghanistan, as Lord describes. A good deal of interplay between the musician and his listeners takes place for two principal, connected reasons: the performer must find out whether he is at home in the role of musician, and the audience needs to check the budding musician's credentials, prodding him to expand his repertoire, improve his skills, and mold his image as performer. The hereditary musicians, for whom this process is not quite so crucial, form a minority of the practicing performers of the North. The bulk of the musicians are almost literally recruited by local audiences from among the broad mass of peasants and nomads, and this process is vital to supplying the large body of listeners with enough musicians to fill the local musical needs. (It would be very useful to have a total survey of the North, subregion by subregion, that would give accurate statistical grounds for determining the number of musicians needed to produce the requisite number of performances per locale per year; unfortunately, such data will not be available for some time to come.)

To summarize the position of the nomad and peasant amateurs, the two key points are: (1) the number of music makers included is large, and (2) they form an active pool of talent from which the ranks of professional musicians are largely filled.

Two other categories of amateurs, the urban bourgeois and the student amateurs, differ considerably in numbers, goals, and repertoire from those just considered. The most obvious difference lies in the basically urban provenience of the bourgeois and student musicians. This fact alone helps explain the other key differences, which stem largely from the urban preference for radio (hence Kabul-related) music over the local folk music of the area. The typical bourgeois amateur is like the shopkeeper of Mazar-i Šarif who invited me to an upstairs room to hear him sing a poem of his own invention in Kabul style, set to a tune markedly similar to that of some radio songs, and accompanied on the *tanbur* (a Kabul-based instrument). On the other hand, students' musical imaginations tend to be fueled by the output of the radio's amateur hour, a program in which Kabul's high school and university students vie for preeminence in a style combining elements of Afghan, Iranian and Western pop music. Students are likely to try their hand on the *armoniā* (harmonium), the ubiquitous accompanying instrument of Indian origin. The piano has taken over this role in the Radio Afghanistan studio, but virtually no pianos exist in Afghanistan outside of Kabul. Occasionally students in the farther provincial towns will employ local folk instruments, but generally in an attempt to produce the radio style.

Unlike the nomad and peasant amateurs, the bourgeois and student dilettantes rarely if ever go on to become professional musicians, unless they should happen to move to Kabul and gain radio stardom. Thus these urban musicians tend to form pockets of Kabul style amid the surrounding mass of nascent and active folk musicians; bridging the two groups are the šowqi professionals, whose repertoire encompasses all available styles.

Before turning to these master musicians we must take up one additional type of urban šowqi, consisting of the small band of lovers of what might be termed Buxaran classical music. The instruments and repertoire of this music have only a small foothold in Afghanistan, but the presence of the art must be taken seriously because of its strong appeal to Uzbeks. Performers of this genre include men of a variety of professions and backgrounds. In the town of Andxoi, the center of the art, three of the finest musicians — Ğafur Xan, Ğafur-i Wafā, and Šoqol Sufi — are a shoemaker, a son of a large landowner, and a shopkeeper, respectively. Some of these šowqis come from families long settled in Afghanistan, while others belong to mohajerin (refugee) families who left Soviet Central Asia in the period ca. 1917– 40. Of particular interest for our present inquiry is the fact that these men, and others like them in towns such as Kunduz and Kabul, maintain the old Uzbek tradition of the gentleman-musician who plays for the love of the art and spurns recompense. Though they may be patronized by wealthy merchants and landowners in the sense of being feted at private parties, it is the respect of the listeners they seek rather than a fee for performance. They all avoid outside public appearances and prefer to play for a select circle.

This attitude toward art music is deep-seated in bourgeois Uzbek families. Badruddin Šarafi, a connoisseur of the Buxaran style, has described to me his family life when he was a child. One feature of the household was regular, frequent evenings of poetry readings, mainly of classical Persian and Uzbek verse. One member of the party would have prepared a poem for analysis, and the verses would be read line by line, with pauses for discussion and analysis by all the members of the men's literary circle. Men would also bring their own poetry to the meetings for critical comment. In such an atmosphere, a talented singer of the poetry was greatly appreciated (see Beliaev 1975 for Transoxanian parallels). It is worth noting that after the introduction of Uzbek programming on Radio Afghanistan in 1972, the two Uzbek singers chosen by listener poll were both performers on the Transoxanian *dutar* lute, rather than on the Afghan dambura. One of them, Ğafur-i Wafa, was mentioned above as a leading šowqi of Buxaran classical music; presumably the pittance he receives for performance does not lower his status as a "pure" musician. The Turkestani and Kabul circles of Buxaran-style connoisseurs overlap to a certain extent, thanks to the radio broadcasts and the travels of performers and connoisseurs.

IIB. Professional Musicians (except those under IB, IC, ID)

Here we have reached the domain of the šowqi professionals. It should be apparent by now that there is no contradiction in linking "šowqi" and "professional," especially if we apply the following definition of "professional" from the Oxford English Dictionary: "One who makes a profession or business of what is ordinarily followed as a pastime." This is a particularly apt definition of the šowqi's professional sphere of activity, for it indicates a commonality of experience for amateur and professional. There are three types of šowqi professionals: the master musicians, often itinerant; the ğaribi-šowqi, who are part-time musicians of lesser standing; and those radio musicians (the majority) who are not in the ustad category.

IIB1. ŠOWQI MASTER MUSICIANS (FULL-TIME)

The master musicians of the North (not to be confused with the ustad "masters" of the radio) are all šowqi; that is, they have arrived at their positions through the kind of informal training and encouragement described above under category IIA, and they cling to the šowqi title tenaciously to avoid identification with the kespi musicians. For example, one of the best-known singers of Badaxšan introduced himself to me as Karim Šowqi Darwazi, giving his status (šowqi) before his place of origin (the Darwaz region of Badaxšan); others in the North referred to him as Karim Darwazi, whereas at Radio Afghanistan he was called simply Karim Badaxši ("from Badaxšan"), a name giving only his broadest point of origin.

Musicians insist on the šowqi label for another reason as well. The state of liveliness implied by the term is a necessary adjunct of their fulfilling of the musician's role. The leading musician of Aqča, Aq Pišak, uses a sobriquet meaning "white cat," apparently an allusion to his abilities as a *masxarabāz,* or comedian, in which role he makes humorous animal noises (examples are recorded on Anthology AST 4001) and generally plays the clown. Such talents can be useful for musicians, though by no means all performers can or do indulge in these professional tricks. It is, however, such indications of liveliness that lead listeners to say appreciatively, "U besiār šowqist" ("He's very šowqi").

Master musicians of this category tend to be itinerant, though there are notable exceptions such as Aq Pišak. Once firmly entrenched in the role of professional, they make their living following the samowad route from town to town, staying in a community as long as there are enough teahouse contracts and party jobs to play. We shall discuss later the ethnic origin and distribution of these musicians and the

*Fig. 1.4 Improvised outdoor teahouse under
Tašqurġan River bridge during 1972 drought*

development of their repertoire; important to note here are their extensive travels and the eclectic nature of the music they play, which embraces the major ethnic and regional musical strains. The widest-ranging tour I know of was that of Bāz Gul Badaxši in 1968; his home town is Kešm, westernmost city of Badaxšan, and I had accounts of him from as far away as Saripul in south-central Turkestan, seven bus or truck stops removed from Kešm. These wandering minstrels cross-pollinate the musical environment, keeping whole species of music alive, and are thus an integral component of the shared music culture of the North.

The work tends to be seasonal, and high points occur at various times of the year. The *Nowruz* (New Year's) season, which begins at the vernal equinox around March 21 brings forty days of celebrations, and music and dance occur much more openly in towns during this festival than at any other time of year, save for the *Ješen* holiday, a week-long festival in late August, commemorating Afghanistan's independence from British influence in 1919. Harvest time is another peak season for musicians. In his calendar of activities for the Tašqurġan region, Centlivres (1970: Plate XLIIb) gives the months of *Sombola, Mizan,* and *Aqrab* (August 23 to November 21) as the "saison des affaires, saison des mariages." On the other hand, the summer is definitely a slack season, for temperatures often rise to the 110°F mark in Turkestan and Katağan, and energy is conserved. Winter may be intermittently good to musicians if the rich landowners *(bāis)* decide to sponsor parties to accompany matches of *buzkaši,* the famed horsemanship contest of Turkestan. Thus by painstakingly following the course of party and teahouse, the itinerant musician can eke out a living, saving money from the fat seasons for the lean months. Financially, a musician can do at least as well as the ordinary worker in the North, and probably a good deal better, since in the course of two nights' work he can earn as much as a casual laborer does in a month: about 600 *afghanis,* or $7.50. The attitude of the šowqi professional is best summed up in the story surrounding Baba Qerān's adoption of his sobriquet. Baba Qeran, who was approximately eighty years old in 1968, is considered the dean of the šowqis. While Baba simply is an honorific applied to old men, *qerān* is a unit of currency (½ afghani, small change). According to some, in his youth the future Baba Qeran was quite popular as an amateur performer, but soon turned into a professional: when asked to perform at parties, he always said, "If there's a qeran in it, I'll go." Here the transformation from dilettante to paid šowqi is most concisely illustrated.

It is not easy to uncover the basic criteria for a master musician's success, but some guidelines can be advanced. The performer is expected to display three basic skills: eclecticism in repertoire, a certain level of instrumental virtuosity, and a good memory. It is on these points that he is judged, rather than on his startling innovations or his elegant style. Let us consider the three items singly.

Eclecticism means familiarity with the three basic sources of northern music: nonurban folk styles, traditional urban music, and outside music. The last category breaks down into two main groupings: the music of Radio Afghanistan and that of Indian films. (The music of the West has as yet had virtually no influence on the styles of northern Afghanistan — or, for that matter, on any Afghan taste beyond that of a tiny fraction of upper-class Kabulis.) The musician is free to blend these three wellsprings of creativity in any order and proportion he chooses. Specific mixtures of styles will be discussed later in this chapter.

The level of instrumental virtuosity required is hard to define. It does not generally involve a great display of technical prowess; there is, as we shall see, little attempt by instrumentalists to think up and execute prodigious feats of virtuosity on their instruments. Of course, people in northern Afghanistan, like listeners everywhere, are impressed by unusually difficult technical feats, but they do not seem to expect it or stress it as an important feature of good performance.

What is required, however, is the ability to hold a steady beat and to project effectively, qualities definitely related to the use of music as accompaniment to dance. Perhaps important reasons for the acknowledged mastery of Baba Qeran's performance are his rock-steady beat and his clear, strong articulation of musical phrasing. Other qualities that strike the Western observer and that are included in the analyses below, such as variation in musical material, seem to be of no particular importance to the audience.

Finally, a good memory is a vital criterion of a performer's success. He may receive requests, like an American band-leader at a wedding, for rarely heard pieces, and he is rated highly if he can produce tune after tune. One comment always made about Baba Qeran is that he knows an unbelievable number of melodies. Aq Pišak, for example, when pressed as to how many purely instrumental pieces he himself knew, estimated the number at perhaps twenty or twenty-five. As for Baba Qeran, Aq Pišak said that he must know at least a hundred tunes. Both figures are considerably lower than the truth, but the attitude is what is of importance here.

Like other factors under consideration, the relationship between playing and singing is somewhat vague. On the one hand, a musician who can both play and sing, like Bangeča Tašqurğani or Baz Gul Badaxši, is at an advantage, as he can impress an audience with both his instrumental and his vocal skills, and he doesn't need to hire helpers. On the other hand, the two other most famous musicians of the region, Baba Qeran and Aq Pišak, never sing at all and have achieved celebrity status through their instrumental exploits (and personality) alone. The ability to play more than one instrument is not particularly valued, and most performers prefer to be known as specialists.

IIB2. ǦARIBI-ŠOWQI MUSICIANS (PART-TIME)

The *ǧaribi-šowqi* form a very large class of musicians. In origin and activities they fall between the amateur šowqi and the full-time professional šowqi performers just described. To get at the concept, we must once again turn to the root meanings of the word employed, *ǧaribi,* and its adjective form, *ǧarib.* Steingass (1970:886) is a useful source:

ǧarib: uncommon, strange, outlandish, foreign; . . . a foreigner, stranger;
      poor, needy, humble. . . .
ǧaribi: foreignness, strangeness, indigence. . . .
ǧaribi kardan: to travel, become a stranger.

Thus, the notion of poverty is linked to that of traveling, wandering, becoming a stranger. The two ideas are clearly linked by the fact of itinerant labor, making a man at once poor and a wayfarer. The technical term for casual labor is *mardikāri*, however, and ğaribi is used with additional nuance in Afghan Persian. Ğaribi definitely means "poor man's work" of any sort; in an essentially poor and unemployed work force (a generous estimate would have one man in five employed), almost any job opportunity outside of the stable, well-paid occupations (as artisan, merchant, official) is referred to as ğaribi. By extension, even those with fortunate employment will self-deprecatingly refer to their work as ğaribi, although both you and he know that the compensation is more than adequate. (The American analogue would be a wealthy shopkeeper modestly indicating his department store with a shrug of the shoulders and the phrase, "Well, it's a living.") That ğaribi also implies travel is shown by the fact that a man can be said to have left town, or even to have gone abroad, for ğaribi.

With this broad definition of ğaribi in mind, it is easy to see how music can also be included. Any poor šowqi, regardless of his main occupation — if he is employed — will not turn down a chance to pick up extra money by displaying his talent. He may be asked to play while at a party, or may pick up the dambura hanging on the teahouse wall, and will be gratified by any recompense. Perhaps his talent is insufficient for him to support himself as a full-time musician, or maybe his personality is not appealing enough to the audience for him to become master šowqi — no matter: if he is a few afghanis ahead in the struggle for survival he has done well enough. For the economy of the North is basically still closed, and the concept of the limited good (Foster 1967) seems relevant to the region. In an area in which a man will walk an extra day to save two cents a pound on the price of sweets he will serve with tea at his samowad, any cash earned is to be taken seriously. Music as ğaribi is thus an important aspect of the art, in that it can keep someone's head above water for another day or month. This was particularly noticeable in the hard times of 1972, following two years of drought and a severe winter that destroyed the bulk of the livestock upon which Turkestan (indeed Afghanistan) depends so heavily. Amid the wreckage of the agriculture and stock-breeding, in a sea of unemployment, those who could purvey music to the still prosperous had a slight edge over those without such skills.

Cementing ğaribi-šowqis' position of importance in the shared music culture is the breadth of its ethnic and occupational base. Virtually all low-paid occupations are represented: I have known ǧaribi-šowqis who were butchers, former teahouse owners, nomads, shopkeepers, and truckdrivers, and they stemmed from a great variety of ethnic groups, including Paštuns, Uzbeks, Tajiks, Arabs, Turkmens, and such splinter groups as Ortoblāqi. A great many, of course, have no trade at all.

IIB3. MOST RADIO MUSICIANS

All radio singers who perform regularly, except for the ustads cited earlier, are paid achieved musicians. Within this general class, however, there is considerable individual variation in earnings. According to radio sources, there were only two singers in the early 1970s who earned their living solely through singing: Žila and Kamar Gul (both female). These two ladies sing frequently on the radio but earn the bulk of their income through private appearances. The rest of the radio singers either have independent incomes or are supported by their husbands. The radio pays very little per song (sometimes as little as one dollar) and gives no royalties for repeated broadcasting of songs.

One special category of radio musicians includes the official musicians, a group of veteran performer-composers who hold full-time, salaried positions in the radio organization (as archivist, assistant music director, etc.) and who occasionally appear as performers themselves. Another class of radio regulars consists of the members of the studio orchestra, who receive fairly small salaries but who make an excellent income by accompanying the ustads at their lucrative private appearances. A third group of performers is the newer body of enthusiastic young amateurs, for whom the nominal radio pay is of little importance; these are mainly the successful student amateurs mentioned earlier, whose ranks are swelling and who include members of the highest strata of Afghan society — for example, the son of Dr. Abdul Zaher, who was Prime Minister in 1975. The existence and activities of this corps of musicians is crucial to the future of music in Afghanistan as a whole.

The radio musicians, then, can all be considered professionals in the sense that they accept at least a nominal payment for their services, but they represent a variety of slots in the increasingly complex spectrum of musicians in contemporary Afghanistan.

IIC. Military, Police, and Municipal Band Musicians

The class of band musicians is rather odd and sui generis. Its roots lie back in the time of the Amir Abdurrahman (1880-1901), the first modernizing ruler of Afghanistan, who introduced the rudi-

Fig. 1.5. Maimana municipal band

ments of European-style music and even developed a notation system for national anthems and patriotic songs. It was, however, not until the days of King Amanullah (1919-29) that serious attempts were made to regularize official music. A musician named Farux Effendi was brought from Atatürk's Turkey to help develop court music; he remained, teaching Western notation to many students over the years, and is still active in Kabul. From this musical ferment a military music training program gradually emerged, spawning brass bands and a curious repertoire of half-Afghan, half-Western music under the general term *bājaxāna* ("hour-house," referring to the positioning of a band on the fortress gates to mark the time of day, a custom practiced with local instruments in the Kingdom of Buxara; see Beliaev 1975).

The national army band of Kabul, which plays for occasions such as the King's departure for state visits abroad, has in turn spun off a series of regional police bands recruited from ex-army-band personnel and permanently stationed in the provinces. These may, like their parent ensemble, be called bajaxana (as in Tašqurǧan), or sometimes simply *muzik* (as in Maimana), one of the rare usages of the Western term for music. The Maimana band is perhaps typical. It has now become a municipal institution under the mayor's office. The mayor himself ordered the instruments from England, a fact of which he is quite proud. The muzik plays for municipal occasions but also provides party music for private festivities. The repertoire of the nine-piece Maimana muzik includes items for every taste: an "Uzbek" piece of unknown origin, a Paštun *attan* (round dance), arrangements of radio tunes, and so on. The players all appear to be Paštuns, which would conform to the disproportionate representation of that ethnic group in the armed forces in general.

Police and municipal bands are a remarkable adaptation of Western music (which appear in glamorous military array) to local taste. What is extraordinary is that the bajaxana represents the only concession to Western influence apparent in the entire music culture of the North. Somewhat ironic is the fact that the Western military band itself originally derived from a Near Eastern model: the Ottoman Turkish janissary band, which terrified the armies of Europe in the sixteenth to eighteenth centuries and whose sounds Mozart, Haydn, and Beethoven incorporated in their compositions.

In terms of the present discussion, the interest of the bajaxana or muzik lies in the anomalous situation of its musicians, who are professionals in the sense that they are paid for regular work as musicians, but who function normally in an entirely different capacity as law enforcement officers. They are neither true professionals nor true ğaribi-šowqi, yet they encroach on the natural domains of both of these categories. Is one to term such a development "musical modernization"? It would be easy to do so, yet neither the repertoire nor the personnel of the police bands is in any sense modern (they play entirely in unison with no application of Western harmonic principles). Indeed, the institution of the quasi-military band of the city is quite old in the Near East and Central Asia, as noted above for the bajaxana of Buxara. It is only the instruments, imported from the West, that are new on the scene and, as noted, the Western ensemble is quite old, actually being Near Eastern in origin. Thus, the bajaxana of brass, while certainly new, hardly qualifies as "modern" in the sense beloved by political scientists and economists.

IID. Religious Singers

The special category of religious singers, like most of the others we have dealt with, includes both amateurs and professionals, but the two groups sing very different types of music. The genre sung mainly by amateurs is called *na't,* or *na'tiya* (Steingass 1970:1411: "The praise of the prophet following the praises of God at the beginning of books; a kind of invocation"). The texts of na't songs are usually in a literary, rather than folk, style, and the melodies seem to stem more from stylized religious recitation — e.g., Qur'anic cantillation — than from folk music sources.

The amateur singers (for whom šowqi is again the appropriate term) fall into two groups. One subgroup, which affects the North only marginally, consists of amateurs of high standing who are šowqi for religious music and who are broadcast over Radio Afghanistan. Holidays such as Muhammad's birthday are the primary occasions for the appearance of these performers, who share the honors with professional radio ustads. The more widespread type of na't singing found in the North is performed by local šowqis. They may sing on request at people's homes for religious occasions or at special gathering places of Sufis called *xānaqā* (the same term that is used in southern Tajikistan for a village religious gathering house; Nemenova 1953:63). Mazar-i Šarif in particular used to boast quite an extensive xānaqa because of the prominence of the shrine of Ali (Muhammad's son-in-law and the major local saint), site of the most important pilgrimage of Afghanistan at Nowruz time (Sultan Ali, Kabul, 1972:p.c.). Xanaqas are scattered at other key points throughout Afghanistan, though the institution is said to be in decline. In addition to na't singing, xanaqas have fostered the performance of Sufi *zikr* rituals, in which repeated, hours-long chanting of short religious formulas leads to ecstasy of the participants.

While na't singing is generally the province of šowqis, is performed only on special occasions and in private (except for the rare radio broadcasts), and is generally accorded respect, the other main type of religious singing is quite different. It is called *madā* and is sung on the street by lower-class itinerant musicians, at any time, and for pay (audience contributions). In both text and melody mada is often closer to local folk music than is na't singing, and in contrast to the more bookish na't texts, mada texts are probably improvised, at least in part, by the performers.

Mada is not relegated to the kespi category, since its practitioners are not ascribed to the role of mendicant singers; however, it is clear that mada singers do not have as much status as either na't singers or the better run of šowqi secular musicians. I would probably rank mada singers in the ğaribi-šowqi category — certainly they belong there economically, for they never seem to get large contributions and depend on the mercy of pious folk for their support. Often mada singers are blind, and perhaps their roles approaches ascription in the sense that the options open to blind people are quite limited.

Mada is generally practiced in the bazaar. The singer stations himself strategically near a teahouse, where there is likely to be a large audience, and proceeds to sing. At times the singer may have an assistant, who chimes in with a stock refrain to the verses; this assistant seems most useful in the case of the blind singers, since he can help collect money and guide the singer through the streets, but he may be found accompanying sighted performers as well. Onlookers generally appear rather uninterested in the performance and speak somewhat cynically of mada. When asked how mada is to be considered, they may merely shrug and say, "Ğaribist" ("It's a living").

Music as a Source of Income

At this stage in our analysis of the musician's role, it might be useful to turn from the ascribed-achieved dichotomy and to regroup the categories of performers differently, on the basis of music as a source of income. This approach is perhaps more familiar to the Western point of view, since we tend to make a rather sharp distinction between amateur and professional in all areas of activity. That such lines are hard to maintain becomes evident when definitions become increasingly arbitrary, as in the controversy over deciding who should be called an amateur athlete.

Here is the list of musicians rearranged on the basis of musical earnings; indicated in parentheses is the position of each category in the ascribed-achieved outline on page 29.

I. Music the sole source of income
   A. full-time šowqis (IIB1)
   B. some radio singers and instrumentalists, including ustads (IIB3, ID)
   C. religious street singers (mada) (IID1)
II. Music a partial source of income
   A. barber-musicians (kespi) (IC)
   B. ğaribi-šowqi (IIB2)
   C. most radio singers (IIB3)
   D. police and municipal bandsmen (IIC)
   E. Gypsies (IB)
III. Music not a source of income
   A. nomad and peasant amateurs (IIA1)
   B. true šowqi of Uzbek classical music (IIA4)
   C. most village and town women (IA)
   D. šowqi religious singers (IID2)
   E. bourgeois and student amateurs (IIA2, IIA3)

Looking at the music culture from this point of view, we find rather unexpected bedfellows in each category: radio stars with barbers and Gypsies, street singers with ustads, and so on. It is obvious that musicians may be included in the same category for radically different reasons, and that the use of one apparently clear criterion, such as money earned, tells little about the underlying motivations and statuses of the individuals involved. Particularly interesting from this point of view is group III, for whom music is not a source of income. There are actually two subcategories in this grouping: those for whom music happens not to be lucrative, but who would appreciate payment if offered (A, B), and those for whom music is not supposed to be connected with money for reasons of status (C, D, E). The nomad and peasant amateurs and the bourgeois and student amateurs form, as we have seen, a pool of potential paid musicians. On the other hand, women, šowqi religious singers, and the true šowqis of Uzbek classical music (like their Kabul counterparts who are devoted to Indian classical music) must spurn any suggestion of payment in order to maintain their social position. For women it is a much more serious matter than for the religious or Uzbek šowqis, since a woman paid for singing or dancing is likely to be considered a prostitute, whereas a šowqi may merely lose prestige, or sink to a lower category of musician. A man who takes it upon himself to raise his image by singing the praises of the prophet in na't songs would probably not like to be confused with the lowly mada street singer. Similarly, in the appreciative amateur circle of lovers of Buxaran music, a respected performer would never bring up the question of money, since it would be tantamount to joining the league of "vulgar" teahouse singers.

Like group III, group II consists of individuals who are in the same category for differing reasons. Whereas the barbers, Gypsies, and police do not expect music to provide more than a partial income, most of the ǧaribi-šowqis and the radio singers would probably not mind increasing their earnings from music if they could. Group I is similarly fragmented. For full-time šowqis and for the ustads and their accompanists, having music as their sole source of income represents a considerable degree of professional success. On the other hand, the lowly mada singer, particularly if blind, cannot take comfort from having attained this sort of success; for him music is a scant sole income, and it is one of the few options open to him at all. I have not interviewed mada singers, but it seems likely that some of them have the compensation of religious devotion to their calling, which the other full-time professionals lack.

Finally, to round out our perspective on the musician's status and activities, we must take into account yet another factor: the contrast between older and newer attitudes towards the musicians and his craft. These fall into two clear zones of pre-radio and post-radio attitudes and practices. Musicians in the pre-radio area, as we have seen, were received with a highly ambivalent public attitude. On the one hand, they were clearly recognized as basic to the celebration of all festivities, public and private. Talented members of the general community were selected and encouraged to become part-time or full-time practitioners, with some ideal number of musicians fixed in the collective mind. In some spheres of musical activity (na't singing, Uzbek art music, etc.), music was looked upon as a praiseworthy activity. Women, who were highly restricted in their range of possible musical performance, pushed for maximal participation under the stringent rules.

On the other hand, the religious leaders *(mullahs)* of the community occasionally fulminated against music as being the road to moral ruin. Police at times cracked down on the more flagrant examples of laxity, such as the abduction and training of young boys for "wanton" dancing. Respectable pillars of society kept their love of music a guarded secret lest they be accused of harboring lower-class tastes or, at worst, identified with the barber or Gypsy category.

All of these manifestations of the older, ambivalent approach to music still hold for contemporary Afghanistan. The authorities in Kunduz still forbid any sort of music in teahouses. Šowqis still fight to keep that title and avoid any identification with the kespi musicians. And there are still mullahs across the land to raise voices against any sort of recreation, indeed against nearly all the šowqi activities: gambling, animal fighting, drinking, games, and music. Likewise, the widespread love of music and unabated participation of šowqis continue. However, superimposed on this traditional, if contradictory, set of values is the new ethic of the Radio Age, which has tipped the scales in favor of the promusic tendencies.

The change brought about by the rise of radio is mirrored in the biography of one of its products, whom I shall call Gunješq. He is a beloved singer of the airwaves and an official of Radio Afghanistan, and he comes from a major city that has been a seat of sophisticated urban music for centuries. He came to Kabul in the mid-1950s to enter the Afghan Institute of Technology (AIT), an American aid project. His arrival during that particular period was crucial to his eventual career, for AIT was then in a process of rapid expansion, fueled by the return of the first group of American-educated teachers. Gunješq's talents as a singer of Herati songs evoked conflicting responses at AIT. While the principal of the school, an older man, violently opposed music on campus and upbraided Gunješq for his efforts, the technological Young Turks at the school supported student recreation and fostered fledgling talent. It is not at all accidental that this situation should have arisen within the most educationally advanced and most technologically oriented sector of Afghanistan: AIT was a major beneficiary of cold-war economic aid, which opened Afghanistan to modernization for the first time since the futile attempts of King Amanullah in the 1920s, and which allowed the first large-scale influx of foreigners and outflow of Afghan students abroad. A final integral component in the changing social situation change was Radio Afghanistan, which had started in the 1930s under limited German aid, and finally came into its own as a national institution during the 1950s. The juncture of these culturally explosive developments has had a major impact on Afghanistan in many spheres of activity, and in none more than in music.

Gunješq was sufficiently encouraged by the atmosphere at AIT to audition at the radio. He proved acceptable, and began to sing regularly. Shortly thereafter, his mother wrote that she had disowned him — "you are no longer my son." This strong action dampened Gunješq's enthusiasm for a radio career, but he eventually returned to active singing. When he looked for a wife during this period he found that even his own relatives were not eager to give a girl to a musician, especially one who was willing to take on the performer's role before a nationwide public. In those days, says Gunješq, children mocked musicians on the street, and even an ustad invited to sing at a private party was treated in about the same way as black musicians in the United States in the recent past. Set apart from the guests and forbidden to eat with them, the singer had to perform exactly what was requested, not daring to venture beyond his host's musical preferences. He was paid poorly, was not allowed to speak with the guests, and was addressed curtly, like a servant.

By the early 1960s attitudes began to change, and by now there has been almost a total reversal of the negative aura surrounding radio singers. "When I used to visit my home town," Gunješq says, "my own uncle would not admit he knew me. Now I have a hundred uncles there. I was able to marry the girl I wanted [rather than being given someone expendable], and if I wanted another wife a thousand women would write and ask for my hand." Gunješq is now invited to parties not to sing, but merely for his presence, and guests — even women — are brought to him for conversation. In short, the near-pariah has become something of a social lion. Gunješq is saluted rather than mocked on the streets and receives a large quantity of fan mail. His picture appears in the newspapers, along with laudatory articles and interviews. Not surprisingly, Gunješq is gratified by this change in status.

However, the glory accorded radio stars of Afghanistan is still far from that given the top singers even of neighboring Iran — not to mention the adulation given Arab superstars such as Um Kalthum of Egypt or Fairuz of Lebanon. While there is no question that the radio has helped satisfy a great musical hunger of people across Afghanistan by providing nearly nonstop entertainment in every nook and cranny, it is unclear how this situation has affected the lot of the average musician in the North. For northerners, the impact of the radio falls into two phases. The first occupied most of the history of broadcasting in the region since its beginning in the 1950s, while the second only began with the adoption of programming in Uzbek and Turkmen in 1972. During the earlier phase, the master šowqis of course adopted the radio music into their wide-ranging repertoire, just as they absorb the songs of Hindi films, the other glamorous component of the shared music culture. Yet teahouse musicians have not been accorded the respect Gunješq now enjoys, nor does it seem that the rich merchants of Aqča would be eager to give their daughters even to a well-known master šowqi such as Aq Pišak, let alone to a barber-musician. Just as the radio, for all its impact, had virtually no connection with the overall socioeconomic structure of Afghanistan in its first contact phase, it has not touched that corner of the status quo occupied by the local musician.

The silver lining in this cloud may be the new Uzbek and Turkmen programming. Now, for the first time, northerners can hear their very own favorite šowqis over the air from Kabul (and nearly all of them have been taped for the radio archives). It has already become clear that Uzbek and Turkmen listeners turn off the Soviet stations broadcasting in their language (from Tashkent and Ashkhabad) for Radio Kabul at least one hour a day, when the new show comes on at 6:00 P.M. The director of regional programming *(program-i mahali)*, Faizullah Aimaq, has shown great sensitivity to the vast quantity of fan mail reaching him from all corners of the North and is doing his best to give northerners the performers and material they have been craving. While it is too early to assess the impact of this new programming on the status of local musicians, it would seem that their position in the social scale can only rise as a result. Certainly the repertoire is being fairly well maintained and restored, and perhaps bourgeois and student amateurs will soon follow suit and take up their own traditional instruments rather than the armonia and *tabla* of Kabul. According to Allah Berdi Surxi, director of Turkmen programming for Radio Afghanistan, the Turkmens have already felt a stirring of renewed interest in the dutar and the Turkmen flutes. Thus, while the radio is still impotent in the crucial questions of national change, in such areas as music and the maintenance of local and ethnic traditions it can play a vital role. In the long run, the sense of participation that groups such as the Uzbeks and Turkmens (as well as the Pušai and Baluch, also represented in the new programming) feel in their own Afghan cultural institutions is bound to bring out some change in attitude. To the extent that these peoples identify with a social order comprising their neighbors in Afghanistan and centered in Kabul, instead of with their fellow ethnics across the Soviet (or Iranian or Pakistani) border, Afghan national consciousness will have been deepened and a step forward in nation building will have taken place.

MUSICAL SPHERES OF INFLUENCE

Details of specific musical repertoires and instruments will be given in both Chapters 2 and 3; our task here is to briefly characterize those bodies of music and musical instruments that tend to be shared by several ethnic groups in the North. These can be grouped into five major complexes: women's music, Kabul music, religious and ritual music, certain secular tales, and samowad (teahouse) music.

Women's Music

Across the North two instruments are the principal available sound producers for women. These are the tambourine (doira) and the jew's harp (čang). As far as I know, among none of the ethnic groups in the region is it customary for women to play any of the numerous varieties of plucked and bowed lutes (fiddles). On the other hand, men are widely allowed to play both the tambourine and jew's harp. The jew's harp is also played by children; most northerners are likely to respond "women and children" when asked, "Who plays the čang?" It is only when pressed that they will admit that men can also perform on the jew's harp. This attitude was documented early in the 1950s by J. C. Lubtschansky. In his recordings of that period he includes a fine specimen of Uzbek jew's harp play, performed by a man, and he notes: "The man playing it on our request felt very much ashamed, for, said he, 'Only women and children play the chang'" (1969:2). Nevertheless, Lubtschansky's Uzbek displayed a high degree of skill on the čang, indicating that men do indeed practice the instrument. The nominal restriction of the jew's harp to women and youths is found in Soviet Central Asia among Tajiks, Kazakhs, and Kirghiz (Vertkov 1963:129, 131, 133).

The doira is less a matter of special northern development than is the čang, since tambourines of varying size and description are played by women all across the Near East, often under the name *doira* or *daf* (the latter is a term also found in Afghanistan, principally in Badaxšan). A particular local feature uniting the North's use of the doira, however, is the manufacture of the instrument by Gypsy artisans. Tambourines are made by Gypsies in locales as far apart as Aqča (Turkestan), Xanabad (Katagan), and the Koh-i Daman (just north of Kabul).

The lesson learned from separate examination of the two women's instruments — tambourine and jew's harp — is that one of two major factors can be at work in determining the place of any shared cultural or musical trait within the general matrix of the North: either the trait emerges as a result of local ethnic accommodation, sometimes on a microgeographic scale, as in the case of the adoption of the jew's harp by groups surrounding the Tajiks, or the trait may be part of an extensive Near Eastern–Islamic network in which northern Afghanistan figures only as a peripheral zone.

The women's repertoire is far less of a shared item than the instrumentarium. Although data for women of various ethnic groups is extremely limited at present, it seems that by and large each group commands its own repertoire of women's songs, with certain exceptions to be discussed presently. This is bound to be the case, because of the high degree of women's isolation within the household walls among the sedentary population. For example, Sakata's writing on Hazaras of Central Afghanistan (1968:35) contrasts men's familiarity with standard Afghan Persian (Dari) with women's reliance on the Hazara dialect (Hazaragi): "In most cases, Hazara men know and use Dari as well as Hazaragi, thus many of their songs are in Dari. . . . The women's songs, on the other hand, are more strictly in Hazaragi, since they are less exposed to other peoples and cultures." It seems likely that research in the North would reveal a similar pattern. The principal exceptions to the pattern are professional women singers, who must cater to more than one ethnic group. Thus Zulaixā and Gulandām of Andxoi sing wedding songs with quatrains in both Uzbek and Persian (examples recorded on Anthology AST 4001); they also sings songs that are purely in Uzbek (their native language) and related to Transoxanian Uzbek repertoires (Lyrichord LIST 7231).

However, despite the differences preserved through women's isolation, common features mark women's songs across the North. One factor influencing commonality is, once again, the radio. The women's wedding song "Astā bero" (analyzed under "Women's Music" in Chapter 3), probably stemming originally from a Kabul Paštun-Tajik milieu, has been popularized by the radio in many different versions — even in an arrangement by male amateurs with Western instruments. The radio has played only a minor role in promoting a joint musical storehouse for women, however. More potent as a unifier is the traditional assignment of two basic musical roles to women: singing lullabies and singing songs at domestic festivities, principally weddings. Unfortunately, scarcely any lullabies have been recorded in the North, so assessment of the nature and scope of the repertoire must await further research. Sakata's (1968) findings among the Hazaras of Central Afghanistan indicates that lullabies form an interesting and extensive body of women's songs. As noted earlier, celebrations such as weddings serve as important outlets for women and may be prolonged for their enjoyment; thus wedding songs form a large part of women's total musical activity. According to Surxi, Turkmen women sing only at weddings. The Uzbek repertoire seems particularly rich in wedding songs, and Tajiks and sedentary Paštuns sing a series of songs for different segments of the wedding ceremony. Beyond the basic unity of lullabies and wedding songs, the ethnic groups once again break into separate traditions for women, to be taken up in Chapter 2.

The Music of Kabul and the Mašreqi

One of the important components of the shared music culture is the body of repertoire and instruments stemming from the area of Kabul and eastern Afghanistan (Mašreqi). In its broadest geographical sense, this region could be considered the concentrated arena of Paštun urban music, which has strong folk song roots. The language and materials drawn upon cover nearly the whole of Paštun country, from Kandahar to Peshawar (Pakistan), but the results are distilled in a roughly triangular region embracing the Logar Valley south of Kabul, Kabul itself, and Lağman and Jalalabad in the east. This rich storehouse of Paštun rural (village and nomadic) and urban poetry and music has been little studied save in Hoerburger's (1969) brief survey and in the periodic collections of Paštun folk poetry issued by the Pašto Tolana (Pašto Academy) of Kabul. Even the dense musical life of Kabul has scarcely been discussed, and the data from Radio Afghanistan offered in the present study are hardly typical. Thus it is impossible to give a well-rounded picture of the fertile Paštun musical soil, whose abundant fruit is one of the principal cultural exports of the Kabul-Mašreqi area to the North.

Let us begin with the musical instruments, about which we are fairly well informed, though we are still far from having a definitive statement of their origin, use, and diffusion. Four instruments stand out as exports from Kabul-Mašreqi: two lute types (the tanbur and *robab*), a drum (the tabla), and the harmonium. The latter two are direct imports from India. The tabla is the standard North Indian set of two drums, and all the tablas in Afghanistan are of Indian origin. Likewise, the harmonium is never locally made. This diminutive relative of the organ was brought to India long ago by European missionaries and used as a tool in spreading Christianity. Once in India, it was soon adopted as a handy accompaniment for native art music, and it was in this guise that the harmonium reached Afghanistan, where it was termed *armonia*. Its use has spread as a result of the radio broadcasts, since it serves as accompaniment to the music of the ustads. Confined until recently to the Kabul-Mašreqi area, the armonia has diffused rapidly through the countryside and is prized among provincial aficionados of radio music. The great advantage of the armonia is that nearly any-one can pick out a tune on its keyboard, or at least hold down a couple of drone pitches and fake an accompaniment to a song. The ease of performance contrasts markedly to the skill needed to play any of the lute or fiddle types alternately available to amateurs.

The importance of the skill necessary for passable play is clear in the case of the tabla, which is by no means as widespread as the harmonium. The complicated drumming technique limits the use of the tabla to a handful of trained performers, and it is played in the North only in touring bands from the Kabul-Mašreqi area and in the ensembles of local musicians who have received special training from Kabul-Mašreqi performers. The tabla seems most indispensable in the Logar Valley style of dance music, the staple accompaniment to the performance of dancing boys. Although on most other occasions the goblet-shaped *zirbağali,* or any large tin can, may substitute for the recondite tabla. I have never seen it used for this *bačabāzi* dancing. It should be noted that few if any Afghan tabla players are so advanced in technical mastery as to be capable of the virtuoso performances offered by North Indian drummers. The tabla is generally used only for basic rhythmic patterns typical of zirbağali drumming, with the possible exception of certain gliding rolls easily played on the tabla; even in the latter case, however, one can find virtuoso zirbağali players (Malang Nejraui, for example) who can match or better Afghan tabla performance. Thus, in the case of the tabla it is the basic sound quality and the repertoire that cause its appearance outside of its basic area rather than the actual musical possibilities of the instrument, which remain largely unexploited by its players.

The case of the tanbur and robab lutes is quite different in most respects, principally in offering musical qualities unavailable in the North. The two lute types are distinctive in construction, playing style, and timbre, and both appear to be among the tiny group of instruments that can probably be said to have originated in Afghanistan. Let us take the tanbur first. None of the lute types of North India, Transoxania, or Iran is constructed precisely like the tanbur (see Figures 4.16–4.19). A tantalizingly similar instrument, called *setar,* is found among the Tajiks of Tajikistan, but the differences between the setar and tanbur are basic enough to preclude a direct connection. The earliest attested date for the existence of the tanbur is the year 1300 of the Persian calendar (A.D. 1821), the date carved on an old tanbur brought to me by Baba Naim of Kabul for inspection. The maker's name was also inscribed clearly and appeared antique, and I have no reason to doubt the instrument's authenticity. Thus it is clear that the tanbur is not a recent invention, and there is substantiation for the statements of older musicians that as far back as they could recall there had always been a tanbur in Afghanistan. Furthermore, the 1821 instrument is almost exactly the size and shape of the tanbur of Figures 4.16–4.19. (For more detail on construction and playing style, see Chapter 3.)

The national focus of tanbur construction and performance is the Kabul-Mašreqi area, but inquiries among Kabul tanbur makers yielded no positive results in pinning down the lute's origin any further. In the North, Mazar-i Šarif is the center of tanbur making and playing. Since both performers and instrument makers state that "whatever Kabul had, Mazar always had," it is reasonable to assume that the tanbur came north along with many other goods from Kabul. Outside of Mazar, this long-necked lute rarely appears, though its spread seems to have increased in the past few years. Confirming the theory of a spread from Kabul is the content of the tanbur repertoire in the North, which consists largely of Kabul-Mašreqi popular music. There is little, if any, purely instrumental music for the tanbur; it is almost always used as accompaniment for song. It may also be used for dance, in which case it is possible that local instrumental (dambura) dance tunes will be used. Here too, though, the repertoire often consists of songs arranged for instrumental use with little alteration or ornamentation. The chief attraction of the tanbur's sound is its metallic twang, produced by using a metal plectrum on the instrument's multitude of melodic and sympathetic wire strings. This sound quality is markedly different from the basic timbre of the dambura, the favorite local lute type, which features finger plucking and strumming on nylon strings combined with knocks on the lid.

The Kabul-Mašreqi robab also offers a special sound. This distinctively shaped instrument is the only Afghan short-necked lute, and save for the rare Pamir robab, it is the only lute type played with a wooden (or bone) plectrum. It is unique in appearance and timbre, as well as in its playing style, which features rapid repeated-note strokes and sharp breaks in sound that contrast sharply with the continuous sound of the dambura and *ğičak*. In the North, the tanbur and robab do not merely represent the appearance of a different music subculture, as does the tabla, but they also contribute a very real acoustic presence whose sound values differ sharply from those of the local music.

The repertoire of all the instruments just discussed consists primarily of Kabul-Mašreqi urban music, with some bending towards the regional northern style if audience demand warrants. The presence of at least the tanbur in pre-radio days in the North testifies to old musical links between that region and the Kabul-Mašreqi area. However, the recent widespread appearance of the harmonium again indicates the explosive nature of the radio impact, which diffused the use of an instrument new to the North within a comparatively short time.

The incursion of Kabul-Mašreqi music goes beyond its association with the instruments just discussed. Perhaps the farthest-reaching impact of the style has been in its adoption by the traditional šowqi performers who use the indigenous instruments of the North (dambura and ǧičak). In this case, it is almost entirely the music broadcast by Radio Afghanistan that is involved rather than folk music or non-broadcast repertoires of the Kabul-Mašreqi area. Radio music has become one of the prime components of the shared culture in the heart of the public music arena, teahouse performance, as well as in the private amateur playing of nonprofessionals or ǧaribi-šowqis across the North. In this eclectic, improvised style, the teahouse dambura player pulls in any and all types of music he knows, varying the length and content of the performance to his own and the audience's taste. Radio songs have become one of the assumed and integral parts of such pieces. Also of interest is the predominance of radio songs among people who sing in the street. Careful listening in any northern town will reveal that very few men sing while working or passing the time of day, and that of those who do, the majority are singing radio music; most important, in nearly all cases of children singing to themselves, radio music is being sung. For the younger generation the radio plays the main role in forming musical taste and repertoire; clearly the future belongs to the radio.

The radio style penetrates to the women's quarters as well. Eagerly taping wedding entertainment in Faizabad, to the consternation of the women performers (though egged on by male spectators), I found that I was recording merely a local variant of a standard radio favorite, "Anār, anār."

Religious and Ritual Music

Of all the little-studied areas of Afghan music, religious and ritual music has been perhaps the most neglected. We know very little about the genres and styles of this important segment of the music culture; indeed, save for Hoerburger's (1969) brief foray into Qur'anic cantillation, there is no literature on the topic whatsoever. Yet no aspect of Afghan music could be more shared than the ceremonial call of the muezzin or the chanting of street mendicants. As mentioned earlier, these varieties of singing are generally not classed as "music" by Afghans themselves, and this seems to be the case across much of the Islamic world. It is primarily outside investigators who take the category "religious music" for granted, basing it on the traditional European dichotomization of sacred and secular music, and thus we take some liberties in applying such categories to Afghan musical life. We can only state our investigative interest in considering all organized manifestations of song as part of the local music culture, while taking careful note of the Afghans' reluctance to include anything other than the genres of secular public male and domestic female songs and dances (and now radio performances, of course) within the domain of "music."

On the subject of Islamic music, we can say little here beyond referring back to the discussion of mada street singing and šowqi na't singing offered earlier as categories of shared public music making. We simply do not have enough available repertoire to make a thorough presentation of the styles and their implications for the joint music culture. It should be mentioned, however, that Persian seems universally preferred for mada street music, thus offering the ethnically mixed spectators-contributors a text in the lingua franca. In sharp contrast are the ethnically distinct religious repertoires (e.g., Uzbek). The mada style focuses on tales easily understood by a broad public, and the tales usually concern Ali, important to both Shi'a and Sunni factions of the audience. Thus mada seems to be a category of music involving catholicity both in its performers, who may be drawn from a variety of ethnic groups, and in its repertoire, which appeals to the broadest segment of the urban male listeners.

Let us turn to a consideration of ritual music. Here we are on more solid ground when it comes to the infrequent, localized, yet highly indicative phenomenon of shamanist practices in the North. Since two coauthors and I have published an extensive report of these data (Centlivres and Slobin 1971), here I shall only summarize the major findings for the town of K. in Afghan Turkestan. Briefly, we uncovered two strikingly different occurrences of shamanism in the town, one for males and the other for females. The male shaman, in approach, local terminology, and musical instrument, can clearly be related to Central Asian shamans, particularly those of the Kirghiz and Kazakhs. The female healer-diviner, on the other hand, seemed the center of a cult similar to those described for various segments of the Near East and neighboring areas (e.g., the Zar cult of Ethiopia). The occurrence of northern shamanism is significant for the present discussion in three ways: (1) it confirms the basic description of the region's cultural traits, which clearly show the intersecting of widespread Islamic and

Near Eastern characteristics with elements of localized Central Asian phenomena; (2) it substantiates our earlier conclusion regarding the use of ceremonial and musical events by women as important expressions of their independence; (3) the fact that the clienteles of both male and female shamans, as well as the shamans themselves, derive from a variety of groups in the multiethnic town of K. gives further support to our hypothesis of a shared music culture in the North. Judging by the available data, we can regard these manifestations of shamanism as being quite anachronistic, even archaic, in the milieu of a present-day Afghan town; indeed, the male variety of shamanism, at least, seems clearly on the decline. The presence of such an old pattern of inter-ethnic ritual participation strengthens our belief in the existence of extensive ethnic accommodation in Afghan Turkestan extending back into earlier times.

Barth has noted that

Stable inter-ethnic relations presuppose . . . a set of prescriptions governing situations of contact, and allowing for articulation in some sectors or domains of activity, and a set of proscriptions on social situations preventing inter-ethnic interaction in other sectors. . . . (1969:16)

It is revealing that so important an area of belief as shamanism should be one of the "prescribed" items in the area of joint activity.

Secular Tales

Once again we are in a little-researched domain when we come to the interethnic distribution of a corpus of secular tales. Preliminary evidence seems to indicate the existence of a shared body of narratives (as distinct from the large number of tales with currency only among a given ethnic group, to be discussed in Chapter 2 under their respective subcultures).

One such tale is the story of Buniyāt-i Palewān, or Buniyat the Wrestler. Wrestling is one of the main arenas of direct interethnic competition in the North, the only other major sport being the buzkaši horsemanship event. Thus a tale about a wrestler is of some ethnic interest, and it calls for a brief description of the sport itself. Wrestling is common all across the North, and may be daily recreational fare in the spring. In Kunduz in May and June, two to three hundred men and boys gather on the *čamān* (the same meadow used for buzkaši in the winter) every afternoon between five and six o'clock for informal wrestling matches *(palewāni)*. The mood on the occasions I have witnessed was quite relaxed, with numerous food vendors pushing carts and boys selling cigarettes; the whole event has a casual after-work air, with considerably more good humor and quiet enjoyment than accompanies such exciting and tense sporting events as partridge or dog fights. No money is exchanged at Kunduz. The crowd slowly forms a neat circle, and it is some time before contestants are separated from observers. The wrestlers strip off their work shirts and put on special jackets made of dense cotton, not unlike judo jackets. As in judo, a belt is tied carefully. The competitors circle round the ring a few times, then kneel and make a brief prayer. Unlike such celebrated occasions as the Turkish greased wrestling matches, northern Afghan wrestling features no musical accompaniment whatsoever. The match begins with one wrestler tugging the other's belt; a stance, again similar to that of judo, is taken, with each contestant grasping the other's lapels, and the struggle to down one's opponent begins. The back touching the ground signals the end of the match. At no time is special force applied for the purpose of inflicting pain. Once I saw a wrestler fall headlong on his nose, producing general consternation and putting a stop to the match until it was clear that no injury had been sustained.

Though contestants stem from any of the many local ethnic groups (I saw Paštun, Hazara, Uzbek, Turkmen, and Loqai contestants) and their identity is well known to the audience, who spot the "regulars," there seemed to be no tension involved in the victory or defeat of a given group's representative. This contrasts with Snesarev's description of Uzbek wrestling, which he sees as "ironically sacred" and as "a struggle of two groups" implicit in the competition between individuals (1971:269). The absence of such tension in Kunduz perhaps underscores the relatively tranquil interethnic relations prevalent in the North.

Turning now to "Buniyat-i Palewan," the tale, like Kunduz wrestling, seems multiethnic in distribution and ambiguous in ethnic content. Basically it seems to reflect an earlier period of greater ethnic confrontation. I have three versions of the tale, one taped in Kunduz from an apparent Uzbek, one taped in a village near Aqča from an apparent Turkmen, and one taped in Sangčerak (by the Tappers) from a Gypsy performer. All three versions are in Persian. Only one of them (the Kunduz version) is lengthy enough and clear enough to present a complete story. Here is a translation of the text as sung by Almas.

BUNIYAT-I PALEWAN

There's a big town called Andijan
Below is a Turkmen tribe with big turbans
From among them came Qader Khan
When he strikes a cypress it trembles

In the royal garden he wrestled much
And he sat there talking
Buniyat came from down there
When he saw Buniyat he trembled
Both come to the square like roaring lions
And they play with their paws like winter wolves
Buniyat has the habit of throwing his opponent over his shoulder
"Ya haidar," he says, and grasps his opponent by the waist
He calls on The Forty
The Farwan blows the trumpet to celebrate
He gives a hundred afghanis in silver to each as a prize
He takes the money to the faqirs around Ali's tomb
He sees three *korons* [small units of money] in the bottom of his pocket
He takes tea and bread and takes it to the Farwan
Before he finishes the tea and bread a decree came
"O please read my decree"
Take this decree to the head clerk
The head clerk read it and saw the name of Amir Mahmud Khan
Take Buniyat to Kabul; it takes thirteen days to Kabul
On a given Wednesday they cleared a large square
On Thursday they were talking about something
Amir Mahmud Khan himself has twenty-four wrestlers
Four together pulled him down like a goat to slaughter
He ordered the cannoneer to tie him to the cannon
"Please dear sir don't tie me to the cannon"
They bared his back and there were the five fingers of Ali
So Amir Mahmud Khan gave him many prizes
All the high-ranking officials gave him robes
And gave him to the police to convey him safely across the borders
When he came to the border there were twelve guards; four Turkmens
       and eight Afghans
"How are you coming, young man?
How did you come from the land of Saxijan [Turkestan]?
Say your last prayers because we are going to shoot you."
He puts his hand to the sheath but the knife doesn't come out
They killed Buniyat the hero on the eve of *Eid-i Qurban* ["Festival of
       the sacrifice," a major religious holiday]
Because of the blessing of Saxi [Ali] may you always be as rich and
       fertile as you are, Turkestan
And may the throne of the king of Afghanistan be secure
We send you greetings Nadir Khan!

A good deal of ambiguity is present in the tale, which no one has been able to clarify thus far. Let us look at some of the unclear points. First, Andijan is a city in the Ferghana Valley, and it is far removed from "the Land of Saxijan," i.e., Afghan Turkestan, where we must assume the rest of the action takes place if we accept the presence of Turkmens. Some Afghans have suggested that there might be a village in Afghan Turkestan named Andijan, and this could well explain the discrepancy since many place names are duplicated on both sides of the present Afghan-Soviet border.

Equally ambiguous and more important to our understanding of the tale is the ethnic identity of Buniyat himself. His name is Persian, if we interpret it as *buniyād,* meaning "a foundation, basis," as in *"bunyad afghandan,* to found, to build up" (Steingass 1970:204). It seems more a mythic than an actual name — I have never heard of a live Buniyat. Furthermore, a Persian name, like the Persian text, adds to the lingua franca aspect of the tale. The version of the tale given above leaves the hero's ethnic affiliation open; all we know is that he can vanquish both his local Turkmen and his royal Kabul opponents. While Buniyat himself is aboveboard in action, his enemies clearly have it in for him; the King, apparently a poor loser, wants to have him executed and is only stopped by divine intervention in the form of the fingerprints of Ali. At the end, the monarch gets his way by having the border guards do Buniyat in. Why the assassins are identified as Turkmens and Paštuns is also unclear. The interesting part of informants' responses to the tale is that they seem unable to clear up the uncertainties, or if they do give explanations, they vary considerably from person to person, leaving the observer with the impression that the tale is meant to be ambiguous in imagery, to fit local situations. The only usable fact in Almas's performance of "Buniyat-i Palewan" is found not in the tale itself but in the tag ending, which mentions Nadir Khan at the very end. Nadir Khan (later Nadir Shah; reigned 1929–33) was the father of the recent king, Zahir Shah, and mention of his name at least dates the tale in some way. The troubled times of 1928–29 (the successful uprising against Amanullah, followed by Nadir Shah's overthrow of the usurper Bača Saqow), were steeped in ethnic unrest. Particularly in the North there was deep division during those years of the uprising and Nadir Shah's reign, and people no longer choose to speak of them. It was the last period of such deep interethnic conflict and as such is well remembered, so it is perhaps not accidental that "Buniyat-i Palewan" relates to those times, that it refers to interethnic strife, and that it is still recounted, if somewhat unclearly by now.

In addition to "Buniyat-i Palewan" there are apparently other tales common to more than one ethnic group that circulate in the North; further research is needed to identify the repertoire and its ethnic meaning. The tale is important for the present discussion because it represents a category of folklore that can be described as part of a shared repertoire and that must be included with other manifestations of the joint music culture under review here. We shall see in Chapter 2 that tales specific to only one ethnic group are a good deal more precise in origin, content, and distribution; it therefore seems likely that tales of the "Buniyat" type represent a special cross-ethnic case.

Interethnic sharing of tales has yet another aspect. One can find the same tale spread among various groups with each version in the basic language of its tellers. The prime example of this trend in northern Afghanistan is the occurrence of the Köroğlu tale. Stories about the outlaw-hero Köroğlu abound from Turkey out into Central Asia (see Chadwick and Zhirmunsky 1969, Karryev 1969), so it is not surprising to find ethnic variants in the Afghan North. There Turkmens, Uzbeks, and Tajiks each preserve their own versions of the same epic subject (Anthology AST includes a recording of an Uzbek version).

Teahouse Music

The music of the teahouse (samowad) is among the most prominent features of the shared music culture. However, the distribution of samowad music is regionally inflected. The stronghold of live teahouse music is Turkestan, where local market towns feature live music on at least one of the two bazaar days each week. In Katağan the picture is somewhat more spotty. At times there has been employment of local musicians in teahouses, but in recent years the custom has faded, largely because of governmental interference. It seems that the guardians of public morals have clamped down on public entertainment more heavily in Katağan than in Turkestan, at least in the larger towns. Farther east in Badaxšan there may be live music at teahouses, but the samowad is not the focal point of musical activity that it is in Turkestan. Instead, sporadic private and public performances are held, often in the form of picnic-like gatherings. Despite this rather erratic spread of the Turkestani samowad complex, the instruments, repertoire, and performance manner typical of the genre have had widespread impact across the North and beyond, to Central and East Afghanistan.

Five basic instruments are employed: the dambura, a two-stringed fretless lute; the ğičak, a two-stringed fiddle; the *zirbağali,* a pottery or (infrequently) wooden goblet-shaped drum; a pair of small finger cymbals (Persian *zang* or *tal,* Uzbek *tüsak*); and a small set of jingles on a string wrapped around the dambura player's right hand *(zang-i kaftar).* These instruments are not all of northern origin and are not equally distributed throughout the neighboring zones. For instance, the zirbağali is nearly universal in Afghanistan, save for some Paštun zones (Hoerburger 1969), where the two-headed *dhol* drum is favored. On the other hand, the tüsak and zang-i kaftar are largely limited to

Fig. 1.6
Teahouse in
Samangan

the North and more particularly to Turkestan and Kataḡan. It is principally the two stringed instruments, the dambura and ḡičak, that symbolize in material terms the spread of the northern teahouse style; we shall return later in this chapter to the ethnic significance of the instruments.

The teahouse repertoire, like the instruments, breaks down into purely local components and those of wider currency. Among the latter is the use of improvised, semi-improvised, and stock quatrains as the main verse form for songs. This genre can be found not only in other areas of Afghanistan, but also across the Persian-speaking world in Azerbaijan and out into Turkic Central Asia. The more recent element in this category is the radio music. Local contributions include regional or subregional melodies, clearly identifiable as such, and used for both songs and instrumental (primarily dance) tunes. Certain characteristics of rhythm may also be localized.

Samowad music is shared by virtually all the ethnic groups in Turkestan, with the possible exception of the tiny Kazakh community, whose members claim to spurn all music save their own Transoxanian style. Performers and audience may be drawn from the major ethnic groups (Tajiks, Uzbeks, Turkmens, Paštuns, Hazaras) and from the smaller groups as well (Arabs, Moğols, Ortoblaqi, etc.). In each case the participants shed their particular ethnic music subculture (if any) to join as full-fledged members of the shared music culture. In so doing, they are of course affirming their interest in a more widespread cultural pattern of which music is only a part: the old, sedentary iranized culture of northern Afghanistan connected at one end to the general Iranian plateau culture and at the other to the history and development of Transoxania. While it is not possible at present to expound a general ethnography of the North, we shall try to get at the roots of the ethnic blend through examining the heart of the musical situation: cultural accommodation between the Uzbeks and the Tajiks, which sets a pattern that has spread to the remaining peoples of the area. It is only in the light of the relationship between these two major groups of the North that one can characterize the milieu in which the newcomer groups (Turkmens, Paštuns) and minority groups (Aimaq, Arabs, etc.) have adjusted.

PATTERNS OF UZBEK-TAJIK CONTACT

To examine the Uzbek-Tajik relationship we must take a broad overview of their patterns of contact over the entire area in which they are immediate neighbors. The map of putative Uzbek-Tajik musical zones (Map 1.1) shows this area. Its outside boundaries (the Khwarizm enclave apart) include all the Tajiks of the USSR and all the northern Tajiks of Afghanistan. The boundaries also include nearly all the Afghan Uzbeks (save for those in the Kabul area), but not all those Persian speakers who are at times called Tajiks (this fact is discussed in the Introduction). We shall first characterize the general historical situation that produced the contemporary patterns of contact, and then review the zones of Map 1.1, adding ethnographic data to clarify the musical situation. The major hurdle in such an enterprise is that for some regions the ethnographic data are almost totally lacking while the musical data are rich (the Afghan North), whereas for other regions the anthropological evidence is much more complete than the musical information (most of Transoxania). The following argument, then, should be seen as a first step in exploring Uzbek-Tajik relations, based on the limited available data, very little of which are directly concerned with the question at hand: how has the fact of living side by side over the course of nearly five centuries worked toward creating a highly symbiotic cultural pattern among Uzbeks and Tajiks? It is hoped that eventually a systematic exploration of this topic will be

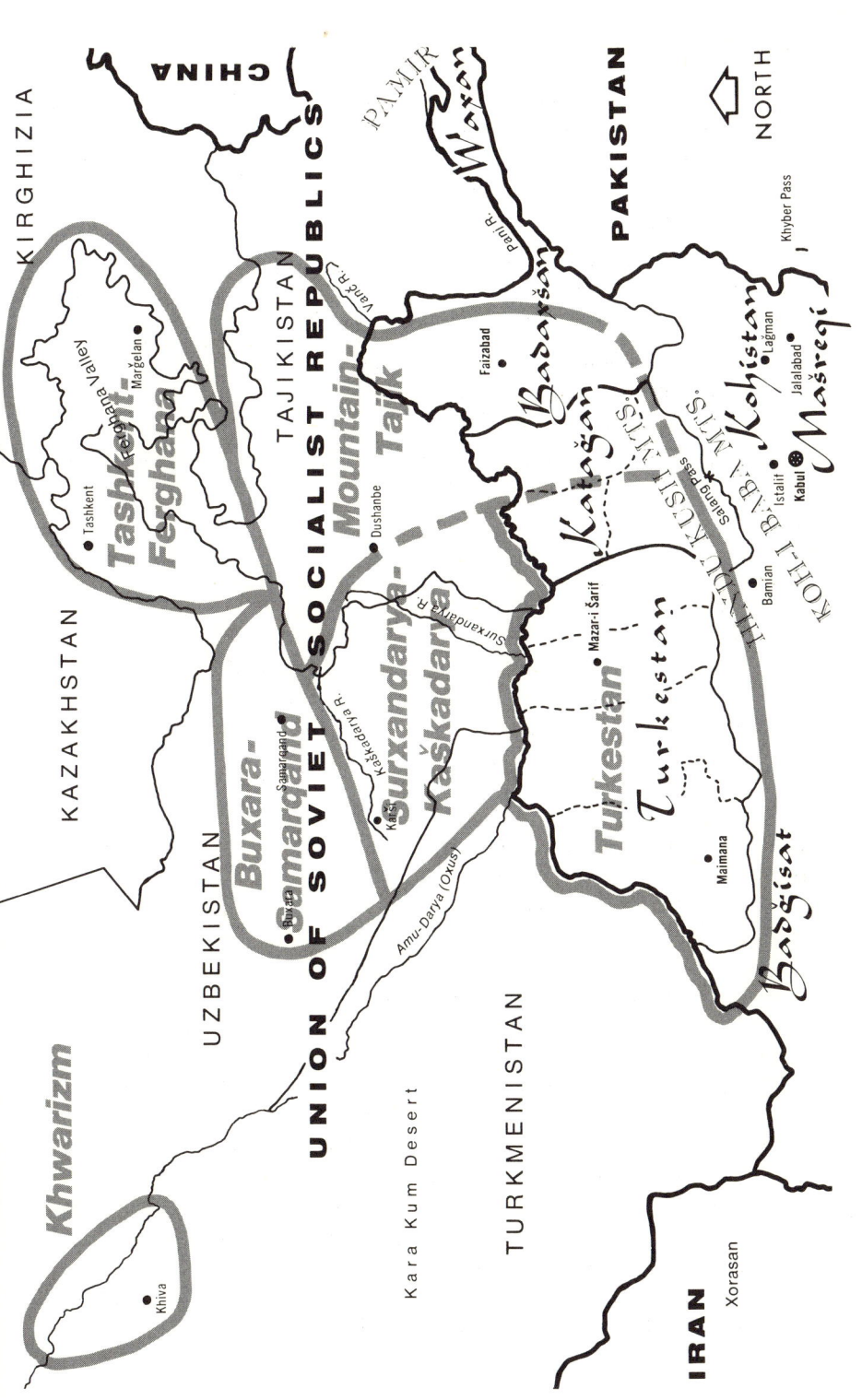

Map 1.1. Uzbek-Tajik Musical Zones

carried out, for it would yield valuable insights into the basic nature of southern Central Asian culture.

In her study of ethnic groups of southern Uzbekistan and Tajikistan, B. Kh. Karmysheva summarizes the factors affecting the ethnography of the area:

The basic ethnocultural process that took place in the broad area studied was the same as in a series of other regions of Central Asia: mutual cultural influence, convergence, and at times fusion of the settled (primarily Iranian-speaking) and nomadic (primarily Turkic-speaking) populations. This process encompassed all sides of the culture: economic, material and spiritual. (1964:100)

To briefly review the historical development of this process, we can perhaps reduce it to three basic stages. The terminology and concept of a three-layered development are derived from *Sprachbund* linguistic theory.

1. *Substratum:* ?1500 B.C.–A.D. 500. This is the period of Iranian predominance from the time of the initial Indo-European invasion of the region under discussion to the time of the major infiltration of Turkic peoples. It was during this period that the cultural pattern of the region was established on the basis of a still earlier underlay: the evolution of agriculture, the creation of village life-styles, and, of course, the spread of Iranian languages.

2. *Superstratum:* ca. A.D. 500–1500. This period saw the large-scale invasions of numerous Turko-Mongol peoples, from the Oghuz confederation of the sixth century through the Seljuq, Mongol, and Timurid upheavals. The heavy Turkic overlay of languages and customs has remained basic to the region, but it seems clear from the available evidence that the history of the period in Transoxania and northern Afghanistan equally involve Turkic adjustment to the substratum culture: Iranian peasant life.

3. *Adstratum:* A.D. 1550–ca. 1940. This period opened with the last Turkic invasion and the appearance of the Uzbeks in the region. It closed with the effective sovietization of the northern part of the area (Transoxania) and the sealing of the border with Afghanistan; both factors ended the traditional patterns of contact between Uzbeks and Tajiks and began a new chapter in the relationship of the two peoples.

In the following zone-by-zone analysis of Uzbek-Tajik contact, the situation must be seen in terms of a continuum of lesser to greater mutual influence. The considerable geographic expanse involved and, more important, the great diversity of the ecology and related life-styles have led to a rather complex articulation of the basic interrelationship of the two peoples. Because of the historically convoluted succession of invasions and assimilations, it is difficult to date any phenomena other than the most basic cultural realities. Thus, while it is obvious that before the advent of the Uzbeks the presence of a large mass of Uzbek words in Tajik Persian would have been unlikely, even linguistic specialists in matters Turco-Iranian (Doerffer 1967:72–79) find themselves hard pressed to determine whether a given word was part of the older superstratum period of contact or represents a clear Uzbek addition to Persian in recent times. To give an idea of the complexity, here is Doerffer's four-part categorization of Uzbek loan words in Tajik (1967:72–79):

1. pre-Uzbek, Čaǧataí layer
2. old dialectic Uzbek layer
3. Kipčak Uzbek layer (Kazakh-related)
4. Uzbek layer stemming from Mongol

The fact that Uzbek itself changed markedly over the centuries before and after 1500 compounds the complexity. Nevertheless, the overall outline is sufficiently clear for us to delineate fundamental patterns.

In terms of language, a major variable, Lazard can confidently note ". . . une convergence remarquable entre cette langue [Tajik] et l'uzbek" (1956:186), while Doerffer (1967:72–79) goes so far as to see some Tajik dialects as "eine Türksprache in statu nascendi," and to remark that an Altaicist of 2100 would find as much similarity between northern Tajik and the Turkic languages as between Turkic and Mongolian languages. Important for the argument being advanced is the opinion of Menges: ". . . the Uzbek dialects clearly exhibit the different degrees of Iranization mirroring their transition from a nomadic to a sedentary way of life . . ." (1967:41). It is on "the different degrees" that we shall rest our attention in order to point out some of the subregional variations of the overall Uzbek-Tajik contact pattern.

It should be noted that the musical zones of Map 1.1 represent the situation at the end of the adstratum (1500–ca. 1940) period — that is, the results of the last four and one-half centuries of cultural accommodation between Uzbeks and Tajiks. We shall have occasion to mention some carry-overs from earlier times that affect the limits of the adstratum period. It is difficult to penetrate the past very deeply in terms of the music culture alone, since our documentation, never plentiful at best even for the immediate past, becomes all too conjectural before classical Islamic times. Nevertheless, it is clear that there is a considerable substratum of performing arts traditions in the region, just as many other, better documented cultural traits can be clearly seen to extend back to quite early times. As data for the existence of such elements one can introduce convergence of phenomena at widely separated points within the area under discussion. For example, Nurjanov notes that highly similar masks were traditionally used for folk dramas among isolated mountain Tajiks and in Khwarizm, near the shores of the Aral Sea, and he states that in general, Khwarizmian comedians' activities paralleled those of the mountain Tajiks. At the same time, he notes that the work of the Tajik masxarabaz comedians was similar to that of Uzbek folk comics *(qiziqči)*, and that there was continuous contact among Tajik comedians out of the Pamirs; he concludes that "the activity of the masxarabazes of the plains did not differ from that of . . . the mountain regions" (Nurjanov 1956:164, 121, 124, 116). In the face of such a similarity of phenomena one can either assume recent diffusion or parallel evolution from a common, older source. The wide spread of the comedian is particularly striking, for there is very, very little carry-over from the Pamirs to Khwarizm in any other aspect of music and entertainment. Since the figure of the comedian is not limited to the immediate Uzbek-Tajik area, nor is a feature such as masked characters in village entertainments (they exist in Rumania, for example), I would tend to identify the element as part of a very old pattern of development. Looking at the situation from another angle, one can find in a given isolated community clear evidence of early substratum contact. A. L. Troitskaia's investigation of secluded Tajik villages of the upper Zerafšan valley showed "an intersection of Turkic and Iranian shamanistic elements," a phenomenon she feels "can be explained only through ancient Turco-Soghdian interrelations" (1971:255); this statement refers to a large area of which the zone under discussion is only one part, just as the Iranian-Turkic linguistic border is a constant across a great many miles and a variety of cultural situations.

We are now ready to turn to the specifics of the adstratum pattern of musical acculturation in the Uzbek-Tajik contact zone. In the case of each zone I shall introduce related ethnographic and linguistic data to indicate that the musical relationships described do in fact bear some connection to more general patterns of acculturation. However, I must stress once again that comparative ethnography of the area is still in its infancy, and that there are whole zones for which both the musical and other cultural data are so sparse as to make any discussion highly conjectural.

The musical zones of Map 1.1. have been substantiated by the findings published by F. Karomatov, director of musicology in the Institute for the Study of the Arts of the Uzbek Academy of Sci-

ences. For the Uzbeks, Karomatov describes " four basic local styles:
. . . Surkhandarya-Kashkadarya, Bukhara-Samarqand, Khwarizm and
Ferghana–Tashkent" (1972a:49); I have used his terminology on my
map, adding the Mountain Tajik zone and Afghan Turkestan. The
borders of each zone, to be discussed below, are mine; Karomatov has
not described precise geographic limits for his zones. Karomatov
does not directly state that his definition of stylistic regions depends
to any great extent on the degree and quality of Uzbek-Tajik contact,
though he does speak of the "shared way of life within various regions,"
and points out the "great popularity of Tajik songs" (1972a:49) whenever such explanations seem relevant. What I hope to accomplish
through presentation of the musical zones is (1) to elaborate on
Karomatov's insights for the Soviet side, extending his remarks to
indicate Uzbek-Tajik contact as an important consideration; and (2)
to use my field observations from the Afghan side in order to depict a
larger ethnic contact situation.

Buxara-Samarqand Zone

Let us begin at the heart of the longest-established region of shared
music culture, in the ancient urban centers of Buxara and Samarqand.
This area was long settled by Iranian peoples before the first possible
Turks, the Hun-related Hephthalites, appeared in the fourth century A.D.
(see Bivar 1969:54 for discussion of the Turkic nature of the Hephthalites). When Alexander the Great encountered the city of Maracanda
— the forerunner of Samarqand — in 329 B.C., it was a major stopping
point along the celebrated Silk Route to China. The high degree of
urbanization and development of crafts in the area during T'ang
Dynasty times (614–907) is well documented in Chinese sources,
especially in the long lists of luxury items imported from the various
Central Asian city-states (see Schaefer 1964). For a detailed account
of the ethnic history of Buxara and Samarqand, the reader may turn to
sources such as Bartol'd (1958) and Frye (1965). The important
point here is to understand the situation as it crystallized after the
settlement of the Uzbeks and the establishment of the Buxaran state in
the sixteenth century, and for this it is best to quote from O. Sukhareva,
who has studied Buxara in depth historically and personally through
extensive interviews over many years. There seems to be no question
that by the nineteenth century the majority of Turkic peoples (mainly
various pre-Uzbek and Uzbek tribal groupings) had assimilated to the
Tajik-speaking, well-established pattern of urban life, creating a special
Buxaran ethnic group:

The local type of the Buxaran was formed in the conditions of long-standing, close neighboring of Tajiks and Uzbeks in Buxara, including those Uzbeks who had gone over to the Tajik language through continuous inter-mixing by means of marriage. (Sukhareva 1966:142)

That this pattern was particularly Buxaran is indicated clearly by Sukhareva:

In this respect the fate of Buxara was sharply differentiated from that of other cities such as Marghelan [in the Ferghana Valley], whose population in recent centuries lost the Tajik language and went over to Uzbek. (1966:149)

On the other hand, the Buxaran Tajiks are themselves of mixed provenience and cannot be said to constitute a "pure" Tajik population:

In general one can scarcely find "pure" Tajiks in Buxara. In every family one can still observe that either in the man's or woman's lineage some ancestor or other was a non-Tajik. (1966:132)

Uzbek-Tajik ethnic boundaries remain undefined in Buxara, though the incorporation of the area into the Uzbek SSR in Soviet times fostered a growth of at least nominal Uzbek consciousness among all sectors of the population. Sukhareva has even recently been able to find Buxarans who formally call themselves Uzbeks but continue to use Tajik as a home language (1966:128). Significantly, this ethnic fusion carries over into the countryside around Buxara and Samarqand; Sukhareva mentions Tajik villages in the Samarqand region whose inhabitants use Tajik as their standard language but who maintain their identities as members of various Uzbek tribes, even claiming kinship and intermarrying with neighboring Uzbek villages (1966:129). I have drawn the line of Buxara-Samarqand to include the steppe area to the south, with its center in the Karši oasis, since that part of the lower Kaškadaryā River seems similar to the rest of the area under discussion (Kisliakov 1960).

Outside of the high incidence of bilingualism cited by many writers, one must also note the heavy influence of each language on the other in this clear Sprachbund situation. Rastorgueva, the chief investigator of Tajik dialectology, particularly for Buxara and Samarqand, notes that "the long-standing neighborship with the Uzbeks and massive bilingualism has not passed without traces on Tajik dialects. They have undergone strong influence from Uzbek" (1964:13). As noted above, Doerffer (1967:57) goes even farther, describing northern Tajik dialects as appearing to be "eine Türksprache in statu nascendi." Going beyond language into folklore, there is abundant evidence of Turkic impact in the northern Tajik areas. Tilavov, who has studied Tajik proverbs, notes that in those regions the influence of Uzbek folklore on Tajik

sayings can easily be seen; it involves outright adoption of Uzbek proverbs as well as creation of Tajik proverbs on Uzbek models (1967:33).

Uzbek has been similarly influenced. Menges notes that "no other
Turkic language, with perhaps the sole exception of the literary language
of the Qarayim, strongly influenced by Hebrew and Slavic, has undergone a comparably powerful extraneous penetration." The effects
have been particularly strong in the cities, where "Iranized dialects"
have their strongholds (1967: 69, 70).

Let us now turn to a brief survey of the musical ramifications of
the Uzbek-Tajik shared culture in the Buxara-Samarqand zone. We
have a fine description of highly cosmopolitan, ethnically mixed music
in Samarqand from the time of Šarux. Tamerlane's son, written by the
historian Hafez Abru (as quoted in Veksler 1965:101):

Golden-tongued singers and sweet-sounding musicians played and sang
to motives in Persian style, to Arab melodies according to Turkic
practice and with Mongol voices following Chinese laws of singing and
Altai meters.

Thus there was fertile ground for the development of Uzbek-Tajik
music in urban Transoxania by the time of the Uzbek invasions.
Already under the Timurids in the late fifteenth century, court Turks
in Samarqand and Herat had developed Čağataí, a Turco-Persian
literary language; it was fostered particularly by Mir Alisher Navoi and
became the basis of Uzbek literature in succeeding centuries. There is
every reason to imagine that when Babur, the first Moghul emperor,
described Navoi as a composer of music (Beliaev: in press), the
pieces involved reflected a joint Turco-Iranian classical music culture of
the sophisticated Timurid courts.

In the sixteenth and seventeenth centuries this tendency toward
fusion was heightened and crystallized in a canonized set of extensive
Buxaran musical-poetic suites called *maqams,* a term clearly pointing to
links with Near Eastern classical musics. There are two ways of looking
at the provenience of the Buxaran maqams and their development.
My own feeling is that when the Safavid dynasty was established in
Iran, cutting off Buxaran Sunnis from their Near Eastern cosectarians,
the succeeding period of isolated cultural development provided ample
occasion for the evolution of a local dialect of Near Eastern classical
forms. As Hambly has noted,

It was the course of the sixteenth century and under Shaybanid rule
that Mawarannahr [Transoxania] became finally isolated from the rest
of the Islamic world as a direct result of the relentless Sunni-Shi'ite
conflict between Shaybanids and Safavids which made it difficult for
contacts to be maintained with the Sunni states beyond Iran. (1969:168)

On the other hand, Laurence Picken (1969:p.c.) has pointed out that the maqams may well be cultural continuations of the age-old Central Asian musical traditions that heavily influenced Chinese music in T'ang times. He feels that Uighur sources at his disposal support the argument for steady maintenance of those traditions in Central Asia apart from Near Eastern Islamic influence, and with that I have no quarrel. Picken's argument and my own theory of the development of Buxaran classical music do not seem to be mutually exclusive: both old Transoxanian and newer Arabo-Persian styles may have fused in creating the unique maqam style.

Debates as to provenience aside, the main point about the maqams for the present discussion is the fact that they are of joint Uzbek-Tajik origin (which is to say Buxaran, in this case), and that they exist in two different forms in the languages of their creators. Pieces with the same title, enshrined within larger musical structures of the same name, and using identical rhythmic formulas based on similar poetic meters exist in both Uzbek and Tajik to this day. These classical compositions have both influenced and been influenced by local folk musics of the Buxara-Samarqand area down to Karši, as substantiated by Karomatov (1972:p.c.). This distribution is the basis for the line I have drawn around the Buxara-Samarqand zone. The western edge of the zone is determined by the heavy impact of Turkmens upon Uzbeks and the falling-off of Uzbek population, while the eastern border is based primarily on increased mountain Tajik representation. As for the boundary with the Kaškadarya-Surxandarya zone, it is mainly set by the topography of that area and the location of the rivers in question.

In the Buxara-Samarqand zone the majority of instruments, particularly those used in maqam performance, are clearly of Near Eastern origin, being variants of Persian types. For example, the local type of hammered dulcimer (called "čang," the name used for the jew's harp in Afghanistan) is directly related to the Persian *santur*. The local tanbur, unlike the Afghan lute of the same name, is also obviously Persian, as is the setar. The main fiddle is the ğičak, similar in name to the Afghan tin-can-bodied fiddle but quite different in appearance, being a form of the Persian-Turkish *kamanča* spike fiddle. Most clearly Uzbek in origin is the ubiquitous dutar, apparently the favorite instrument of the area. This handsome lute seems to be a cross between long-necked lutes of other Central Asian Turks (particularly Kazakhs and Turkmens) and Persian models; both influences have apparently been at work in the case of nearly all the long-necked lutes of northern Afghanistan and Soviet Central Asia.

Tashkent–Ferghana Valley Zone

In the Tashkent–Ferghana Valley area Tajiks drop to a much more modest component of the population, and the tendency towards strong acculturation, even assimilation, seems to be reversed, with the Tajiks becoming Uzbekized. V. I. Masal'ski noted this in 1918 when he told how Tajiks in the Tashkent area were being called *qul* ("slave") by Uzbeks and were glad to lose such a title and become Turkic (presumably Uzbek) speakers; this Turkicization occurred mainly in the cities (1908:405–6). Menges notes that the Ferghana Uzbek dialects are only "semi-iranized" (1967:71), and Sukhareva has already been cited to the effect that in Marghelan Tajiks tended towards Uzbekization. Rastorgueva (1964:152) describes the Tajik language of various districts of this area as being more heavily influenced by Uzbek than it is in Buxara and Samarqand. Nevertheless, although ethnically the shoe may be on the other foot in Tashkent–Ferghana, a considerable degree of mixture and acculturation has been reported by observers. Menges (1967:69) describes the dissatisfaction of some nationalist Uzbeks in the 1920s when the Tashkent dialect was chosen as the basis for modern literary Uzbek; they felt it was too iranized, as opposed to "the Uzbek dialects of the nomadic population . . . almost free of Iranian influences." It is worth noting that a considerable proportion of the still nomadic, noniranized Uzbek population lived in the Tashkent–Ferghana area in the 1920s, though they have now fused with the majority Uzbek population (Babushkin 1967:73). One must also take into account the impact of neighboring Kazakhs and Kirghiz, a substantial linguistic if not cultural influence in the Tashkent–Ferghana area, and a strong counterbalance to the Tajik presence. Schuyler, among other nineteenth-century observers, clearly indicated that the Tajik population was smaller and of lower status in Tashkent–Ferghana than in Buxara, but he noted as well that "intermarriages . . . are not uncommon," and, in summary, that "the Uzbeks look upon the Tajiks with contempt, but at the same time they are dependent upon them; the Tajiks treat the Uzbeks as fools and children of nature, and smilingly say that they have them entirely in their power" (Schuyler 1877:108). Regardless of how one is to interpret these subjective ethnographic remarks, it is evident that considerable mutual acculturation was at work in the area.

Musically, the Tashkent–Ferghana area shows two distinct characteristics that tally with the brief ethnographic summary above. On the one hand, it has a wealth of diverse and broadly used genres of vocal and instrumental music that are purely Uzbek. Such song types as the *katta ašula, čublama,* and *yalla* are local in origin and relate only to an Uzbek world, which in some ways seems quite Central Asian-Turkic in character. For example, in the men's genre of the katta ašula, a striking aspect is the nature of the singing, in which soloists compete at top range and full voice for the climactic sections of the song. It is hard not to see in this a connection with the well-established Kazakh, Kirghiz, and Mongol practice of singing contests.

On the other hand, as Karomatov notes, "the exception to this pattern was the cultural center of the Ferghana Valley, Kokand, where the maqams and other varieties of Uzbek professional music were introduced from Bukhara" (Karomatov 1972a:51). This observation reveals the prestigiousness of Buxaran culture, which was used as a cultural prop for the weak Kokand Khanate, most tenuous of the Uzbek kingdoms. Here we find vocal variants of the Buxaran maqams, involving different modes, structures, and arrangements of the classical storehouse. Tashkent–Ferghana, then, was an intermediate zone for Uzbek-Tajik musical contact, much as Menges (1967:71) has indicated for language by labeling the local dialects "transitional."

It is appropriate here to mention another Uzbek zone, Khwarizm (near the mouth of the Amu-Darya), home of major kingdoms and populations since Achaemenid times. Its relevance for our discussion is in providing a further example of the trend outlined above for the Tashkent–Ferghana area: Uzbekization of the Tajiks and the development of a strong regional Uzbek culture with only limited reference to Tajik models. Vambery (1970:400) observed the zone in its heyday, when it was the center of the Khivan Khanate. Of the Tajiks he wrote, "Their number here is small. They have, by degrees, exchanged their Persian language for the Turkish . . . (they are) no great favorite with the Özberg, and in spite of the Sart [Tajiks] and Özbek having lived five centuries together, very few mixed marriages have taken place between them." The situation was clearly far removed from that of Buxara.

To briefly survey the musical scene, Karomatov says of the Buxaran *Shashmaqam* (six maqams) canon: "It is typical that in Khwarizm the Shashmaqam contains so many sharp local traits that it is no longer common to two peoples, but must be considered a purely Khwarizm Uzbek phenomenon. . . ." Of the whole music culture of Khwarizm, he says, "Though many traits are shared by the music of Bukhara and Khwarizm and the level of performance is equal, the Khwarizmian style stands out due to distinctive local color" (1972a:50). Thus for Khwarizm, distance, demographic predominance of Uzbeks, and strong local tradition have neutralized the heavy impact of Tajik culture more effectively than in Tashkent and Ferghana.

Surxandaryā–Kaškadarya Zone

Surxandaryā–Kaškadarya is the last of the wholly Transoxanian musical zones. It is almost the most difficult to summarize briefly, since the ethnic background is so complex and the groups interrelate in so dense a network of associations that generalization is difficult. Nevertheless, the possible extrapolations provide interesting matter for comparison with other regions.

We are fortunate to have the results of the careful ethnographic research of B. Kh. Karmysheva for this area of southern Uzbekistan. Basically we are concerned here with the region of several tributaries to the Amu-Darya (the Surxandaryā, the Sherabaddarya, the Kafirnigan), in which there is a complex ethnic mix dominated by Uzbeks (75 percent according to Babushkin 1967:225). Historically, it is the old Tokharistan. Topographically it is a mixture of desert, steppe, steep river valleys, and, in the east, highlands linking up to the Hissar and other ridges of Tajikistan. Therefore it is not surprising to find a variety of ecological and ethnic solutions involving considerable accommodation. According to Karmysheva (1964:98–99) this accommodation took the form of topographical stratification, with a pre-Uzbek Turkic group named Türk occupying most of the higher ground, topped only by mountain Tajiks, with the somewhat mysterious Čagatais (in two varieties, Uzbek and Tajik) below, and Uzbeks in the bottoms of the river valleys. It appears that acculturation has proceeded unevenly. According to Karmysheva, while the Türks have fairly well assimilated to mountain Tajiks, the latter know very little Uzbek, and by no means all of the Uzbek-Čagatais and seminomadic Uzbeks have "mastered the Tajik language" (1964:101).

In the north of the zone under discussion we find yet another ethnic group, the Tagowi (from the word *tagow,* "narrow river valley"), in the direction of the upper Zerafšan valley; they are Uzbek speakers. The urban centers to the northwest (basically above Karši) I have previously assigned to the Buxara-Samarqand region, since the population seems to belong to the highly Tajikized Uzbeks mentioned earlier; as Karmysheva notes,

All the true urban and village population is called Tajik, regardless what language its representatives speak — Tajik or Uzbek. (1960:52)

Musically we find the same ambiguities of ethnic contact expressed in the ethnographic literature. On the one hand there is strong evidence for purely Uzbek styles and even instruments of a particularly Surxandaryā-Kaškadarya type, with a suggestion of considerable Turkmen contact on the western side (Karomatov 1962; 1972:p.c.). On the other hand, the same authority cites such a high degree of musical similarity among ethnic groups in the region that he says "separating the music into corresponding groups is not possible" (Karomatov 1972:p.c.). Let us look at the evidence for both sides. For an example on the fusion side, Karomatov says, "In the Surxandarya region the Tajiks basically play on the Uzbek dombra, though the [Tajik] dumbrak is also in use there. At the same time the Uzbeks also play the dumbrak" (1972:p.c.). As for the particular local Uzbek music culture, it is quite rich and unique. Most noteworthy is the preeminence of the Uzbek *dombra*, little used in the rest of Uzbekistan. The appearance of the *qobuz*, a horsehair fiddle more common among the Kazakhs and Kirghiz, is also quite suggestive, as is the fact that epic recitation, so strong among the peoples just mentioned, is quite well developed in the Surxandaryā area. Other instruments used, such as the jew's harp (čangkobuz) and shepherd's flutes *(čupon nai, ğajir nai)* are rarely found in urban areas. Conversely, "it is characteristic that the art of Bukhara . . . was not able to significantly affect the nomadic population of Surkhandarya" (Karomatov 1972a:50); as in northern Afghanistan, the local Uzbeks were not at all involved in the classical tradition of the great urban cultural centers. All of the above suggests a strongly archaic strain in the music culture of the Surxandaryā-Kaškadarya region. In that it relates more closely to the northern Turkic nomads (Kirghiz, Kazakhs) than to sedentary Uzbeks, it seems to reflect a common Turkic past more than it does an Uzbek-Tajik present. These data jibe with the assortment of pre-Uzbek and seminomadic Uzbek components of the population cited by Karmysheva. Unfortunately, I do not know of any extensive studies of villages in the region that would give more complete information on specific ethnographic details. Clear enough, for our purposes, is the picture of an Uzbek-Tajik contact zone of distinctive character.

Mountain Tajik Zone

With the mountain Tajik zone we enter an area that straddles the present Afghan-Soviet border, which was fixed only in 1895. Kisliakov and Pisarchik (1966:213) have interviewed old-timers in the southern part of the Soviet side (Darwaz) who have affirmed that the area was an unbroken region up to that date. This confirms the observations of Burnes (1835:179) and other nineteenth-century travelers that Darwaz

was under the rule of independent Tajik chieftains, though much of
Badaxšan, to the south, was devastated by the conquests of Murad Beg
just after Burnes's time. Today the Soviet side of the region outlined
in Map 1.1 is the ethnic inverse of the Surxandaryā-Kaškadarya zone
in that it is at least two-thirds Tajik to one-third Uzbek, at a conservative estimate (Karmysheva 1964:96); the proportion of Tajiks goes
much higher once Afghan Badaxšan is taken into account, though
there are some Turks (Uzbeks, Türk, Loqai) on the Afghan side as
well (Karmysheva 1964:6; Kuškeki 1926).

Delineating this zone either ethnographically or musically is perhaps more difficult than for any of the other zones presented here,
and I hold no brief for the compromise reflected in Map 1.1. The
entire eastern flank represents a borderline with the Pamirs. This line
is based on a combination of Schultz's map of the Pamir peoples
(Schultz 1914) and Kisliakov's delineation of the adjacent mountain
Tajik zones, Karategin and Darwaz, since I feel those sources along
with others (e.g., Rastorgueva 1964) give adequate data for the
Pamirs. The southern edge of mountain Tajik country is the most
difficult; as I pointed out in the Introduction, the literature is less than
clear on the possible cultural differences between various types between
the Bamian area and Badaxšan. Robert Canfield (1968:p.c.) has
pointed out that the Doši area jut north of the Salang Pass is a religious
dividing line among Tajiks (between Sunnis and Ismailis), but this is
only one of several possible criteria; thus I have used a noncommittal
dotted line for that intra-Tajik demarcation.

The northeastern edge of the zone is dictated solely by the distribution of Tajiks, who give way to Kirghiz there. The northwestern
edge reflects the distinction between mountain and plains Tajiks, the
latter in this case being those of the Ferghana Valley. This is a differentiation commonly made in Soviet research and seems justified by
dialectic and cultural differences among Transoxanian Tajiks. The
western border is nearly as unclear as the southern edge shown by the
dotted line; it is almost an arbitrary distinction based largely on general population distribution (Tajiks fade out to the west) and data
such as Karmysheva's citing of differences between mountain and
plains Tajiks in the Kaškadarya area (Karmysheva 1960:52). Finally,
at the southwestern edge, the mountain Tajik musical complex spills
over from Badaxšan into Katağan, hence the location of the boundary
between the Mountain Tajik and Afghan Turkestan zones in Katağan.

While there are negative bounds on the region (presence or
absence of Tajiks, Pamir peoples, and Uzbeks), I feel there is also a
strong cultural identity to the zone, which emerges clearly in research

such as the dialectological investigations of Kisliakov and Pisarchik (e.g., 1966) and Rastorgueva. The latter, for example, speaks of bilingualism as being heavy only north of the Turkestan Ridge and west towards Buxara and Samarqand (1964:13). Kisliakov and Pisarchik minimize the intrusion of outside cultures in the mountain fastnesses of Karategin and Darwaz and cite the physical rarity of outsiders: for example, in Garm, the only major bazaar town of the area, the main "foreigners" were an Armenian tinsmith, a Samarqand Tajik and a Jew, both bootmakers, and a Buxaran Jewish barber (Kisliakov and Pisarchik 1966:196). Similarly, on the Afghan side, in Badaxšan, one is struck by the unity of appearance and custom among mountain Tajiks. The use of the term *Galča* for the mountain Tajiks in pre-Revolutionary times indicates that they were accepted as a distinct ethnic entity in those days. One trait noticed by Kisliakov and Pisarchik (1966:51) that indicates the greater isolation of the mountain Tajiks is their less orthodox variety of Islam, as compared to that of plains Tajiks.

Within the large zone indicated in Map 1.1, of course, there is significant variation in the extent of Uzbek impact. Karategin, the northernmost sector, seems to have been more greatly affected because of its proximity to the Ferghana Valley. Kisliakov and Pisarchik (1966:63) describe systematic outmigration for seasonal labor from Karategin towards Ferghana and Tashkent, which led to some Tajiks settling and establishing families in those areas or returning to their home region with Uzbek (and sometimes even Turkmen) wives.

Musically, this pattern is carried out in both instruments and repertoires, as far as the scanty data will allow us to generalize. For Karategin and Darwaz, Kisliakov and Pisarchik note a significant number of instruments related to the plains culture (dutar, robab, setar). Dansker, in the only extensive study of music Karategin and Darwaz, notes that the former region calls the lute related to the Badaxšani dambura *dutar-i maida* (small dutar), a term that links it to the plains instrument, while the term *dumbrak* is more common in Darwaz. Similarly, the plains čang (dulcimer) is most widespread in northern areas (Dansker 1965:247, 257).

Dansker's study is most valuable in linking Karategin and Darwaz musically to Afghan Badaxšan in many vital respects. Chief among these in terms of instruments is the appearance of the dumbrak (called dambura on the Afghan side), meaning here the version of that instrument in the specific shape identified with mountain Tajiks, as distinct from the dombra of the Surxandarya region and its Afghan relative, the Turkestani dambura. Dansker flatly states that the dumbrak-dambura is the most widespread and popular instrument in his zone

(1965:249), and the same holds for Badaxšan. The popularity of the tin-can ğičak on both sides is another important instrumental link. Methods of ornamentation of these instruments are identical (1965:263). The sexual ascription of instruments also tallies with Afghan practice: tambourines and jew's harps but no lutes for women; mountain Tajiks even believe "that a dutar will lose its resonance if a woman plays on it" (1965:247) — in clear contrast with the widespread custom of women's dutar playing among the Ferghana Valley Uzbeks (Romanovskaia 1959:66).

In terms of repertoire, the existence of a widespread genre titled *felak* (see Chapter 3) links the Soviet and Afghan sides of the zone, as does the common practice of playing felaks on pastoral flutes (Dansker 1965:225). Sung felaks, called *Raği* in Darwaz (Dansker 1965:203), seem to have characteristics identical to those of Afghan songs, and the connection between a genre prevalent in Soviet Darwaz and the Afghan town of Rāğ (near Faizabad) is indicative of the overall relationship presented here. One can even find song texts with nearly identical words on both sides and instrumental tunes of remarkable similarity.

I am not aware of data relating to Uzbeks in the Mountain Tajik zone, either ethnographically or musically, other than the remarks in Karmysheva (1964), so it is difficult to assess the nature of Tajik influence on the Uzbek population. What emerges for our purposes from the available data is the picture of a strong mountain Tajik culture, influenced moderately by plains Tajik-Uzbek elements in the northern areas of the region.

Afghan Turkestan

After this long digression to set the stage, we are now in a position to properly evaluate the nature of Uzbek-Tajik contact in Afghan Turkestan and its role in developing a basic music culture to which minority groups in the area respond. It is clear from the above discussion that Badaxšan must be discounted as an area of shared music culture from this particular point of view, though we have had and will continue to have occasion to indicate that musical values, instruments, and repertoires of the area both reflect concerns shared by other groups and have in fact influenced the activity of those groups.

In the Introduction I have already indicated the terms on which Uzbeks and Tajiks coexist in Turkestan, namely an original accommodation by Uzbeks to a preexisting Tajik sedentary agricultural village model. We can now add supportive data, such as linguistic interchange. Like Buxara, Afghan Turkestan offers a picture of a well-integrated

Sprachbund, in which both the degree of bilingualism and of mutual linguistic influence has been and remains high. Again, data are scanty, but Jarring 1939: iii), for example, states that Andxoi Uzbek is an iranized dialect; on the other hand, investigators such as C. Kieffer (1971:p.c.) feel strongly that Turkestani Persian dialects are heavily influenced by Turkic influxes — a factor plain to anyone used to Kabul Persian who travels to the North. Place names and lexical items in northern Persian abound in Turkic loan words, and the two elements are often simply strung together, as in Qarabāğ, where Turkic *qara* ("black") combines with Persian *bāğ,* ("garden"), or in the name of a major musician, Aq (Turkic "white") Pišak (Persian "cat"). In terms of social category and self-declared ethnic identity, Centlivres (1968: p.c.) has noted the tendency of aspiring urban middle-class Uzbeks in Tašqurğan to designate themselves as Tajiks; I have observed this in the case of Bangeča Tašqurğani, a musician whose father was Uzbek but who declares himself a Tajik. Like most Uzbeks and Tajiks in Turkestan, Bangeča is bilingual.

Song texts are valuable sources of evidence for linguistic interchange. One finds both alternate verses in Uzbek and Persian (an example is recorded on Anthology AST 4001, side 1, track 1), and mixed lines, as in the following excerpt from a widely known stock song of Turkestan, named "Kelingayar" from its Uzbek refrain, "kelingayar uinang" ("come dance with me, my dear"). The performance was by Šarif, a Tašqurğani Tajik.

Samawārga āb-i juš	Boiling water in the samovar
Biš afğani čāinak gušt.	Five afghanis for a teapot of meat
Čurtingni xarāb qelma	Don't worry;
Xoda uzi parda puš	God keeps our secrets

In line 1, the ending on *samawarga* is Uzbek, though the word is Russian (i.e., international), while *āb-i juš* is pure Persian. In line 2, *biš* ("five") is Uzbek, while *čāinak gušt* is Persian. Line 3 is similarly mixed, with *čurtingni* and *qelma* being Uzbek and *xarāb* Persian, while in line 4 *xoda* and *parda puš* are Persian and *uzi* is Uzbek. Such song texts mirror the linguistic blurring in Turkestan. It is to be hoped that linguistic researchers will take up this fascinating Sprachbund situation on a rigorous basis, and that ethnographers will supply more extensive data on the nature and extent of Uzbek-Tajik interplay in the region. Even preliminary reports (Centlivres 1972: p.c.) on kinship terminology in Turkestan show a Turco-Iranian mixture both in the terms and in the kinship systems themselves.

Turkestani teahouse songs not only are bilingual and bicultural in content, but they indicate significant formal interchange as well. Quatrains (*rubāi,* or commonly in Afghanistan, *čārbaiti*) are an old and quite widespread verse form among Persian speakers (see Slobin 1970), one that continues to be practiced in Xorasan to the west, out in Badaxšan beyond Uzbek influence, and down in Kabul; they are also an essential verse form among Central Asian Turks and they appear to be deeply rooted among both peoples. For example, they are the form used for Uzbek agricultural work songs in widely scattered areas of southern Uzbekistan (Karmysheva 1960) and for incantations to protect livestock against the evil eye among isolated mountain Tajiks (Rakhimov 1960). In both these usages *a a b a* rhyme schemes are prevalent. A major difference seems to be that Tajiks adhere less carefully to six- and seven-syllable lines and favor longer counts. It is hardly accidental, then, that the chosen idiom of interethnic performers of Turkestan should be the quatrain, a favored genre of both Uzbeks and Tajiks.

In the performance of quatrains, one can notice preferences in presentation that perhaps reflect a divergence of Uzbek and Tajik taste. Most Tajik musicians sing their verses solo and are proud of their ability to compose endless quatrains on demand, even relating them to the immediate occasion. Uzbek singers, equally confident of their abilities, like to show off their talent in a competitive framework. In an Aqča teahouse two Uzbek singers will sit face-to-face, singing alternate quatrains to the deadpan accompaniment of a dambura player, while marking off the beats with the small finger cymbals (Uzbek tüsak), which are rarely employed by Tajik singers. This competition seems to show the same echo of old Central Asian Turkic singing contests that I suggested for Tashkent katta ašula performance. Thus, within the shared framework of instruments and genres just outlined, there is always enough difference in usage to indicate that just below the joint music culture can be found extensive music subcultures, to which we shall turn our attention in Chapter 2.

Let us now examine the material-culture aspect of musical sharing in Turkestan, the dambura lute type, as it represents in microcosm the problems of disentangling the strands of the Uzbek-Tajik cultural knot.

The dambura of Turkestan bears a definite relationship to similar instruments found among mountain Tajiks and southern Uzbeks, and these three dambura types stand out as highly distinctive in the complex set of long-necked lutes of the Afghan-Transoxanian world: they are the only fretless lutes of the entire area save for the remote and very different Kirghiz *komuz,* with which no link is apparent.

Such a coincidence of construction calls attention to itself. Within the dambura world, many small features of playing style link or separate the three lute types in various ways. For example, Turkestani and Badaxšani dambura players share a technique for playing on both strings at once (one finger on both strings, in contrast to the thumb and opposed fingers used by Uzbek and Turkmen dutarists). However, only the mountain Tajik lute players use a special right-hand stroke involving four fingers together on the down stroke and two or three fingers separately on the upstroke for individual notes. Many more examples of such small variations could be adduced to indicate independent lines of instrumental development among the various Uzbek and Tajik groupings of the three zones mentioned. What should be borne in mind is that (1) the adjacent Surxandarya-Kaškadarya, Mountain Tajik, and Afghan Turkestan zones are linked through their very similar lute types, each of which is the most widespread instrument in its own area, and (2) the complex interrelationship among the basically similar damburas mirrors the dense web of associations between Uzbeks and Tajiks in the area.

Let us examine the manner of construction, one material way to approach the issue. Turning first to Afghan Turkestan, we have considerable information from Jurai Qul, an old Tajik dambura maker of Darā-i Zendān (near Samangan), the center of Turkestani dambura construction. Jurai Qul feels that an Uzbek and a Tajik type can be distinguished within the category "Turkestani dambura." He points to the juncture of neck and belly as the critical spot. The Uzbek type features a pointed region at the back of the neck and a flat area where the neck joins the belly, whereas the Tajik model is flat at the back of the neck and peaked where the neck joins the belly. My own dambura was identified by Jurai Qul as being of Uzbek origin, perhaps from the Rustāq area. Mention of Rustaq is noteworthy, since Uzbeks of that region, which is included in Badaxšan by some observers (e.g., Kushkekei 1926), are somewhat cut off from the main body of Afghan Uzbeks, and since the area is also a site of pre-Uzbek Turkic population (Karmysheva 1960:6). Though I have not had the opportunity of examining Surxandarya dombras, I am tempted to associate the Rustaq specimen with that variety of lute. First field reports from P. and M. Centlivres (1972:p.c.) support Rustaq's intermediate position. Apparently the Türk group and a considerable number of Qarluqs (also pre-Uzbek Turks) live in the area. In such a situation one would expect a mixture of dambura types, and the early findings of the Centlivres indicate that two types are indeed in use: one they term "typically badaxši, about 75 centimeters long," which tallies with normal

Badaxšani measurements, while the other is shorter (about two-thirds as long). Unfortunately, none of the standard descriptions of the Uzbek dombra (Karomatov 1962, 1972; Vertkov 1963) gives its dimensions, but in pictures it appears rather small, certainly smaller than the Turkestani dambura. It can perhaps be assumed that the instrument the Centlivres say is of the Surxandarya (southern Uzbek) types; at any rate, the diversity and complexity of damburas is well illustrated by this information from Rustaq. The possibility of such microevolution of instrument types within a small ecological zone and within a framework of shared instrument types underscores the fragmentation of cultural traits and the instability of ethnic boundaries across the North.

Returning to the dambura question, Jurai Qul gave additional valuable information regarding the Turkestani type. When asked about the appearance of damburas he made fifty years ago, he responded that he made a type that was considerably narrower, shorter, and lighter than the damburas he and his son make today. Such a dambura would have been much closer in appearance to the Surxandarya and particularly to the mountain Tajik damburas. The existence of this type of instrument in the recent past considerably blurs the picture of divergence noted in present-day damburas. If the Turkestani dambura of two generations back leaned towards the current version of its northern and eastern neighbors, the implication is that at one time all three lutes looked even more alike than they do now. Interesting, Karomatov feels that distinguishing Uzbek and Tajik lutes in the Surxandarya area is not useful: "In general, I have not distinguished the dombra into Uzbek and Tajik. In folk practice there is no such division" (Karomatov 1972:p.c.); this goes along with his statement that Uzbeks and Tajiks exchange instruments in the area.

It is possible that in Jurai Qul's youth such a situation prevailed for northern Afghanistan, but today there is a considerable distinction made by players between Turkestani and Badaxšani types, with each one said to belong only to its area of provenience. The juncture, not surprisingly, is in Katagan. In Xanabad I found both types of dambura hanging in one shop for sale; the shopkeeper said he had them ready for customers with differing musical tastes. In fact, the recent trend toward elephantine Turkestani damburas would require a customer to think twice before buying if he was used to the Badaxšani version. The sharp physical difference now observable between Turkestani and Badaxšani damburas underscores the regional distinctiveness of the two zones and the extent to which northern Afghan Tajiks must be considered as consisting of two large groups — mountain and

Fig. 1.7. Musical instruments in a shop in Xanabad, a crossroads region (left to right: *Turkestani dambura, Badaxšani dambura, tanbur, zirbağali*)

plains — just as the Transoxanian Tajiks have been distinguished for many years both by themselves and by observers. Again, data simply are not now available to approach such a typology on a serious basis. I merely bring up the subject as an important topic for future investigation. At the heart of the matter once more is our lack of information concerning not only the past of the so-called Tajiks (their provenience and diffusion), but even their present interrelationships as members of a geographically continuous but apparently culturally discontinuous ethnic group.

To summarize the dambura question, we find a distinctive lute named *dombra* (also, locally, *dumbura*) in a heavily Uzbek area (Surxandarya-Kaškadarya), where it is used interchangeably among Uzbeks and Tajiks with a lute called *dumbrak* or *dambura,* which is of similar construction and is based in a heavily Tajik area (Karategin-Darwaz-Badaxšan). Finally, in an area where Uzbeks and Tajiks are fairly equally mixed (the Samangan area of Afghan Turkestan), we find an intermediate lute type, the dambura, which is made by Tajiks and used by both ethnic groups, and which a prominent maker tells us was less distinctive in construction fifty years ago than it is today. We cannot by now state which group provided the stimulus for the first two-stringed fretless lute of the region, nor can we say when it appeared, since as a folk instrument it was not recorded by court theorists or historians. Whether there was a dambura when the area was called Bactria in classic times or whether it only evolved in the Kingdom of Buxara is simply unknowable at present. We do know, however, that it gives evidence of a fairly long-term convergence of Uzbek and Tajik approaches to instrumental music. Why in Turkestan this convergence — and the craft of dambura making — should have centered in the Samangan area is not clear. Perhaps it reflects that region's earlier importance as a center of north-south trade, or maybe it was only a fairly balanced Uzbek-Tajik population distribution that allowed the craft to prosper. What is clear is that the evolution in Samangan of a lute type which is not exactly like either the Uzbek dombra or the mountain Tajik dumbrak-dambura and which is played by both groups in northern Afghanistan is symbolic of a considerable degree of Uzbek-Tajik cultural accommodation. That this accommodation then carries a strong charge becomes clear when we examine the spread of the Turkestani dambura beyond its area of origin. It has become the basic lute of the Hazarajat (Sakata 1968) and can be found among Paštuns down to the Urozgan area (Hoerburger 1969) and as far east as the Lağman area (my own observation), having displaced many other available types of long-necked lutes.

The strength of northern music culture is also displayed in the appearance of the ǧičak. According to Baba Naim and others, the ǧičak originated in Badaxšan, perhaps specifically in the Šuǧnan area. Soviet data (Dansker 1965; Vertkov 1963) clearly tie this tin-can fiddle to the mountain rather than the plains Tajiks. Baba Naim cites a genealogy of ǧičak masters and their students to explain the spread of the fiddle in recent times (perhaps during the 1930s) from its home in Badaxšan to Kataǧan (Xanabad) — where Lola Akbar, the reigning virtuoso, confirmed Baba Naim's story. Old Hakim of Mazar, a venerable musician, also verified the account of the spread of the ǧičak by a handful of traveling Badaxšani musicians in the 1930s. Today the manufacture of the wooden body piece that forms the basis of the ǧičak (Figure 4.23) is restricted entirely to Tašqurǧan. This crossroads town par excellence can be seen as the diffusion point for many regional items. From Tašqurǧan the Tajik ǧičak became interethnic, spreading throughout Turkestan, down to the Harazajat, and out into Paštun country, paralleling the diffusion of the Turkestani dambura, which perhaps occurred earlier, and displaying the same ability of the dambura to displace local instruments of the same type. Once again, an Uzbek-Tajik accommodation can be seen at work in the musical instruments of the North.

CHAPTER 2

The Music Subcultures

THE PAŠTUNS

Thus far I have had little to say about Paštun music beyond that created in Kabul. Now it is time to turn to Paštun folk music, which stands out sharply from the shared music culture of the North. Of course, there is no single Paštun folk music; as an ethnic group, Paštuns are extraordinarily fragmented along lineage, tribal, and confederation lines, which shift over the years, and they "exhibit a great range of cultural and social forms" (Barth 1969:117) over the wide area they inhabit (cf. Barth 1969a). Nevertheless, when a thorough study of Paštun music has been completed, I believe the interesting factor that will emerge concerning ethnic boundaries is the existence of a strong pan-Paštun stream of folklore, including tales, poems, and songs. Barth has noted "the Pathans' self-image as a characteristic and distinctive ethnic unit with unambiguous social and distributional boundaries" (1969a:119), and he cites "Pathan custom" as one of the chief atributes of Paštunhood cited by Paštuns themselves. I would argue that among the items included in "Pathan custom," along with the celebrated Paštun code of behavior *(Paštunwali),* is an intimate familiarity with the rich Paštun folklore. Here one can perhaps make an analogy of the importance of oral expression often noted among the Arabs:

The Arab's virtual obsession with oral functions can hardly escape notice; it strikes the observer in Arab reverence for language and oral arts. . . . Oral testimony in Islamic law is superior to circumstantial evidence . . . an Arab political scientist . . . has gone so far as to claim that esthetic appreciation of the language has hindered its use as a means of conveying ideas clearly. (Berger 1962:139–40)

I would not wish to state the case so strongly for Afghanistan, but even limited acquaintance with Paštuns will impress an outside observer with their respect for and interest in effective use of language; the Tappers (1973:p.c.) have noted that language (specifically the Kandahar dialect of Pašto) is a key determinant in Paštun self-identification in the Saripul area of Turkestan. It is worth noting Barth's feeling that in the case of a spread-out ethnic group like the Paštuns, the more obvious outward structures of social life may not be the key to understanding the underlying cultural pattern:

. . . We must expect to find that one ethnic group, spread over a territory with varying ecologic circumstances, will exhibit regional diversities of overt institutionalized behaviour which do not reflect differences in cultural orientation. . . . It is thus inadequate to regard overt institutional forms as constituting the cultural features which at any time distinguish an ethnic group. (1969:13)

Following Barth's line of thought, then, it may not be out of place to suggest that the study of oral expressive behavior might be useful for understanding Paštun ethnic boundary maintenance.

To get at the heart of the Paštun oral phenomena referred to, we might turn to the *landai,* the most widespread poetic-musical genre among Paštuns. While each area of Paštun habitation (Laǧman, Kandahar, etc.) appears to have a flourishing regional school of songwriters and tale-tellers, "every Paxtoon everywhere knows some landey by heart and molds them into songs when the occasion demands" (Shpoon 1968:44). According to Shpoon, the tunes to which the landai are set vary from one region to another, but the basic pattern of landai composition remains the same throughout the entire Pašto-speaking area.

The distinctiveness of the landai lies in its verse structure. Every landai consists of two lines only, with the second line longer than the first (generally thirteen and nine syllables, respectively). Furthermore, the second line always ends in certain syllables: *ma* or *na.* To state Shpoon's formal definition, the landai is "a non-rhymed two lined catalectic verse with five anapestic paeon feet, two in the first line and three in the second, ending in MA or NA" (1968:43). The strictness of the form, its brevity, and its tendency to be epigrammatic have led some observers to compare the landai to the haiku of Japan. Like the haiku, the landai first sets up an image and then clarifies and deepens its meaning. Here are two typical landai as transcribed and translated by Shpoon (1968:46):

> Golaab che pre she bea raa shin she
> Zzre che Zakhmi she tol wojood wer sara mrina

> You cut a flower and another grows
> As red, as tender as the first;
> This is not the way with hearts.

> Pe loyo ghro de Khudaay nazar dai
> Pe sar-ye waawre warawi chaaper goloona

> God has an affair [lit.: an eye] with lofty mountains,
> With snow he caps them and around them plants flowers.

The stylistic uniqueness of the landai is matched by its social context, which also stands out sharply from general Afghan practice. Shpoon found that of the landais he collected among Paštun nomads in central Afghanistan, approximately 80 percent, to the best of his knowledge, had been composed by women. Two aspects of this evidence strike the observer immediately: first, that women occupy such an important position in the creation of folksong, and second, that men find no objection to singing the poems composed by women. Indeed, most of the landais are decidedly female in orientation: ". . . landey describes beauty from a woman's point of view and no creator of landey has tried to depart from her feminine emotions" (Shpoon 1968:44). Shpoon contrasts this orientation with that of those few female poets (non-Paštuns) writing in Persian, who invariably adopt the traditional male stance in composing verse.

The landai seems virtually universal among Paštuns. I have recorded examples in as distant and non-Paštun an area as Badaxšan (e.g., Anthology AST 4004 and Chapter 3, p. 179). Though Shpoon found that my Badaxšani performer (Baba Naim) was unorthodox in his musical setting of the landai, and that his arrangement of landai lines and refrain text was not standard, there was no question that the basic texts were those familiar to Paštuns across Afghanistan. I have seen two Paštuns from regions hundreds of miles apart get together and sing landais they both knew well. Particularly interesting in this respect is the manner of performing landais, since the singer must necessarily string together several of these brief couplets to create a song-length composition. Generally landais are compiled topically on such occasions, and (according to Shpoon) a man's excellence as a singer may be judged by his ability to put together a rich and subtle combination of landais.

As must be evident from the above description, two of the hallmarks of the Paštun musical subculture seem to be a high regard for song as an aspect of expressive behavior, particularly of verbal expression, and an apparent universality of basic competence among the population. This profile again marks off Paštun practice from that of the surrounding peoples, among whom music is by no means so widely respected or so frequently performed. One cannot help wonder whether this "musical egalitarianism," which extends to the lack of male musical dominance, is not a part of a larger pattern of Paštun culture. Two of the main forms of Paštun settlement described are "villages of mixed agriculturalists, organized in egalitarian patrilineal descent segments with an acephalous political form," and a pattern in which "a large sector of the ethnic group lives a pastoral nomadic life, politically organized as tribes with, in part, very great autonomy." Another

*Fig. 2.1. Paštun nomads traveling to summer pasture
(Turkestan steppe, looking south)*

grouping of Paštuns consists of a small number of landowners, who are
also organized "in some places in acephalous systems," while the
remainder are Paštuns who "live as administrators, traders, craftsmen or
labourers in the towns of Afghanistan and Pakistan, as an integrated
part of those two states" (Barth 1969a:119). The latter group, by virtue
of their integration into the traditional sedentary, largely urban sector
of Afghan (or Pakistani) life, have in fact lost many of the basic Paštun
characteristics Barth describes, and they have also dropped the musical
practices exemplified by the landai complex.

Thus in the North, those Paštuns who are nomadic transients,
mixing temporarily each year with the local populace, tend to maintain
their customary way of life, even inflicting it on the surrounding non-
Paštuns by expanding their grazing lands at the expense of the local
farmers (see Ferdinand 1962 for details of this process in central
Afghanistan). Somewhat different is the situation of other Paštuns
from the southwestern, southern, and eastern regions of Afghanistan
who have claimed new lands in the North (principally in Katağan)
and have setled down as landowners and merchants. These Paštuns
have became northernized in many ways. Shpoon is fond of quoting a
poem by a southern Paštun, addressed to his compatriots who have
moved to the North; in it the poet warns the reader that he will learn

to wear a čapan (the traditional Central Asian long-sleeved cloak) and eat vegetable oil (as opposed to the sheep fat beloved by the nomads). Indeed, Paštuns in northern bazaars who wear čapans and take up the local eating habits become to a great extent indistinguishable from the local ethnic groups. It is quite possible that they will learn Persian along with Pašto as children, and they are likely to pick up Uzbek as well in some locales. One horsecart driver I met in Aqča was quadrilingual, alternately speaking Pašto, Persian, Uzbek, and Turkmen with his customers. We have already noted that Paštuns may become performers in the local teahouse style in the North as well.

It is clear that in speaking of a Paštun musical subculture one must first define which Paštuns are being discussed. For any given Paštun in the North, one must first note his general relationship to the region and its population before assessing his musical tendencies. Even among established northern Paštuns the situation is not uniform. For example, Shpoon's family, though resident in the Xanabad area of Katağan for some fifty years, has maintained strong Paštun identity: witness Shpoon's activity as a Pašto poet and as a folklorist. Ethnographic investigation into the overall cultural situation of northern Paštuns is only now beginning, and until we have data on the distribution of Paštun social structure and patterns of ecological accommodation in the North, we cannot properly assess the role of musical behavior in the general cultural orientation. It is already clear, however, that in addition to reaching a musical accommodation with the local population of the North, Paštuns (to a greater or lesser extent, regionally and individually) maintain a considerable interest in preserving their characteristic folklore and music.

THE KAZAKHS

The Kazakhs, of all the groups under discussion, tend to come the closest to maintaining a closed musical subculture. The preservation by a small minority people of its musical traditions on alien soil is not unusual; one need only think of the case of the Nekrasov Cossacks (see Listopadov 1953), who returned to their homeland singing their old songs after two centuries in Turkey. The case of the Afghan Kazakhs, however, is a bit more surprising, since they are surrounded not by hostile ethnic groups but by their Central Asian Turkic brethren, the Uzbeks and Turkmens, whose languages they well understand.

Unfortunately, we have so far only the word of the Mazar-i Šarif Kazakhs that their musical world is a sealed one. We would need considerably more research into Kazakh family life in Afghanistan to properly assess the musical situation. Thus, when musicians and

Fig. 2.2. Kazakh musician in his textile shop

merchants say that they take no interest in the shared urban music culture of Mazar, and play no Uzbek-Tajik teahouse favorites at their weddings, we must take the statements with a grain of salt at present. In fact, Sakata (1971:2) reports that among the Kazakhs of the Herat area "those born in Afghanistan are more interested in Persian and Uzbek songs." Nevertheless, the fact that some Kazakhs still sing and play songs of the Alma-Ata homeland in authentic style after forty-odd years in Afghanistan is remarkable. Perhaps the Mazar community is more conservative in this respect than the Herati Kazakhs, since one of the best musicians I recorded there, Kengšilbāi, was a young man who was born in Afghanistan. In 1972 I was told that Kengšilbāi had gone to Turkey for "ğaribi" (business); it would be interesting to follow up on his trip and gain his impressions of the musical world of Turkish Kazakhs, about which there is presently no literature to my knowledge.

The Mazar Kazakhs seem quite eager to perform their music. Thus far I have been unable to make direct correlations between their repertoire and that available in published sources of the music of Kazakhstan. This is hardly surprising, given the breadth of the Kazakh repertoire and its variegated regional inflection. However, many of the names of songs and instrumental pieces (e.g., "Qiz-žibek," "Kokšetau") are familiar enough to anyone who knows Kazakh music. The Mazar Kazakhs' interest in keeping up their traditions is particularly well illustrated by their choice of lutes. Unable for many years to find an authentic *dümbra* to replace the much-repaired specimen they had brought from their homeland, they modified a Turkestani dambura by planing down the neck to the proper shape and adding frets. By 1972, however, they had managed to send one of their number to Kazakhstan and, much to their delight, had obtained a handsome new Soviet Kazakh dümbra. The playing style seems purely Kazakh, and it contrasts markedly with the plucking and strumming styles of the other lutes common to the Afghan North.

Despite the presence of a younger performer in Mazar, it seems unlikely that the Kazakhs can long maintain a distinct music subculture in the face of the homogenization created by the radio. Here again the new ethnic programming of Radio Afghanistan may be decisive. Aimaq, the director of the regional programming, agreed to my suggestion that Kazakh music, even if only in small quantities, be included alongside Uzbek and Turkmen selections in the broadcasts. We must wait some time for the results of such an introduction of Kazakh music over the airwaves. The Mazar Kazakhs indicated to me that they would be pleased by such a gesture and had in fact noticed the bit of their music that had already been broadcast. As noted earlier, even a very minor addition to radio programming can have important results in strengthening a group's interest in its ethnic identity.

THE TURKMENS

I noted in the Introduction that the Turkmens are the only people of the North to live in three lands (Iran, the USSR, and Afghanistan). For Iran, data on the Turkmen music culture are extremely limited, and there had been no publications as of 1973. For Soviet Turkmenistan, curiously, the picture is not much brighter. Since the excellent work by Beliaev and Uspenskii of 1928 *(Turkmenskaia muzyka),* there has been practically no publication on Turkmen music and, as far as I could tell in a brief visit to Ashkhabad, little current scholarship is in progress. Thus it is quite difficult to assess the earlier social side of music in pre-Soviet days, before the Turkmens had clearly split off into "national" groups and had adapted to varying acculturational situations. Most of my information, then, draws on *Turkmenskaia muzyka,* Soviet recordings, my own fieldwork in northern Afghanistan, and data from Afghan Turkmen informants, particularly Allah Berdi Surxi, director of Turkmen programming for Radio Afghanistan.

Though the distribution and tribal identification of Afghan Turkmens has been well documented and a certain amount of historical reconstruction has been done (Bregel 1959; Jarring 1939a), the ethnographic data for Afghan Turkmens are remarkably sparse, particularly on the aspect of greatest interest to the present discussion: Turkmen acculturation to the patterns of living in the Afghan North. More than any other of the major northern groups, the Turkmens are still isolated in that region. Surxi puts the number of Turkmen students at Kabul University at less than ten, and there are not enough Turkmens in bureaucratic or military positions to consider as being culturally significant. Though no statistics are available (we do not even know the total number of Turkmens in Afghanistan), it seems that Turkmens are undereducated even by Afghan standards. There is still time for proper evaluation of Turkmen life in the large number of domed-roof villages scattered across the North, and it is to be hoped that anthropologists will shift their attention from the Paštun nomads, the perennial goal of so many fieldworkers, to the question of the once-nomadic Turkmens of the northern qišlaqs.

Although the Turkmens have turned toward teahouse music as part of a general pattern of adaptation into the basically Uzbek-Tajik culture of the North, it should not be assumed that they have jettisoned their own music culture. Since the Turkmens are by and large isolated from the main stream of change in Afghanistan, they have preserved in large measure their own approach to music. Surxi feels that teahouse music was adopted for two basic reasons: first, teahouse music is technically a good deal easier to perform than is traditional Turkmen music, and second, one can draw a crowd — in other words, make a living — only with Uzbek-Tajik music, the major musical current of the North. I find this evaluation perfectly reasonable. Part of the success of teahouse music certainly lies in the technical accessibility of the instruments used (dambura and ǧičak), at least at the basic level necessary for ǧaribi-šowqi competence; and Turkmen music unquestionably requires a greater virtuosity in both its vocal and its instrumental performance than do the samowad favorites. As to Surxi's second point, it is of course true that no urban audience will listen for long to Turkmen music, which is both linguistically and musically too alien from the lingua franca of the bazaar.

Turkmen music is a complete world unto itself. The three basic instruments employed are shared by no other ethnic group, and the vocal style, particularly the ornamental wordless sounds (vocalise) introduced at the ends of stanzas, is not paralleled in any neighboring music culture. As to the functions and attitudes associated with music,

Fig. 2.3. A Turkmen village

we are on much weaker ground due to the paucity of the data, but I will attempt to summarize the available information.

As is the case with the other peoples of the North, Turkmen musical roles are sexually ascribed. Women are restricted to roles as tambourine and jew's harp players and perform only at weddings, where the music reflects the interethnic music culture. Women also take part in two distinct dance styles, one a group round dance and one a dance for two girls using wooden spoon-castanets (cf. the Uzbek *qošiq* percussion; Karomatov 1972:51); the dances, like women's songs, are performed only at weddings. Presumably lullabies round out the female repertoire. Paradoxically, then, it is the males, who are in contact with outside ethnic groups, who preserve the particularly Turkmen instruments and repertoires, whereas the more isolated women's musical life belongs clearly to the shared music culture of the North.

Men's amateurism spans a variety of settings, occasions, genres, and musical instruments. Shepherds play solo tunes on either of the two distinctive Turkmen wind instruments, the *tüidük* (lit. "reed") and the *dili-tüidük* (lit. "tongue-reed"). Both instruments are made of readily available steppe grasses by the performers themselves. The tüidük is a very long (as much as one meter) open end-blown flute related most closely to various Near Eastern flutes of similar construction that are generally termed *nai* (Persian for "reed"). The dili-tüidük is a very short (pencil-length), much thinner single-reed pipe, related

most closely to the Uzbek *sibiziq*. Both the dili-tüidük and the sibiziq
are rare in being unpaired single-reed pipes; most such aerophones in
Europe and the Near East are lashed together in pairs. The existence
of pastoral tunes and instruments tends to set off Turkmen music,
since Uzbeks and Tajiks of Turkestan seem to lack shepherd's music.
Here the Turkmens are closer to the Paštuns and Baluch of the southern
and southwestern regions of Afghanistan; these nomadic groups play
a much smaller version of the tüidük known as the *nal* (Pašto: "reed").
Turkmen shepherds, however, not only pipe tunes but also dance a
distinctive round dance employing gestures with their staffs; I have not
seen this dance, nor do I know a non-Turkmen who has witnessed it.

Outside the pastoral sphere, Turkmens are musically active principally around the hearth in the long winter nights. Surxi says that
music making takes place nearly every night, and he cites a high
degree of amateurism among males, most of whom have at least a
nodding acquaintance with the dutar, the third member of the Turkmen
instrumentarium. This long-necked fretted lute, like its Uzbek counterpart of the same name, has two strings, but it differs from its Uzbek
namesake principally in its much smaller dimensions.

Turkmen amateurs who become recognized as master musicians
have a special title, *baxši,* bestowed on them by the public at large.
This practice is interesting in reflecting the Turkmens' respect for
music, and also as it points up the lack of such titles for master performers in the shared music culture. We have noted that *ustad,* as a term
of respect, is reserved for a handful of distinctive Kabul musicians;
northerners, however, have no honorific term for their own musicians,
be they dambura players or singers. The Turkmens' use of the term
baxši is therefore highly suggestive. The word stems originally from
the Chinese (Menges 1968) and was used for Uighur functionaries
under Mongol rule. Later the Central Asian Turks adapted the term
to a variety of functions (summarized in Centlivres and Slobin 1971),
but it has been reduced to three basic usages at the present: (1) epic
singer among Uzbeks; (2) master musician among Turkmens; and
(3) shaman among Kirghiz, Kazakhs, and residents of the town of
K. in northern Afghanistan. Beliaev (1975) states that *baxši* might at
one time have denoted shaman among Turkmens as well. The argument
advanced here is that the use of such an historic and affective term for
musicians of a certain grade of excellence speaks for the intrinsic
importance attached to music making among Turkmens. It is not
accidental that among the Uzbeks epic singing and shamanizing were
formerly practiced by the same man (Chadwick and Zhirmunsky
1969:334), that the Kazakhs and Kirghiz use the same horsehair

Fig. 2.4. Turkmen bazaar, Qizilayaq

fiddle (qobuz or *kiak*) both for healing and for musical performance, and that the qobuz was once in use among the Turkmens (Beliaev 1975). The Central Asian inheritance reflected among Afghan Turkmens by the persistence of the *baxši* term for superior musicians sets them off from Afghan Uzbeks, who have lost much of the heritage of their Transoxanian past in adapting to Tajik sedentary life.

Another distinctive aspect of Turkmen practice seems to be the diminished degree of conflict between music and religion as compared to the shared music culture described earlier. I found this particularly striking in the town of Qizilayaq, a major religious center for Afghan Turkmens and the home of the Xalifa of Qizilayaq, the personage most important to devout Turkmens throughout Afghanistan. Qizilayaq is also well known as a musical center, producing many celebrated performers, and the Xalifa gave his brother permission to produce performers for me, a non-Muslim foreigner. The music played was by no means religious but drew from various secular Turkmen traditions, and I was allowed to take photographs as well. By contrast, many informants among other ethnic groups and in other regions of Afghanistan have cited the religious leaders of villages and towns as being key opponents of music.

In addition to singing songs, another popular diversion during long winter nights is reading aloud poems and tales from published versions of Turkmen texts. In Afghanistan this is rather difficult; to my knowledge there have been no books published there in Turkmen (a similar situation applies in Iran), and Afghan Turkmens must rely principally on Soviet Turkmen books, published in Cyrillic script, which must be inaccessible to all save a handful of villagers. Nevertheless, Surxi states that such readings do take place on a regular basis. The importance of the readings is that they furnish source material for song texts. As Chadwick has noted,

The Turkmens are said to have been especially pre-eminent in the art of memorization. Their professional reciters were as remarkable for their highly specialized memories, and the verbal exactitude of their traditions, as the poets of the Kirghiz for their facility in improvisation. In the preservation of the past history of their tribes also the Turkmens were said to excel. . . . In regards to the songs the tradition seems to be one of verbal memorization rather than improvisation, and even in regard to the prose stories the form seems to be strictly memorized. (Chadwick and Zhirmunsky 1969:18, 216)

The emphasis on memorization stressed by Chadwick (who relies on earlier authorities such as Chodzko and Radloff) is distinctively Turkmen and is in contrast to the Kirghiz penchant for improvisation. Yet among Afghan Turkmens, at least, such excessive emphasis on memorization is not characteristic today. Rather, the Turkmens make a clear distinction between song texts that are memorized and that stem from the literary tradition *(xalqi)* and those that are the property of an individual singer *(uzduridan)*. Thus the works of the great Turkmen poets such as Maxtum-quli, Nepes, and Žalili are considered xalqi, while the songs of outstanding baxšis (master performers) would be termed uzduridan. Surxi admits to the possibility that uzuridan compositions may eventually become xalqi through popularity.

The xalqi-uzduridan dichotomy points up major features of the Turkmen music subculture. The xalqi texts show the importance of the literary canon of the Turkmens and indicate strong pantribal unity in poetic matters, and the role of memorization indicated by Chadwick is seen to be verified in the spread and maintenance of the xalqi repertoire. On the other hand, the uzduridan songs confirm the existence of local and personal styles valued for their individuality. Here tribal and personal stylistic traits, dialects, and melodies come into play, factors of considerable importance to Turkmen culture.

Let us look at excerpts of xalqi and uzuridan song texts to gain some perspective on the styles involved. Both types of song are in the repertoire of Axmad-baxši, an outstanding dutarist and singer who was chosen by a listener poll of Radio Afghanistan as the major Turkmen performer. The xalqi selection is from one of the numerous tales of recent centuries that circulate principally in written rather than oral versions. These have been termed "popular novels" by scholars, and their development has been well summarized by Zhirmunsky:

In the Near East popular novels *(Volksromane)*, which are very widespread in Turkmenia, Azerbaijan and Turkey, have practically superseded the old heroic epos. Their plots draw in the main upon the novella and romantic love themes . . . Of great importance in the development of this genre were classical literary versions of medieval love-tales, presented first by Persian and later by Turkic poets *(Leila and Majnun, Farhad and Shirin, Yusuf and Zuleika)* which were then partly remodelled as popular chap-books *(kissa)*. Most of the popular novels either go back to concrete written sources *(Seipul Melik, Hemra, Gul and Sanuabar)*, or have undergone literary adaptation . . . *(Tahir and Zuhra)* not only by word of mouth, but also in the written texts which used to be read aloud by special-reciters. . . . (Chadwick and Zhirmunsky 1969:316)

These "popular novels" are quite popular among Afghan Turkmens; particular favorites are *Tahir and Zuhra* and *Hemra and Hurluqā* (which Zhirmunsky cites just as *Hemra*). It is from this latter tale that our xalqi excerpt comes:

Dur qardašim sanden xabar alayen
Ārtiq niyāz yārim qarim amānme
Sarwadak builaring oidek yuzlaring
Āq yuzingda betan tārim amānme.
Mesering ilingden gelen xanlarim
Xabar bergen bizing iler amānme.

Stop, dear friend, I am inquiring of you.
Is my beautiful sweetheart well or not?
Her figure is like a cypress; her cheek is like a flower.
Are the two moles on her face well or not?
Friend, when you leave Egypt
Tell me if my people are well or not.

At the point in the plot where this song occurs, Hemra is being held captive in Egypt like Joseph in the Bible, who is the hero of the Near Eastern tale *Yusuf and Zulaixa* — one of the sources Zhirmunsky cites for the "popular novels" such as *Hemra*. Stylistically, the striking element of the excerpt cited above is its formalized structure and heavy dependence on the poetic imagery of classical Persian verse. Line 3 is particularly obvious in this respect, repeating in Turkmen the stock epithets for beauty used countless times in Persian poetry and folksong texts. The introduction of a standard tag ending for every second line (the word "amanme") is a device probably also borrowed from Persian verse. I must here refer to my original assessment of the Turkmens as a people heavily influenced by close proximity to Near Eastern, primarily Persian, culture. The overlay in the case of poetry and tales is particularly clear. To the extent that this situation holds, then, the Turkmen music subculture could be seen as merely a dialect of a more general regional trend.

However, on balance, Turkmen music is more distinctive than shared. Let us turn to an uzuridan composition by Axmad-baxši. The song, "Kardašim," is an impassioned lament for a love who died young:

> Buldum yaning ulmazasen bilmai uti wādarix
> Indi gulning šaxasi ačilmai uti wādarix
> Salanat bizdan xabar almai uti wādarix
> Ikki zalemning elinen gulmai ute wādarix
> Izlasem yalğuz bašem xirdan taparman kārdašim
> Hasratingdan qaldi atam zār o ogiryān ulup.

> Woe that she left, not tasting the pleasures of this world
> The buds did not flower and she left
> Asleep, she did not inquire of me and left
> She did not smile to her mother and father and left
> If I search for you where will I find you?
> My father was grief-stricken and left in tears.

This is a private song, perhaps even prompted by a private grief. Structurally, we must take note of the four-line segment at the beginning of the excerpt, with the lengthy repeated ending "uti wadarix." As Zhirmunsky has noted,

The basis of rhythmization in Turkic folk-verse lies in the rhythmic-syntactic parallelism of consecutive verse lines . . . the principle of repetition, of variation and parallelism as regards both sense and grammar, constitutes an important means in the development of epic narration as well. (Chadwick and Zhirmunsky 1969:337)

In the twenty-six lines of "Kardašim," there are no fewer than five such ending patterns for three- to five-line segments of text. On three of the occasions, four-line sections are involved, exemplifying Zhirmunsky's stress on "the emergence of strophes of different types, more frequently of four lines . . . bound up with the influence of lyrical forms, songs and the like . . ." (ibid). Axmad-baxši, then, as song composer, seems squarely in the mainstream of Turkic folk poetry. There is also a lower incidence of Persian-derived imagery in "Kardašim," though it is apparent from the *Hemra* excerpt that Axmad-baxši is well aware of the Persian literary tradition. The difference clearly lies in the distinction the performer makes between the xalqi and uzduridan repertoires. Though evidence is still limited, it is possible to delineate a dichotomy between pan-Turkmen, memorized, Persian-influenced song texts and private, probably tribal, composed or improvised, more Turkic poetry, and we have seen that the two approaches to song texts can coexist in the repertoire of a single master performer. Details of musical structure will be discussed below, but it should be mentioned here that in musical terms every aspect of Axmad-baxši's performances is uniquely Turkmen, bearing little resemblance to either Persian or Afghan Turkestani styles. Particularly distinctive is the style of playing on the dutar, which is unparalleled in even so closely neighboring a style as that of the Uzbek dutar.

We know very little about the precise nature of the special ties existing between the Turkmens and their fellow Turks across the Caspian Sea, the Azerbaijanis. Azerbaijani culture seems to have had a particular appeal for the Turkmens, and the musical side of the relationship was well described by Vambery in 1865:

It is remarkable that, in spite of the bitter hostility reigning between the Turkomans and their Shiite brethren in Persia, the former still always especially name Azerbaydjan as the seat of a higher civilization; and whenever the Bakhshi is asked to sing something more than usually beautiful and original, Azerbaydjanian songs are always called for; nay, even the captive Irani, if of Turkish origin, may always expect more merciful treatment, for the Turkoman says, "He is our brother, this unbeliever." (1970:375).

Unfortunately, research on Turkmen music to date has neither substantiated nor disproved Vambery's statement.

THE UZBEKS

Afghan Uzbeks are divided into two fairly clear-cut groups: the majority, long settled in the country, and the minority, recent émigrés from the Soviet Union. Though the line between the two blurs increasingly each year, it still remains an important factor. In custom, dialect, and even music the émigrés (mohajerin) form a fairly compact group, often with close internal ties. In recent years, the mohajerin have reestablished links with their homeland through visits to their families in Tashkent and Samarqand. Zia Xoja, the noted dutarist, used such a trip as an occasion to buy himself a prize antique instrument (recalling the efforts of the Kazakh émigrés of Mazar-i Šarif to procure a genuine Kazakhstani dümbra). The cultural tenacity of the mohajerin

Uzbeks is somewhat more striking than that of the Kazakhs, since the former are surrounded by a large number of fellow Uzbeks. Another difference setting off the émigré Uzbeks from the Kazakh community is the much higher socioeconomic levels attained by the Uzbeks. The latter have in many cases acquired wealth by becoming merchants and money changers, particularly in Kabul.

Let us examine the musical attitudes and practices of the émigré community before turning to the native Afghan Uzbeks. The mohajerin brought with them a whole set of musical values that pertain to Transoxanian Uzbeks but not to the Afghan situation. Chief among these is the complex of interests related to the maintenance of an art music tradition, unknown in Afghanistan save for the limited practice of North Indian classical music. The Uzbek tradition relates to the world of the Buxaran maqam mentioned in the discussion of musical zones in Chapter 1. Briefly, this involves a canon of six lengthy, modally organized suites of instrumental and vocal music performed by a highly trained group of professional singers and instrumentalists; the tradition is backed up by extensive theoretical writings that go back over several centuries. Allied with this repertoire is considerable respect for its practitioners and a serious interest in matters musical and poetic.

The master musician achieves a special status within the mohajerin community. Though the Uzbeks do not have a term analogous to the Turkmen "baxši" for performers of high distinction, the concept is nevertheless clear in their minds: certain performers are singled out for special commendation. For example, the Uzbeks honored Ğafur-i Wafa of Andxoi by choosing him as one of two performers for the new Uzbek programming on Radio Afghanistan. Ğafur, though an Afghan Uzbek, plays exclusively in the Transoxanian tradition, whereas the other official Radio Uzbek performer, Saidullah Ağa Kunduzi, tends to play a more Afghan Uzbek repertoire. The major difference between the Turkmen and Uzbek attitudes towards the master musicians is that the Uzbek virtuoso is expected to disdain compensation for his work, whereas Turkmens are invariably paid for performing. This concept of the true amateur is a special mohajerin value far removed from that of the working šowqi Uzbek of the Turkestani teahouse. Ğafur-i Wafa is himself the son of a rich land and sheep owner of Andxoi, and is thus a true gentlemen-musician akin to the old troubadour-artistocrats of twelfth-century France, or to minnesingers like Oswald von Wolken-stein. In an interview for *žwandoon* magazine (5/13/72:23), Ğafur notes that he took up the dutar only in his late teens and was for a long time quite shy of public performance, not expecting to be well received. Musicians like Ğafur-i Wafa perform by invitation only, usually at the homes of bais (land and livestock owners like Ğafur's father) and merchants, for a select circle of guests. Andxoi is particularly rich in musicians and patrons of Transoxanian Uzbek music, and the town is famous across the North as a center of Uzbek culture. Badruddin Šarafi (the connoisseur who spent some childhood years in Andxoi) feels it is "the most Uzbek" of towns, and even a self-proclaimed non-Uzbek, Bangeča Tašqurǧani, says "all the Uzbek music comes from Andxoi." Indeed, outside of Kabul, it is only in Andxoi that one glimpses the Transoxanian attitudes toward music and musicians. None of the Andxoi dutarists would deign to play in a teahouse, or even for a general audience; all are proud of their achieved status as appreciated master musicians. One leading musician, Šoqol Sufi, refused to play for me or even to admit to his identity, despite prompting by his friends. Both Ǧafur-i Wafa and Ǧafur Xan, another leading dutarist, have made tours of Mazar-i Šarif, Kunduz, and Xanabad at the request of prominent mohajerin Uzbeks who long for the music of their homeland. I have been reliably told that they are not paid on such trips, though in the case of Ǧafur Xan, a poor shoemaker, I imagine that at least his expenses are covered. Judging by the enthusiasm with which this dutarist was received in Kunduz, where twenty-odd guests were invited to his performance, it seems likely that he is the recipient of some gifts, if not cash payment; however, the tradition is clearly against such remuneration for musical services.

The relationship of such performers to Uzbekistan, the true homeland of the musical style they favor, is somewhat ambiguous. They would rather not admit to being avid listeners of Radio Tashkent (which is easily heard in northern towns such as Andxoi), but when I played tapes of Ǧafur Xan to musicologists in Tashkent, they dismissed him as a not especially gifted imitator of Uzbekistani performers. Even allowing for a certain amount of local chauvinism in Uzbekistan, it does seem clear that Andxoi musicians learn much of their repertoire from Radio Tashkent, mixing it with material learned from their native Afghan or mohajerin fathers and acquaintances. Some listeners rely heavily on Uzbekistani broadcasting, tuning in to Radio Tashkent all day long in shops or homes. However, the new Radio Afghanistan Uzbek broadcasts will proabably influence these listening patterns, at least for that one hour per day, particularly since Transoxanian music is included along with Afghan styles. Faizullah Aimaq, the director of the ethnic programming, is himself an Andxoi Uzbek and therefore leans toward inclusion of both basic Uzbek repertoires. In the long run, the radio may have a decisive effect in eradicating some of the cultural differences between Afghan and Transoxanian Uzbeks by acquainting each group more closely with the dialects and repertoire of the other.

The dutar is not the only uniquely Uzbek instrument found in Afghanistan. Çagatay (pseudonym of B. Šarafi) cites a special type of ğičak "made from a large gourd, the top of which has been sliced off. . . . Over the opening is stretched a dried sheepskin . . . and three strings" (Çagatay and Sjoberg 1955:107). I have never seen such an instrument nor heard of one used, but have no reason to doubt Çagatay's statement. The interesting feature of the ğičak he describes is its three strings, which would relate the instrument closely to Uzbekistani practice rather than to the standard tin-can, Tašqurğani-made ğičak usually used in Afghanistan. However, Çagatay's added statement that ". . . a metal container may be employed instead" (1955:107) points to a convergence of the type of ğičak he describes and the common model usually seen.

More specifically traceable as Uzbek is the *qošnai* mentioned by the same author (Çagatay and Sjoberg 1955:107). This is a paired single-reed aerophone most closely related to similar Near Eastern pipes. The instrument described by Çagatay, however, is interesting for its deviation from the Uzbekistani norm: "The qosnay is an instrument of brass or wood consisting of two tubes connected to form a V" (1955:107). The standard qošnai as described by Karomatov (1972: 72–73) is quite different and always features reed construction and parallel tubing. Thus the Afghan qošnai, like the ğičak just cited, seems to be a local adaptation of the Transoxanian model. Çagatay also notes that the qošnai "is rarely used in Kabul," which again suggests its particularly northern affiliation. Also "not used in Kabul" is the Turkestani version of the Uzbek *karnai,* which the author gives as *"kannay* . . . a wood-wind instrument of copper with a bass tone. It is extremely long, at times over ten feet . . . it is employed by Uzbeks in northern Afghanistan at marriage ceremonies, wrestling matches, and other games" (1955:107). This time Çagatay's description matches those of the standard Soviet Uzbek references (Karomatov 1972:90), with the exception that the instrument is cited there as being used primarily for alarms or for military purposes (in the old Buxaran Khanate) rather than for ordinary entertainment. The karnai is another instrument that has just about gone out of use in northern Afghanistan; I have not been able to even locate a specimen for observation, though Aimaq remembers seeing a karnai in Andxoi when he was a boy, in the 1950s.

Summarizing the discussion of musical instruments, it seems that there is considerable material evidence to indicate old ties between Afghan and Transoxanian Uzbeks, even though the former have tended to modify their instruments to suit local conditions. It is unfortunate that we have no data regarding the musical life in the city-states of

Afghan Turkestan in the nineteenth century. Most of those towns, from Maimana to Kunduz, were ruled by local Uzbeks for some time; it seems unlikely that, in the course of intensive contact with Buxara, none of the strong Transoxanian music culture would have rubbed off on the petty potentates of Andxoi, Maimana, and other towns. One can imagine them patronizing local musicians who played in Buxaran style and evolved a local dialect of Transoxanian art music. However, there is no hard evidence for the survival of such a tradition, so we must be content with speculations. The survival of musical values, instrument making, and repertoire in Andxoi even today, however, does point to the possibility that more than just émigré influence has been at work, especially since some of the musicians (Ğafur-i Wafa, for example) come from old Afghan Uzbek families.

Let us turn now to examination of the native Afghan Uzbek music subculture. We have already discussed at length the repertoire of the teahouse, in which a strong Uzbek component has fused with Tajik elements to form a major contribution to the shared musical life, at least in Turkestan. When it comes to distinctively Uzbek elements, there is an equally rich field of investigation, at least in the area of repertoire. Unlike the mohajerin, the Afghan Uzbeks do not seem to have any special attitudes toward the practice of music to set them off from surrounding peoples, nor are there special instrument types other than the qošnai and karnai just cited. The dambura and to a lesser extent the ğičak remain the major lute types, with the doira and čang still reserved for women and children. Perhaps a special case might be made for the tüsak (Persian: zang or tal), the finger cymbals that accompany the teahouse songs. Although they form a part of the samowad presentation described here as part of the joint music culture, it is nearly always Uzbeks who are seen playing the tüsak; yet the instrument is probably Indian in origin. Noticeably absent from the instruments one might expect among Uzbeks are the percussion (idiophone) sets of spoons and stones commonly found in Uzbekistan (Karomatov 1972) under the names qairaq and qošiq, respectively. Paradoxically enough, only Turkmens seem to use the qošiq, as accompaniment to a girl's wedding dance, and the only practitioner of qairaq I found in the North was a Tajik from the Samangan area (recorded on Anthology AST 4007). Such irregularities point up the mixing of instruments that is typical of northern Afghanistan, and they underscore the presence of considerable acculturation.

Within the specifically Afghan Uzbek repertoires, four principal areas of interest can be defined: urban ğazals as song texts, na't religious songs, secular tales, and instrumental dance music. Let us examine them individually.

Urban Ğazals

The ğazal is a basic genre of literary Persian verse, perhaps most classically exemplified in the works of Hafez (d. 1389). It is still widely used by poets in all the Persian-speaking regions and has been adopted by writers of Uzbek, Pašto, and Urdu poetry in Afghanistan, Soviet Central Asia, Pakistan, and India. In Afghanistan the Uzbek urban ğazal seems to be a direct counterpart to the urban Tajik ğazal of the same region. Thus the ğazal repertoire tends basically to confirm the existence of a joint music culture rather than that of a distinct subculture. Nevertheless, the fact that the ğazals are held by Uzbeks to be part of their own heritage and their exclusion of Tajiks from full appreciation of the genre seem to point to a "separate-but-equal" position, which at once confirms acculturation and denies it.

Not surprisingly, Andxoi is seen by some as the center of the urban Uzbek ğazal. Performers in Aqča, for example, spoke of a whole school of poets in Andxoi who turned out ğazals that could be set as song texts. Singled out as exceptional was Kamal Andxoi, father of Ğafur Xan, the shoemaker-dutarist mentioned above. As in the case of Andxoi dutar music, there seems to be some connection with the Transoxanian classical tradition — in this case, with the heritage of classical Uzbek poetry. However, like the art music, the poetry has at least geographic roots in Afghanistan proper, since the great Uzbek classic poet, Mir Alisher Navoi (d. 1501), lived, worked, and died in Herat under the last of the Timurid rulers. Structurally, both the works of Navoi and recent urban ğazals tend to be highly imitative of classical Persian verse models, including a large number of Persian words and principles of prosody.

Na't Religious Songs

Here again we find Uzbek practice running parallel to that of other groups. Basically, Uzbek na't song seems to be quite similar in function and structure to the religious song outlined in Chapter 1. However, Uzbeks compose texts in their own language for sacred use, bypassing the pan-Islamic Arabic and the Persian lingua franca of Afghanistan. Because of the high degree of interrelationship with Tajiks, a separate Uzbek na't repertoire calls attention to itself as a distinctive feature, especially since the occasions for na't singing — major Islamic holidays — would seem to suggest shared public songs rather than individualized ethnic compositions. We thus return again to the home as the guardian of distinctive ethnic traits as opposed to the intergroup accommodation of the bazaar.

Secular Tales

The body of secular tales falls into two distinct categories: the various Uzbek versions of the widespread, multiethnic tale "Köroğlu," and the purely Uzbek tales. "Köroğlu" seems to be diminishing in popularity in Afghanistan, as the older tellers have died and do not seem to have been replaced by younger reciters. Unlike the situation in Uzbekistan, where epic recitation is widely supported, the Afghan outlook is somewhat bleaker. Whether this relates to change in taste or to the disappearance of the older members of the first émigré generation is hard to tell; there are simply not enough data to properly judge the case. Nevertheless, there are still singers of "Köroğlu," such as Xodai Qul, a young man of Andxoi (recorded on Anthology AST 4001). A striking feature of Xodai Qul's performance is his insertion of an introduction in Persian before beginning the Uzbek segment of his tale. Here again the tendency towards ethnic accommodation becomes evident. Xodai Qul knows little of the epic, having learned only selected passages from an old reciter before the latter's death in the mid-1960s.

In the case of the local Afghan Uzbek tales the situation is quite different, and the tradition is still flourishing in areas of heavy Uzbek population. Local tales can be subdivided into two genres: quasi-literary "popular novels" related to a Transoxanian Uzbek repertoire ("Zibājān"), and stories based on actual events and personages of the locale of origin (" Bāijura"). Let us examine them separately.

Zibajan is the female side of a standard pair of star-crossed lovers, whose male half is Yāzi. "Zibajan" and similar tales, according to Aimaq, tend to be identified with particular locales; thus "Zibajan" is sung primarily in Fariab province, particularly in the Qaisar area. Karmysheva (1960a:74) indicates that in Uzbekistan similar localization of the heroes occurs. The local Uzbeks speak of Ziba's home as the qišlaq of Birqa, near Qaisar. The time and setting for women's performance of "Zibajan" is distinctive and constitutes a special area of Afghan Uzbek music culture. Women sing "Zibajan" at several times: while cooking, while grinding flour (not all towns have ready access to mills), at weddings, and while weaving carpets (a skill quite recently learned from neighboring Turkmens). The combination of singing at work and performance at weddings is particularly notable, in that it indicates a continuity of women's customs and music. This tends to confirm our earlier identification of a special women's sector, and the tendency of women to expand the sector of musical expression to a multiplicity of occasions.

If Aimaq's observation for the Andxoi area can be generalized for other Uzbek areas (which seems reasonable, given the wide spread of the local tradition), it would appear that Uzbek women maintain a considerable body of musical activity, both work-related and occasional. Such a picture would strongly link Afghan Uzbeks to those of regions of Uzbekistan such as the Ferghana Valley, which has been studied by Soviet researchers. In 1931, Romanovskaia collected an extensive repertoire from women of Andijan, Osh, and Margelan, covering a wide variety of genres (ceremonial, lyric, game and dance, Soviet topics). Yet the Ferghana situation differs from that of the Afghan Uzbeks in several important ways. First, the Ferghana women's repertoire apparently contains neither tales such as "Zibajan" nor songs sung during work. Second, the Ferghana Valley women commonly play the dutar, albeit a smaller version of the instrument, and with a more limited repertoire, than is common among men (Romanovskaia 1959:66). As far as I can tell, no Afghan Uzbek women play any stringed instrument; they are limited, as noted earlier, to the tambourine and jew's harp. Finally, the tradition of professional female performers seems to have been much more comprehensive in scope and more widespread in Uzbekistan than in Afghanistan. Romanovskaia (1959) cites the high number of professional women performers in the Ferghana Valley. Kadyrov also describes women's theaters for various areas of the country in recent years: ". . . in many towns and villages of Uzbekistan there existed . . . theatre companies, of which about twenty continue to function nowadays." The repertoire of these female troupes is quite broad, consisting of comedies, dramatic stories, comic songs, comic dances, dramatic parodies, and pantomimes; in addition, each local company has its own genres (Kadryov 1969:94). In Afghanistan one finds occasional female professional performers, such as Zulaixa and Gulandam in Andxoi, mentioned earlier; however, such entertainment is extremely limited in scope (to singing only), in number of performers, and in social acceptability. Thus, while it seems clear that Uzbek women everywhere have a strong stake in musical expression, Afghanistan presents a much more limited spectrum of outlets and repertoires than does the Uzbek heartland in Uzbekistan.

Turning to male performance of "Zibajan" — or, more properly, "Yazi and Zibajan" — once again the Transoxanian usage seems more functional and widespread. Karmysheva (1960:72–73) describes the tale as being sung by the Uzbeks in numerous regions of Uzbekistan and Tajikistan as an accompaniment to harvesting, with noted singers (*yazigui,* "yazi-tellers") being invited to perform this task. On the

Afghan side, I have not witnessed nor have I heard of such Uzbek work parties with tale-singing soloists.

The tale of "Zibajan" itself pulls in two directions stylistically. On the one hand, there are the elements that tend toward the multi-ethnic concept of the tale: a plot turning around a highly romanticized couple, the introduction of a great many turns of phrase related to the stock epithets of Persian classical verse, and a basic verse form organized in couplets like the Persian ğazal rather than in the typically Turkic folk quatrains of the Turkmen tale. These elements Karmysheva does not describe for the Transoxanian version. On the other hand, there are elements of "Zibajan" that are strongly local in imagery and even locale. Let us look at some sample lines to pinpoint both elements of "Zibajan:"

Zibājān howli saldi pas pas ğina
Gul ikubān yā ekan birdas gina
Gulidan iskeidisan tekānebār
Labidan upaidisam čārxālebār.

Duganamni šaftāluzar qarsibār
Mastiwāna arqasida sālibar.

Borup aiting motarwāni uziga
Akagenam Mazār saxi kitida.

Zibajan built a house below;
Her low house was full of flowers,
If you try to smell them, they're thorny
I can't kiss her because of her moles.

Her shawl is peach-colored;
It is more beautiful than the trappings of a fighting-camel.

When the drivers cross the bridge
Tell them to take my friend [Yazi] to the pilgrimage at Mazar.

The first four lines cited seem Persian-related in presenting an image of flowers and thorns and then tying it to the standard beauty spots of the Persian lover's face. The second couplet cited is more localized. Noting the color of a woman's veil (the all-encompassing Afghan *čadri*) is a local pastime, since in a village or town one can identify women only through such features of dress. The comparison to a fighting-camel is also regional; Turkestan is famous for such tournaments, and it would be typical for a male to make such a metaphor. According to Jarring's informants in Andxoi, in the 1930s every *bai* had about ten fighting-camels (1939a:79). Even more localized is the last couplet quoted, which refers to the annual spring pilgrimage to the putative grave of Ali in Mazar-i Šarif, the major religious event of northern Afghanistan. The switch from the male to female point of view apparent in the excerpts above perhaps indicates the catholicity of the tale and illustrates how segments can be sung by men or women. Here the Uzbeks seem to differ from the Turkmens, among whom it seems women do not recite tales at all, but an analogy can be seen with the Paštun approach, in which men and women share a repertoire largely related to the women's realm. It would be useful to research the authorship of tales such as "Zibajan" to substantiate the feeling gained from informants that they are primarily female in origin.

Turning now to "Baijura," we find the most localized type of Uzbek tale. The tale is sung across Turkestan, with excerpts performed to dambura accompaniment by professionals and nonprofessionals alike. It refers to an actual drowning of a shepherd during the

"BAIJURA"

Bāijureya bāijura senang senamga jura
Iki kuzing qabqara dowreia kulugara
Bāila čeǧu tulālde teira siya pulālde
Sangalaǧni gulida bāijurani seilālde
Igar uzde tāidan pākat kelde bāidan
Bāijurana seilāldi yātu qālian jāidan
Āstanāni čulida qizilputa beilida
Bāijurana seilāldi sangalāǧni kulida
Beilda puta beilgardān qulda rumāl qulgardān
Bāijurani seilādi qaum o xiši sargardān
Zardālune dānase kup yāzilyen šānasen
Seil ičida saragardān bāijura ānasi
Kup čaini šamase zardālune tammasi
Balamlaidi yiǧlaidi bāijuraina amasi
Uzul qildi tāqlari gup be sini čaklari
Kitidan yeǧlaow qāldi jurana bibālarai
Budanani qapasi čigukiti napasi
Ukam dide yiǧlaidi bāijurana āpasi
Māšinqantai čakasi quytartade sirkasi
Ukam didi yiǧlaidi bāijuranai akasi
Kalawani āhāri yilda kilyen bāhāri
Akam didi yiǧlaidi bāijurani xāhari
Bāǧimumen araiǧi šildilaida barǧe
Turam didi yiǧlaidi baijurana qallare
Dalāq lani pāksi qulida tamāksi
Waxjiendi yiǧlidi jurana amaksi
Zardālune šaxasi bātaigen paraxisi
Wāxjiendi yiǧlaidi bāijurana tāǧasi
Telārgarni qāši kisildi quinibāši
Kitidan yuǧlin qāldi jurana qarandāškan
Bāǧdan uzdi ǧurani aiting mullā tarane

flood season some fifty years ago in the area of Širin Tagow, a village along the Andxoi-Maimana road. In the version of the tale presented here (as performed by Mati Sagir from Širin Tagow and broadcast over Radio Afghanistan) Baijura appears only in the past tense, and the content could be seen as an extended lament over a fallen hero. Throughout, there is an extraordinary likeness to the techniques and imagery of the Central Asian Turkic epic tale, in contrast to the heavy iranization apparent in the Uzbek urban ğazal and (to a lesser extent) in the "popular novel" tales of both the Afghan Turkmens and Uzbeks. Mati Sagir's text is presented below in toto, both for its interesting epic style and as a contribution to the still nearly nonexistent ethnography of Afghan Uzbek life.

The description of Baijura's funeral proceedings jibes with Çagatay's

---

"BAIJURA"

Baijura o Baijura let us be together
Your eyes are black; look at me
During the sheepherding time
Baijura was carried away by a flood
Letters came from all the *bais*
That Baijura was taken by the flood while asleep
In the Astana steppe wearing his red belt
The flood carried him to the stony riverbank
While he wore his belt and held a kerchief
The flood carried him off causing all his relatives unhappiness
His shoulders were broad; he was handsome like an apricot
His distracted mother looked for him down by the flood plain
Green tea leaves; apricot bough
His father's sister cries "Balam, Baijura!"
His arbor yielded grapes; he wore a *gup* [Uzbek shirt]
All his friends lamented Baijura
Baijura's soul flew out like a quail from a cage
His little brother cried, saying "Older brother!"
His face was white like sugar cubes
His sheep were led by a bellwether
His older brother cried "Baijura!"
His life became like a tangled ball of thread
Another spring will not come
His little sister cried, saying "Brother!"
Even the fishes of the Bagmumen river cried
His fiance cries, saying "Husband!"
Barbers came crying with their razors
Smokers came crying with their tobacco
The apricot bough and twigs scraped "Baijura"
His uncle cried, saying "Nephew!"
For his death they killed sheep
His relatives and tribe cried for him

["BAIJURA"—Continued]

Xasgirya band gālwakan taptila bāijurana
Xirman naxurdasina yāǧena dardesini
Daryādan tāpa āldi jurana murdasim
Bāijura qilda qazā ātasib bulda razā
Bāijurai āqulda unming nafar janāza
Xirmanni zāti yermi bulyen nāoti
Asel činardan akan bāijurana taoti
Guyabaǧrani telow tarsiya qara qulo
Taotini duzatyan ikita najār kelo
Maimanain yigiti ayāǧilde bār buti
Quldan qulya ti maida bāijurana taoti
Yuldum baru parina kursati hunarini
Dowrešiya quidila katārdaki narina
Širinšakar suzāni iki xumār quzini
Talašān qelan birdi ikinni hokuzini
Gačkāreqil uyina xinčadai qadbuina
Xairat qelo birdala suridaki quyina
Tarifitai bāina piyālani čaini
Isqātya quidāla anbārni buǧdai yini
Dušmanam dustini ālāl maida qustini
Mulālai birdala tamām hasto bustina
Ketsala xoda yāri dumburagi nātāri
Kiči qunduz yātipti yetim mullā qarāri
Hawāya čeǧar yalduz terama kitsai qunduz
Yetim mulla qarāri hamkeča o ham qunduz
Xareidan kilyan maxi unbirātarne sixi
Dunqqizdai tuyukiti audiyāsina šixi
Yenuqildem yeništan kizanyeqil kamištan
Jurajani qaori yetming bešix xištdan
Jānqutiya qawalyan salalari čuwalyan
Jurajāni qaori simintmenam suwalyan
Sizye biryan sālani kisasida kalami
Yetiǧaz darāida hawāsini alimi
Tarif itai bāine ičalmaidi čaini
Bairaq qelow quyčakam yetigaz durāini
Dušman manam dustiya harflar jelustiya
Xaimani yettu urdi qowrami ustiya
Čupana eštim čalow biz emas maqsad palow
Jurani juma siya damlandi unqainā palow
Bašiya saldi alās turkman tuqida palās
Bāijurani ksasi šuyerda buldi xatas.

["BAIJURA"—Continued]

They picked the raw grapes from his arbor
Tell the mullah to sing a lament
They found him in an eddy of the river
People gathered as for a harvest
The people remain but Baijura has left [simile: butter sediment]
They found dead Baijura in the river
Baijura died; his father had to accept it
Ten thousand people sang his lament
He had goods, all of it was lost to people
They made his coffin from good plane-tree wood
All his dear ones' hearts were as if cut
They ordered two carpenters to make his coffin
The young men of Maimana came wearing boots
There were so many not all could be pallbearers
His father showed his art by giving things away [simile: plucking bird]
He gave all his camels as lament-gifts
His speech was sugar, his eyes were love-drunk
His father gave away his plough oxen
All his houses were beautiful and spacious
His figure was like a sapling
He gave all his sheep away
The *bais* and even his teacups are worth recounting
He gave away all the grain in his granary
His death cannot be laid to friend or foe
He gave everything away to mullahs
I play my dambura and may God bless Baijura
Mullahs pray in his house night and day
Stars are in the sky; in autumn we go towards Kunduz
Seven mullahs pray night and day in Baijura's house
He even gave away his good rifle
The grave guarders became fat as pigs
We make spurs so we won't fall on the way
His grave was made from seven thousand precious stones
His turban became raveled and his soul was lost
His grave was made of cement
He greeted everyone and had a pen in his pocket
Seven meters of *qanawi* fabric went in his grave-cover
I sing of Baijura who can't drink his tea
They put a *yurt* over his grave
All his friends and foes were sad at his death
I go eat *chalow* [rice] with shepherds
I don't intend to go to his grave
On Friday they gathered people and gave *palow* [meat dish]
Seven pots, each of twelve *sirs* [1 *sir* = 16 lbs.]
Everyone wore veils and Turkmens cried weaving carpets
The story of Baijura is ended.

description of Afghan Uzbek custom (Çagatay and Sjoberg 1955:97–99). Perhaps the extensive lament presented here relates to the tradition of having a close friend tell "the story of the person's life and his or her contributions to family and society." Çagatay notes that "on the fortieth day after the death the family will, if financially able, hold a large feast for the poor." *"Pilaw* with *qawrma* is the principal dish served," and it corresponds to the killing of sheep for a feast in "Baijura." Also found in the tale is the custom of setting aside a special place for prayers for the deceased. Çagatay does not mention giving away the deceased's possessions, which is probably added into the narrative to further the image of wealth imputed to Baijura's family. Schuyler (1877:151) describes Uzbek funeral customs that also fit well with those described in "Baijura." He speaks of burial "chambers . . . made of bricks plastered over with clay, in different forms, usually square or oblong, and sometimes with a pavillion or temple over them," which would correspond to the special tent mentioned in "Baijura." It is the high degree of hyerbole that lends the true epic flavor to 'Baijura." It must be "ten thousand people" who sing the lament, and "seven mullahs" praying night and day, plus "seven thousand precious stones" to make up the grave. The addition of cement as the building material is a contemporary hyperbolic touch as well, as Çagatay simply speaks of "a rounded mound of earth . . . topped by a large stone" (Çagatay and Sjoberg 1955:98).

Laments have an old history among Turkic peoples. Chadwick mentions an eleventh-century manuscript with laments for heroes, "probably from an earlier copy" (Chadwick and Zhirmunsky 1969:77). She quotes Radlov to the effect that "among the Kirghiz the wife sings elegies . . . for a whole week beside the clothes of her dead husband, and a dead man is always celebrated in poetry . . . professional minstrels . . . will sing in public assemblies in honour of a famous man" (1969:71). It is interesting to note Chadwick's statement that "elegiac poetry is commonly composed by women in celebration of the dead" (1969:70); one wonders to what extent this Turkic custom might hold true for Afghan Uzbeks. In the case of "Baijura," the singer identifies himself as a dambura-playing male, and attributes singing and lamenting to members of both sexes.

Dance and Dance Music

Uzbek dance is associated with the long-established custom of training dancing boys. We are fortunate to have a description of this practice from Andxoi in the 1930s, as told to Gunnar Jarring:

. . . among Turkmens or Uzbeks the habit is this: the men tie bells at the feet of young boys and dress them in women's clothes, and keep them in a cellar. Having caused them to stay there for some years, they take them away whenever they want, and having assembled people in the night they play the dutar and tambur and beat tambourines and have these children dance. This is very current in all Turkestan. And if young boys are to be found, they never let women dance. Having decorated the dancing-rooms beautifully, and having spent money on it, they enjoy themselves. For this reason, ever so many boys at the age of ten or fifteen disappear. Because they bring the young children in the night or at day-time from hidden places and imprison them in some place. In many cases their father and mothers are not able to find them. In some cases their children came back after fifteen or twenty years. (Jarring 1939:159–160)

Dancing boys are an old Uzbek-Tajik tradition, described numerous times by nineteenth-century travelers to the Kingdom of Buxara. Schuyler (1877:132–37) has given the most extensive and vivid description of the Buxaran dancing-boy tradition; it is worth quoting some passages to indicate the pervasiveness of the practice among Uzbeks:

These *batchas,* or dancing-boys, are a recognized institution throughout the whole of the settled portions of Central Asia, though they are most in vogue in Bukhara, and the neighbouring Samarkand . . . the mere rumor that there would be a *bazem,* or dance, was sufficient to draw great crowds. . . . These *batchas* are as much respected as the greatest singers and *artistes* are with us. Every movement they make is followed and applauded, and I have never seen such breathless interest as they excite, for the whole crowd seems to devour them with their eyes, while their hands beat time to every step. . . . Even when a *batcha* passes through the bazaar all who know him rise to salute him with hands upon their hearts. . . . In all large towns *batchas* are very numerous, for it is as much the custom for a Bokhariot gentlemen to keep one as it was in the Middle Ages for each knight to have his squire. In fact no establishment of a man of rank or position would be complete without one; and men of small means club together to keep one among them. . . . The dances, so far as I was able to judge, were by no means indecent, though they were often very lascivious. . . . The songs sung during the dances are always about love, and are frequently responsive between the *batcha* and the musicians. . . . The *batcha* practice their profession from a very early age until sometimes so late as twenty or twenty-five. . . . Rarely do they lay up any money, and more rarely still are they able to profit by it afterwards. . . . Occasionally one succeeds, and becomes a prosperous man . . . in the old days . . . a handsome dancer might easily become . . . Grand Vizier. More often a *batcha* takes to smoking opium or drinking *kukhnar* and soon dies of dissipation.

From Schuyler's picture we can perhaps gain a glimpse of the status of bačabazi in former times in northern Afghanistan, even if the "backwoods" courts of Turkestani city-states could not have maintained the level of dissipation of Buxara. His picture of the post-*bača* life of dancers would seem somewhat overdrawn for the Afghan situation. Though information on boy dancers' careers is rather limited, it appears that they may simply take up ordinary working lives after they have passed their days of stardom, rather than rising meteorically or declining disastrously. Occasionally they may stay in the field as adult performers; one such example is Faiz Andxoi, who continues to dance and play instruments and is also known as a dance teacher for boys in Andxoi. Faiz may be an exceptional case, in that he is known to come from a kespi (hereditary-professional) family of performers in Andxoi, which includes the female wedding singers Zulaixa and Gulandam. Another former dancing boy from Andxoi, Mowlanqul, works in the bazaar and occasionally performs musically around town. In any case, the boy dancer finds it hard to live down his career; as Schuyler stated, "The remembrance of his past life will frequently place the then odious affix batcha to his name" (1877).

In Afghan Turkestan today the institution of the zirxana, the cellar in which fledgling dancing boys are kept, is said to be considerably diminished since the days of Jarring's informant. This is perhaps due more to the efforts of the central government and provincial authorities than to a change in the interests of local Uzbeks. Doubtless the custom has not entirely died out. Informants in towns such as Kunduz and Xanabad still respond with knowing smiles when asked about dancing boys and will admit to the existence of private parties attended by such performers. In those towns I have been told that dancing boys are to be found in the *atrāf,* the environs of the town, rather than in the bazaar area, because of restrictions by the authorities. Paštun villagers near Xanabad declined any knowledge of dancing boys in their area, confirming the general feeling that the custom in the North is generally connected to Uzbek surroundings.

It is difficult to distinguish between the superficially similar Paštun and Uzbek dancing-boy traditions, if one relies solely on the outer trappings: an atmosphere rife with immorality and suggestive of lewd behavior, and the appearance of young nubile boys dancing to accompaniment of folk music. However, significant differences separate the two ethnically related expression of a single institution. Paštun performances in the North tend to feature dancing boys from the Kabul-Mašreqi zone rather than northern Paštuns. The accompanying band, though it may include some local pickup musicians, is largely from that same region, and the music played is usually Logar Valley style rather than northern. At one performance in Tašqurğan, a major local musician (Bangeča), who was earning a small fee as an accessory player, looked and sounded quite out of place as he tried to fit in with the Logar musicians and their style.

More central to the distinction between Paštun and Uzbek dancing boys is the place and occasion of performance. Paštun troupes may appear in the spring holiday season or at other relaxed times of year. They perform in public in the center of a town and charge a fixed admission price, and they expect spontaneous donations from devotees of one or another dancing boy, who may then make his own arrangements for private appearances. Uzbek boys, on the other hand, may well find considerable employment in the long winter months, when many Uzbek circumcisions are held as major pastimes complete with horsemanship matches and feasts. Their appearances are privately arranged, with no standard cover charge for the entertainment. In the absence of reliable evidence, I would hazard the guess that in the case of both Paštun and Uzbek performers, the dancers operate with considerable independence and under different contract arrangements from those of the band members. The latter are hired for a fixed fee arranged in advance by the host or entrepeneur, while the former seem free to wheel and deal with admirers. As mentioned in Chapter 1, northerners may view attachment to dancing boys as a form of šowqi enthusiasm — almost a type of hobby — rather than necessarily as a sign of debauched homosexual activity. Nevertheless, a certain stigma hangs over the performers and their appearance; it seems to stem from an understanding that a breach of public morality is involved, one that might be looked at askance by the local guardians of Islamic ethics. Here the Uzbek and Paštun versions of bačabazi diverge again, in that I have not heard of northern performances by Paštun troupes being actively suppressed by local police, whereas similar Uzbek performances have been quite effectively curbed, at least in the urban situation. It is hard to say whether the fact that custodians of morality tend to be Paštuns plays a role in this policy or whether some other, unexplained principle is at work. As to the type of dance itself, there are considerable differences between Uzbek and Paštun styles. Unlike the style of Paštun dancing boys and their Uzbek and Tajik imitators, which is derived from Indian films, true Uzbek dance relies hardly at all on serious shoulder rolls, eyebrow wiggles, and neck jerks. The dance unfolds as a series of discrete gestures performed in a free sequence under the general guidance of a dambura player.

This brings us to the question of dance music. Outside of the dancing-boy situation, the Uzbek instrumental pieces that accompany dance must be considered on their own terms as expressions of a clearly Uzbek music subculture. The tunes are universally acknowledged in the North as being Uzbek in origin, and they tend in some cases to be specifically linked to a given place of origin. Tunes are named "Aqčai," "Sangčeraki," "Maimanegi," and so on, in reference to a town that has made the piece famous. This name is often the only designation one can obtain from either musicians or laymen for any given musical entity, apart from an occasional ascription to a specific musician who has popularized a piece of his own composition. Often the same tune may be ascribed to different towns with complete confidence by different informants. This seems due partly to the strong melodic overlap in the repertoire, which tends towards confusing one tune with another, and partly to a blurring of the musical boundaries in recent times. The latter phenomenon could be traceable to several causes: (1) the great increase in mobility in the North since the 1950s, thanks to motorized transport, allowing for more exchange of regional repertoires; (2) the impact of the radio, which has minimized local differences by introducing a variety of outside repertoires as background against which subtle distinctions between, say, Aqča and Sangčerak tunes lose their meaning; and (3) the general homogenization of northern culture through cultural accommodation, advanced by the absorption of Turkmen and Uzbek émigrés after the northern border was effectively sealed in the late 1930s. There is no doubt that these three factors overlap in various ways and have a combined effect on the musical situation, certainly leading to so simple a manifestation as loss of local identification of tune types, in addition to more serious effects detailed in other sections of the present study.

Nonetheless, a certain degree of local color remains in the repertoire whenever a strong hometown musician achieves a high degree of recognition for performing in a traditional manner. The main examples of this trend would be the songs of Baz Gul Badaxši, associated with the Kešm border area between Badaxšan and Katağan, and the work of Aq Pišak of Aqča, who is almost single-handedly preserving the traditional instrumental music of his town. Indeed, a large part of his total repertoire consist of Aqčai tunes used for dance accompaniment, and in Chapter 3 we shall examine a large number of his variants of these tunes.

Summarizing our foray into the world of Afghan Uzbek music, it is apparent that this ethnic group has maintained a highly diverse and comprehensive music subculture above and beyond the components of the shared music culture of the North. The extent to which this situation will continue to obtain depends at least in part once again on the success of the ethnic broadcasting of Radio Afghanistan. Even from very tentative preliminary soundings it seems that the programming, directed by an Afghan Uzbek, has been extremely well received by its intended audience. Aimaq has received a disproportionately heavy volume of mail from Uzbek listeners (considering the high rate of illiteracy) commenting favorably or critically upon the early programs he has produced, and he has shown himself highly sensitive to listeners' interests. My impression is that Aimaq's work will have considerable impact upon Uzbek musical practices in the North as well as in Kabul, and may well spark a renascence of ethnic pride, perhaps to the extent of turning Uzbek youth towards performance of their own traditional music rather than simple adoption of Kabul musical styles. In the long run, this situation cannot but help to increase national unity, by ending the alienation from Kabul which had led the older generation to tuning in Radio Tashkent, and by giving ethnic groups such as the Uzbeks a feeling of participation in the shaping of Afghan culture.

PAMIR PEOPLES

To date there has been no musical investigation of the Pamir peoples, whose rich storehouse of archaic languages has been well-mined by linguists (Morgenstierne 1938). The data at my disposal is based on conversations with Nizam Nurjanov of the Tajik Academy of Sciences, who has done extensive collecting in the Soviet side of the Pamirs, and on travelers' accounts for both Afghan and Soviet sides from the nineteenth century. Turning to the latter first, Schultz (1918) is particularly voluble on the subject of music, giving extensive illustration of the instruments he saw. Some of these — Afghan robab, Kašgar robab, Tajikistani tanbur, daf (tambourine) — relate to outside neighboring music cultures, but one instrument also named robab is strikingly different and purely Pamir in provenience (Schultz 1914:79–80). I have seen a specimen of this instrument (Figure 4.20) that was brought back by the French Hindu Kush Expedition of 1968 from the village of Sarkan, near Qala-i Panja in the mid-Waxan area, and it tallies closely with the "Pamir robab" pictured in the Soviet *Atlas of Musical Instruments* (Vertkov 1963:Plate 639). The only linguistic evidence I am aware of for the instrument being called robab in local languages is among Parači speakers (Morgenstierne 1938:27*); Morgenstierne (1938:27*) gives *tubur* (dambura?) for "guitar" in Yidǧa-Munji. The broad neck, bent pegbox, protruding spurs, and thick leather-covered belly are characteristic. Another early observer (Capus 1884:115) said the instrument was played by the women of Kašgar, which indicates a wide range of distribution. It is difficult not to see a connection between the Pamir robab and the *damyan* lute of Nepal, found as far as Sikkim; Lieberman, the chief investigator of Sikkimese music, says he feels the identification of the two lutes is indisputable (1972:p.c.). The Tibetan lute of similar construction also appears to bear some relationship to the Pamir and Nepalese instruments, which suggests that the Pamir robab belongs to a series of high-mountain lute types in a special musical region at "the roof of the world." The music played on the robab, at least in the examples kindly supplied by Nurjanov, is quite distinctive, and bears little resemblance to Badaxšani styles.

An important component of Pamir music culture is the dance tradition cited by Schultz (1914:83–84). This includes a number of "action" dances such as a vigorous sword dance and dance-staff numbers. He was particularly impressed with the virtuosity of the latter: "Der Stocktanz erfordert einige Kunstfertigkeit, da die heftigen Schläge leicht die Hand des Partners treffen können." I have not seen descriptions of Badaxšani dances that would parallel these Pamir performances. Other dances mentioned by Schultz and, more recently, by Andreev (1953) — spoon dances and masked animal dances — may well relate to forms widespread among mountain Tajiks (Nurjanov 1956) and perhaps point to an old Iranian substratum of dance and mime performances, especially since totemic associations tend to be imputed to masked and animal dances. Schultz (1914:83–85) lists the following dances of this type: a horseman dance (in which the performer plays both horse and rider), a camel dance (with two men as camel and rider) a chicken dance, a bird dance, and a devil-madman dance (Schultz is not clear as to which is involved). Also perhaps tied to mountain Tajik practice are small dance-theatrical scenes, such as one portraying an old husband and young wife (Schultz 1914:83–85). Other entertainments mentioned by Schultz and Andreev similarly betray outside connections, such as the buzkaši horsemanship game (Schultz 1914:86). In terms of epic, Nurjanov (1968:p.c.) sees a strong demarcation between Pamir peoples and mountain Tajiks. The former have never had the Guroğli epic, which is basic to the latter; furthermore, the Pamir peoples have their own *dastān* (tale) tradition. It is based on extensive narrative passages frequently punctuated by songs.

Unfortunately, I have not recorded nor have had access to any archives of songs in the local languages of the Pamir peoples. There seems to be a tendency for the songs to use Persian as a lingua franca and to meld with the general mountain Tajik repertoire, at least in the case of a Waxi performer I met in Faizabad. It was only with great difficulty that I coaxed a few words of his native tongue from him, and I was totally unable to elicit songs in Waxi: he played the Badaxšani dambura (a small Waxi model) and sang the types of quatrains generally heard among mountain Tajiks. Linguistics data from Morgenstierne (1938: glossary) confirm a strong Persian influence on musical terminology: e.g., *meila* for festival, *nagara* for drum in Parači. *Sazinge,* the Suğni word, for music, is close to Persian *sāz* as well. A quatrain in Sangliči-Iškaši given by the same authority (1938:378) is in lines of 11, 12, and 13 syllables, has an *a a b a* rhyme scheme, and contains some Persian words, supporting further a supposition of considerable mountain Tajik influence in the Pamir peoples' music. To cite one more illustration from Morgenstierne (1938:179), he gives a tale in Yidğa-Munji that is prefaced by a stanza in Persian. This is reminiscent of a similar practice of a Uzbek singer from Andxoi, who introduced a segment of the Köroğlu epic tale with a short Persian declamation (recorded on Anthology AST 4001). In both cases the primacy of Persian as the lingua franca is felt at the extreme west and east of the Afghan North. For Pamir peoples of Tajikistan, Nurjanov (1968: p.c.) notes that in recent years mountain Tajik influence has increased thanks to the mass media and improved transportation.

One interesting song type collected by Nurjanov is women's work songs, performed during agricultural labor. Nurjanov says that women show no reticence in singing out of doors or hesitation in having their songs recorded. If part of a general trend, this would indicate a substantial difference between Pamir music culture and the shared culture of northern Afghanistan. Doubtless there are a considerable number of other factors setting off these isolated peoples, for it is hard to imagine them maintaining their highly archaic languages over the course of so many centuries without also maintaining at least a minimal body of musical attitudes and repertoire idiomatic to their language and culture. We can only hope that research will be completed soon among these peoples, as on the Soviet side there already appears a tendency of the Pamir peoples to merge with the general Tajikistani Soviet culture. There are also unexpected acculturational factors such as the directed migration of the Yağnobis, an isolated Pamir-like mountain people who speak an archaic Iranian language and live in the Hissar Mountains. According to the *New York Times* (5/3/71), 4,000 Yağnobis have been resettled by the Soviet government in the Zafarobod cotton irrigation district in the Ferghana Valley region of Tajikistan.

MOUNTAIN TAJIKS

In terms of attitudes, we simply do not have enough data to sufficiently delineate a separate mountain Tajik musical subculture. Lorraine Sakata's extensive fieldwork of late 1972 may produce the material necessary for such an endeavor. At present, we must rely largely on repertoire and instruments and some hearsay evidence.

Perhaps the clearest expression of mountain Tajik individuality is the widespread and popular genre called *felak* (lit. "starry firmament"; Steingass 1970:938). Felak seems to imply fate, the heavens here seen as the source of good or ill fortune, in the folk poetry of Badaxšan, as shown in the following lines from a song of the Afghan Darwaz region:

Emsāl či sāl-i nāsana kard felak.
Yārān o barādarān jodā saxt felak.
Guftam kerawam piše felak, geryā konam.

What a bad year the heavens made this year.
The heavens separated lovers and brothers.
Once I decided to go to the heavens and cry.

This poetry of desolation is common among the mountain Tajiks, adding a fatalistic tinge to the sadness of requited love bemoaned in Turkestani folk verses. The felak is a form dear to the backwoods population of Badaxšan and is sung in various ways (solo, with instrumental accompaniment) in mountain pastures and fields. Much Badaxšani instrumental music is modeled on the unaccompanied song and is thus given the name felak as well. Dansker (1967:255) has noted that the local flute is so associated with this genre that the natives say of it that "faqat čizha-i felaki navoxtan mumken ast" ("only felak things can be played on it"). As I have written elsewhere on the structure of the felak (Slobin 1970), here I would like only to summarize my impressions of the genre's development and spread. First, it seems to me remarkable that in an area basically marked by difficulty of transportation because of mountains, which produce a range of microecologies, a particular genre and its musical accompaniment (both music and instrument; see Chapters 3 and 4) should be so nearly uniform across the entire length and breadth of Badaxšan, from Darwaz to Kešm to the Waxan. Second, it is interesting that apparently in each subregion the felak has its proponents among various strata of society. Though, as noted above, data are far from complete, one has the impression speaking to Badaxšanis and noting the variety of performers that the felak is basic musical currency for everyone, and that there is a particularly high degree of amateurism. When I stood in the Faizabad bazaar tootling on some newly bought flutes to elicit amateurs, it appeared that nearly everyone around could either play the flute or judge performance critically. I have been told that wealthy landowners throw picnics with general invitation, and great numbers participate in the music making recreation. As one young Badaxšani put it, "Everyone brings a dambura, since everyone can play it."

We have already discussed the Badaxšani dambura at length. The other principal instruments are the ubiquitous large tambourine, called *daf* here as in other areas of the Near East and Central Asia, and the *tulā,* a block flute, found only in Badaxšan. Significantly, the instrumentarium of the mountain Tajiks includes one element found even outside Afghanistan (daf), one relating only to nearby Uzbeks and Tajiks (dambura), and one of seemingly local provenience (tula), again demonstrating the shared vs. discrete aspects of all of the music of the North.

Stylistically, Badaxšani music is quite distinctive. Its rhythmic basis, often a 4 + 3 beat, is found among Paštuns but not in Turkestan, among either Tajiks or Uzbeks. Its scalar emphasis on extremely narrow melodic lines with considerable half-step motion is similarly un-Turkestani, but is also non-Paštun as well. Of particular interest is the Badaxšani voice quality, which is a combination of tenseness, nasality, and a guttural timbre unlike that used in Turkestani music. Also peculiar to Badaxšan is the presence of a considerable body of felaks sung in parlando-rubato style (rhythm associated with declamatory speech patterns rather than with fixed musical meter). Virtually all Uzbek-Tajik Turkestani music is in tempo giusto, or fixed rhythm, style. Again, the mountain Tajiks here seem closer to the Paštuns, whose up-country songs tend towards free rhythm. Perhaps it is not surprising that the nonurban Paštuns and mountain Tajiks display some musical affinities that set them apart from the oasis dwellers of Turkestan, though I would certainly reject an ecological-determinist cause for such an effect.

Perhaps the clearest link to old Turkic developments is the presence of the Köroğlu epic tale, here titled "Guroğli," in which Persian *gur* ("grave") is combined with Turkic *oğli* ("son of") to form a folk etymology of the hero's name. Performances of "Guroğli" by special singers appropriately titled *guroğligu* ("Guroğli tellers") are quite close in sound quality to those given in an extremely and tense voice by some Uzbek epic reciters, perhaps most notably those of the Surxandarya area. The only solid data regarding contemporary "Guroğli" recitation in Afghanistan comes from Rustaq, in Katağan just west of the Badaxšan border. According to a preliminary field report from P. and M. Centlivres (1972:p.c.), "the whole recitation is said to last three evenings, being divided into seven *sāx* (parts). Both Tajiks and Qarluqs claim to possess this epos in their culture." It is noteworthy that the Qarluqs, a small pre-Uzbek Turkic group, claim "Guroğli"; this indicates the type of acculturation to Tajik ways noted by Karmysheva (1964) for such splinter groups in southern Uzbekistan-Tajikistan. The case is particularly strong in the "Guroğli" itself, as noted above, represents a Tajik borrowing of Uzbek material. It is significant that the Qarluqs nevertheless lean toward the Tajik rather than the equally accessible Uzbek version.

To summarize Badaxšan, there is great distinctiveness of the music subculture combined with a wide spread of certain of its aspects. The ğičak has been cited as a mountain Tajik export, and the Badaxšani dambura seems to have played a part in the development of the Turkestani lute of the same name. Similarly, Badaxšani repertoire has spread beyond the border area of Kešm, most notably to Katağan. For example, in Xanabad one can hear non-Badaxšani performers using aspects of Badaxšani melody and timbre in singing non-Badaxšani verses. Katağani style in general is much given to such striking elements of Badaxšani music as consistent playing on dambura and ğičak in parallel fourths or fifths by placing the finger across both strings, a practice eschewed by Uzbek Turkestani players in their repertoire. Thus, while the isolated Badaxšanis have maintained a clear identity of style at home, they have played their part in the formation of a mixed interethnic style in Katağan; this style in turn has been spread by non-Uzbek performers to Turkestan and eventually beyond (in the case of the ğičak) to many other areas of Afghanistan.

THE URBAN ENCLAVE

Thus far I have tended to present the music culture and subcultures of the North more or less as a unit and without making an urban-rural distinction. This is partly due to a general reluctance in the recent literature on Near Eastern cities to stress such a dichotomy: "The fact that formerly popular conceptions of a sharp rural-urban dichotomy have come under heavy attack from a number of related social science disciplines has become a commonplace"; the current trend is towards seeing "cities not as isolated organisms but as constituents in a wide ecosytem" (Adams 1969:191, 192). Perhaps the most extreme case of such urban analysis has been English's (1966) study of Kerman, Iran. As will be noted in the discussion below, I think that it is wise to go along with this scholarly trend for the present in the case of northern Afghanistan. Even a casual observer of the region will note the vital role of urban-rural interaction to the life of the towns. In the one oasis for which data are available (Tašqurğan), there is a strikingly high ratio of urban to rural population (35,000:50,000; Centlivres 1970:26)

The towns of the North fall into an intermediate position in their role as centers, if one visualizes a continuum from the temporary open-air markets of Morocco (Mikesell 1958), which lack all urban focus, to the Near Eastern city, either in classical Islamic times, with its highly complex internal structuring, or today, with the massive population and intensive technology characteristic of the modern metropolis. Northern towns incorporate elements from both extremes of the urban spectrum, functioning as simple gathering places for nearby trade and as fairly complicated but limited bundles of permanent settlement having religious-cum-administrative significance.

The purpose of the present section is to describe the urban (town) musical scene in some detail so as to more closely identify aspects of the music culture with their immediate setting, and to indicate the extent to which town life relates to musical life, since so many authors (e.g., Adams 1967:188) have cited the well-known premise that Near Eastern culture has always been intimately tied to an urban way of life.

Before approaching the details of music within towns, we must first confront the question of a possible urban-rural differentiation. I must again first cite the extreme poverty of data relating to such theoretical questions for Afghanistan. We are fortunate, however, to have the valuable study of Tašqurğan by P. Centlivres, which includes among many other useful discussions an introduction to the relationships between a given northern Afghan town and its hinterland. Outside of that book, I can draw only on the older travelers' literature, disconnected references in recent publications, and my own observations. None of the accessible data except for those of Centlivres include statistical support, the results of exhaustive interviews or questionnaires, or even reliable census information. It is clear that we are in the infancy of understanding Afghan urban life beyond Tašqurğan and Kabul (for Kabul, see Jung 1971; Hahn 1964–65:177). The theorizing found below must be taken as speculative attempts toward analyzing the towns of the North.

Centlivres has well summarized the problem of defining "town" in northern Afghanistan (1970:31). He sees the literature on Near Eastern urban life as stressing one or two of three possible crucial elements for an urban center: the market, the Friday mosque, and the administrative headquarters. As Centlivres points out (1970:32), for the North, all three components tend to be combined:

On peut alors songer à définir la ville centre-asiatique par le réunion en un lieu d'un bazar, d'un centre religieux et d'un centre politique ou administratif. . . .La taille de la ville, son rôle, le territoire qu'elle domine, son réseau de communications, tous ces éléments nous ramènent au bazar à qui ils sont associés; c'est dans cette perspective que le paysan, lorsqu'il part pour le bazar à l'aube du jour de marche, prend place dans le mouvement général des citadins et ruraux vers le coeur de la ville où les activitités économique, politique, religieuse ou sociale sont pour lui indissociables.

I find this concept of the town as indissociable nexus of economic, religious, and administrative life persuasive for the North, though it does not necessarily hold even for other areas of Afghanistan (nor does its author intend it to). For the peasants of outlying villages, the town is simply "the center" to which they turn regularly on a weekly basis to conduct all affairs that are not related to their immediate daily routines and family contacts. Also useful is the remark by Centlivres that the villager judges the town by a combination of factors (size, situation, environs, administrative power, available goods, etc.), among which distance is perhaps not the key element. In this aspect we must differ from a cardinal assumption of central-place theory (to which the study of Afghan towns belongs), which states that "consumers who must visit the market place on a regular basis want a location that permits them to conduct their business with a minimum of effort, and if a choice of location is available will always prefer the one which involves least effort" (Berry 1967:3). For members of the rather closed economy of northern Afghanistan, a day's walk to a more distant market to save a penny a pound on some vital commodity is a realistic choice that belies the customer's supposed interest in "a minimum of effort." There simply is no other way to save the pennies involved.

The nearly unexplored world of the northern towns must be seen at least tentatively as a complex of interrelated urban conglomerations, each offering a special blend of attractions to the villager or nomad. What I will present next is a schematization of the differential pull of various northern towns to get at the nature of urban life in the region. Music will be singled out for special description as a component of the urban complex in order to show how a single element such as public entertainment fits into a more general matrix: the special relationship of towns to their own inhabitants and to the outlying rural folk. As the towns of the North are undergoing continual metamorphoses due to recent change, the description offered here must stand only as an approximation of a situation perceived at one point in time — basically 1968 with updating from 1971–72.

In beginning a survey of northern towns, it is useful to visualize two urban hierarchies, a system observed by Skinner (1964) for rural China. One is the marketing hierarchy, which encompasses a series of urban markets of varying importance, while the other involves an administrative ranking, according to which towns are placed in order of governmental importance. As in the case for China, in the northern Afghan case "the two hierarchies occasionally meet at the same level in the same cities, although this is not a necessity" (Berry 1967:95). Let us examine the two continua of urban importance. The marketing hierarchy can tentatively be presented in the following framework:

Marketing Hierarchy

A. Village center
B. Local center
   1. Standard oasis
   2. Interregional border town
   3. Subregional center
C. Regional center
D. National center (Kabul only)

The Afghan administrative hierarchy consists of three basic types of communities, ranging from least to greatest importance: *alaqadari; woleswali* (fourth to first degree, according to population); and provincial capital (which need not be the largest in population).

The congruence and lack thereof between the two hierarchies can be indicated by the following diagram:

Marketing		*Administrative*
village center	⟶	alaqadari
local center	⟶	woleswali
regional center	⟶	provincial capital

It can be seen that: (1) markets I have classed as village centers can be located in either an alaqadari (e.g., Aliabad, Kunduz province) or a woleswali (Mungiček, a fourth degree woleswali in Jozjan province); (2) local centers can be situated in either a woleswali (Aqča, a first degree woleswali in Jozjan province) or a provincial capital (Taluqan, Taxor province); and (3) regional centers (Mazar-i Šarif, Balx province) are always also provincial capitals. The findings indicate that woleswali-sized towns form the main body of market centers and can be seen as the backbone of ordinary marketing activities.

However, our survey of town styles is not yet complete. We must add a kind of urban center that is nontraditional and thus extra-hierarchical, fitting neither into the marketing continuum nor into a single administrative slot. This is the industrial and communications hub, a type of town intimately linked to recent technological and political developments. The clearest examples of this trend are Kunduz and Pul-i Xumri, both in Katagan. Neither features a market of the traditional type that fits into our hierarchy. Administratively, Kunduz figures as a provincial capital, whereas Pul-i Xumri is a first degree woleswali. We shall detail the special cases of these towns below; let us return now to defining the traditional town types given above, first with a general outline of each type and then with specific case studies, including musical life.

Village center is a term I employ for small marketing centers that exist primarily to fulfill immediate needs on the off days of the larger local center bazaars. Here we enter the domain of scheduled markets with synchronized periodicity, but on a much more modest scale than observed for Morocco by Mikesell or for China by Skinner. There exists no elaborate day-by-day periodicity in northern Afghanistan whereby markets of roughly equal size stagger their market days to serve local clienteles, nor is there extensive synchronization between lower- and higher-order markets in the hierarchy. The village center represents limited response to local marketing conditions, and as far as I know it relates only to one given nearby a larger center as a satellite. To extend the astronomical analogy, the Friday market in Mungiček represents the reflected glow of the great Aqča bazaar, but it is only a single moon like Earth's, not part of a complex set of satellites near a metropolis, like the many moons near great Jupiter. Unfortunately, the distribution of such village centers is not well documented, since there has been no thorough survey of marketing functions of northern communities, so the case rests only on observation of towns such as Mungiček, or Almar (an alaqadari) near Maimana.

As can be seen by its three subdivisions, the *local center* is a set of town types unified by a similar position in the hierarchy. I have labeled type 1 "standard oasis" to indicate it is the majority case, as opposed to the less common varieties under type 2 and type 3. Classic northern local centers that could be called standard oases are the Turkestani steppe towns of Aqča and Andxoi. Each has a bazaar twice a week and draws on a large number of surrounding villages for clientele. These towns act as major intermediaries between rural populations and the outside world, putting peasants (and, seasonally, nomads) in contact with the regional center (the wholesaler) and, ultimately, with the national market in Kabul, with its extensive import-export functions. The feeder region may extend at least as far as the 20 miles noted by Mikesell (1958) for the Moroccan *suq,* and perhaps up to 30 miles, a considerable distance for traffic that is largely nonmotorized. As I have noted elsewhere (Slobin 1969:451), "the infusion of activity on market days is the lifeblood of the town." Customers flock to some two thousand shops in the central bazaar, which is built to handle heavy traffic. On off days, the market is largely deserted, underscoring the tidal nature of the commerce. The custom of periodic market days in a local market center is an old one in Turkestan, as witnessed by Burnes's remarks of 1835:

The custom of having market days is uncommon in India and Cabool, but of universal use in Toorkistan; it perhaps gives a stimulus to trade, and is most convenient; since all the people of the country, for miles around, assemble on the occasion. Every person seems to think it incumbent upon him to be present. The different articles are arranged in separate parts of the bazaar with as much regularity as in Bokhara itself. (1835:8)

The interregional border town functions like the standard oasis, but may have added distinguishing features. The prime example of such a town is Tašqurǧan. Situated between the major regions of Turkestan and Katagǎn, Tašqurǧan acts both as broker for the zones involved and as producer of consumer goods exported to all neighboring areas.

Finally, subregional centers also function like the standard oasis but edge towards regional centers in importance by gathering products from a number of smaller local markets. Maimana is a good example of this kind of town. Though clearly subordinate to the regional center of Turkestan (Mazar-i Šarif), Maimana draws in goods and activities from such nearby bazaars as Qaisar and Belčerāǧ, then transmits commercial flow to Mazar. For its own subregion of Turkestan, Maimana acts as a center, but must eventually funnel its mercantile wealth to the regional marketing headquarters.

Turning to the *regional center,* we have already mentioned its command of the total trading energy of its constituent local centers. Mazar is the major middleman between Kabul and the North, and in every parameter of size and commercial flow stands in a category apart from the smaller oasis and subregional towns. Mazar and its Badaxšani counterpart, Faizabad, fit the description of "central market" described for China by Skinner: "The central market receives imported items and distributes them to its market area via the lower-order centers, and it collects local products and exports them to other central markets and higher-order centers . . . central markets . . . are the highest order and are located at strategic points on the transport network, providing important wholesaling functions" (Berry 1967:94). With the proviso that only Kabul is a "higher-order center" than the regional market (or central market, in Skinner's terms), Skinner's outline fits the northern Afghan situation. Also similar is the appearance of "permanent shops in addition to . . . periodic markets, and . . . smaller business centers at each of the four gates of the city" (Berry 1967:94).

Before turning to closer examination of the market types just surveyed, a brief commentary on administrative importance is in order. As noted above, while alaqadaris and woleswalis are assigned according to population, provincial capitals receive their designation for other reasons. This is primarily a political matter. Up until quite recently (1964), the North consisted of only three provinces: Mazar-i Šarif (comprising all of the present Fariab, Jozjan, Balx, and Samangan provinces), Katagan (including the present Bağlan, Kunduz, and Taxor provinces), and Badaxšan, actually only a minor province (*hukumat-i alā*) then. Apparently as a result of interest in breaking up such huge concentrations of governors' authority, the new provinces were created, necessitating the assignment of provincial capital status to towns previously lower in the hierarchy. Rather in the manner of early American legislatures designating less important (often obscure) towns as state capitals (e.g., Springfield instead of Chicago in Illinois), Afghan officials overlooked prominent towns in two provinces and bestowed administrative blessings on communities of lesser magnitude in both population and marketing power. The chief beneficiaries of this policy were Samangan in Samangan province, clearly less important than Tašqurğan, and Šiberğan in Jozjan Province, inferior to both Aqča and Saripul (and perhaps even Sangčerak) in traditional importance. Šibergan's subordinate marketing status relative to Saripul was noted by Ferrier (1860:381), who pointed out that the latter town's control of the local river always left the former town at a disadvantage. Thus, these towns became local centers with a particular status belying their position in the marketing hierarchy; we shall have occasion to discuss this peculiar position below. It should also be noted that downgrading of administrative status can debilitate a community. Dupree (1966: 16) cites the example of Aq Kupruk (Balx province), which lost its status as woleswali site to Šolgan in 1961; the result was the economic downfall of the former town and a great growth of population for the latter.

Let us turn now to a detailed look at the major types of towns, using selected examples. One must bear in mind that: (1) all the towns in question are quite old, many of them having been sites of trade in earliest recorded times; (2) up to recent times (1880s) the towns of Turkestan were semiautonomous city-states, each with a different history and special set of circumstances; and (3) the closed northern border with only a tiny number of designated (generally nontraditional) ports for transfer of goods, is an even more recent development (dating from about 1940). These three factors ensure that any general schematization will quickly spring leaks if stretched to describe more than a restricted situation. Like any generalization, the typing of towns suggested here is meant primarily as a temporary tool for future economic and cultural geographers of the North rather than as the last word in urban classifications. We shall begin with the local center viewing the satellite village market as an adaptive mechanism related to the more central market town in its vicinity.

The Local Market Center

This type of town is the backbone of Afghan domestic commerce. The concentric-circle model given by Centlivres for Tašqurġan (Figure 2.5) is a useful starting point for analyzing this type of town.

In Figure 2.5, the *Tim* is the cupola-like central covered bazaar of Tašqurġan; the *madrasa* is the Islamic school. Tašqurġan is useful as an example because it is the last town in the North to retain so classic a town structure, with its eighteenth century architecture preserved. Tašqurġan is archaic and unique in many ways, e.g., in its custom of closing off the bazaar each night and maintaining two different, named types of watchmen (those on roofs and those in courtyards) to guard the central market. Most of the other towns of the North have changed from this earlier model to the more commonly found recent pattern of a totally uncovered bazaar constructed along the lines of a well-organized main shopping street; it is located away from the traditional

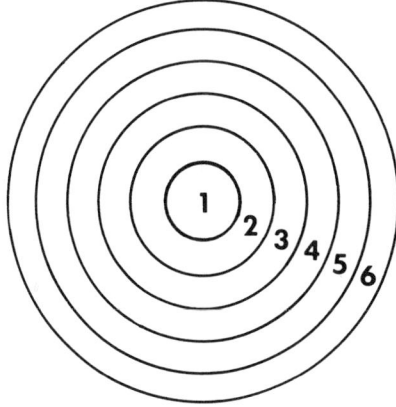

1. covered bazaar (*Tim*), *madrasa*, baths, municipality
2. uncovered bazaar, livestock market
3. zone of contiguous habitations
4. zone of discontinuous habitations and gardens
5. suburbs, villages recently annexed to the town
6. zone of villages and grain cultivation

Fig. 2.5. Model of the Tašqurġan oasis (from Centlivres 1970:31)

Fig. 2.6. The Tašqurğan bazaar

town center near the citadel and usually culminates at a large cross-roads where the two main roads cut through the town. Generally a *šār-i now,* or "new city," is built apart from the older center to include a hotel, which doubles as municipal headquarters, and the offices and homes of the local officials.

Let us look at the map of Aqča (Map 2.1), the local market town of the "standard oasis" type that we shall examine at length, to see how its layout both reflects and differs from the model given by Centlivres (Figure 2.5).

In the map, the grid just north of the juncture of two main roads near the heavy lettering AQCHA is the new bazaar, which supplanted Aqča's covered market somewhere in the 1950s. The oval gray blob just above with the smaller AQCHA label is the old town citadel, consisting of ruins from the days of the town's independent status as Turkestani city-state. As Centlivres indicates in his model for Tašqurğan, the density of town population radiates from the older center concentrically, from contiguous to noncontiguous zones of housing, becoming at last individual, highly scattered villages separated by spaces of dusty steppe zone along the traces of dried watercourses.

The extent to which the water source may determine the demography of an oasis is clearly indicated in the map of Andxoi, another important local market center of the steppe, one that is even more water-poor than Aqča and considerably drier than Tašqurğan, our original model. In Map 2.2 it is clear that the population hugs the

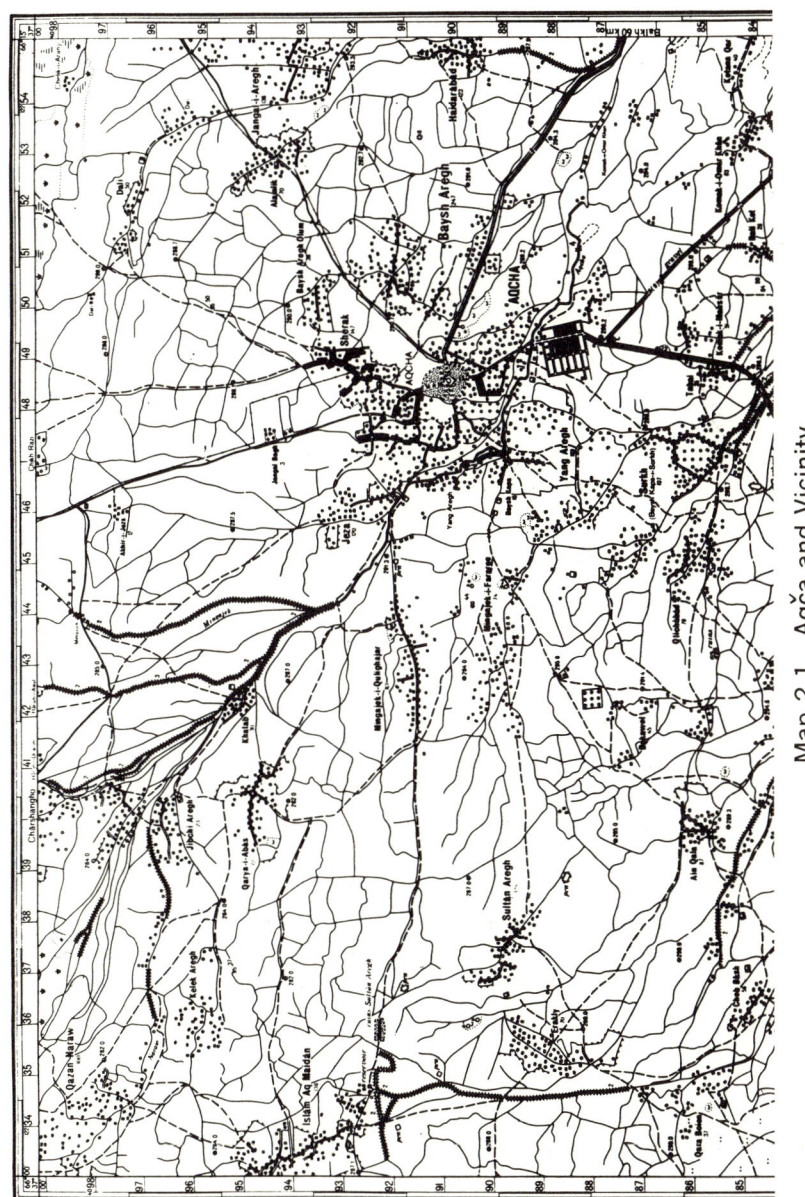

Map 2.1. Aqča and Vicinity

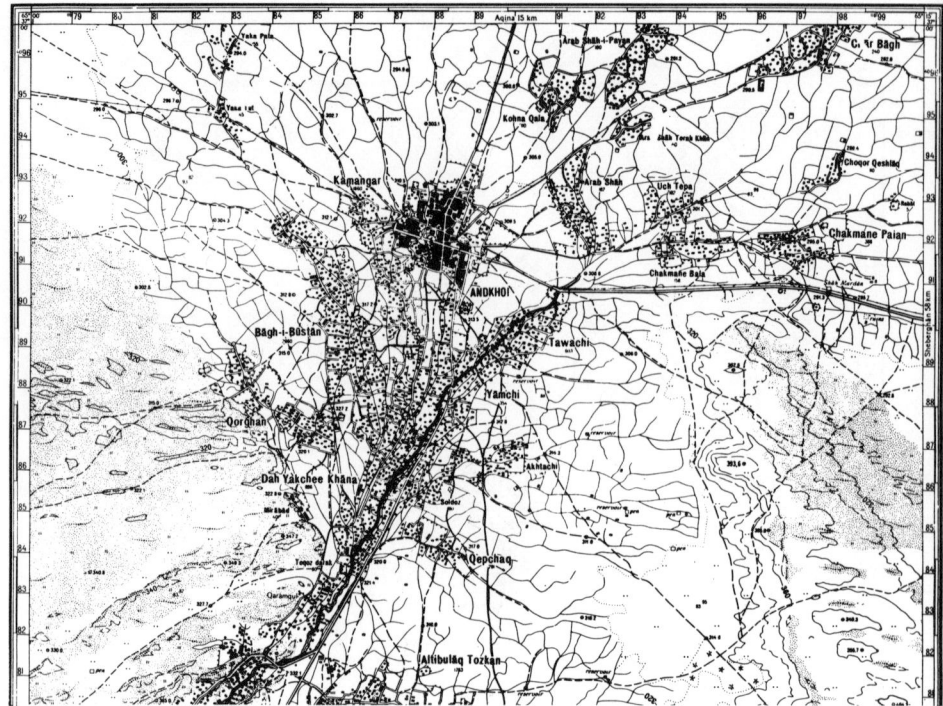

Map 2.2. Andxoi and Vicinity

trickle of water that comes up from Maimana (145 kilometers distant)
every fifteen days. Near the center of the map is the new bazaar,
in black. Satellite Turkmen villages can be seen primarily to the east,
where the water is more plentiful. To the west, northwest, and southeast, however, there are practically no habitations in the vast desert
tracts (actually the southernmost extension of the Kara Kum Desert,
which stretches far beyond the Soviet border, some 20 kilometers off).
Thus, while the traditional model is still operative for Tašqurğan, it can
be seen that geographic circumstances and recent administratively
inspired remodeling have had their effect on the invidual configurations
of local market centers across the North.

What towns of this type share is the ebb and flow of market-day
activity, based on the centrality of the town in its oasis setting. The
relative prosperity of each town, reflected in the abundance and wealth
of shopkeepers and artisans, fluctuates in relation to several factors:
(1) the effect of weather on local crops (and thus on the availability
of pasturage and the health of livestock), which strained towns almost
to the breaking point in the drought period 1970–72; (2) the outside

demand for the local products, which since about 1940 has meant transshipment of such goods to Kabul for export; and (3) the internal demand both for goods from within the local agricultural production area and for those traditionally manufactured by local town artisans, such as jewelry, iron goods, and items of carpentry. While these factors may vary considerably from year to year, the town remains an indispensable forum for exchange of goods and services even in the worst times, and has probably always done so since urbanization first emerged in the region under discussion.

There is no need to detail the economic organization of such towns, since Centlivres has provided ample evidence for Tašqurğan. It should be noted, however, that the proliferation of artisans evident in his analysis probably relates to the special role that town has taken on, which we shall return to below. It should be mentioned that the location of trades and the ethnic ingredient of market personnel varies widely from town to town; thus the data for Tašqurğan must be taken as valid only for that community. In his brief study of Saripul in 1968, Centlivres (1968:p.c.) found that many of the occupational roles had settled at different levels in the urban marketing hierarchy, and that their ethnic composition was unlike that of Tašqurğan.

An outstanding feature of local market centers is the careful ordering of its activity. As noted by Burnes above, the bazaar area is divided precisely by craft and type of goods. Each craft has its own guild structure, presided over by an elected head *(kalontar)*. The rural customer knows exactly where to find the ironmongers, imported fabric sellers, tea-and-sweets merchants, or the large *mundai* area for sale of staple commodities (grain, rice, produce). In short, the bazaar can supply every need of the villager or nomad, and will furnish him with a modest amount of capital by purchasing whatever he can produce that is marketable, from eggs to homemade caps to valuable Turkmen ("Bokhara") carpets. Entertainment is seen as a stape commodity of the bazaar, catering to the customers' hunger for glamour and diversion. In the present-day town the movie theater has become the principal attraction; indeed it has become the status symbol and mark of identification of the urban center. The vast majority of films are of Indian origin and portray love and war, with songs and dance scenes in Hindi — a language none of the viewers can understand (and subtitles are useless for a population that is 95 percent illiterate). Seeing a life totally divorced from Afghan village existence — with kings and princesses or upper-class modern urbanites, dancing girls openly performing sensuous motions, epic battle scenes and fast car chases — gives intense enjoyment to town and country folk alike.

The obverse side of the coin is the local, highly traditional entertainment of the town teahouse (samowad), described in Chapter 1. It is the antithesis of the glamorous imported film. Here local performers of village origin blend newer tunes (often from the films themselves) with long-standing favorites as part of an older pattern of diversion, or sa'at-tiri. In the all-male world of the bazaar, the teahouse is the ideal place for men to rest, drink endless cups of liquid refreshment (black tea in winter, green in summer), and gossip with friends, while occasionally listening to the music of the small band. Sometimes the teahouse is equipped with *karambul* boards (a billiards-like game played with small flat discs), but most gambling with dice, cards, and sheep bones takes place on the streets. Many teahouses avoid the expense of live music and strategically deploy a radio and loudspeaker; more rarely one finds the ancient gramophone with a repertoire of scratchy Indian Victor records of antique film songs.

In Aqča, if live music is to be heard, chances are that Aq Pišak, the finest musician of the oasis and one of the leading performers of the North, will be leading the band. We shall focus on Aq Pišak's career and repertoire to gain an understanding of how the musical life of Aqča reflects the particular pattern of that town's general activity as a local market center.

Aq Pišak is a Turkmen, from the village of Čakeč near Aqča. He belongs to the Čekiji sugbroup of the Ersari tribe. He was approximately forty years of age in 1968 and had been playing the dambura for over twenty years. His career follows the model of the successful šowqi outlined in Chapter 1. Beginning life as a shepherd, the musician played the dambura for private enjoyment. He also amused friends with his animal imitations, for which he probably earned his epithet of Aq Pišak, "white cat"; by now his original name has been forgotten. As he played for celebrations and earned money, he began to acquire a reputation as an outstanding entertainer. Eventually he graduated from ğaribi-šowqi to full-time musician. He has never traveled beyond Šibergan to the south and Mazar to the east, rarely has a chance to listen carefully to the radio, and doesn't often have the twelve cents necessary to enter the cinema. He has a wife and several children.

Aq Pišak's public personality seems shaped by his career. He is treated as a clown: mention his name and people smile. He wears the old-fashioned tall fur Turkmen cap no longer worn by local villagers, which gives him a comic appearance, and knows how to make his audience roar with laughter at imitations of sheep, cats and well-known people. "Offstage" he is grave and quiet, with the look of a sad clown. Though a Turkmen, Aq Pišak performs only the Uzbek-Tajik teahouse repertoire, the musical lingua franca of the North, thus strengthening the cross-ethnic aspect of Aqča's musical life. He cannot play any of the purely Turkmen instruments; however, he was very pleased to introduce me to a fine Turkmen musician (Axmad-baxši), and after long acquaintance finally consented to sing an excerpt from the Turkmen version of the Köroğlu tale. Aq Pišak would confirm Surxi's comment that Turkmens play Uzbek-Tajik music simply as a pragmatic matter: one can earn a living that way.

Aq Pišak's band varies with the available talent, but always includes the bare minimum of two Uzbek singers who alternate verses in the improvised quatrain songs that make up the bulk of the repertoire. The damburači plays from about 10:00 A.M. to 3:00 P.M. on market days, and was paid the equivalent of sixty cents per day in 1968 by the teahouse owner. In addition to his role as urban music maker, Aq Pišak serves as village entertainer for domestic festivities. The latter role, though seasonal, nets him a larger income than the former. During the winter, when a bai throws a party (often for a circumcision), he may go to great lengths to entertain guests, even to including a buzkaši horsemanship match. At such occasions, according to Aq Pišak, each *čapandoz* (buzkaši rider) will contribute money for the entertainment, and a first-rate musician may also be awarded a silken čapan (cloak) by the host in reward for his long night's work. As far as I can tell, Aq Pišak plays the same repertoire with the same band for many of the same people at village festivities and in the Aqča teahouse; it is the occasion that determines the different pay scales.

Aq Pišak's repertoire is made up of three distinct components. One is the purely local Aqčai Uzbek dance tunes, to be analyzed in Chapter 3. The second includes items from the remaining northern repertoire, picked up from traveling musicians, while the third consists of music from two outside sources: Radio Afghanistan and Indian films.

Aqča and its native son Aq Pišak offer an exceptionally clear example of local talent and the local market center. Variants of this model abound; a major local market center such as Xanabad, though rich in talent, features no live teahouse music because of governmental proscription; on the other hand, for special reasons outlined below, the native musicians of Tašqurğan seek employment in other towns. What is important for the present discussion is the extent to which in Aqča one can sense a clear interrelationship between the musical life and the socioeconomic position of the town, which at least in theory holds for many other towns of similar position in the marketing hierarchy. Just as Aqča provides villagers with stock goods available all across the North, so it gives them a brand of music that connects them to listeners of the entire larger area. From time to time, new wares are introduced, as are new songs. At the same time, the town gives country folk a chance to see familiar faces, friends and kinsmen who come in from other villages for shopping and gossiping. It also provides an opportunity for customers to be entertained with the kind of live music associated with home festivities, and it is important to note that the music is played by fellow villagers rather than outsiders. The local market center, a place largely familiar but simultaneously an important link with the outside world, has a musical life that is in many ways homespun, but it also features a considerable degree of innovation based on external stimuli.

The resistance of this pattern to change is fairly high, even surviving technological inroads if they pose no direct threat. In 1969 I was not sanguine about the survival of local market center music because of the extension of paved roads through Turkestan (Slobin 1969:42). A return visit to Aqča in 1971 did not support this doleful hypothesis. Curiously enough, the reason that bringing a highway from Mazar to Šibergǎn via Aqča did not basically affect the town was the excessive modernity of the traffic engineering solution devised by Russian planners. The Soviet advisors applied the latest approach to urban road placement, creating bypasses of important northern towns (Samangan, Tašqurǧan, Aqča) rather than bringing the road straight through the heart of the urban center as did older highways in Europe and America. This "interstate highway" approach left these towns high and dry. The crucial motorized freight and passenger traffic of the North is channeled directly to far-separated destinations rather than filtered through a series of market towns. The preliminary result in Aqča has been a marked decline of the bazaar, coinciding with a tentative relocation of shops closer to the roadway, some three miles down a "business spur" road. One can estimate that some five to ten years will elapse before the bypassed towns of the North can adapt to the too-advanced road technology thrust upon them; in the meantime, the older patterns of town life will remain, perhaps even in more impacted and isolated form. We shall see below how the more traditional method of highway placement resulted in important benefits to other northern towns (Kunduz, Pul-i Vumri) in earlier years.

Before leaving the local market center, we must pay a brief visit to the satellite market centers (designated "village centers" in our hierarchy) often associated with these towns. Čaršangay, seat of the

Mungiček woleswali, about six kilometers northeast of Aqča, is a good example of such a market. The area is at the center of the Turkmen silk-weaving trade, an important local cottage industry. Around 1960 the subgovernor of Mungiček, recognizing the great volume of business passing through the village on the way to Aqča twice a week, decided to build a small bazaar in Čaršangay to provide a further trade outlet for surrounding villagers. Suitably, the bazaar day was set for only once a week, on Wednesdays, an off day for Aqča. This administratively instigated change answered a need for adequate channeling of existing mercantile activity — the same need that is filled by the scheduling of satellite markets of other major towns, such as Aliabad for Kunduz and Almar for Maimana.

Musically, the Čaršangay bazaar closely mirrors Aqča in featuring a Turkmen damburači and Uzbek singers. Their repertoire, like that of Aq Pišak's band, is strictly in the samowad tradition, even more markedly "out of place" than in Aqča in the sense that the listeners are almost all Turkmens used to hearing Turkmen music at home.

Let us examine briefly the other two main types of local market center: the interregional border town and the subregional center. The latter presents less divergence from the Aqča pattern outlined above. A brief survey of Maimana, for instance, seems to show a greater breadth of trading possibilities — largely because its situation in verdant foothills is more favored than Aqča's or Andxoi's steppe location — but no major differences in basic configuration. The greater importance of Maimana seems reflected musically only in its role as instrument producer, a trait I associate mainly with major urban centers like Mazar and Kabul or special traditional sites of instrument export (Tašqurǧan and Samangan). Maimana is far enough from the area of origin of most Turkestani instruments and boasts enough amateurs to produce its own supply of damburas. It is worth noting that they are not used anywhere except in the immediate Maimana area. Even in Širin Tagow, the first sizable town on the road north towards Andxoi, I saw a Samangan rather than a Maimana instrument hanging in the local teahouse.

Turning to the interregional market town, we come to the case of Tašqurǧan. This community was long famous as a crossroads town. Writing in the 1880s, Yate described the town as follows:

Tashkurghan is the great trade-mart of Afghan Turkistan, and about its most important place. Here the caravans from India on the one hand, and Bokhara on the other, all break bulk and from here the merchandise is distributed all over the country. Nothing is obtainable at Mazar even, except through Tashkurghan. (1888:315)

In addition to serving as port for international trade and as regional market center, Tašqurğan was traditionally the border town between Katağan and Turkestan. It is only this latter role that remains, for the town's more glamorous trade status was stripped away by the sealing of the Soviet border and the designation of ports farther east and west as the only approved international trade points.

As a result, Tašqurğan fell back on its established internal market as a means of survival, stressing domestic export by relying on the large body of skilled artisans built up in former times. Tašqurğani goods, particularly the characteristic red, green, and black painted carpentry objects, are found at least as far southwest as Saripul in Turkestan, as far east as Taluqan in Katağan, and as far south as Kabul. The painted wooden cradles, slingshots, and significantly for the present study, ğičak (fiddle) components are found all across the North, spread primarily by itinterant Tašqurğani merchants who may well settle down in towns such as Aqča as tradesmen. Such colonies of Tašqurğanis can be found in many towns, including Kabul. Out-migration is not new for Tašqurğanis; Ferrier (1860:399) reported meeting Tašqurğanis as far away as Herat and Meshed (Iran). In the agricultural sector, Tašqurğan turns its celebrated gardens into profit by exporting large quantities of figs, almonds, and pomegranates. No other town of the North depends so extensively on export for a living as does Tašqurğan, though the town keeps up its full status as major local market center at the same time, drawing customers from as far off as the foothills west of Samangan.

Is it surprising, then, to find that many of the most famous and successful musicians of the North come from Tašqurğan? Baba Qeran and Bangeča Tašqurğani, perhaps the two best-known northern performers, are natives of the town, as are Šarif and Hakim, major musicians of the Mazar area. The composer of the well-known song "Bulbulak-i sangšekan" (he is now known as "Bulbul," thanks to his song) is a Tašqurğani, as is Abdullah Buz-baz, itinerant master of the musical marionette (see Slobin 1975). Another well-known traveling damburači, Abdul Nazar, has retired to his home town, Tašqurğan. No other town can boast such a concentration of talent, and the reason probably lies in the pivotal geographical position of Tašqurğan, where the styles of Turkestan and Katağan (and consequently of Badaxšan) meet. Musicians growing up in Tašqurğan have the benefit of a varied repertoire from the start. Indeed, much of the music that forms the basic Uzbek-Tajik repertoire was spread by, and probably originated with men, such as Baba Qeran, now an octogenarian.

The town itself hosts little live entertainment. Occasionally

Bangeča, resting between tours, or Baba Qeran, whiling away his retirement years, will play a bit, much to the delight of Tašqurğanis, but little regular performance is available to the public. Of some importance, however, is the existence of local poets; Quramali Xuram, for example, supplies Bangeča with song texts. This tradition of urban poetry, in the ğazal form, is an important hallmark of town culture, marking one of the few areas in which urban and rural styles clearly diverge. It is perhaps again Tašqurğan's central position that affects its musical life. Located midway between two powerful large centers, Mazar and Kunduz, and having its talent siphoned off to serve other regions, Tašqurğan must needs lack its own vital live music performance.

In summary, Tašqurğan's emphasis is on outward activity, expansion of its own commerce, and exportation of artisans, including musicians, and objects, including musical instruments. At the same time, the town, as so amply demonstrated by Centlivres, is a repository of traditional northern structures and customs; likewise, Tašqurğan remains a storehouse of traditional northern musics, which it exports by means of talented performers to enrich the repertoire of urban music all across the North.

Perhaps only one other town can be considered analogous to Tašqurğan in functioning as a local market center with strong interregional overtones. That town is Kešm, less well known and by nature less flamboyant than Tašqurğan. It is an important meeting place for the two eastern areas of the North, Katağan and Badaxšan. Just east of Kalafğan, the last local market center of Katağan, lies a small pass sometimes called the Kutal-i gunješqan ("Sparrows' Pass"), which is generally thought of as the gateway to Badaxšan. Just beyond this natural dividing point lies Kešm, a large oasis of green in a rough brown rocky landscape. Past Kešm stretches the long desolate Kokča River valley, with Faizabad lying farther up. In this central if somewhat isolated position, Kešm is neither here nor there regionally. Some Kešmis may say "yes" when asked if their town lies in Badaxšan, but others may say "no," pointing upstream towards Faizabad. The latter view may remain from the days in the nineteenth century when Faizabad, according to many travelers' accounts, was itself called Badaxšan. Inhabitants of Katağan and of Faizabad are equally vague in ascribing a particular reference name to Kešm.

Musically this ambiguous status of Kešm reflected in the town's repertoire of instruments and pieces. Both Turkestani and Badaxšani types of damburas are in use, and styles of the regions on both sides can be heard.

Kešm is well known in Faizabad as the home of a particular

subregional Badaxšani style, while to the rest of the North Kešm is best known as an exporter of music. This role is exemplified by two performers, Baz Gul Badaxši and Drai Kešmi. Baz Gul is one of the best-known northern musicians, having attained national fame when one of his Kešmi songs was played on Radio Afghanistan. He has followed up his success with tours that have taken him as far as Saripul in Turkestan. Drai Kešmi is not so famous, but a tape of his performance is treasured by a teahouse owner in Xanabad, for example, who plays it regularly for his customers. Thus, while Kešm is a pivot community quite different in nature from Tašqurǧan, it is interesting to note that its interregional positioning also seems reflected in its musical life.

The Regional Market Center

The regional market center is a kind of super-bazaar for a larger geographical unit. Into it flow the peoples and goods of an entire district composed of several local market centers and perhaps several provinces. Regional centers can also serve as rallying places for special religious or patriotic events that bring together large segments of the population, perhaps even attracting people from the far ends of Afghanistan. Such centers thus put an entire section of the country into contact with Kabul, the national capital, and with the rest of the world.

In the North, there are only two clearly definable regional market centers. One is Mazar-i Šarif, capital of Balx province and unofficial center of Turkestan, and the other is Faizabad, provincial capital and center of Badaxšan. The two are markedly different in almost every detail, but similar in their basic function as regional focal points and in the type of musical life they support.

Mazar-i Šarif, usually referred to as just Mazar, attained its present position of prominence only within the last century. Writing in 1835, Alexander Burnes (1835:200) described Mazar as a small village, which "contains about 500 houses." At that time, Balx, some 12 kilometers from Mazar, was the center of Turkestan, as it had been for countless centuries, dating back to the time when the whole region was called Bactria by the Greeks. However, the "mother of cities," as Balx was known, had so declined in population and importance by the mid-nineteenth century, largely because of the abnormally high incidence of malaria, that the regime of Sher Ali Khan decided in 1866 to make Mazar-i Šarif the new administrative center (Dupree 1967:48).

Mazar had one main drawing card: the alleged grave of Ali,

son-in-law of the prophet Muhammad, which is still the main religious attraction of all Afghanistan. Each year at Nowruz, the New Year's Day of the Persian solar calendar, which falls on March 21 (the first day of spring), thousands of pilgrims make their way to Mazar for the ritual of the raising of the *janda,* the standard of Ali. In 1968, authorities estimated the crowd at approximately 50,000, with pious Muslims coming from as far away as Pakistan. A source in the Ministry of Foreign Affairs indicated that many more Pakistanis would make the trip if unlimited entry were allowed.

This striking religious occurrence has its roots in the twelfth century, when "a man by the name of Mohammad came upon ancient evidence that Hazrat Ali had in reality been buried in a village near Balkh. . . . This information was immediately communicated to Sultan Sanjar, who commanded that a shrine be built over the grave. His order was carried out in 1136" (Dupree 1967:50). An impressive blue-tiled shrine dating from 1481, beautifully restored by the Afghan government in recent years, stands at the center of Mazar-i Šarif on the site of the original shrine. It is the finest architectural complex standing in Afghan Turkestan.

Thus Mazar assumed the mantle of Balx, which today is an unimportant local market center with extensive stretches of ruined masonry. Mazar, on the other hand, is the nearest thing to a city, in the Western (or even the classical Near Eastern) sense, in northern Afghanistan. The population of the town itself is often judged to be near the 100,000 mark, and Mazar forms the northern point of the diamond-shaped distribution of the four major cites of Afghanistan: Kabul, Kandahar, Herat, and Mazar. Flights leave Kabul for Mazar daily, and there are regular air connections with Herat and Kunduz as well. Paved highway reached Mazar from Kabul in 1969.

At Nowruz time the pilgrimage makes one aware of Mazar as a national center, yet the city has a special character all year long. Products from every town and region of Turkestan reach Mazar, and it is from Mazar, with its extensive warehouse capacity and a chamber of commerce, that goods are distributed to all of Turkestan. Oranges from Pakistan and Jalalabad reach Qaisar, at the far western end of Turkestan, from Mazar, and carpets of the famous "Mowri" variety, produced near Qaisar, find their way back to Mazar. The carpet bazaar of Mazar features every type of Turkestani rug, and the modern-goods shops stock items such as Western toilet paper that are unobtainable anywhere else in Turkestan. Even shopkeepers in towns such as Samangan and Tašqurǧan, further down the road to Kabul, watch trucks going by to Mazar with goods, and must wait for merchandise to be brought back for sale after unloading in Mazar (with a resulting increase in price).

Though Mazar does serve as a local market center for an extensive belt of satellite towns, one is not readily aware of the bazaar-day traffic, since it accounts for a relatively unimportant share of the total commercial activity of the town. However, Mazar's position as the center of a fairly rich agricultural area is an important reason for its high permanent population figure. The fact that much of the local fruit crop is exported to other regions of Afghanistan lends Mazar additional weight as a commercial center. For example, Mazar ships large quantities of melons to Kabul, whereas those of Andxoi and Aqča are never seen outside their local areas.

This unique status of Mazar-i Šarif is reflected in a special kind of musical life enjoyed by the townspeople. In its role as area center, Mazar offers the utmost in regional entertainment at suitable times. Just as the local market center provides music for its regular customers, so Mazar furnishes extensive recreational facilities when it attracts the bulk of its visitors: namely at Nowruz time. For the combined New Year's and pilgrimage tourist crowd Mazar goes out of its way to set up a special entertainment quarter, a kind of tent city called Čārbāǧ, quite near the focal point of town, the shrine and mosque of Ali. For the traditional forty days of New Year's, starting March 21, there is continuous entertainment into the night at Čārbāǧ. Musicians, dancers, storytellers, magicians, gypsies, holy men of every description — all flock to Mazar to see the miracles at the raising of the janda and to find ready customers. It is the only time of the year when musical instruments — mainly tambourines, flutes, and toy drums for children (see Chapter 4) — are sold on the streets of Mazar. Medicine men and amulet writers appear all round the great central square, and though they fade away after a week or ten days, the musical entertainment continues for the full forty days. Famous musicians such as Bangeča Tašqurǧani are lured to Mazar by the prospect of steady work. Bangeča earned from $1.50 to $2.00 a day for performing during Nowruz in 1968 — a figure that compares quite favorably with Aq Pišak's sixty cents for a day's playing in an Aqča teahouse — and says his wages have risen considerably since. In addition, the crowds are numerous and enthusiastic, and may throw the musician more money. Paštun dancing boys from the Kabul-Logar region appear, adding an especially festive touch to the occasion. Temporary kitchens supplying huge cauldrons of rice palow or fried fish do a thriving business as well.

When the holiday merriment tapers off, enough permanent entertainment is left for the citizens of Mazar. The town is so large, compared to local market centers, that it can support a variety of performers catering to different audiences in various quarters of town. The 500 Kazakhs of Mazar, refugees of 1932 from the Alma-Ata region of Kazakhstan, have their own musicians and musical traditions, and have maintained these intact up to the present. Émigré Uzbeks who long for the tones of the Uzbek dutar invite Ğafur Xan to come from Andxoi to perform. Thus the importance of Mazar can also be judged by the fact that it imports entertainment from any preferred region of the constituent area.

Mazar supports a large number of semiemployed professional musicians, far more than can be supported in a local market center. They split into two fairly distinct camps, thus offering customers a choice of programming not available in, say, Aqča. The more traditional group of performers sticks to the local repertoire, such as can be found in the local market teahouse, while an equally large, if not larger, set of musicians plays only the music of Kabul. It does not appear that either of the groups is paid more or works more steadily than the other; both average perhaps $4.50 to $5.00 per night. The Kabul-oriented group, on the whole, seems younger and more purely local in origin; two of the main members of the traditional set are Hakim and Šarif, older Tajik Tašqurğanis who have settled in Mazar where work is fairly steady, whereas the Kabul-style musicians tend to be middle-class Mazar Paštuns and Tajiks who are struck by the chic of radio music. There are also "refugees" from Kabul itself who find it easier to make a living in the North — Lali, for example, whose brother Majid has remained in the Radio Afghanistan orchestra back in the capital. Lali and the young Mazar players use only Kabul-based instruments (tanbur, harmonium, robab).

One final type of musician should be noted. This is the entrepeneur-performer, who does not rely on music for his sole means of support. The prime example is Sekundar, a flutist and tanburist, who also owns a bathhouse adjacent to the teahouse where musicians tend to gather. Considering that the bath costs five afghanis (six cents) and that hundreds of customers traipse through weekly, Sekundar must be fairly prosperous without musical income. Abdul Mazari, another local player and a friend of Sekundar's, once owned a shop (in 1968), though apparently he no longer does. This special type of performer can be spotted by at least one outward sign: they all tend to wear the karakul hat of officialdom and the aspiring middle class, rather than the ordinary turban of poorer musicians and the majority of the local populace.

Another sign of Mazar's importance as a musical center is its ability to support two full-time instrument makers. Aǧā Mohmad and his apprentice Said Maidin have a small shop in a poor section of Mazar, near the Darwāz-i Tašqurǧan ("Tašqurǧan Gate"). Aǧa Mohmad learned his trade from his father and represents the third generation of instrument makers in his family. He has worked forty-five years in the trade. He makes primarily robabs, tanburs, and damburas, and will make anything else (such as an Indian *sarinda*) if commissioned, and if he can get a model to work from. Mazar is the only town outside Kabul where one can have just about any instrument made. Aǧa Mohmad's technique is the same for every type of instrument. He always uses mulberry wood, and always hews the body of the instrument from a single block (for details of instrument construction, see Chapter 4). He categorizes the different types of instruments mainly in terms of the length of time needed and the price charged. The scale runs from the dambura (ten days, up to $3.40) to the robab (one month, up to $40.00). As far as Aǧa Mohmad and older musicians of Mazar remember, Mazar always had the kinds of music it does today. The incursion of Kabul style is not a new phenomenon. Old Hakim, the tanbur player, says that even fifty years ago "whatever was in Kabul was here too."

Thus Mazar, in both economic and musical terms, is a major collecting point for the products of a large service area and is the major link with Kabul for Turkestan. It is large enough and varied enough to provide a whole range of services for its inhabitants, and offers its size and facilities to the larger area for the biggest yearly event, the Nowruz pilgrimage, much as Chicago used to earn its name of Convention City.

Faizabad functions for Badaxšan much as Mazar does for Turkestan, but on a much more modest scale. This is partly due to the town's smaller population, which probably does not exceed 25,000, but is due equally to the nature of its location and its hinterland. Badaxšan is a mountainous, inhospitable, and poor area, largely cut off from the rest of Afghanistan. The major truck route from Kabul ends at Faizabad, and there is little up-to-date internal transportation. Faizabad can boast no great national event like the Nowruz pilgrimage of Mazar, and scheduled flights to the town run at about 25 percent efficiency. As can be seen on Map 2.3, Faizabad lies on the bend of the Kokča River, completely hemmed in by the Hindu Kush, with peaks of up to 2,500 meters in the immediate vicinity. Access to Faizabad is provided by the circuitous road that hugs the cliffside along the Kokca and is easily washed out in flood season. There are few towns away from the main road, and villagers in the hinterland reach Faizabad with great difficulty.

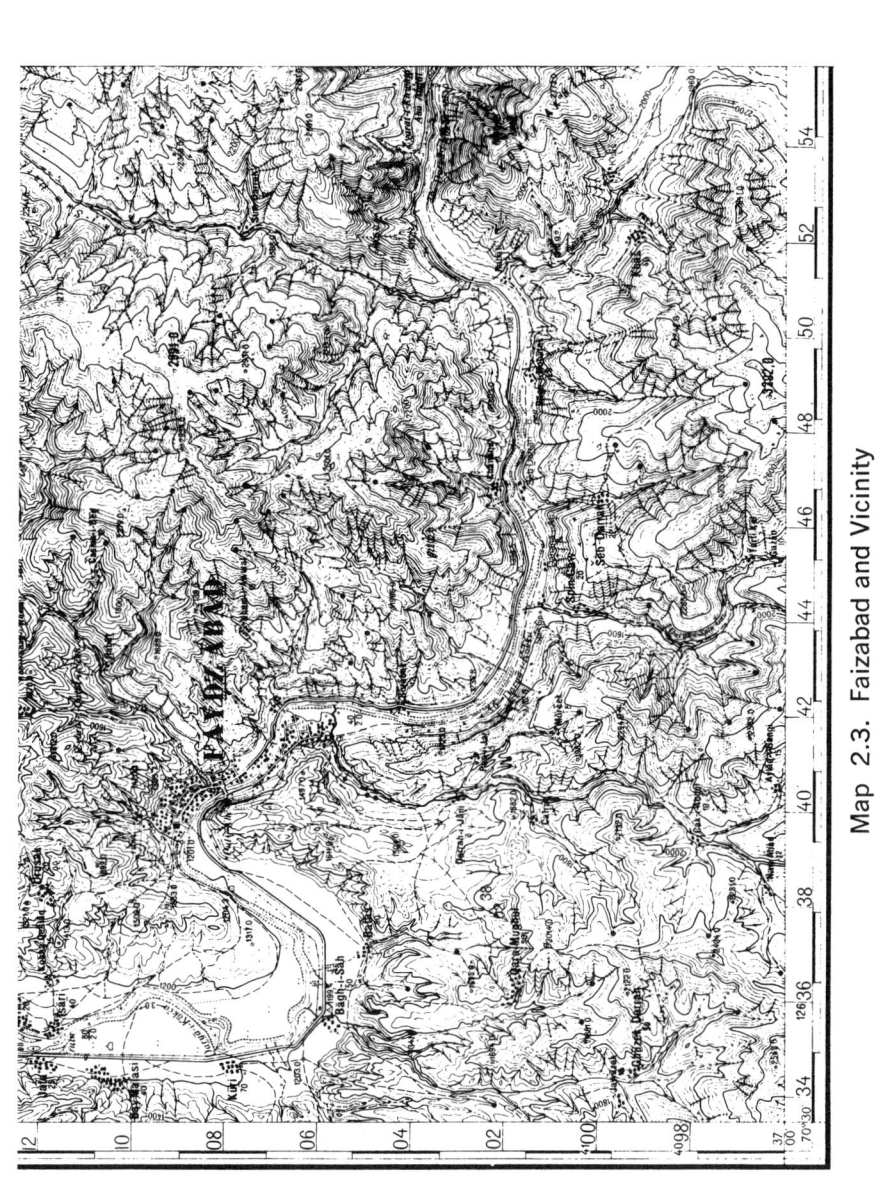

Map 2.3. Faizabad and Vicinity

In short, it is hard to imagine a greater contrast than is offered by the settings of Faizabad and of steppe towns like Aqča and Mazar-i Šarif.

Despite the differences, however, basic similarities enable the observer to recognize Faizabad and Mazar as sister cities. Faizabad is not only spiritually, but economically, geographically, and administratively the center of Badaxšan. Although peasants and shepherds of the far reaches of the province may never personally reach Faizabad, they know of it from friends who spend time in the capital as recruits in the army, or from merchants who get down to the city to replenish their stock.

Once a year Faizabad, like Mazar, serves as host to its entire client area. This occurs at the time of Ješen, a period in late August set aside by the government as a time for celebrating national independence (actual Independence Day occurs in May). During Ješen, the best performers of Badaxšan flock to Faizabad, and the public at large takes over the town in a manner reminiscent of Mazar crowds at Nowruz, though on a much smaller scale. It is the one time in the year when Badaxšanis from different regions meet for entertainment and business en masse, and Faizabad is ready for this friendly invasion. The provincial officials clear a large space near the center of town as a parade ground and exhibition area, and the word goes out to subgovernors to collar all the available talent in their regions for entertainment.

Like Mazar, Faizabad has its own urban musician-shopkeeepers, who perform a type of music not heard in the local market centers. Akbar is Faizabad's counterpart of Abdul of Mazar. He runs a typical *banjāra,* or mixed-goods shop, on the main street, and is widely known as a musician and comedian who is on tap for festivities. Akbar and his good friend Kākā ("Uncle"), a talented damburači from Katağan, play at Ješen on contract for a sizable sum of money. Their repertoire includes some folk music but mainly stresses songs to texts of urban poets. Town poets write in the ğazal form, a traditional literary style of the Persian world, instead of in the folk čarbaiti or quatrain genre. In many towns, amateur poets write specifically for musicians, casting their verse in forms easy to sing to the standard tunes that float around the North for years under different titles.

As there are fewer sizable local market centers in Badaxšan than Turkestan, there is an even sharper disparity between the music of Faizabad and its hinterland than between that of Mazar and, say, Aqča. In Faizabad, one either hears the urban songs of Akbar or the up-country shepherd tunes called felak (see Chapter 3); there is no intermediate "buffer" style like the teahouse music of Turkestan. There is also a much more limited selection of professional and public music in Faizabad on an ordinary bazaar day. The only people likely to be strumming a dambura in a teahouse are backwoods visitors or occasional town amateurs, rather than organized professional groups. There are said to be instrument makers in the suburbs, but most people feel that instruments coming from backwoods regions like Šuğnan or Darwaz are superior to those made in the Faizabad area.

Faizabad is clearly the regional market center of Badaxšan and a focus for cultural activity of the entire area, and yet because of the nature of the region it serves it is neither so active nor so magnetic a center as Mazar-i Šarif, and because of its geographical position it will never be so important or so large a city. However, because of its close connections with the countryside, Faizabad will long remain a storehouse of traditional Badaxšani culture.

Before leaving the regional market center, let us briefly examine Samangan and Šiberğan, two towns in which the marketing and administrative hierarchies fail to coincide. As mentioned earlier, these communities had governmental importance thrust upon them in the reorganization of provinces completed in 1964, when they were made provincial capitals.

Samangan is not the center of any major market or traditional craft (the nearby dambura production being the sole exception). I met a man from the Čārkent area (in the foothills west of Samangan) who bypassed Samangan to shop in Tašqurğan, then half a day's ride farther on, because the prices were better there. He and others belittle the role of Samangan in the local area's economy and thinking. Yet the town boasts a newly built bazaar, the governor's headquarters, and the provincial military garrison. Until the Soviet planners bypassed the town in 1970, the paved road was making Samangan an important truck stop; now one must make a special effort to get to the town. Though located in a fertile agricultural area, Samangan holds no valuable economic cards like the carpets and karakul skins of Andxoi and Aqča.

The music of Samangan reflects its ambiguous status. As a minor local center, it neither produces nor exports entertainment. In fact, it is so poor in musical resources that the only available public music in 1968 came from outside, in this case from army recruits. On Fridays (their day off) draftees sometimes form bands to supplement their meager pay (less than one dollar per month). Since market days are of little importance to the life of the community, no special musical arrangements are made. Instead, the government provides blanket musical coverage for Samangan to parallel the administrative status it has introduced. This comes in the form of loudspeakers placed at intervals along the one-street bazaar, broadcasting Radio Afghanistan from early morning to late in the evening. The radio is such a dominant

Fig. 2.7. Samangan soldiers on their day off, performing as musicians to supplement their pay (instruments include zirbağali, dambura, and zang).

factor that only teahouses at the far end of the bazaar, past the last loudspeaker, support live music — a striking illustration of the predominance of modern conventions over traditional patterns in the town's life. It is interesting to note that despite the presence of the public amplification system, some shopkeepers still keep expensive radios going in their shops to demonstrate their wealth.

Šiberğan, like Samangan, has entered a period of change in recent years. Lying between the powerful towns of Aqča to the north and Saripul to the south, Šiberğan has never had much drawing power as a market center. Its designation as provincial capital has brought the town some added prominence, in the form of a movie theater and two or three shops with some modern goods for sale. An interesting additional feature of Šiberğan's situation that differentiates it from Samangan is the stationing of a considerable body of Russian technicians in the town to work on the natural gas pipeline to the Soviet Union. In the late 1960s, 180 specialists and their families were living in a separate enclave, representing a large increase in the number of consumers. A tall television tower — a striking sight in a Turkestani town — was built for the Russians to receive transmissions from across the border, and its presence underlines the isolation of the Russian community. The complete lack of social contact between the local populace and the Russian workers has kept a potentially dynamic situation from having any effect on the basic structure of the town, even while it underscores the nontraditional nature of Šiberğan today.

Šibergan's role has been strengthened, however, by another group of Russians, in this case the highway builders who completed the Mazar-Šibergan road in 1971. Though I have not revisited the town, it seems clear from conversations that Šibergan's commercial importance has increased thanks to the paved road, which allows goods to be brought in directly from Mazar. Perhaps the town will now become a type of subregional wholesaling center, since Aqča remains bypassed and the other main nearby towns, Saripul and Sangčerak, are still cut off from paving. Eventually Šibergan's place in the marketing hierarchy may match its administrative status, again through direct intervention by the government in the form of the highway.

The Industrial and Communications Center

Last in our survey of urban enclaves is the type of town that could be considered "the wave of the future" if Afghanistan eventually moves towards further modernization of the North. These are towns born or resuscitated in recent years, designed with an eye to modern technological needs and populated with a mixture of elements not found in other areas of the country. Basically we are dealing here with Katağan, and specifically with three of its principal towns — Kunduz, Pul-i Xumri, and Bağlan.

Kunduz is an old settled area. Especially during the early nineteenth century it was the center of a far-reaching principality, then ruled by the Uzbek chieftain Murad Beg, whose dominions stretched from the Waxan to Balx and who exacted a yearly slave tribute from the Hazarajat, as mentioned earlier. Even at the time (in the 1830s) Kunduz, though center of such an important kingdom, was never properly equipped as a capital. Captain Wood's disparaging remarks about the town can be recalled (1872:138): "Kunduz, the capital of Murad Beg, is one of the most wretched in his dominions. Five or six hundred mud hovels contain its fixed population . . . nothing, in short, can be imagined less resembling a metropolis." The reason for this sad state of affairs was the same that brought down the ancient city of Balx: malarial swamplands around the town. According to Dr. Ğoŝwand of the Afghan Institute of Health, the malaria rate in the Kunduz area was as high as 95 percent in the early 1930s, and while the disease has largely been checked, Kunduz province still registers more malaria patients than any other region each year.

With the completion of the antimalaria campaign and the establishment in 1925 of the Spinzar Company (cotton, textiles, and by-products such as edible oil), Kunduz rapidly changed from a tumbledown, sleepy village to a major center of Afghan industrial activity. In a country that is still 95 percent agrarian, development of a new industrial center is an achievement of great importance, and Kunduz does have great significance for Afghanistan. With the arrival of the road from Kabul to the Soviet border via the Salang Pass and Kunduz in 1964, the importance of Kunduz was solidly established by its threefold role as home of the Spinzar Company, clearinghouse for trade with the Soviet Union, and major transportation-communications hub of Katağan. In addition, the role of the local market in supplying Kunduz with produce for export must not be minimized. Kunduz is the center of Afghanistan's major rice-producing region, and Kunduz melons compete with fruits from Mazar in the Kabul marketplace. To these functions of the town must be added its important role as provincial capital. Taken together, these many facets of its economic-administrative position make Kunduz a town of major national significance, and that importance is enhanced by the fact that it is a modern, capitalist role that has been assumed by the town.

Looking at Map 2.4, one can easily see the reasons for the prosperity of Kunduz. The great north-south axis of the paved road, which links Kunduz to Kabul through Bağlan to the south and knifes across the desert north to the Soviet border, and the rather wide zone of well-watered, fertile land that surrounds Kunduz stand out clearly from the adjacent arid zones.

Also clearly visible on Map 2.4 is the development of Bağlan. Farthest north is the site of old Bağlan, a thriving town in Kushan times (second to fifth centuries A.D.), marked BAGHLAN (ŠAHR-I-KOHNA) on the map. Just to the south is the new administrative center and capital of Bağlan province, BAGHLAN (ŠAHR-I-JADID). Here a model new bazaar has been built, and the governor's office is perched on a mound "which produced many stone sculptures . . . typical of the Kushan period" (N. Dupree 1971:256). Still farther south (in heaviest type) is BAGLAN (SANA'ATI), clearly visible as a strong gridiron of new structures; it is the commercial center related to the large local sugar factory.

The ethnic complexion of this part of Katağan strongly reflects its recent past. In Kunduz and Pul-i Xumri a variety of ethnic groups of diverse geographic origin have settled down in company towns. While keeping a certain degree of ethnic distinctiveness, the town population has assimilated to a way of life that is somewhat strange to all the groups involved. We noted earlier the adjustment northern Paštuns have made to Katağan. In addition, a large body of Soviet émigrés (perhaps the largest in Afghanistan), including many Uzbeks, some Tajiks, Kazakhs, and others, has settled in the Kunduz area. Kunduz cries out for sociological study of interethnic relations; it is

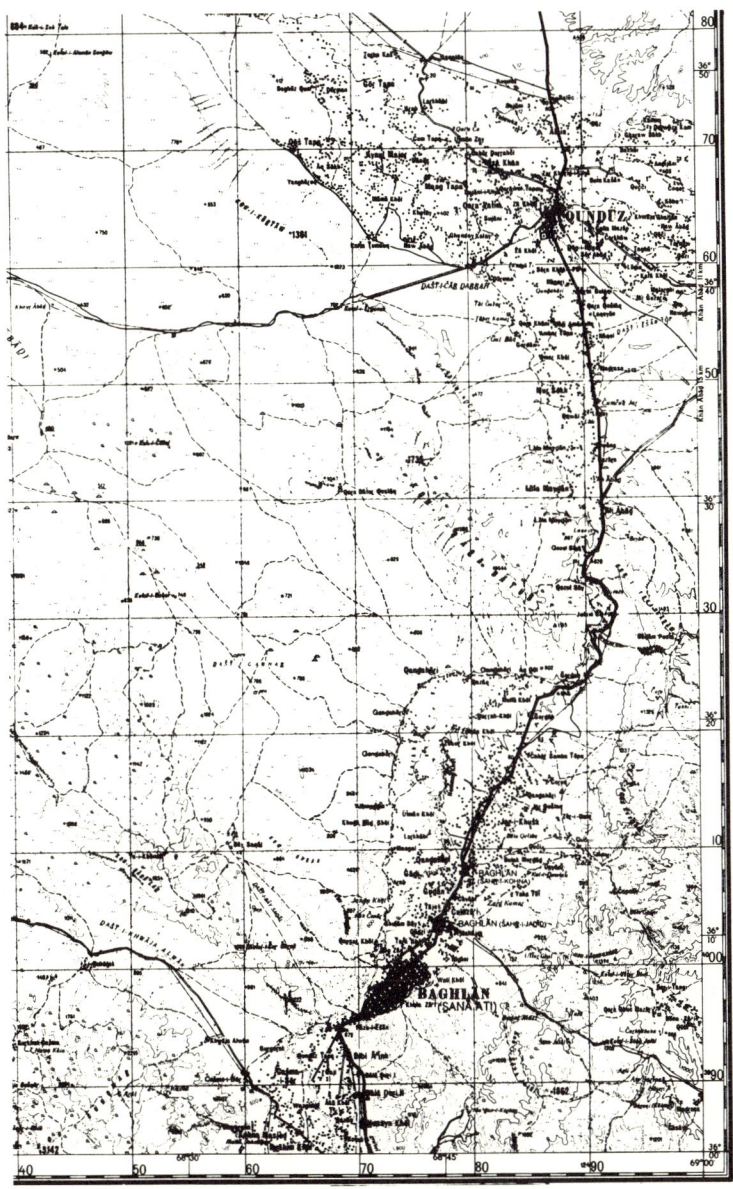

Map 2.4 Kunduz and Bağlan Areas

certainly too early now to make generalizations about the evolving social structure. It is apparent that the presence of a large industrial concern (the Spinzar Company), with its emphasis on modern technology, along with the quasi-modern governmental apparatus and the import-export activities of the vital Soviet trade, creates an unusually high concentration of nationally oriented rather than locally centered activity, and that the Kunduzis are exposed to the wide outside world to a far greater extent than are any other northern townspeople. A native of Kunduz can take a taxi or a plane (at low domestic rates) to Kabul, which is less than a six-hour drive and only a one-hour flight away. By contrast, until 1964 it took travelers two weeks or longer at times to travel between Kunduz and Kabul.

The effect of all this progressive activity on the musical life of the town has been drastic. Kunduz, though surrounded by a densely populated hinterland containing a wide variety of ethnic groups, no longer keeps up live performance of traditional music. In this region, radios are so popular because of affluence, and bazaar days are of such slight significance, that there is no longer any real need for the teahouse music of the local market center. Kunduz, like Mazar, views Kabul music as a necessary cultural acquisition, but unlike Mazar the town prefers to invite musicians from Kabul itself rather than to support local musicians who have learned the capital's style. For Ješen of 1968, for example, Kunduz brought up a large contingent of Kabul musicians, while Mazar was content to rely on local talent. Folk musicians from the Kunduz area went to Taluqan, the capital of the province, which lies between Kunduz and Badaxšan.

Part of the lack of live music in Kunduz is administratively inspired. It seems that Katağani officials take their job as guardians of public morality more seriously than do their Turkestani counterparts, for in Xanabad, hardly an industrial-communications hub, townsfolk complained of governmental interference in musical performance as much as did Kunduzis. However, the latter indicated direct involvement of Spinzar management in the musical crackdown, and censorship seems more long-lasting and effective in Kunduz than in Xanabad. One has the impression that a clean and quiet company town is the aim of Spinzar and local officials alike; in no other community does one see such eager dredging of sidewalk ditches and cleaning of streets.

One can find a certain amount of performance in traditional regional styles in Kunduz, but only with great effort and for brief periods. During my first visit in 1967, for example, I was fortunate enough to record Karim Badaxši, a fine traditional musician of the Darwaz area of Badaxšan who was at the time unemployed in Kunduz. By the time of my second visit in 1968, Karim had left for parts unknown. Other wandering players pass through Kunduz, probably in the hopes of finding a welcome among their countrymen, as Karim did among his fellow Badaxšanis, but it is hard to find any who have settled and still keep up their musical activity.

Kunduz might be termed a kind of Afghan California, where people have drifted in from all parts of the country for jobs and new land, and have developed a generalized dialect and way of life, while keeping roots in the old homeland and maintaining some local traditions. If Afghanistan has further development along the lines of effective, patient modernization, it will probably occur in the northern area of the country, and will produce more towns like Kunduz.

Pul-i Xumri, some 100 kilometers further down the road to Kabul (see Map I), is perhaps even more of a forward-looking community. Unlike Kunduz, it does not have even a past of any interest, is not an administrative center, and has fewer connections with the agrarian base. It is a town created by Afghan-Russian city planning, with a textile plant, a large hydroelectric station, a cement factory (built with Czech aid), and a huge silo for grain storage. There are quarters for company workers, and until 1971 there was another area marked off for Russian advisers on the Turkestan road project. Pul-i Xumri is probably the most important truckstop in the country, since the great majority of Afghan trucking goes over the Salang Pass and forks off at Pul-i Xumri towards either Mazar or Kunduz. It is a mere four hours' ride to Kabul, and taxis are numerous. It is in Pul-i Xumri more than any other place in Afghanistan that one is aware of the power of paved roads to create new patterns of population distribution and new, potent economic factors that can lead to social change. It need scarcely be added that there seems to be no local music at Pul-i Xumri whatsoever; when necessary, as at Ješen time, musicians are hired to come up from Kabul.

*   *   *

In surveying the types of towns in the North, I have tried to show: (1) that the urban enclave is the product of particular geographic and economic settings in which individual ethnic strands are less important than basic socioeconomic functions; (2) that a considerable variety of urban communities still function in northern Afghanistan, thanks to a complex interrelationship of marketing and administrative hierarchies and despite recent technological trends and improvements in transportation; and (3) that in any one trait of town life, such as entertainment, consistencies of behavior will be found that are compatible with the specific structure and function of a given community in the general northern setting.

CHAPTER 3

Analysis of Selected Musical Styles

INTRODUCTION

In this chapter some musical examples from the shared music culture will be presented with transcription and analysis, followed by examples from representative music subcultures. Of the subcultures, only the Kazakhs have been omitted, because (1) their musical style is so highly restricted in distribution, and (2) there has been apparently no Afghan input for Kazakh style, the music resting solely on repertoire remembered from the émigrés' home region of Alma-Ata, Kazakhstan. For like reasons Uzbek classical music of the Buxaran style is not discussed here. In presenting shared musics, I have chosen examples that clearly show heterogeneous origin rather than music of single-ethnic origin that is purveyed to a multiethnic audience. I have tried to balance vocal and instrumental music for purposes of illustration, but it should be remembered that vocal music greatly predominates over instrumental throughout the region under discussion. At times instrumental music will be stressed, both because that was my original area of investigation in the North and because instrumental music, particularly dance tunes, most clearly exemplifies basic structural aspects of musical style. In the discussion below, the songs presented will emphasize the importance of textual questions in the matter of musical ethnicity. In terms of balance, there will be considerable diversity of emphasis among the shared musics and subcultures, which reflects both a bias towards the larger or more distinctive groups and relative lack of information about the others.

Before proceeding to examples of individual styles, it is worth looking at the music of northern Afghanistan as a unit in its regional context. As is the case of musical instruments (see Chapter 4), styles relate to patterns extending well beyond the borders of Afghanistan to the north, east, and west. To take one example, the playing of polyphonic music on lutes and fiddles occurs in an extremely wide, unbroken band from central Siberia (among the Tuvins) to Anatolia and beyond, into Macedonia (among the Pontic Greeks) and up into the Transcaucasus (among the Georgians) (see Slobin 1969 for a survey); thus in this case northern Afghanistan is a central way station for an extensive musical practice, and northern Afghan polyphonic instrumental music must be seen in light of data from surrounding areas. Similarly, even subtypes of instrumental polyphony (parallel intervals only, upper-string melody vs. lower-string drone, etc.) occur at various points in the greater region just outlined as well as in the Afghan North.

Unfortunately, ethnomusicology has not reached a point of systematization precise enough to quickly compare intra- and interregional data. The only extensive attempt to arrive at cross-cultural classification has been that of Alan Lomax's cantometrics project. According to Lomax's findings (1966:96ff.), Northern Afghanistan would fit into a vast area labeled "Old High Culture" (Mediterranean Europe, North Africa, the Near East, Central Asia, and East and Southeast Asia plus Australia), which is characterized in the following way:

Probably the most important theme is "exclusive and elaborated dominance" where a solo performer, accompanied by an orchestra (frequently playing in heterophony), sings a precisely enunciated, long, and complex text. The length, wordiness, and precision of the text is combined with a complex, multiphrased melodic structure, extreme ornamentation, frequent use of rubato and a constricted vocal style, all of which effectively prevent participation by others. Such, apparently, has been the style long employed by plowmen in harvest songs, and by priests and bards for the praise of gods, great beauties, and princes. Within this stylistic framework, great virtuosos and aestheticians developed scales and musical systems, poetic forms and refinements of instrumental structure and technique. . . . The songs of Old High Culture are frequently grave and serious in tone, an effect produced by the combined use of intervals of a second or less, slow tempo, and embellishments, melismas, glissandos and glottal tremolo.

It is not my purpose here to examine the totality of Lomax's theories, which deal with the interrelationship of song style (in all its aspects) and social structure, using Murdock's system of organizing cultures. I would only like to indicate the extent to which Lomax's generalizations about world style areas are relevant for the region under discussion. Only a few of the traits Lomax finds for Old High Culture musical styles fit the northern Afghan situation, or indeed that of Afghanistan as a whole. In the North there are no soloists accompanied by an orchestra either frequently or infrequently playing in heterophony. Song texts tend to be short and uncomplicated rather than long and complex, and enunciated sloppily as often as clearly. Melodic structure (as we shall see below) tends to be fairly simple, all in all. Except in the case of the Turkmens, ornamentation is modest rather than "extreme," and outside of some Badaxšani and Turkmen examples, rubato is rarely used. No great virtuosos or aestheticians are present, though the influence of those in the past in nearby regions (particularly in Persia) is not to be discounted. Slow tempos are rare rather than common.

The principal features of northern practice that jibe with Lomax's description are the almost total predominance of solo rather than group song and the constricted vocal style, which is extremely common. It should be noted in Lomax's favor that those two characteristics are basic to the correlations he finds between song style and social structure and not merely incidental or unimportant features of the musical system of the North. Thus Lomax's generalization, while hopelessly general for the vast geographic and cultural framework he sets up, nevertheless rings true for criteria important to his way of looking at music in culture.

So far I have only mentioned rather gross features of northern musical styles in relationship in those of neighboring areas: the presence of certain types of polyphony played on certain types of instruments, and the tendency toward solo rather than group vocal performance and toward constricted voice quality. The plain truth that must be restated is that ethnomusicology does not offer meaningful ways of categorizing the spread of elements other than such macrofeatures of styles. For example, we shall observe below that northern dance tunes often proceed from a slower to a faster tempo, and that they therefore have two easily definable components. Such a feature can be found in the music of Renaissance Europe, and among the Bashkirs in the Urals (Lebedinskii 1964); however, we have no methodology for making meaningful statements either about possible diffusion of such elements of music making (rather unlikely in the case just cited) or about relationships of such structural devices of social structure, aesthetic evaluation, economic organization, or any other possible pertinent cultural phenomena. Thus, connections between northern Afghan music and that of adjacent regions are still best defined in terms of material culture — i.e., musical instruments — though even in the case of artifacts the usual problems of origin, evolution, and diffusion cloud the basic issues.

In the transcriptions to be presented, it should be noted that for instrumental pieces, only basic sections (A, B, etc.) are presented, and for songs, only one stanza of melody. These are sufficient because of the basically strophic nature of the music, again excepting only certain Turkmen and Badaxšani genres. In terms of notation, all dambura, ǧičak, and dutar parts sound an octave lower than written. Figure 3.1 gives the notational symbols used in the musical examples. Additional symbols for specific technical features (e.g., dambura accen-

Fig. 3.1. Symbols used in the musical examples

tuation) are given in the examples themselves. Throughout, transcriptions are *"skeletal"* so as to focus easily on the basic structural principles discussed. In the text, a single prime indicates the octave ascending from middle c, and double and triple primes indicate the succeeding octaves.

THE SHARED MUSIC CULTURE

Teahouse Music

In examining the Uzbek-Tajik urban style discussed at length in Chapter 1, we shall look at three instrumental and two vocal selections. The purpose of Examples 1 and 2 is to introduce the reader to the basic components of Turkestani musical style. Example 4, representing a mixture of Turkestani and outside musics, leads to the discussion of two songs (Examples 5 and 6) that exemplify interethnic characteristics.

Example 1 (recorded on Anthology AST 4001) is typical of many Uzbek dance tunes of simple structure. It was performed strophically and in unison by Bangeča Tašqurğani (dambura) and Abdul Mazari (tanbur) in Mazar-i Šarif. The piece is divided into two sections by the rhythm, but there is no melodic difference between parts I and II. The only change is a shift from a duple (here 4/4) to triple (6/8)

Example 1. Uzbek Dance Tune (dambura, tanbur)

division of the beat. This basic rhythmic variation is probably related to the needs of the dance, which, as we shall see, are responsible for many of the facets of musical structure in instrumental works. Here, the triple-meter section serves merely as an accelerando for the dancer, who speeds up his motions accordingly.

Let us examine the musical material of Example 1 in detail. First, the ending of both sections A and B on the same note, g′, provides strong tonal orientation. Next, it can be noted that sections A and B occupy two almost mutually exclusive melodic ranges: A covers the interval of a fifth from d′ to a′, except for minor deviations, while B takes a higher-pitched fifth, g′–d″, for its tessitura. Aside from this difference, the two sections are remarkably similar: each occupies four measures of 4/4 time, which can be subdivided into two two-measure phrases. In addition, both sections present the upper notes of their basic interval span (a′ and d″ respectively) in half-note value at the end of measure 2, and reach g′, the strongest pitch, again given as a half-note, at the end of measure 4. The rhythmic figuration of each measure of both sections is remarkably close as well. Note, for example, the matching rests in the second measures of A and B in section I and the matching ties in measures 1–2 and 3–4 of section II.

Example 1 gives an unusually lucid illustration of binary structure on the simplest level of dambura music. Particularly interesting is the one feature that differentiates the two sections, besides the factor of range already cited: the tonal switch from the b♭′ of A to the b♮′ of B, which turns back to b♭′ at the close of B as g′, the home base, nears. As we shall see, both range and varied shading of a single pitch are key factors throughout Turkestani instrumental music and provide basic materials for distinguishing sections of a piece.

Before leaving Example 1, let us further examine the tonal structure. Several striking features come to view. One is the lack of the pitch e′ in the piece and the very weak presence of its neighbor, f′, which gives the impression of a rather empty fourth (d′–g′) in the bottom region of the scale. This feature is typical of much Turkestani music, and it points to a general emphasis on fourths and fifths as basic structural intervals that provide the skeletal outline of the music. To a certain extent, the constant tuning of the dambura's two strings to the interval of a fourth can be introduced as an explanation for this scalar phenomenon. In this feature of melodic structure, we can perhaps find a link between the music of the dambura and that of other Central Asian lutes. In particular, one is reminded of the great prevalence of empty fourths between the lower and upper open-string pitches in the literature of the Kirghiz komuz.

This gap of a fourth, attended by a lack of stress on the lower open-string pitch d', confers upon g' the role of tonic (of this, more below). Thus, we can look at scalar structure from two points of view: in terms of total range we find the breakdown into overlapping fifths (d'–a' and g'–d") cited above as characteristic of binary structure, while we can also look at the intervallic relationships holding between g', the tonic, and the pitches above it as constituting the other principal tonal dimension of the piece. From the latter point of view, we find that section A gives us the alternation of a' and g' as strong pitches, while section B outlines a chain of conjunct thirds (b'–d" and b [alias b♭']–g') as the tonal skeleton. We shall see that both alternation between two strong pitches and emphasis on thirds as a basic melodic interval characterize Turkestani instrumental music.

Music of the dambura and ğičak always seems to move on two planes, because of the construction and favorite tuning of the instrument. In Example 1, as in many other pieces, the first plane, that of the lower string, is of minor importance. A tune may begin at the bottom (as does Example 1) and soon leave it for the upper range of the top string, where most of the melodic activity takes place. The continual return to g' at the end of each phrase and the stress on g' created by such melodic factors as the cadential formula a'–g'–f♯'–g' clearly mark the upper open-string pitch as tonic, and this case is typical of a great many tunes. The presence of the lower open-string pitch, and use of the lower string in brief turns of phrase (as in the descent to f♯' in measure 3), indicate that instrumentalists continually think of the parallel planes provided by the tessituras of the two strings of their lutes. When we term an upper-string pitch "tonic," then, we are recognizing the durational and melodic importance of that pitch, but we must not forget that the lower open-string tone carries a potent charge of stability as well.

Thus, in the two-voiced (here termed polyphonic) pieces to be discussed below, in which the lower open-string pitch takes on the role of drone, the simultaneous sounding of the upper and lower open-string notes as a chord is the most stable possible musical structure, and the drone tone continuously provides "home-base" support for the upper-string melodic activity. Nevertheless, we shall continue to reserve the term "tonic" for the focus of the higher tessitura, which is often the open upper-string pitch, located one fourth above the drone. Occasionally, when the lower-string pitch emerges as a melodic focus for some time, the term "lower tonic" may be used to describe its role.

By examining a simple two-part dance tune (Example 1), we have been able to outline all of the basic factors underlying the more complex manifestations of Turkestani instrumental style. Only one more factor needs to be introduced to complete the picture. This is the relative weight given to each section in terms of overall duration (time) and number of repetitions (stress). In this small piece, which lasts only 137 seconds in the performance being examined, section A occurs 19 times, for a total of 81 seconds, while B appears 12 times in 56 seconds (counting both parts I and II). The resulting proportion, A:B = 3:2 (roughly), in both number of statements and total duration, is common to many binary dambura pieces, and shows the clear prevalence of the A section. Baba Naim, a northern musician familiar with the styles of all regions of the North, once told me that all music is divided into *raft* ("going") and *āmad* ("coming"), and that the amad is the more stable and important of the two. Section A, which stresses the open-string pitches (d′ and g′), can be viewed as the amad in this and other like tunes. We shall find the terms raft and amad useful in analyzing other types of pieces as well.

Example 2, a solo dambura tune, is a dance melody invariably termed "Uzbek" by performers and audience, yet extensively played by musicians of every ethnic group. Because it is one of the most widespread stock items of the shared musical repertoire, I have dubbed it "The Uzbek Rag." In order to get at the essence of variability and stability in musical style, twelve versions by ten different performers are presented. It should be pointed out that I have sharply delimited the discussion by providing the piece in cut-and-dried form, namely by presenting its division into three components as an a priori assumption and by giving only a single one of the manifold microvariations of the tune that unfolded in each live performance. The resulting comparative score, though obviously arbitrary, becomes a revealing indicator of musical style.

In analyzing the performances, we can take version 1 as the standard because of the age and status of the performer, Baba Qeran, universally recognized as the doyen of damburačis. Let us examine parts A and B, referring to the analysis of Example 1 arrived at earlier for two-part structures. We find that A, as in the A section of Example 1, covers the basic interval of a fifth (here e′–b′). The main difference between the A section of Example 1 and that of the Uzbek Rag is that the latter proceeds stepwise up the fifth, thus avoiding the empty interval that characterized the earlier example. We notice also the stress on the third beat of each measure, a favored place for playing an important pitch, which was typical of Example 1 as well. Here the lower open-string pitch fills in the fourth beat of the measure as a kind of drone note. That this filler is not necessary to the melody can be seen in version 3 of Example 2, where quarter-note rests take up the weak beat and e′, in its sole appearance, is relegated to the minor task of beginning a stepwise approach to the tonic b′. Another salient feature is the distance of a (minor) third between b′ and d″, corroborating my earlier conclusion as to the importance of thirds in the melodic skeleton above the tonic.

Moving to the B section of the Uzbek Rag, we find that the

Example 2. "The Uzbek Rag" (dambura)

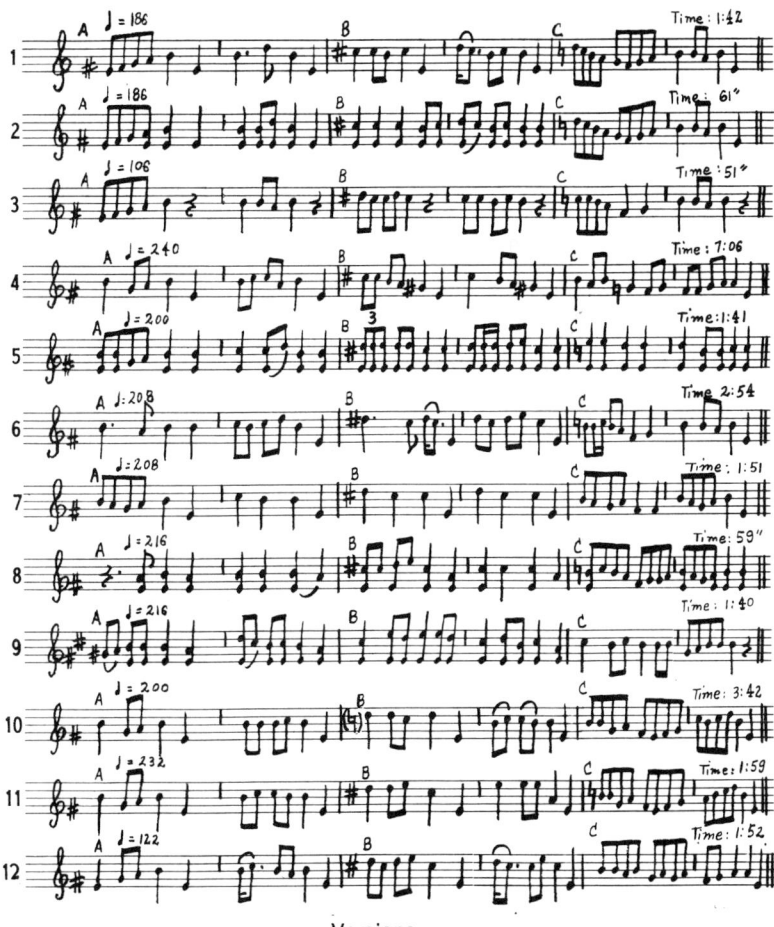

Versions

1. Bābā Qerān (Balx)
2. Bābā Qerān (Tašqurǧan)
3. Ḥakim Mazari (Mazar-i Šarif)
4. Ǧulam Nabi (Maimana)
5. Selim Diwāna (Samangan)
6. Abdul Nazar (Tašqurǧan)
7. Abdur Rahman (Saripul)
8. Bangeča Tašqurǧani (Kabul)
9. Bangeča Tašqurǧani (Mazar-i Šarif)
10. Rahmatullah (Andxoi)
11. Naimullah (Sangčerak)
12. Šer Mohmad (Maimana)

feature of pitch alteration cited in Example 1 holds equally true for
Example 2: after the c♮″ of section A in most versions, c♯″ is heard
for the first time, making the new section distinctive. Another aspect
of structure common to Examples 1 and 2 is the ending of both the
A and B sections on the tonic (b′ in Example 2).

What then is the function of the C section, a new component,
since Example 1 was basically binary in structure? C merely provides
an elaboration of principles already defined. First, it returns to the
c♮″ of section A, rounding out the tonal material. Second, it swoops
down to f♯′ and g′, reintroducing the range below the tonic. Third,
by setting up the interval g′–b′ the third b′–d″ (introduced in section A)
is given new importance as part of a chain of thirds, which is now seen
to be possible both above and below the tonic. C stands as a completing
section, creating the amad, or return, after the raft, or departure, of section B. It is only in such microelements of structure as the presence or
absence of c♯″ or of the pitches above or below b′ that one can differentiate basic structural elements of the Uzbek Rag; this is typical
of much Turkestani instrumental music, which avoids large or dramatic
breaks in the musical line and strives to keep the music on an even
keel, most probably in response to the needs of the dance.

With this basic analysis, largely founded on version 1 of Example 2
to work with, let us turn to a comparative discussion of the twelve
versions at hand. What is most striking is the amount of their similarity,
despite the fact that they were recorded by so many different performers
at different places and times. This similarity becomes apparent if we
examine the weighted scales extracted from the twelve Uzbek Rag
performances (Example 3). Looking at the scale pitch by pitch, we

Example 3. Weighted Scales from Example 2

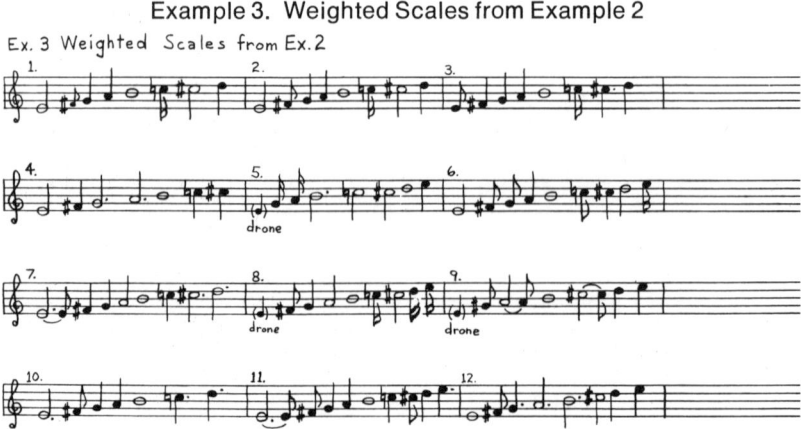

arrive at a fairly definite role for each tone. E′ is always of great importance (except, oddly enough, in version 1), showing the strength of the lower open-string pitch. F♯′ and g′ are weak in all the variants, thus vindicating the principle of the empty lower fourth temporarily discarded above.

A′ is our first ambiguous pitch, being strong in five versions (4, 7, 8, 10, 12) and weak in the other seven. The reason for this vague status of a′ can be found at the very roots of tonal thinking. A′ as the upper open-string pitch, and as the note lying a fourth above the fundamental of the instrument, is bound to carry a certain weight; we noted in connection with Example 1 that the upper open-string pitch is often the tonic of dambura pieces. In addition, a′ lies next to b′, the tonic of Example 2. Pitting a′ against b′ as a rival center of tonal significance provides a certain degree of dynamism in the music by creating an inherent instability that must eventually be resolved. This is the tactic employed by Bangeča, for example (version 9), who closes both the A and B sections of the tune with a′ (albeit on the weak beat), resolving the ambiguity only in C, where b′ alone is heard at the end, set off by a rest. Here is confirmation of the principle of alternation of pitches as an important tonal concept, as stated in the analysis of Example 1. We can even go so far as to say that such alternation provides a keystone of musical structure in the North.

Turning now to the pitch b′ in our survey of tones, we find almost unanimous agreement as to the importance of b′ for the Uzbek Rag. The only exceptions are versions 5 and 12. In the complete performance of version 5, the player uses C as a brief passing phrase leading to the return of an oft-repeated A section, strengthening the suspense of the return to tonic. The deviation from b′ at the close of version 12, found also in version 4, may well be a regional variant of the tune, since both performances are from Maimana. Also noteworthy is the reversion to the common practice of making the open upper-string pitch (here a′) a key tone of the melody, which is atypical in the case of the Uzbek Rag.

Moving on to c♮″, it appears that this pitch is always weakly expressed. Its main role is restricted to being the alter ego of c♯″, and thus it need not be strongly emphasized. On c♯″ falls the burden of innovation, and it is necessary to have heard c♮″ only briefly to be aware that a new contrasting pitch has been introduced. Indeed, when we look at c♯″ we find that it is a strong pitch in nearly all twelve variants. An interesting modification of this outline occurs in version 11, in which the performer, Naimullah of Sangčerak, chooses to move up to e″ as an important pitch, creating a chain of thirds, a′ ♯″–e″, which is an effective counterweight to the tonal material of sections A and C.

D″ and e″, the final elements in the scalar resources, are both weak pitches. When d″ does appear more frequently, as in version 6, it is as an alternating tone to c♯″, which only serves to highlight c♯″ the more. We have already noted the creative use of e″ by Naimullah (version 11), an outstanding exception to the general weakness of the pitch. Indeed, half of the variants do not even include e″ at all. The fact that only 50 percent of the versions reach a full octave range is significant, in that it indicates a basically narrow compass of instrumental music in the North. A span of a sixth or seventh is frequently found, and tunes are heard as exceptional if they range as widely as a tenth or twelfth.

Thus far we have concentrated on the features that make performances of the Uzbek Rag fairly similar. Let us now turn to the disparities, which occur in the parameters of tempo, overall distribution of time among the sections, and total duration. Tempo is indeed variable, ranging from MM 106 to MM 240 for the quarter-note value. This seems to be a function of individual taste, as both Baba Qeran and Bangeča, the most experienced damburačis, stick to exactly the same beat for both of their performances (MM 186 and 216 respectively) recorded months apart; this is strong testimony for the stability of individual style.

Variation in overall duration is more problematic than differences in tempo, since public musical performance depends to a great extent on outside stimuli. Yet the wide variability expressed in Example 2 is certainly indicative of artistic freedom in determining duration. Performances of the Uzbek Rag range from a mere 51 seconds (version 3) to 7 minutes, 6 seconds (version 4), creating a proportion of 8:1 for longest to shortest. However, two-thirds of the versions fall between 1 and 2 minutes, which can perhaps be taken as the average length of performance.

In examining the proportions holding between sections of the tune, there are three possible patterns of duration for a complete performance of the Uzbek Rag, all of which occur in Example 2. In the first, section A receives the most weight, B somewhat less, and C the least. This pattern occurs only once (version 1). The second possibility is for C to be the most important section in terms of time, and this also occurs only once (version 8). The third structuring, under which B is the principal section, occurs in the other ten versions and is thus the standard approach. The proportions run from A:B:C = 6.5:14:1, the highest predominance of B over the other sections, to A:B:C = 2.5:3:1, the lowest. It is interesting that there is so much agreement among performers on the need to stress section B. There is probably a simple answer to this finding: A and C are both amad (return), or tonic-based sections, and together they form an equal counterweight to B, which must by itself provide all of the tonal interest of the Uzbek Rag.

One more factor of variability must be taken into account. This is the presence or absence of an e' (open lower string) drone among the variants. This element may appear unimportant at first glance, but it provides the first glimpse of a factor that will prove to be of considerable interest in later discussion. It should be noted that Baba Qeran's versions differ: the first features only one-string play, while the second introduces the drone style, indicating that both approaches are equally "legitimate" for the piece. The large majority of performances in Example 2 (eight of twelve) are monophonic, and informants expressed the view that this was the authentic mode of presentation. What is notable about the application of the drone pitch in Example 2 is that it is often an all-or-nothing technique — that is, either with the drone used throughout or with no drone at all — and the drone is rarely added as an artistic device for variety of tone color. We shall see later, in the case of Aq Pišak, that within the Uzbek tradition polyphony (as expressed by a drone) can indeed become an important structural factor.

For the next example of teahouse music we turn to a genre of greater scope than Examples 1 and 2. This is a multisectional piece that consists of units such as Example 1 or Example 2 strung together in a kind of suite. I have termed this form a *quodlibet,* a term adopted from Western music history; Apel partially defines it in the *Harvard Dictionary of Music* (1961:621–2) as "a . . . type of music characterized by the quotation of well-known melodies. . . ," and he speaks particularly of "the successive quodlibet . . . in which various melodies are quoted in succession, much in the manner of a potpourri." It is to this latter type of quodlibet that certain Turkestani instrumental pieces belong. They consist of a series of popular songs, or *nagmas,* strung together without a break, played by a solo dambura or a combination of dambura and gičak. These quodlibets have no special name and, indeed, it is often hard even to identify the component parts of the piece. When the content can be established, it turns out to be composed of the most variegated possible sources open to a Turkestani musician. Local nagmas, local songs, songs from other regions of the North, Kabuli songs, and Indian film music may all be drawn in to provide source material for a quodlibet, the instrumental piece par excellence of the shared music culture.

The performer of Example 4 (recorded on Anthology AST 4007) is Baba Qeran of Tašqurgan. The piece is in three parts, with each section deriving from a different repertoire. Section I will not surprise the reader, since it is the Uzbek Rag and served as version 2 in the comparative score; in Example 4 are seen a few variant phrases not included in the abbreviated score of Example 2. Section II is taken from quite a different source: the music of Radio Afghanistan. Here we can see how Baba Qeran dresses up a simple song with a bit of instrumental elaboration. The first part of the actual song can be found

Example 4. Quodlibet (dambura)

here in the A section in only slightly altered fashion. The second part of the radio song is a four-measure standard "reply" phrase, completely bypassed in section B of this instrumental version, which is a pure Qeranian invention. Part II of the quodlibet moves to part III without a break, indicating the alternative solution to the one used between parts I and II, where a subtle modulatory passage was inserted to connect the pieces.

Section III turns to teahouse songs for source material. The tune is "Alpaqadar tular," which we shall examine below in its vocal version (Example 5). It is a particular favorite of Uzbek singers and features some attractive scalar features, notably the alternation of the c♮″ and c♯″ of its part A, which changes to a steady c♯″ at the beginning of section B and reverts to c♮″ as a transition to part a_1. The division of part A into two unequal sections is also interesting and points up the vocal origin of the tune: in the song, part B is the refrain, with the division of A made to accommodate an entire quatrain of text before the refrain.

Example 4 combines traditional Turkestani instrumental music, the new style of Radio Afghanistan, and a typical teahouse song as source material, all blended with ease by Baba Qeran. This art of composing the potpourri is a basic prerequisite to becoming an accomplished professional musician, and it sharply differentiates him from the majority of bumbling amateurs, who at best can play through one simple nağma at a time. We return here to one of the basic criteria of excellence mentioned earlier: breadth of memory, which is often associated with Baba Qeran's name.

Turning to vocal styles, let us first look at "Alpaqadar tular" in its sung version (Example 5). Immediately it is clear that folk songs of the North show little of Lomax's "extreme ornamentation" and "frequent use of vibrato." Instead, they present a crisp, syllabic text setting with only the last syllable of the lines briefly extended (of which more below). The song is divided into two basic sections that may be called verse and refrain, since the text of the final two lines of the latter remains unchanged in each stanza. Like the sections of Examples 1 and 2, the verse and refrain of Example 5 are set off by an obvious pitch distinction, in this case between the d♮ and d♯; the return to d♮ at the end of the refrain is quite similar to the confirmation of original pitch in section C of Example 2. The overall range (a major sixth) is narrower than the octave of Examples 1 and 2, and is typical of numerous Turkestani songs, contrasting with the even narrower range of many Badaxšani songs on the one hand and the wider compass of Turkmen melodies on the other.

Text is distributed across the melody in a fairly intricate pattern.

In the verse section, the first two lines of text each take up four beats; then a two-beat infix ("bulbul jan") is added before and after the recurrence of the second line. In the refrain, however, a full quatrain (čarbaiti) is stated (with a rest after each line to mark it off) before a closing couplet, and "bulbul jan" again appears before and after the last line. This structure gives the singer considerable latitude in building quatrains, which are partially or completely improvised.

Of particular interest is the nature of the song text in this version of "Alpaqadar tular." Here we find a mixture of Uzbek and Persian, reflecting the dual ethnic origin and diffusion of the style. In the section covered by the transcription, the entire verse is in Persian, whereas the refrain is evenly divided between Persian and Uzbek. Here are the first verse and some later quatrains of the performance (Persian lines and words are italicized):

1.
(Verse)

Sištim sare namāzi	We sat in the afternoon
čand gap zadim ğalati (bulbul jan).	just chatting.

(Refrain)

Alpaqadar tular	Multicolored clothes
sairidi bulbular	the singing of the nightingales
awar barmu mendik	is there another so lost as I
mesāle kauki zar	like a golden partridge
tu asti čučai pari (bulbul jan)	you are a fairy's child
dilaike man meibari (bulbul jan).	you take my heart away.

Example 5. "Alpaqadar tular"

2.

Cand čekepow xāna xāna	Some dice with holes
keldi yuroka xāna	[my love] has made holes in my heart
uše *zamin bi hāsel*	on fallow ground
bir mailar *tanhā banā.*	don't pay taxes.

3.

Ulder gani kelding mu	Did you come to kill me
kuider gani kelding mu	or to see me
učkan *čerāğ* laremni	the lamp which was put out
yander ğani kelding mu.	you came to light it.

In these verses considerable fluctuation of Persian content can be seen, ranging from very high to very low. What is important to note is that the quatrains are structured so that both languages fit the verse lines comfortably. It seems from the evidence that the basic pattern is an Uzbek one, for the following reasons: (1) a seven-syllable line (particularly with lengthening of the final syllable) is highly characteristic of Turkic folk poetry from the Crimean Tatars (Samoilovich 1914) to Azerbaijan (Mamedbekov 1954:4), to the Kirghiz (Vinogradov 1958), and up to the Čuvaš of the Volga region (Maksimov 1964); (2) neighboring Tajik folk quatrains performed in similar situations in Badaxšan display a wide variety of syllable distributions, with no fixed number per line (see Slobin 1970 for a discussion).

Of particular interest is the structure of the quatrains, which break into two two-liners, often with apparently unrelated meanings. This again is a widespread Turkic phenomenon. D. Mamedbekov (1965:4) has noted for Azerbaijani folk verse that the first two lines of a quatrain are arbitrary in content but set up the rhythm and meter, whereas the second two lines convey the basic meaning and unify the entire stanza. Similar views are expressed by northern Afghan Uzbek informants, who state that the opening two-liner is often there to set the stage for a loosely connected yet definitive second half of the quatrain. Without specific information regarding a certain verse, it is often difficult for an outsider to sense the inner link, though at times the connection is clear enough — as in quatrain 3 above, where the overall meaning seems continuous. In quatrain 2, the first half and second half are linked by a common topic (unrequited love); in this case, the explicit vs. implicit approach of the two-liners allows the singer to cast differing lights on a single topic in the course of a quatrain.

Of course, expediency often dictates the content of quatrains. This became very clear when I asked Bangeča Tašqurğani to extemporize quatrains for me. In doing so, he used stock lines and common Persian word endings at a quick rate to produce standard quatrains such as the following:

Āmadim ruye maidān	We came to the square
guš konad xurd o kalān	Let big and little listen
misterā beguyam	I tell the Mister
Āmadam be Tašqurǧān	I came to Tašqurǧan.
Az tu porsān meikonam	I ask you
čand waxt asti Tašqurǧan	How long will you be in Tašqurǧan
bexeir kodom sui miri	Which way are you heading
asli mikonam porsān.	I ask you.
Āmadam ruye maidān	I came to the square
ina dambura Samangān	Here's a dambura from Samangan
in zulfirā mibini	See this chain lock?
in aslan az Badaxšān.	It's really from Badaxšan.
Unā xarbuza piše rui	There's a melon in front
če xub kardi, nuše jān	well done, bon appetit!
in še'ra az jur karda	this poem was put together
Bangeča az Tašqurǧān.	by Bangeča from Tašqurǧan.

These completely impromptu quatrains are clearly roughhewn. Gramatically, they are elliptic at times (e.g., *dambura Samangan* instead of *dambura-i Samangan*) and stay at the most colloquial level of local speech instead of breaking into the semipoetic style that characterizes more deliberately composed folk verses. In quatrain 1 Bangeča establishes the standard *a a b a* rhyme scheme of a čarbaiti, and he manages to keep to it in quatrain 3. In the other two quatrains he uses an *a b c b* rhyme, which is less typical but nonetheless maintains the rhyming of second and fourth lines that is basic in čarbaitis. Note that all the rhymes depend on the *-ān* ending of Persian, a common last syllable of many words and place names (Tašqurǧān, Samangān, Badaxšān); this is quite typical of even the most polished of Persian čarbaitis. All the lines of Bangeča's extemporaneous poetry are seven or eight syllables long, again a stereotype pattern for the style. The hurriedness of construction is responsible for the obvious repetitions of words (*Āmadam* in verse 1, *porsān* in verse 2).

Most interesting is the content. All the verses revolve around my arrival in Tašqurǧan on a brief visit (in 1971). Both Bangeča himself and I (the "Mister" of verse 1) are mentioned, and details from the immediate environment (the melon, the chain lock on the hotel room door) are brought in. References to place names of nearby regions (Samangan and Badaxšan) appear along with three citations of Tašqurǧan itself. This penchant for immediacy is a key feature of the čarbaiti and relates intimately to its function of providing general entertainment in the teahouse setting. As two singers alternate verses in the full ensemble situation, each picks up topics from the audience, singling out one man as a butt of humor or discussing the local situation, and a competition in satire may result. Here one can see most clearly the similarity to Central Asian singing contests (which may be a genetic relationship in this case) and to such competitive and satirical musical commentary in various parts of the world. Music here conveys a social message, one that deserves deeper investigation in a given community, where local circumstances and song texts may shed light on one another; at present there are not enough data to undertake such an analysis.

Women's Music

Wedding songs form the core of women's music, so it is appropriate to take perhaps the most widespread song of that genre. "Astā bero" ("Go slowly") as our example for female music making. The first version (Example 6) is in Kabul style, as sung by the women of a Paštun family of high status temporarily resident in Šibergǎn, where the man in the family was an official. Here the women are singing for their own amusement. The second version of "Asta bero" (Example 7) stems from quite a different source — two professional Uzbek singers of Andxoi, Zulaixā and Gulandām. These performers were mentioned in Chapter 1 as typifying low-status families engaged in music making for money. They may or may not be prostitutes, but they are at the least considered so.

Here is a translation of the excerpts from the two "Astā bero" variants:

Example 6: I sit, sit, until you come from the road.
Walk slowly, my moon, walk slowly.

Example 7: My darling, your figure is like a flower.
Walk slowly, my moon, walk slowly.

The lesson to be gained from examination of Examples 6 and 7 is that despite the extreme difference in ethnic and social background, the two sets of singers perform "Astā bero" in a remarkably similar manner. Most important, both versions are completely in Persian. The two refrains are textually identical and musically nearly so, and both occur after a short one-line verse. In both versions the verse line is made up of twelve syllables divided 5 + 7, with a melodic range of a fourth, and both feature markedly rhythmic drum accompaniments and the same tempo level. In addition, the verse line in each case follows roughly the same pattern, indicating the generic connection between the two versions. The differences, however, illustrate the sharp ethnic and regional distinctions that can separate performances of a single song. Among these, the most obvious is the text; there is no overlap in verse lines in the two versions of "Asta bero" under discussion. Also of particular interest is the sharp difference in word accentuation: the Kabul version is close to normal speech, as in the accenting of the last syllable of *xiābān* and in the iambic pattern of *astā*. On the other hand, the Andxoi "Astā bero" often strongly contradicts speech rhythm, as in the protracting of the middle, normally unaccented, syllable of *mimonad* instead of the initial syllable. These differences may be due to the Andxoi singers' lack of native status as Persian speakers, in contrast to the Paštun family's Kabuli familiarity with the language. The somewhat more complex rhythmic relationship of drum pattern to melody in the Kabuli version is less easily explained; it probably relates to the component of individual variation inherent in every performance of a song, for the drum pattern is not definitively ethnic or regional in outline in either version.

It is interesting that "Astā bero" is the wedding song found most widespread, since unlike many wedding songs, which are sung only at a certain moment in the course of the long evening of ceremony-cum-entertainment, "Astā bero" may be sung (at least in Kabul) at various points in the proceedings: by the family when the group assembles to decorate the bride's and groom's hands with henna, or when the bride leaves for the groom's home, or by a professional singer as part of the general entertainment. It is also significant that "Astā bero" has been taken up as a radio song by a leading male performer (Hamāhang), who may sing it in the course of more modern weddings held at restaurants or hotels as well as on the air at any random point in programming. There is even a recent version with a rather European-

Example 6. "Astā bero" (Kabuli version)

Example 7. "Astā bero" (Andxoi version)

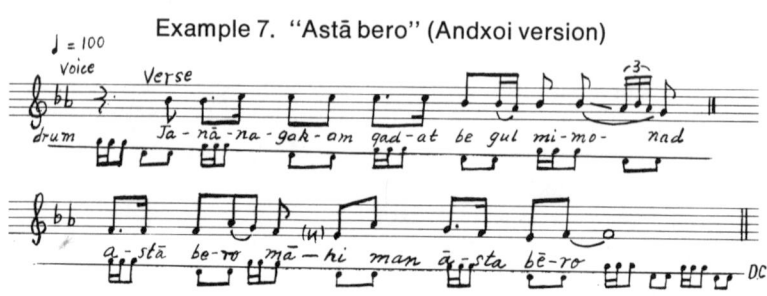

sounding arrangement on the radio amateur hour. In this case a specifically feminine and ceremonial song has been transmuted into a generalized sentimental "asexual" component of the mass media, highlighting and continuing the process of interethnic sharing that first brought the song to prominence. The concept of marketing a sentimental song to a primarily female audience is beginning to spread over the radio, a notable example being Rahimbaxš's song about mothers, which is on the order of European or American flowery tributes to Mom. In one family a woman lonely for her mother (who lived in a distant town) chose to sing me this mother-song. Here again the radio has responded to a cultural pattern of expressing feminine emotions in music.

Religious Music

Rounding out our survey of shared musics, let us briefly examine a bit of religious street-singing, or mada. The example comes from Šibergan and was performed by a door-to-door *sadhu*, or holy man, on the occasion of the tenth and last day of *Muharam*, the commemoration of the slaying of Husein (Ali's son and Muhammad's grandson) at Kerbala in Iraq. Muharam is a major religious occasion in Shi'ite Iran, where *ta'zia* passion play is performed and groups throng the streets for mass self-flagellation. In Kabul, Shi'a Afghans congregate in their gathering house *(tekexāna)* for extensive services. In the heavily Sunni North, however, I did not observe any special public marking of Muharam. Nevertheless, the itinerant sadhu found it an occasion to make the rounds of the courtyards of affluent families to chant and collect alms. Unfortunately, I was not able to ascertain whether he himself was Sunni or Shi'a, but the significant point is that he did not care to which sect the households he visited belonged, and his attitude underscores the cross-sectarian and interethnic nature of mada singing.

The chant itself (Example 8) is marked by extreme narrowness of range (basically a minor third with a rare excursion another whole step up), considerable instability of pitch, and a high degree of melisma. None of these qualities is common by itself, and they are certainly not found in combination in any of the local musics of Šibergan. The musical style seems more related to Qur'anic chanting and other types of religious vocal expression than to any one secular music of the North. Important, however, is the fact that mada singing is almost always entirely in Persian, rather than in the Arabic of the Qur'anic cantillation or call to prayer *(azan)*. Once again Persian is selected as the lingua franca of the multiethnic North, insuring maximum intelligibility to a mixed audience.

Example 8. *Madā* Song (Šiberğan)

The text of Example 8 is as follows:

> O Imam, O Husein, today is the day of battle.
> The soul is exalted today.
> Husein the oppressed is alone at Kerbala today.

THE MUSIC SUBCULTURES

The Paštuns

To illustrate Paštun music of the North, let us return to an example, cited in Chapter 2, by Baba Naim, a Paštun of Faizabad. Though he has lived in various parts of Afghanistan, and has been so far from Paštun roots as to find it hard to remember songs of his childhood, the Paštun poet Saduddin Shpoon and I were able to coax the old performer into singing landai poems, accompanying himself on the ğičak, the northern fiddle. I have chosen a Badaxšani Paštun for two reasons: (1) the musical style of less isolated Paštuns is probably less distinctive from the Paštuns' own point of view, and (2) Paštuns in the steppe country have probably tended to adopt the local non-Paštun style to a greater extent. Both of these assumptions are rather speculative at this point.

One of Baba Naim's performances is given in Example 9. Here is the text, with an unpolished translation by Shpoon:

Landai text:

Māde asmān spina spuğmaike	Make me the white moon of the sky
čede janā paqi dar tul nalarena	So that I always stand at my love's ford

Framing line:

Sabādei šemāle gigi wine pāne	It's morning and the breeze is blowing

As mentioned in Chapter 2, Shpoon found Baba Naim's presentation of the poem, a string of landais known to Paštuns all over Afghanistan, unorthodox. To what extent this represents an original amalgam of musical styles by Baba Naim, a strongly individualistic performer, and to what extent it is typically Badaxšani Paštun I cannot say; the musical evidence points in both directions. The treatment of the text, whereby one line of the landai is stated, and followed by a framing, non-landai line, recalls a structure we have noted for certain northern songs, in which a refrain breaks up basic units of the text stanza. In Baba Naim's landais this feature becomes quite marked. In later verses (not given in the transcription) the second line of the couplet may appear in place of the second half of the framing line in the refrain. This may be a personal touch on Baba Naim's part; at any rate Shpoon did not find it in accordance with general Paštun practice. In landais I have heard sung, there is generally a straightforward statement of both lines of the verse, after which the singer moves on to another landai. Occasionally the framing-line technique appears in radio versions of landai songs, but not to the extent that Baba Naim applies it.

The melody in Example 9 is particularly non-Badaxšani. The slow descending curve of the first two song phrases (A and B), followed by a final stabilizing section, simply does not occur in any Badaxšani music with which I am familiar. Neither does it seem

Example 9. *Landai* from Badaxšan

typically non-Badaxšani Paštun. The use of the ğičak, on the other hand, is in itself northern (particularly Badaxšani), though the music allotted to the fiddle, which consists of two variants of the melody of the vocal section, is, like the entire song, ambiguous. The free-rhythm introduction is not unusual for a Badaxšani song with ğičak; the use of a vamp (the repeated fourths) at the opening and again before the voice begins is typical. However, the accompaniment (not notated) during the song, which is restricted to straight melodic duplication of main pitches, is not very common in Badaxšani pieces I have heard; it is a feature I associate more strongly with Turkestan (a region in which Baba Naim has also lived for about ten years).

All in all, Baba Naim's landai songs perhaps represent an inter-ethnic and also individualized musical style strongly Paštun in association, since the text is considered the focal point of landai songs. Considerably more research among northern Paštuns is needed to determine whether such an eclectic style can be found among other gifted Paštun musicians of the North.

The Uzbeks

We shall look at two examples of the Afghan Uzbek "exclusive" repertoire, or at least musical styles that are clearly identified by everyone as purely Uzbek in origin. The first of these is an instrumental piece, a dance tune for solo dambura (Example 10), while the second is an excerpt from a secular tale (Example 11).

Example 10 cames from the repertoire of Aq Pišak of Aqča, one of the finest damburačis of Afghanistan and a leading exponent of traditional instrument music. A large part of Aq Pišak's repertoire consists of "Aqčais," pieces named for his home town. Over a long period of time I gathered ten such tunes. All of them feature almost identical melodic material. We shall dissect one performance and present the overall findings of seven of the ten versions comparatively in Table 3.1 below. In this way we can approach individual variability and continuity of tradition in a way complementary to the collective scrutiny of twelve performers offered in Example 2.

To fully understand the working of the Aqčais, we must introduce a brief discussion of the Uzbek dance. Unfortunately for the outside observer, dance (as noted in Chapter 1) is considered a shameful act, to be performed only under private circumstances. Not only do the tenets of the strongly religious Northerners militate against public dance, but the government has issued administrative decrees against as it as well. Whereas Paštun dancing boys are allowed to travel freely across the countryside, making stops in towns for general entertainment, Uzbek dancing has in the past been severely censured and was at times even considered a punishable offense.

Nevertheless, I was able to witness some dance performances by special arrangement. Through these brief glimpses and by means of discussion with musicians, I have pieced together the salient features of Uzbek dance, especially as they relate to instrumental performance. The main factor to be remembered is that the music determines the steps of the dancer, rather than the routine of the dance deciding what the instrumentalist must play. The whim of the damburači is the soul of the dance. If he plays in a leisurely manner, the dance proceeds slowly, and when he speeds up, the pace quickens. Beyond this basic control, the damburači has additional means of guidance at hand. For example, certain strokes tell the dancer to kneel and perform gestures in a semisitting position, and a counterstroke compels him to rise again. The basic repertoire of dance activity consists of innumerable well-defined gestures of the hands and arms, combined with quite restricted foot and leg motion. The gestures are usually presented two or three times over the length of two or three musical phrases, and are then changed. Thus succession of novel motions is formed, and it is easy for the dancer to vary his routine according to the music: he has only to introduce more and more items of his basic stock of gestures for as long as the damburači feels like playing (gestures can, of course, be repeated as well).

It is thus the interest in creating a lively and interesting dance that motivates the damburači in performing his instrumental tunes. Even where there is no dancer present (as was usually the case at recording sessions), it seems that the artist keeps a dance routine in mind while varying his phrases. In the case of a fine performer like Aq Pišak, this means that, for example, seven performances of a basic Aqčai will come out markedly different as he stretches or curtails sections to fit his fancy.

Let us now turn to Aq Pišak's Aqčai (Example 10, and nağma 2 in Table 3.1 below). Only the basic sections are given, in their simplest forms, for purposes of analysis. Preceding section A is a brief introduction, which is worthy of mention because of its extreme simplicity: it merely outlines the basic fourth (d'–g') of the open strings, which is the tonic sound of the entire piece. Section A initially presents the pitch f', thus stressing the third between d' and f', and adds, in turn, g' and a' as additional pitches; with the introduction of a', a new third (f'–a') is established. The subsequent measures of section A represent a stepwise descent to the lower tonic, d', returning the nağma to its opening state. A is thus a self-enclosed segment, in which a modest degree of departure and return is suggested through the stress on f′ (and its upper auxiliary a′). Of particular interest is the type of stroke in section A. This is a careful strum using only the index finger for plucking the string, while the middle finger regularly taps on the resonant lid of the dambura to produce a distinctive accentuation pattern and timbre. Also important is the fact that section A is played without any lower-string drone.

B provides as much contrast as possible in the world of the dambura. First to strike the ear are the changes in texture and accentuation: the lower-string pitch now becomes a drone, and a new type of stress is introduced. This is the full-bodied accent (marked >), which is the simultaneous striking of three or four fingers on the lid in a kind of scraping follow-through of the whole-hand stroke. The dambura is thus being used at maximum volume to define the new section. Another integral part of B is the shift in register we have come by now to expect of new segments of the nağma. First to be heard is the pitch a′, only briefly referred to before, but now stressed for two full measures. Next, the entire span of a′–d″ is suddenly introduced in a descending sequence that finally brings us down to g′, the upper tonic. The rhythmic figuration of B is also novel: triplet sixteenths take the place of even eighths as the basic time unit.

Aq Pišak now needs a way to get back to section A. Thinking back to the dance situation, we note that he has shifted from a steady-paced, quiet section to one that is more agitated and louder; translated into dance steps, this implies slower to faster motion. The damburači must now supply a bridge to bring the dancer back to the original pace of the nağma, or risk an uncoordinated shift of steps.

Example 10. "Aqčai" (dambura)

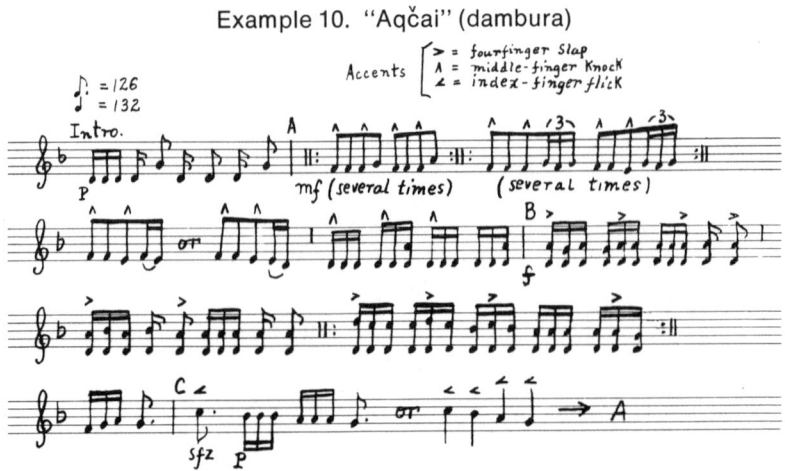

Section C provides the needed transition. It introduces no new pitches, but achieves tonal distinctiveness by stressing the range of a fourth between c″ and g′, a hitherto neglected tessitura. In addition, the feature of accent again appears as a major structural determinant, as Aq Pišak comes up with yet another stroke — the third basic available coloring. The stroke, called *kār-i naxun,* consists of a flick with the index finger against the uppermost part of the dambura lid, near the neck. A hard, dry, dead sound results, which is almost pitchless and highly distinctive. It may, of course, be possible analytically to link section C with B and explain it as a bridge phrase, usually quite brief, with no independent status. However, on a theoretical basis, the pitch content and accent type of section C seem to qualify it for special labeling. In addition, we shall see in Table 3.1 that section C can live a life of its own in some of the versions of the Aqčai nağma.

Table 3.1 gives the findings of a comparison of seven Aqčai nağmas by Aq Pišak. It may be added that these "seven pieces" (in effect only one nağma played seven ways) constitute perhaps up to one-third of Aq Pišak's total repertoire of purely instrumental compositions, according to his tally.

To supplement the table, it should be noted that the length of versions ranges from 4 minutes, 1 second to 8 minutes, 10 seconds, making the longest Aqčai roughly twice as extensive as the shortest variant. Tempo remains fairly constant, with MM 116 to the quarter-note about average.

Table 3.1 provides both a norm for performance and grounds for evidence of significant variability. The norm can be seen in versions 1–4, with some deviation in version 2: the number of statements is quite close for all three sections, and the average time per statement runs in the order A,B,C, — from longest to shortest. Finally, the percentage of section A in the total time is remarkably constant in the first four Aqčais (58 percent for the first three, 60 percent for the fourth), as is the proportion holding between sections B and C. Thus a considerable degree of uniformity is present.

Turning to versions 5–7, however, we find that a marked degree of variability can also occur. This falls into two main categories: one, represented by versions 5 and 7, exhibits an increased emphasis on section A, which now takes up roughly three-quarters of the total time and lasts up to 42 seconds per statement. C remains constant at its lowest level, at 6 percent of the total time and about 3 seconds per statement. The other area of variation is reflected in version 6, in which "the worm turns," as C comes quite close to the figures for A, leaving B a poor third. Translated into musical terms, these figures

TABLE 3.1

Comparison of Seven "Aqčai" Nağmas by Aq Pišak

Nağma	Section	Number of Statements	Average Time per Statement (In Secs.)	Percentage of Total Time	Order of Sections
1	A	8	17	58	
	B	8	9	30	:ABC:
	C	8	4	12	(8x)
2	A	8	17	58	:ABCAC: ABCA
	B	4	4	24	(4x)
	C	7	6	18	
3	A	8	22	58	
	B	7	14	31	:ABC: A
	C	7	3	11	(7x)
4	A	8	26	60	
	B	8	12	27	
	C	7	5.5	13	:ABC: AB
5	A	7	27	72	
	B	6	19	22	:ABC: A
	C	6	2.5	6	(6x)
6	A	12	15	46	AC :ABCAC:
	B	6	10	15	(4x)
	C	11	13	39	
7	A	9	42	77	BCABC :ABC: A
	B	9	9	17	(7x)
	C	9	3	6	

indicate Aq Pišak's interest in making his bridge section, C, an interesting and highly elaborated part of the piece, rather than just a few perfunctory flicks of the finger to warn the dancer.

In another area of structural interest (shown in the column marked "Order of Sections"), the existence both of a standard method of performance and of significant variation is also manifested. Here the standard seems to be strong reliance on the straightforward sequential presentation of sections A, B, and C (in versions 1, 3, 4, 5, 7). Variability takes two main forms. One is in the choice of sections to precede or follow the repetitions of the ABC ordering: thus, whereas versions 3, 4, and 5 merely add on an extra A or AB at the end, version 7 begins the whole structure with the chain BCABC, and version 1 keeps to just the ABC alone. The other type of variability is the substitution of a different basic unit, ABCAC, for the simpler ABC (versions 2, 6). Even this scheme is not uniformly carried out, for in version 2 Aq Pišak adds an ABCA grouping to the basic unit, while in version 6 he begins the unit with an AC statement.

Such a creative approach to structure is rare among damburačis; even among Aq Pišak's variants there is a standard approach. When a break with the usual is effected, however, as in the lengthening of the C section in version 6, it is always appreciated by the members of the audience, who nod their heads and utter laudatory interjections. One wonders whether it is merely the recent increase in outside musical influence that has so restricted the flexibility of the dambura repertoire, or whether it has always been the case that a very few musicians have been able to make the nağma a plastic, individualized means of expression.

Turning to the secular tale "Zibajan," we shall only comment briefly on the musical setting of the excerpt that was discussed fully from the textual point of view in Chapter 2. Example 11 shows a pattern of text distribution and melody that we have not seen heretofore. Four lines of text form the basic strophic unit, but unlike the Uzbek quatrain setting we examined earlier (Example 4), it has no refrain; the story moves ahead at a steady pace. In addition, the *a a b b* rhyme scheme of the tale, unlike that of the teahouse čarbaiti, seems to lend itself to two-line groupings in melodic terms. Thus, the four lines are organized 2 + 2 with a melodic AA′ pattern in which the main difference between the two halves of the strophe consists of the ending. It is rather more like the Western concept of "question and answer" phrases than like the verse-refrain structure of the čarbaiti or the melodic-differentiation principle of binary instrumental tunes (Example 1). The very steady 2/4 drum beat combined with the very nearly syllabic text adds to the narrative quality of the setting. Taken as a

Example 11. "Zibājān" excerpt

whole, this setting of "Zibajan" by Xodaiqul Širintagowi seems musically distinctive within the Turkestani context and can perhaps be labeled "Uzbek" in conception.

The Turkmens

For reasons of balance, the following presentation of Turkmen music is far from complete, though thorough discussion of Turkmen music (whether of Iranian, Afghan, or Soviet Turkmens) is practically nonexistent outside a single seminal book (Beliaev and Uspenskii 1928). The range of Turkmen vocal and instrumental music and its structural complexity render the task of condensed presentation difficult, but I shall attempt to summarize the key points in the exposition below. For a more comprehensive survey of instrumental music the reader is referred to Slobin 1969.

To focus on the considerable difference between Turkmen music and that of various other subcultures, it is useful to begin with the heart of the instrumental tradition; the repertoire of the dutar, the principal lute used by Turkmens and the single lute common only to Turkmens.

Turkmen music differs sharply from most of Uzbek-Tajik music of Turkestan, Katağan, and Badaxšan in three main areas: (1) the basic structural approaches (outlined below), (2) the existence of modes (defined below) as a foundation for tonal orientation instead of the focus on single tonic and alternating pitches found in Uzbek-Tajik music, and (3) the frequent appearance of wavering or free rhythms instead of a fixed musical-metrical pattern. Individual pieces will serve as examples of all three points.

Our first specimen is the nağma called "Nawai" (Example 12). Though it does not have a wavering or free rhythm, it furnishes fine examples of basic structural and modal characteristics, which are the main facets of Turkmen music to be discussed.

The basis of "Nawai," a typical dutar piece, is a series of returns to the tonic. Each section (marked A-D in Example 12) is distinguished by its point of departure, i.e., distance from the tonic; hence segments can be lined up by their endings, rather than by their beginnings, as would be the case with Uzbek-Tajik music. Figure 3.2 represents schematically the structural difference between hypothetical dutar and dambura pieces. In the "converging-line" structure of a dutar piece, the successive sections each start at a different point above the plane of the tonic, only to descend gradually, with the frequent use of melodic sequence, to the basic pitch level. In our hypothetical dambura piece, on the other hand, sections A and B follow parallel, rather than converging, lines, with each firmly entrenched in its own particular ambit.

Example 12. "Nawai"

(continued)

188

Example 12. "Nawai" *(continued)*

Let us turn to the concrete example at hand, "Nawai." Example 13 reduces this nağma to a schematic score, which shows the key pitches of each section in terms of frequency of repetition. The score shows that while sections A and D represent a small ambitus, ranging as far as a fifth from the tonic (a′), parts B and D range much farther, reaching up to the octave (a″) before sinking back down to home base. "Nawai" has a rather simple structural outline; we shall see below that its divi-

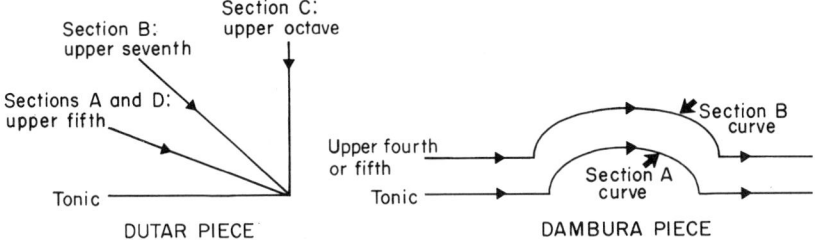

Fig. 3.2. Diagram of hypothetical dutar and dambura tunes

sion into merely four sections, in such a clear pattern as A = D, B = C, is somewhat atypical in its low degree of complexity.

We have defined the tonic as the pitch a'; yet the piece begins with a short introduction that has as its object the stressing of the pitch g', in the chord d'–g' (the open-string sound), and the work closes with a clear return to d'–g' as cadential sound. Does this not point to a clear affinity to dambura music, as described above, instead of to a distinctive modal system? The answer is yes and no. While it is true that the simultaneous sounding of the two open-string pitches forms the most "stable" or "tonic-like" tonal grouping of all dutar pieces, the data show that throughout the greater part of a piece the player may ignore this chord as tonal basis, preferring another pitch, which I call the provisional tonic.

In "Nawai" this provisional tonic is the note a', the second degree of the scale employed; in other pieces it may be the third, or another degree. Such reliance on pitches other than the lowest as the basis of tonal orientation is characteristic of many "modes" of the Near East, and it allows us to consider classifying the Turkmen way of tonal thinking as a modal approach. Axmad-baxši told me that each piece has a particular beginning, resting spot, and ending point. As it happens, seven of the thirteen pieces he played use the lowest pitches both as beginning and ending tonic and as provisional resting point. While this indicates the strength of the open-string notes, the presence of as many as six out of thirteen pieces that do not rely on the lowest melodic pitch confirms the existence of a modal way of tonal thinking. Among these

Example 13. Outline of Example 12 ("Nawai")

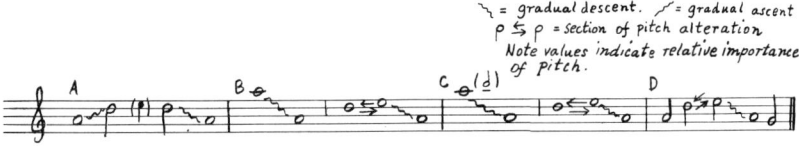

six works, two rely on the second degree, three on the third degree, and one of the second plus the fifth degree as the provisional tonic.

If we look again at the division of "Nawai" into four sections, we find that Axmad-baxši has provided an extensive codetta for each section, which emphasizes dramatically the return to the tonic. It comes in the form of a series of triplet figures that stand out sharply against the primarily duple time maintained in the earlier segments of each major section. These codettas merely serve to stress the tonic pitch. Another feature setting off the parts of each section is the use of the lower-string drone. At the opening of major units, the open-string drone is maintained; then, as the descent to the tonic, or further elaboration of the upper tessitura, begins, the lower-string pitch shifts, at times attaining considerable mobility. This flexible approach to the lower string sets off the music of the Turkmens sharply from that of their Uzbek and Tajik neighbors. It also links the style of the Turkmen dutar to that of most other Central Asian lute types, including the Uzbek dutar, Kazakh dümbra, and Kirghiz komuz (but excepting the dambura). The Turkmen use of the lower string is largely a matter of establishing temporary drone pitches, rather than maintaining a chain of parallel intervals (fourths and fifths), though the latter technique is also open to the dutarist.

Looking at the overall melodic skeleton of "Nawai" given in Example 13, it becomes apparent that fourths and fifths provide the basic tonal outline, as is the case of all Central Asian lute music. Of particular interest tonally is the alteration between d″ and e″ in all four sections; this changing off of the fourth and fifth above the tonic is a feature previously noted in dambura music, and applies as well to other neighboring lute styles. The basic compass of an octave is also a familiar aspect of instrumental play.

Finally, the melodic arch formed by the overall design of "Nawai" should not be overlooked. As a basic contour of instrumental music, the arch typifies nine out of the thirteen pieces played by Axmad-baxši, and once again links Turkmen lute music to other regional styles, notably those of the Kazakhs and Kirghiz, and to the basic form of "classical" Uzbekistani music, in which the principle of a major rise at the middle of the piece is given a special name *(auj)*. The arched contour of "Nawai" is emphasized by the great amount of time spent on sections B and C, in which the upper tessitura is presented: together, they occupy 2 minutes, 16 seconds of the total 3 minutes, 20 seconds of "Nawai." In this respect, "Nawai" is somewhat atypical of Turkmen dutar style.

"Nawai" has provided us with the basic outlines of the dutar tradition. Clearly, that tradition is based on a more complex musical germ than is the repertoire of the Turkestani dambura. Here, instead of the standard tonic-centered strophic forms of the Uzbek-Tajik style, we find a well-expressed modal approach, coupled with what could be called a twofold formal design. One facet of this structure calls for a series of near- and far-ranging departures from the tonic, with well-marked returns, while the other specifies an overall pattern which, in "Nawai," takes the shape of an arched contour.

Thanks to the cooperation of the Union of Composers of the Turkmen SSR, "Nawai" provides material for a comparison of the music of contemporary Soviet Turkmens with that of Axmad-baxši. Officials of the Union were kind enough to present some live music for me during a brief visit to Ashkhabad in December, 1968, and I prevailed upon the doyen of Turkmen dutarists, Chari Tashmahmedov, to play a version of "Nawai" for me.

It was gratifyingly to find that Tashmahmedov's performance of "Nawai" is remarkably similar to Axmad-baxši's. Both feature the same mode, based on the second degree of the scale, and the same skeletal outline of tonal orientation, although the Ashkhabad virtuoso rises to the climatic topmost pitches only once in the course of performance rather than twice, as in Example 12. This high concurrence of basic structural elements confirms the importance of overall contour and tonal orientation of sections as the defining traits of a given Turkmen piece, particularly since in every other detail (rhythmic figuration, length of sections, treatment of polyphony, etc.) the two versions of "Nawai" differ widely. Thus, despite these personal (or tribal?) differences of style, Turkmen music can be seen as basically similar on both sides of the Afghan-Soviet border today. This is not the case for music of the Uzbeks and Tajiks of Afghan Turkestan, whose styles find no obvious parallels in Transoxania. The situation of the Turkmens is closer to that of the Badaxšanis in respect to transborder similarities, as we shall see below.

Before leaving "Nawai," it is worthwhile mentioning the tradition connected with the piece cited by Axmad-baxši. According to him, if "Nawai" is played a thousand times, a *peri* (fairy) will appear. It is necessary to play another piece, "Baiqara," to send the peri back to fairyland.

Let us turn to a second example of dutar style for comparison and contrast. This is the piece "Uğulbeg" (Example 14), a favorite tune of all Turkmens, derived from the song of the same name. A. Rejepov

192

Example 14. "Uǧulbeg" (dutar version)

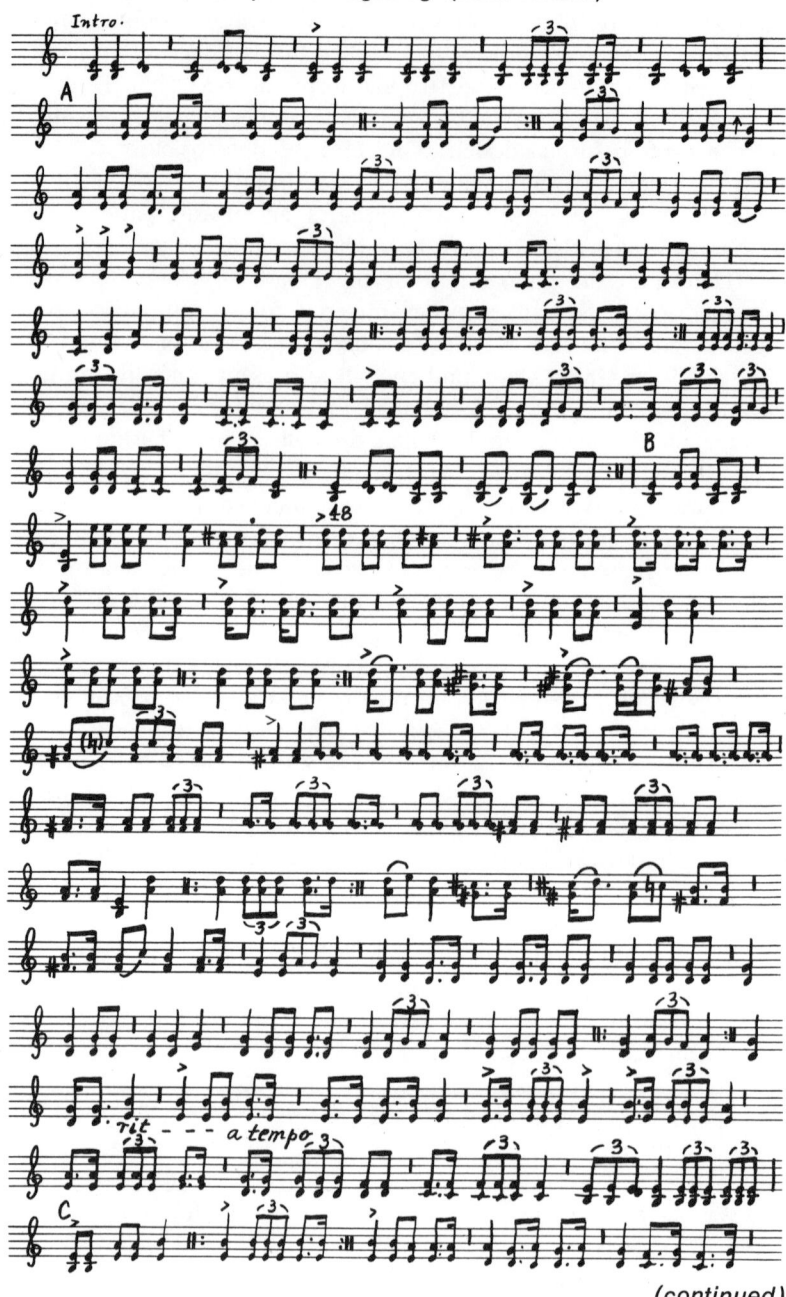

(continued)

Example 14. "Uğulbeg" (dutar version) *(continued)*

(continued)

Example 14. "Uğulbeg" (dutar version) *(continued)*

(1966:5) notes that "every Turkmen knows the song 'Ogul-beg' to the words of Kemine, composed by the baxši Kior-Kojali." A song of the same name is included in Beliaev and Uspenskii's *Turkmenskaia muzyka* (1928). Axmad-baxši showed particular respect for "Uğulbeg."

In contrast to "Nawai," "Ugulbeg" is firmly based on the lowest melodic pitch (e′) as tonic. Also quite different from Example 13 is the structural scheme of "Uğulbeg," which is presented in Example 15. Here, instead of a clear-cut four-part design, we find an eight-part, somewhat more ambiguous patterning of musical elements. Unequivocal is the descent of each section to the tonic in the converging-line method noted above as typical of dutar style. Though "Uğulbeg" lasts considerably longer than "Nawai" (4 minutes, 5 seconds vs. 3 minutes, 20 seconds), there is no dominant lengthy section, but rather a succession of episodes of varying lengths, ranging from 12 to 53 seconds in duration.

Looking more closely at the structure, it becomes apparent that certain similarities link specific sections. Parts A, C, E, G, and H are near-ranging, while B, D and F are far-ranging. The former segments are the shortest in length of the piece, while the latter are considerably longer on the average. Statistically, this is reflected in the fact that the three sections B, D, and F outweigh the remaining segments in total time (133 seconds vs. 102 seconds) and in average length (44 seconds vs. 20 seconds) by a considerable margin. Hence, though the stability of the lower, more tonic-affirming range is assured by more repetitions (five sections vs. three), the far-ranging, less tonic-centered sections carry greater overall weight in terms of duration.

Of the far-ranging sections, F is the most important, both in duration and in structural significance, since it reaches the highest pitch of the piece (f♯″) and takes the longest time getting back down to the tonic. If, then, we visualize the overall structure as being one of alternation of near- and far-ranging sections, we can also notice a certain tendency toward a slight arch in the rise of F to greatest heights and its stress of the upper register. Structurally, "Uğulbeg" is thus rather close to "Nawai" in general design.

In terms of scalar patterning, "Uğulbeg" furnishes material for several conclusions. These refer to the type of interval considered basic in dutar playing. Looking over Example 14, it can be seen that the tonic (e′) can be approached two ways: from the upper fourth (a′) and from the upped fifth (b′). Of these possibilities, the first is used five times and the second three times, clearly pointing up the importance of the interval between the lower and upper open-string pitches, noted earlier as a key factor in dambura music and as a unifying element

Example 15. Outline of Example 14. ("Uğulbeg")

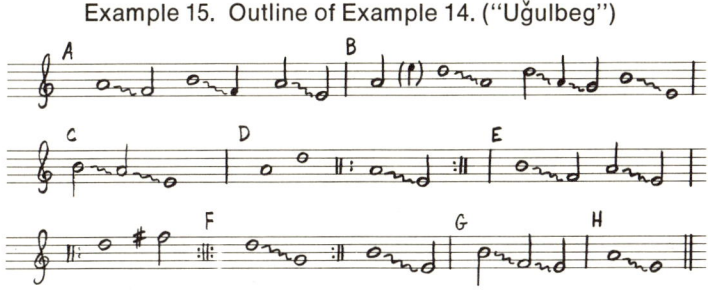

among various Central Asian lute styles. We have also noted that alternation between the upper fourth and fifth constitutes a standard tonal tendency.

A further look at Example 14 shows some other possible foci of tonal orientation. One of these is the fourth (a′–d″) above that just cited (e′–a′), which presents a logical extension, in a higher range, of a tonal relationship set up at the level of the tonic. A second auxiliary interval is the topmost extension of the scale, in the form of the third d″–f♯″. This expression of the second degree of the scale (f) in a raised form in the upper octave is typical not only for Turkmen music, but for several Central Asian styles (Uzbek dutar music, some dambura pieces, etc.). It must be considered a particular tonal habit among the peoples concerned. D″ is also the upper tone of a fifth g′–d″ in the latter half of section F. Thus, a profile of key pitches describes, for the most part, a chain of thirds running e′–g′–b′–d″–f♯″, with the only notable exception being the important note a′, whose role in the tonic-upper-fourth axis was just discussed. Such a tendency to create a chain of thirds links the tradition of the Turkmen dutar once more to that of the Turkestani dambura and the Kirghiz komuz.

Turning from this structural and scalar analysis to other aspects of "Uǧulbeg," we find that Axmad-baxši has once again employed a simple marked rhythm, here given as 3/4, with a regular accent on beat one of each measure. The performer's penchant for introducing triplet figurations is again noticeable, though here it serves to break up the steady quarter-note pulse instead of to define a codetta section, as in "Nawai."

An important trait of dutar style exhibited in "Nawai" and in "Uǧulbeg" is the ample length of time spent in establishing key melodic pitches, a characteristic that makes it possible to construct skeletal outlines such as those of Examples 13 and 15. In "Uǧulbeg" note, for example, the repetitive stressing of the important e′–a′ chord at the outset of the piece (measures 8–17) before the tune turns toward greater mobility. The same is true of the appearance of nearly every main pitch of the piece, e.g., the nearly twelve measures spent in emphasizing d″ as the main note of the first part of section B (measures 48–59) or the six important measures (171–176) devoted to hammering out the tonic before the onset of section F, the segment with the farthest departure from home base. Hanging the tune on such strong nails gives dutar music its unmistakable structure, against which the continual motion of the melody away from and back toward the tonic stands out in clear relief.

The pitch content of "Uǧulbeg" describes a scale that is basically

Phrygian. Phrygian scales characterize nine out of the thirteen pieces played by Axmad-baxši, with the rest split between major-like and minor-like patterns. Considering e′ as the tonic of Example 14, we have a fourth below and a tenth above; such a wide overall range characterizes most of Turkmen music, in sharp contrast to Uzbek-Tajik tradition, particularly that of Badaxšan. The f♯′, g♯′, and c♯′ found in "Uğulbeg" do not upset the Phrygian orientation of the scale, since they occur almost exlusively to create perfect fourths with other pitches, and do not have a major autonomous role in the melody. This changing of tones to fit vertical tonal needs points up the importance of polyphony in the lute styles of Central Asia. The c♯″ and f♯″ of section F, on the other hand, do not stem from requirements of polyphony. These pitches serve to mark off F as a section of special interest and could perhaps be interpreted as a scalar modulation; unfortunately, there are not enough examples of such shifts in the available repertoire to enable us to draw conclusions about this aspect of tonal thinking.

Looking more closely at the polyphony introduced in "Uğulbeg," several principles become apparent. Most obvious is the strong predilection for parallel fourths, which occur to a much higher degree than in "Nawai." Another principle, however, is also in use: the establishment of temporary drone pitches to create islands of stability in the flux of the melody. Thus, for example, the main melodic phrase of "Uğulbeg," as given in measures 14–27 for the first time, consists of a stepwise descent of drone pitches (e′–d′–c′) over which the melodic figuration runs.

In addition to providing this smoothly flowing sequence of parallel fourths and shifting drone-tones, polyphony can also serve to produce sudden stress. A good example of this approach occurs at measure 185, where Axmad-baxši reaches out for the highest pitch of the piece (f♯″) and simultaneously lets the drone fall a whole fourth, cutting the musical ground away to emphasize the high point.

We can examine Turkmen song in the light of instrumental music by comparing vocal and instrumental versions of the same piece. Example 16 is the song we just looked at in dutar arrangement, "Uğulbeg." It should first be noted that the dutar takes up an average of 27 percent of the total time in an accompanied song (this figure is based on a sample of six key songs of Axmad-baxši); dutar activity consists of a prelude, a postlude, and numerous interludes, some of which can be seen in Example 16. These instrumental sections are considered by performers to be essential components of a song. Though instrumental interpositions occur in various repertoires of the North, nowhere are they as systematic nor do they occupy as much time as in Turkmen music.

Vocal versions of a given piece tend to be much longer than purely instrumental renditions (20–40 percent longer) and to rely on a quite different structural principle from the intricate multisectional arrangement of dutar performances: all songs are strophic, and thus squarely in the mainstream of northern music. The distinguishing

Example 16. "Uǧulbeg" (vocal version)

(hummed)

marks of Turkmen songs are: (1) the great length of the strophe, which is much larger in scale than any stanzas of Uzbek or Tajik songs, and (2) the sharply defined profile of the strophe, which consists of a melodic, dynamic, and expressive fall from an initial peak of register and intensity to a section of highly stylized vocalise ornamentation at the end of each verse. Generally under such conditions of protracted strophic development a song cannot contain more than two or three verses.

Looking at Example 16, one can easily spot the intense opening cry on a single long pitch; this is followed by a brief dutar interlude setting the tessitura, which is maintained for one more line of text, then the vocal line proceeds to unwind its long melismatic descent, stopping at key pitches highlighted by instrumental underscoring and ending in a brief hummed passage at the lowest, tonic level before the arduous declamatory process begins again as the second strophe. Humming is a rather modest form of verse-closing ornamentation (*gul*, "flower"); performers stock a variety of short repeated cries on single syllables ("i, i, i," "ei, ei, ei," etc.). A brief discussion of Turkmen forms of verse was included in Chapter 2; below is the full text of "Uğulbeg." Interestingly, Axmad-baxši's performance seems to combine the characteristics of both xalqi (shared) and uzuridan (private) verse styles, since according to Turkmen sources the first ten lines are standard while the last five are weaker, personal additions to the text.

Asmāning gunisan zemining ai
Gulum rošan tofar gurdigum sai
Dunyāning zinati san yārim ai
Gara ğarai guzler bilan
Guzleš masek bāl mağali
Sirin šakaria suzler bilen
Suzleš masek bāl mağali
Tarxi xinali quallar menam
Tutu masa bāl mağali
Dunyāning zinati Uğulbeg.
Salaranda sačbāğ laring seseda
Qiğirinda qišgularni yazada
Basqadam dida ustundan yar
Jup basan ayaq lerindan
Qoyun sagmana čekupsen.

You are the sun, the moon and the earth
When I see you my eyes brighten
My love is the beauty of the world
If we don't look at each other's black eyes
There can be nothing

If we don't speak with sweet tongues
There can be nothing
If we don't take each other by henna'd hands
There can be nothing
Uğulbeg is the beauty of the world
The hanging braids are rustling
When you call me winter turns to spring
Put your foot on my eyes
Put both feet together
You went milking sheep.

Let us round out this brief survey of Turkmen vocal styles with an
example of epic recitation (unaccompanied). Here we shall look at
an excerpt from the widespread "Köroğlu" tale, (Example 17) as
performed by Said Murad of Qizilayaq.

Example 17 indicates that Said Murad's approach to epic recitation
contains elements found in various local narrative traditions: narrowness of range and paucity of melodic elements, creating a parlando-
rubato style that highlights the clear projection of text. It might be
useful to compare the "Köroğlu" excerpt with the sample of an Uzbek
tale given earlier (Example 11). Both are based on two fundamental
melodic lines that alternate, but the differences within this approach
are significant. The Uzbek lines differ at the end, making a complete
unit through a cadential formula after the second line. The Turkmen
lines, on the other hand, have the same cadence but are basically different at their beginnings, spaced a neutral third apart (c′–low e″).
The Turkmen approach seems to correspond to the formal concept
underlying the dutar pieces we have examined, with their sections
marked by varied beginnings and identical cadences; perhaps the stylistic
overlap in two Turkmen genres indicates a general approach to musical
structure. Below is the text of Said Murad's excerpt from "Köroğlu,"
as translated by Karim Jigar of Kabul. (Said Murad's dialect has been
standardized.)

Example 17. "Köroğlu" excerpt

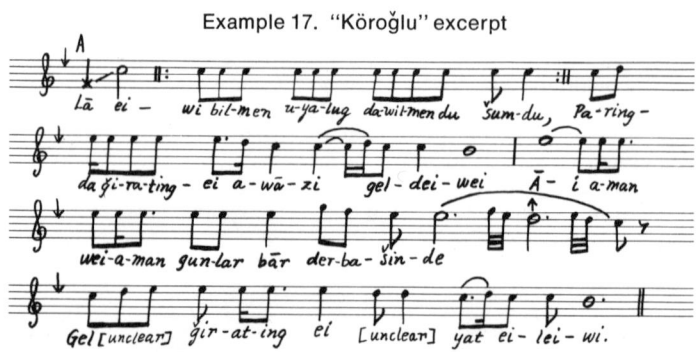

Bilmen uyaluq dawil men dušunda
Parangda ğirating awazi geldi*
Aman gunlar bar der mening bāšinda
Gel Guroğlu ğiratangni yat eila
Gira sis barma dāğlara seila
Parišan qesmatim yazuldi seila
Aqlayuq ğirating awāzi geldi
Ğiratim bar unuč untort yāšinda
Dila tila jigasi barder bāšinda
Yezid maskan tutar unin dāšinda
Indi man nadayin dunyā wa genji
Ber awāzi geldi yiğlap narenji.

I do not know if I am asleep or awake
The voice of Girat [Guroğlu's horse] came from the mountain
Woe, a bad day has befallen me
Come, Guroğlu, remember your horse
Do not go into the mountain without your horse
My fate, afflicted, has been written this way
I hear the weeping voice of Ğirat.
I have one Ğirat, thirteen-fourteen years old
The horse has a golden topknot
The troops of my enemy surround my horse
Of what use are jewels and the world without my horse?
I hear a horse's weeping voice.

*This line sometimes repeated between lines, and appears at last line of complete text.

Before leaving Turkmen music, let us look at two short examples representing the flute and pipe traditions. Turning first to the repertoire of the tüidük (long open end-blown flute), we shall investigate a brief piece, "Wāğelbeg" (Example 18), to delineate the basic structural elements.

Like all Tüidük pieces, "Wağelbeg" opens with a short introduction on one breath and moves through a sequence of additional single-breath phrases, each about 5 seconds in length. Groups of phrases make up distinct sections of the piece, definable in the same terms as the sections of a dutar nağma, i.e., by departure and return relative to a tonic pitch, and sections are differentiated by the tessitura they take as a launching point for the inevitable return to home base.

"Wağelbeg" contains four basic sections. A and B consist of two breaths and are near-ranging, while C takes up five breath-phrases and is clearly the climactic section of the piece. The concluding section D, four phrases long, consists of a somewhat less steep descent than in C and stresses the tonic (g') briefly (end of phrase 12) before descending for the last time.

In terms of basic structure there is little or no difference between a tüidük piece and a dutar piece. There is, however, a certain necessary degree of variation in the approach to the form. The tüidük must do without the polyphonic resources of the dutar and thus relies completely on melodic emphasis for stress of key notes. This is accomplished by introducing carefully placed melismatic turns around the important pitches, and by spending entire breath-phrases on the stressing of these notes. For example, phrase 4 consists merely of an ornamented c″, and phrase 6, which carries the burden of introducing the new tessitura of section C, does nothing more than underline the main pitch, f″. In all, six of the fourteen phrases of "Waǧelbeg" exist primarily to emphasize a single pitch.

The extreme brevity of "Waǧelbeg," which is shared by most tüidük tunes, forces the player to come to a cadence fairly often in order to accommodate four sections in such a short time. Thus, four of the fourteen phrases are devoted merely to the cadential drop of a fifth from d″ to the tonic, g′. If the six pitch-affirming phrases mentioned above are then added to the four cadential phases, only four breaths remain in which the player can introduce tonal variety. These must

Example 18. "Waǧelbeg" (tüidük)

perforce serve as bridges between pitches. For example, phrase 8 takes the listener down from the heights of the pitch f″, stressed for two consecutive previous phrases, and leads the ear to c″, the subject of the following pitch-affirming phrase (9). It can readily be seen that tüidük pieces are a good testing ground for theories of scalar outline in Turkmen music. Looking over the basic intervals, we find no surprises. The fourth and fifth above the tonic (c″ and d″ respectively) are the main centers of tonal orientation, and the two notes are presented in alternation. Perhaps the great stress laid on f″, a fourth above the fourth above the tonic (an interval totaling a minor seventh), is not quite so familiar from the pieces analyzed previously. Emphasis on the seventh above the tonic seems to typify tüidük tunes more than dutar naǧmas, but it is found in a variety of musical styles of the North, and in other Central Asian musical styles as well. For example, a chain of two, or even three, fourths is a basic structure in Kirghiz instrumental music.

That Soviet Turkmen music is similar to styles analyzed here is indicated by Beliaev's description of tüidük pieces (1975):

Tüidük pieces are built like professional vocal compositions, with descending melodic contour. They are often instrumental versions of these songs . . . broad descending melodies, beginning in the upper register, are often cast in recitative vein and end with refrain-like turns of phrase.

"Waǧelbeg" could as easily be approached from Beliaev's description as from the analysis given above; this would be particularly fruitful if the song from which the piece is taken were available.

As for the reed pipe (dili-tüidük), Beliaev states that it "is originally a pastoral instrument, and it is mostly pastoral tunes and folk songs that are played on it." Indeed, dili-tüidük tunes seem freer and more dance-like in character, a trait confirmed by Surxi's description of the use of the reed pipe as occasional accompaniment to dance. Example 19 is a dili-tüidük tune by Ana Durdi of Quizilayaq, who is so accomplished a pipe player as to merit the sobriquet of "baxši," rarely accorded dili-tüidük players.

Ana Durdi's tune seems divided between a drawn-out phrase (A), typical of vocal or perhaps tüidük music, and a rhythmic repeated phrase of differing character (B); the two alternate with some variation at each statement. The opening line, akin to A in material, has an introductory character that is common to many beginning phrases of tüidük pieces.

Summarizing Turkmen music after so cursory an investigation is not easy. The point germane to the general argument of the present

Example 19. Dili-Tüidük Tune

study is that while certain elements of Turkmen music relate to surrounding music cultures (e.g., the long-necked lute polyphony per se is related to styles ranging from Anatolia to Kirghizia), there is a remarkably solid core of distinctive musical thought. Turkmen music remains one of the most distinctive of the subcultures in the North, just as the entire Turkmen way of life continues to be fairly remote from the mainstream of an emerging national Afghan consciousness.

Pamir Peoples and Mountain Tajiks

I do not wish at this point to present a case for a distinctive Pamir music subculture, for three reasons: (1) I have not myself collected purely Pamir music, and would rather not introduce extensive examples from the Soviet side (save for counterpart materials) in a study devoted to Afghanistan; (2) available data do not yield a clear picture of what a Pamir music might include, beyond special tunes on the local lute (the Pamir robab); and (3) a good deal of the Badaxšani music presented below is also shared by Pamir peoples.

For Badaxšan I shall first present an instrumental tune, to introduce the basic stylistic characteristics, followed by a song by the same performer, and then take a short look at the Badaxšani flute repertoire with a complementary Soviet selection. The first performer is Adinabeg, an amateur dambura player from Darwaz, the northernmost region of Badaxšan. As noted in Chapter 2, the most uniquely Badaxšani of forms is the felak, a genre that embraces sung quatrains and instrumental variants thereof.

Example 20 is a fine example of up-country instrumental style. The A section is the true Badaxšani vamp, consisting of the alternation of two chords: one is merely the strumming of the open strings (e' and a'), while the other g'–a') is the most prominent major second of all northern Afghanistan. This fourth-second refrain is a hallmark of Badaxšani style. Also highly characteristic of the A section is the fluctuating rhythmic pattern of the phrases. Each phrase ends with a quarter-note e'–a' chord, yet the length of the statements varies from three beats to nine in strophe 1 and from two beats to sixteen in strophe 3. Section A is the true amad cited by Baba Naim in his analysis of Badaxšani music. It provides basic stability for the piece, and gives the performer some time to think between strophes; this latter function is particularly important for the vocal felak (see Example 21), in which the player must think up the next verse of the song.

The B section of Adinabeg's felak differs most markedly from its A segment in tonal materials. A principal distinction is made in

Example 20. Adinabeg's *Felak* (dambura)

scalar terms by the introduction of a drone pitch (f♯′) above the lower open-string tonic (e′) stressed by A, and by the opening up of three new pitches (a♯′, b′, and c♯″) previously unheard. Tonally, a workable amount of variety has been achieved by the use of remarkably few tones and a very narrow melodic range. The total supradrone compass comprises only the major third from a′ to c♯″. This extraordinary economy of ambit is quite typical of Badax̌sani music and is one of its outstanding characteristics. Against this meager setting, even the fifth and sixth of Turkestani tunes seem wide-ranging.

Turning to other aspects of Example 20, we note that B hardly diverges from A in rhythmic patterning. The brief outburst of short note values heard in strophe 1 can be seen as exceptional, and the bulk of B moves in the same eighth-note pairs that characterize most of A. The uneven phrase lengths of B also match those of A. Another noticeable trait is the extreme austerity of phrasing, which allows for practically no ornamentation of basic pitches. The single grace note heard in section B stands out sharply in relief against the progression of plain notes. The main interest of B, as noted above, is tonal; the slight melodic turn provided by the downward half-step b′–a♯′, which is reciprocated by the upward turn b′–c♯″, is heard as a striking departure in the tune.

In terms of durational stress, section B occupies 56 percent of the total time, and section A only 44 percent; the average statement of B takes 21 seconds, while that of A lasts only 13 seconds. Though the amad provided by A gives great stability to the felak, it is the divergence from the vamp that takes up most of the time in the piece. This is another feature linking Adinabeg's felak to general Badax̌sani practice.

Adinabeg's felak, this time in song form (Example 21), can be used to indicate the relationship between vocal and instrumental styles in the case of a single performer. Here is the text and translation:

> Zardalui zard (ei) (ke) jigar buryānam (ei)
> Dar mulke musāferi ajab heirānam (ei)
> Yak panjai xat (ei) namiyād az suye watan (ei)
> Yak yāre aziz guftam o faryād kunam (ei)

> My fried liver is like a yellow apricot
> I am at a loss in a strange place
> I don't get any letters from home
> I say "dear friend" and cry.

The text is characteristic of a great many čarbaiti, or quatrains, used for the felak. The content is the usual desolation, here in the form of the loneliness of the traveler, a common theme. The *a a b a* rhyme scheme is standard, as are the interjections (in parentheses) at the middle and at the end of lines. The reference to "fried liver" is not culinary; Persian poetry and colloquial speech refers to the liver much as English uses the heart as the bodily center of emotions, and "fried" indicates a state of extreme grief.

Turning to musical analysis, we see that the text is preceded and succeeded by the very vamp that characterizes the instrumental felak

Example 21. Adinabeg's *Felak* Song (with dambura)

(alternation of e′–a′ and g′–a′ chords). The quatrain is divided into two parts by an instrumental interlude; the first and second pairs of lines are divided by an extremely long held note on the interjectory syllable "ei." The same interjection marks the halfway point of lines 1 and 3, thus giving the entire verse a highly symmetrical setting based on binary subdivisions. Such a construction recalls the two-part structure of most instrumental pieces. The main break in this pattern occurs at the beginning of line 4, where a considerable rest in the vocal part (six measures) follows the first half of the line of text. This breaking of the line is commonly heard in vocal felaks; perhaps it is intended as a stress of the final line, the "punch" line of the quatrain.

The melodic content of the song is slight, and is close to Adinabeg's solo dambura version (Example 20) in its extreme narrowness of range. The principal melodic activity consists only of an alternation of the two pitches a′ and b♭′, only a minor second apart.

The activity of the instrumental accompaniment, beyond the vamp already noted, consists of a continuous rhythmic figure of two eighth notes, pitched only on the two basic tones of the melody. How close, then, in Adinabeg's instrumental felak to his vocal version, if just the instrumental accompaniment of the latter is considered? The narrow range, the rhythmic figure, the content of the two sections (vamp and

Example 22. Safar Mahdi's *Felak*, "boland" (flute)

melody) — all point to a remarkable similarity, which leads to the obvious conclusion that the instrumental version is merely meant as a "song without words," i.e., a straight adaptation of the vocal felak. Indeed, this is what performers often express when speaking of the felak. When one listens to the instrumental version alone, it is hard to imagine a vocal counterpart, but it is easy to see the relationship of the two when one discovers that it is the vocal part that provides the only legato element of the music.

Let us round out the survey of the felak by looking into music for the Badaxšani tula, a recorder-like flute. Example 22 is a brief felak performed by Safar Mahdi, from the Šuǧnan area; he named it *boland* ("high"). Such highly melismatic felaks are among the most orna-mented music in all of northern Afghanistan. Basically, they present us with nothing new in the concept of the felak, showing the same narrow range and emphasis on alternation of two adjacent pitches noted earlier.

Safar Mahdi's tune opens the way to comparing the Badaxšani music of Afghanistan with that of Soviet Tajikstan, just across the border. Nizam Nurjanov, head of the arts section of the Institute of History of the Tajik Academy of Sciences, and himself an expert on folk drama and dance, was kind enough to furnish me with examples of Badaxšani music taped by the Academy's expedition of 1967. Among the pieces included in this sampling were some specimens of flute music, including a tune specifically labeled *felak*. Through the good offices of Mr. Nurjanov, it is possible for the first time to make an exact comparison of pieces of the same repertoire on opposite banks of the River Panj, which forms the Afghan-Soviet border. The felak of Example 23, performed by Baba Ilbam, was taped in the village of Iemts in the Rošan region, which is adjacent to the Šuǧnan area, Safar Mahdi's home; it thus provides a perfect counterpart to Example 22.

Even a cursory glance at Example 23 shows the very close affinity between the Tajikistani felak and Safar Mahdi's tune. We find a similar melismatic treatment, the same resting on key pitches, and a like insistence on a very narrow range, through Example 23 has a somewhat greater compass than Example 22. This great similarity is welcome confirmation of the unity of style that persists on both sides of the Afghan-Soviet Badaxšani border. Such unity is only to be expected, since it was as recently as the 1890s that the present border on the Panj was fully established.

The following comparison of Badaxšani and Uzbek-Tajik styles will help to summarize this account.

DIVERGENCE OF BADAXŠANI AND UZBEK-TAJIK TURKESTANI STYLES

Badaxšan	Turkestan
Consistent texture, usually polyphonic (drone, organum)	If consistent texture, usually monophonic; mixed texture also common
Binary structure nearly universal	Binary structure common, but three- and multi-part forms also in use
Narrow melodic range frequent	Range moderate, may be wide
Minor and augmented seconds common	Minor and augmented seconds rare
Seven-beat meter frequent	Seven-beat meter rare
Some free-rhythm styles	No free-rhythm styles

CONVERGENCE OF BADAXŠANI AND UZBEK-TAJIK TURKESTANI STYLES

Vocal music based on folk quatrain verse
Close connection between vocal and instrumental styles
Use of instrumental music in three ways:
    (1) as accompaniment to song
    (2) in performance of songs without words
    (3) as accompaniment to dance
Concept of raft and amad, or departure and return to a very stable tonic, as defined by the sounding of the open strings in lute music or of the fundamental pitch in flute music

It can be seen that while the two styles diverge in terms of the working out of basic principles, those principles hold equally for both regional musics. The isolation of Turkmen music in the North thus stands out even more sharply in view of the underlying unity of the principal northern styles, Badaxšani and Uzbek-Tajik Turkestani. Perhaps the cultural affinities of Uzbeks and Tajiks cited in Chapter 1 have gained musical corroboration in our account, while at the same time the distinctiveness of the mountain Tajiks from those of the steppe country has been upheld.

Example 23. Flute *Felak* from Tajikistan

CHAPTER 4

The Musical Instruments

LUTES

The Turkestani Dambura

The Turkestani dambura (Figures 4.1–4.3) is the most widespread lute type of Afghan Turkestan. It is a two-stringed fretless lute with two lateral pegs. It is almost always strung with nylon cord; generally one long stretch of cord is used for both strings by means of the following procedure: the cord is attached to one peg, brought over the bridge and down to the notched fastening point at the base of the lid, then brought back up over the bridge to form the second string, and is finally tied to the second peg. One celebrated musician of the North, Bangeča Tašqurğani, prefers gut strings on his instrument, and is in somewhat the same position as those few violinists today who prefer pure gut to metal-wound strings. It does not seem that silk was ever used for dambura strings, as it still is on the Uzbek and Turkmen dutars. Usually, large quantities of nylon cord are wound over the tips of the peg and around the body of the peg. When a string breaks, the player merely winds off another length of cord. In this way, a performer can go for long periods of time without restringing his lute.

Peg shape varies little among Turkestani damburas. The most common form, with three points, is called *sepāra*. A notched triangular shape may also be found.

The Turkestani dambura is made in three parts: neck, belly, and lid. It is interesting to note that the local term for neck is the Persian word *dasta,* "handle," which well suits our terms "handle lute." Table 4.1 gives the terms for parts of lutes, in Persian and Uzbek.

Xarak and *eišak* both man "little donkey," indicating the role of the bridge as beast of burden. *Gušak* means "little ear," perhaps indicating an analogy between tuning and ear-twisting.

Body measurements for Turkestani damburas vary considerably; figures for a few sample instruments are given in Table 4.2 to indicate the general range in size.

Fig. 4.1. Turkestani dambura

Fig. 4.2. Turkestani dambura lid

Fig. 4.3. Turkestani dambura back

TABLE 4.1

Local Terms for Parts of Lutes

English	Persian	Uzbek
neck	dasta	dasta
lid	kāse	kasnak
belly	pošt	kasi
string	tār	tar, ziye
bridge	xarak	eišak
upper bridge	tārgir	?
peg	gušak	kulaq

From Table 4.2 can be seen not only that overall measurements vary considerably, but that the proportions between length, width, and depth can differ greatly. For example, whereas instruments 2 and 3 have almost the same overall length, instrument 3 is much wider and deeper than instrument 2 and has a considerably shorter neck. It should be added that the Turkestani dambura has a rather thick and wide neck in general. Instrument 3, which is typical in most respects, has a fingerboard 4.3 centimeters wide and 3.5 centimeters deep. Dambura makers say that in the past, the instrument was a good deal smaller and lighter. They describe its sound as having been more *zil,* or treble, in the old days.

Most of today's larger, heavier Turkestani damburas are decorated with small areas of cow-bone inlay, usually small concentric circles. They may be arranged as a group of three circles inside a triangular piece of bone inlay. Such a design is called *šeraz,* a term that has wide currency in Turkestan for various sorts of ornamentation in handicrafts, including pottery, clothing, etc. Recent Turkestani damburas have a smear of color over the bone inlay, most often in a bright reddish shade. The color is compounded of corn flour and watercolor and is daubed on quite freely over the inlaid sections, usually coloring some of the wood as well. The inlay occurs frequently on the neck,

TABLE 4.2

**Dimensions of Selected Turkestani Damburas
(In Centimeters)**

Instrument	Overall Length	Length of Neck	Greatest Width	Greatest Depth
1	97	64	21	14
2	102	69	20.5	13
3	103	66	23	16
4	110	71	26	19

and may also be found near the peak at the back of the belly, on the back of the neck, or at the point where the neck joins the belly. Inlay is almost never placed on the lid. This is probably due to the fact that the lid is made of an unfinished, rather soft, quite thin wooden sheet which could not stand inlay.

A large sound hole is placed in the belly at the apex of the peak (see Figure 4.3). Sometimes a slight ridge is placed around this sound hole so that it can be decorated with bone inlay. Instrument builders and performers alike maintain that the hole serves to improve resonance rather than to fulfill an ornamental function.

The sound holes in the lid are the last work to be completed on the instrument. Several holes are drilled, usually in a given pattern; most frequent is a pattern of four holes in a diamond shape, placed on either side of the bridge (see Figure 4.2). Sound holes are rarely arranged as fancifully as they are on tanbur lids (see below). According to Turkestani dambura makers, the holes must be sunk a few months after the instrument has been in use, "to let the sound out." The craftsmen seems to feel that each dambura develops a tone quality of its own, which will be rounded out by the placing of holes when the instrument has reached a certain stage of maturity.

Turkestani damburas are made in family workshops, and the craft is hereditary. Among the craftsmen I visited at Dara-i Zendan, near Samangan, the old father, Jurai Qul, a septuagenarian, said that his family had been dambura makers as far back as he could tell. Of his seven sons, only one is involved in the instrument trade. The others are peasants, working the family plot located back of the workshop and living area in the rolling upland cliff country of southeastern Afghan Turkestan.

Jurai Qul and his son Šarif say they can make up to twenty instruments in a month, but put the amount of time needed for one dambura at five days. They make instruments both on commission from professional musicians and amateurs and for general market sale. Their damburas and those of other local makers can be seen in the shops of Samangan, which is the center of dambura construction for all of Afghanistan.

In making damburas, they use mulberry wood almost exclusively. However, more discriminating (and wealthier) customers will ask for apricot, pine, or walnut to be used in making the neck of the instrument. The main criterion for choice of wood seems to be durability. Hardwoods such as apricot or walnut last much longer than mulberry, though the latter is in fact a fairly tough wood. Mulberry trees are found in great quantity in northern Afghanistan, and are handy multipurpose trees: the fruit is widely consumed in both fresh form and dried (dried mulberries can be ground into a kind of flour in the winter); the leaves are fed to silkworms; and the wood can be used for various construction purposes. The shade value of a large old mulberry tree is highly respected as well.

Mulberry was extensively used by the craftsmen of Tajikistan and Uzbekistan as well. In N. A. Avedova's valuable study of Uzbek instrument making, one learns that in the seventeenth-century treatise on Central Asian music by Derviš-ali, mulberry was cited as the main wood for instrument construction, and Avedova adds that "old stringed instruments were almost exclusively made of mulberry" (1966:28–29). Modern makers of Soviet Central Asia use a wider range of woods, but mulberry remains a favorite.

Damburas are hewn from a single large block of wood. The block is patiently whittled down and hollowed out by means of a single tool — an axe *(kajkord)* with a wooden handle approximately one foot long and a wide, arched metal blade, about nine inches long, which ends in a flared, curved edge. Figure 4.4 shows the father-and-son team of Jurai Qul and Šarif hard at work. "It takes a thousand strokes to make a dambura," says the old man resentfully, and the actual number is probably considerably higher. All of the lutes of Afghanistan

Fig. 4.4 Turkestani dambura makers of Samangan

Fig. 4.5 Finished Turkestani dambura lids (fore-ground) *and bellies* (rear) *drying in the sun*

are made in this painstaking way, and the traditional method on the Soviet side of the border is identical.

It does not seem that great stress is laid on the lack of imperfections in the wood, for knots, wormholes, and other defects are allowed to remain in the finished dambura. I was not able to detect the presence of a significant body of lore about selection and processing of wood for damburas. Makers express a basic interest in using timber that is somewhat green. They prefer to have the instrumental darken and season with use, rather than choose more mature woods for the basic construction. Such a preference is somewhat at odds with information about instrument making in other areas of the Near East and Central Asia. For example, Avedova speaks of the celebrated Uzbek master, Usta Usman, as keeping his timber in a dry place for two to three years, and notes that the seasoning period may last up to five years (1966:58).

Jurai Qul finishes the surface of the belly and neck with a rather heavy file. As a result, his (and most other) Turkestani damburas are quite roughhewn affairs, becoming smooth only after long years of cradling against a performer's body. I once made the mistake of bringing Jurai Qul a large quantity of sandpaper from Kabul as a present, and was greeted with a lengthy outburst of hilarity. He felt that such feeble paper could never improve his sturdy mulberry wood.

The lid is added to the belly at the end of the construction process, having been briefly dried in the sun (Figure 4.5) while the belly and neck were being made and joined with glue. The lid is also attached with glue. As noted above, the sinking of sound holes in the lid is the final stage in the making of a dambura, and is done after some months of use. It should be added that not all makers are as careful in this respect as is Jurai Qul.

Lids, like bellies, are smoothed by filing. Whereas the file marks on the belly radiate in several directions (with the grain, against the grain, and diagonally), those on the lid go only at right angles against the grain. The scrape marks on the neck are mostly with the grain, and a finer file has been used. Perhaps the coarsest woodwork on Jurai Qul's instruments is at the very end of the neck, above the pegbox. The instrument ends abruptly, and is cut off at a careless angle, with little attempt having been made to smooth down the unplaned surface at right angles to the back of the neck. All the damburas I examined were similarly made.

A bridge is added, made of any scrap of available wood, since so much of Afghan Turkestan is wood-free steppe and desert. There is no standardization of bridge shapes.

Once a dambura is finished, it is rarely altered in any way. If, in the course of time, a dambura "goes bad," expert players are familiar with some tricks to remedy the defect. For example, Abdullah Buz-baz of Tašqurğan advised me to cover the lid of my dambura with egg yolk, let it dry, and then scrape the yolk off to raise the level of the lid, which had become slightly concave. The method worked with considerable success.

The Turkestani dambura is the most widely used lute of northern Afghanistan. It is also found beyond the North within Afghanistan, perhaps most commonly in the Hazarajat of central Afghanistan. To the southeast, it can be found even in strongly Paštun areas of the country such as Lagman. To the east, distribution of the Turkestani dambura tapers off and overlaps with the spread of the Badaxšani dambura. To the north, the Turkestani dambura borders with the region of the Uzbek dombra, a closely related two-stringed fretless lute. To the west, the Turkestani dambura is played in the mountains of Badğis (the Paropamisus range) and reaches the zone of the Herati dutar.

A variety of ethnic groups use the Turkestani dambura. The bulk of the players are Uzbeks and Tajiks of Afghan Turkestan; however, the instrument enjoys wide popularity among the minority groups of the region — Paštuns, Hazaras, and Aimaq tribesmen — and has been adopted by the Turkmens to a certain extent as well. It is the teahouse instrument par excellence, usually occupying a handy position hanging on a nail, ready to be taken down by anyone who feels like strumming.

The Badaxšani Dambura

The Badaxšani dambura (Figures 4.6–4.8) is considerably smaller in all its dimensions than the Turkestani lute, and has one important structural difference: the body and neck are generally made of only one piece, to which the lid is attached. In addition, some Badaxšani damburas have bellies planed into a ribbed pattern of broad surfaces, tapering off towards the neck. No Turkestani damburas are ribbed, and the only ribbed lute belly found in the North, that of the Uzbek dutar, is actually composed of separate strips of wood rather than of different planes of one whole piece of wood.

As in the case of the Turkestani dambura, the dimensions of the Badaxšani instrument vary significantly. Table 4.3 gives basic measurements for selected Badaxšani damburas.

Overall variation in length can be significant: 10 centimeters between instruments 1 and 2. Variation of dimension among instruments of similar length can be seen to be greatest in the case of width and depth. Thus, while instruments 4 and 5 are nearly the same in length, instrument 4 exceeds number 5 by 7 centimeters in both width and depth. Differentiation of dimension is a factor of regional variation among Badaxšani instrument makers. For example, the smallest of the instruments cited, number 3, is from the far eastern area of Badaxšan, the Waxan corridor, while the largest, number 1, comes from Darwaz, the most northerly area. Number 4 is from the Šuğnan area, northeast of Faizabad, the provincial capital, and numbers 2 and 5 are either from the Faizabad area, in the center of the province, or from Kešm, the most westerly region of Badaxšan. What is particularly surprising is the fact that instruments 1 and 3 are almost identical in shape, type of wood, and construction, although they are so different in dimension and come from the far north and east respectively.

In differentiating the Badaxšani dambura from its Turkestani counterpart, one must note the following factors in addition to the considerations of dimension and belly shape noted above: the Badaxšani type is much more carefully finished, giving the wood a smooth polished surface; the wood seems to be more thoroughly seasoned to begin with; and the sound holes are placed at the center, instead of at the sides, of the lid (see Figure 4.7). In addition, the belly is much thinner, to the point of almost eggshell fragility in some instruments, and the lute is consequently much lighter than the Turkestani dambura. The fastening point of the strings on most Badaxšani damburas consists of a protuberance with slits for the strings, instead of an inserted peg as on Jurai Qul's instruments. Also, the neck flares out above the pegbox rather than tapering off, and is generally narrower, facilitating the playing of fourths, which is a hallmark of much of Badaxšani music. Badaxšani

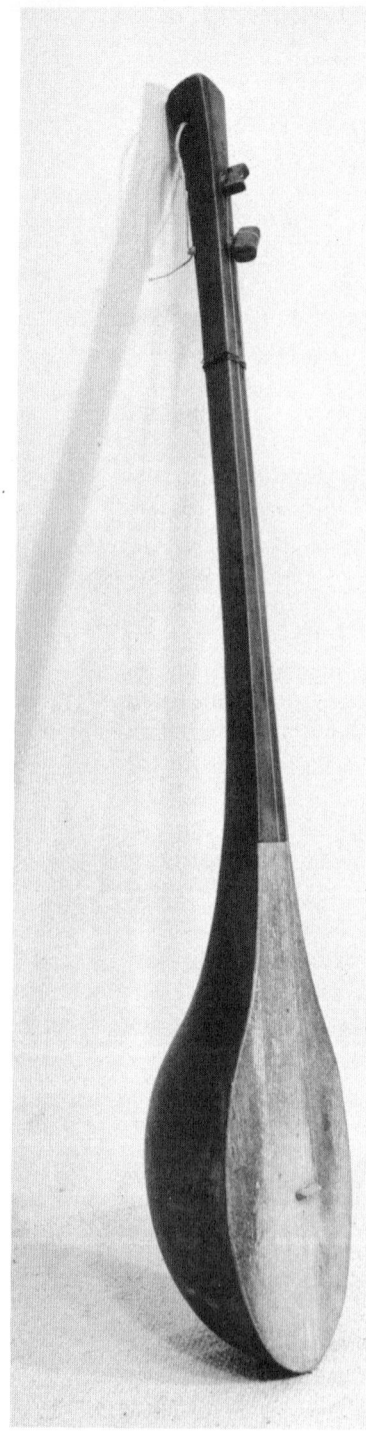

Fig. 4.7. Badaxšani dambura lid

Fig. 4.8. Badaxšani dambura back

Carol Reck

Fig. 4.6. Badaxšani dambura

TABLE 4.3

**Dimensions of Selected Badaxšani Damburas
(In Centimeters)**

Instrument	Overall Length	Length of Neck	Greatest Width	Greatest Depth
1	78	49	17	11
2	68	39	12	8
3	66.5	39	13	10
4	75	44	20	17
5	74	42	13	10

damburas come to a sharp point at the back of the neck, in contrast to the flat-backed neck cited by Jurai Qul as a criterion of Tajik-made Turkestani damburas. The *targir* or *gulband* (upper bridge) of the Badaxšani instrument is generally of gut, rather than nylon, perhaps because nylon cord is less available in Badaxšan.

It is also worth noting that there is no single center of instrument production in Badaxšan comparable to Samangan for Turkestan. This may well be due to the great difficulty of moving from one place to another in Badaxšan: for example, to get from Faizabad to Šuǧnan, a distance of perhaps fifty kilometers as the crow flies, requires three to four days' journey on horseback in the summer, ten to twelve days in the winter. A comparable distance on the Turkestani steppe could be covered in three hours by the ubiquitous jeep taxis, even over rugged desert roads.

The Badaxšani dambura is quite similar in many respects to the Tajikistani dumbrak (*-ak* is a diminutive suffix in Persian). O. Dansker, in his study of the music culture of the mountain Tajiks of the Karategin and Darwaz regions of southern Tajikistan (adjacent to Afghanistan), says that there the dumbrak is "the most widespread and popular instrument" (Dansker 1965:249). Here is the description of the dumbrak from the *Atlas* (Vertkov 1963:125):

. . . [The dumbrak is] a two-stringed instrument with a length of about 700–800 millimeters, with a pear-shaped body and a comparatively long neck. It is made of mulberry wood. The body is hollowed out, and the back side is convex; two or three groups of small round resonating opening are drilled on the lid. The neck is round, without frets; wooden pegs are placed at its far end (head). The neck and body are made of one piece of wood. The strings are silk, sometimes gut; they are tuned to a fourth. The sound is marked by rattling. The right-hand technique is rather varied and consists of alternating striking of the strings with one or with all the fingers, and of the motions of the hand above, below, and on both strings. For the most part, three fingers (the thumb, first, and middle) take part in the left-hand play, more rarely the fourth finger and, as an exception, all five fingers. As a rule, it is played only in first position. The sound of the dumbrak is not loud, and is accompanied by noises arising from the striking of the nails on the lid.

The dumbrak is played sitting or, at times, while standing on horseback while traveling; it is held in front of oneself in a horizontal position and by slightly raising (or lowering) the neck. The dumbrak is a very portable instrument; fastening it to his belt, the musician can easily handle it while walking or riding. This could not better suit the conditions of life of the Tajiks of the mountain regions, where the dumbrak is most widespread. On it, songs are accompanied, and dances and instrumental variants of songs are performed. Its role in the musical life of the inhabitants of mountainous Tajikistan is approximately that which the dutar plays among the Tajiks of the valley regions of the Republic.

The general description of dimensions and physical characteristics of the dumbrak fits those given above for the Badaxšani dambura. It should be added, however, that not all Badaxšani damburas feature one-piece construction for neck and belly. Some instruments, from the Šuǧnan region, are made in three pieces — neck, belly, and lid — like the Turkestani dambura.

The description in the *Atlas* does not go into detail regarding the exact shape of the belly of the dumbrak; we have seen that the Badaxšani dambura may have a smooth, peaked back or a ribbed one. Such distinctions apply as well to the dumbrak. The instrument pictured in the *Atlas* is similar to the Badaxšani dambura of Figures 4.6–4.8; however, Dansker illustrates a dumbrak with ribbed back. A new instrument I purchased in Dushanbe (the capital of Tajikistan) also had the same construction, though it was somewhat longer and thinner than both the dumbrak in the *Atlas* and the typical Badaxšani dambura, as may be seen in Figure 4.9, in which the Soviet instrument stands next to a large Badaxšani dambura (instrument 1 of Table 4.3). It should be added that the new Soviet-made dumbrak was highly esteemed for its superior resonance by Badaxšani musicians when I introduced it to Faizabad. It enabled me to make a trade for a Waxan dambura, much to the delight of both the Waxi performer and myself.

Returning to the data given in the *Atlas,* it is interesting to note that silk and gut strings are apparently still widely used in Tajikistan, whereas the Badaxšani instruments tend to be strung with nylon cord, like the new Soviet dumbrak of the Dushanbe department store. The reference to use of the thumb in dumbrak left-hand technique is somewhat surprising, as the thumb is never brought into play on the Badaxšani dambura. The frequent parallel fourths in Badaxšani style are

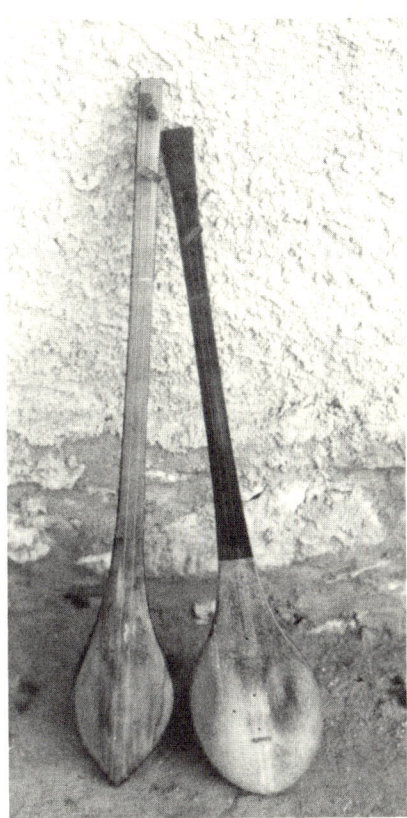

Fig. 4.9   Soviet Tajikistani
dumbrak (left) *with*
Badaxšani dambura (right)

always produced by placing the index, middle, or ring finger across both strings simultaneously, a practice facilitated by the narrowness of the instrument's neck, as noted earlier. In shunning the little finger in left-hand play, Tajikistani and Badaxšani players are both in agreement with Turkestani lutenists.

Dansker gives further details linking the dumbrak of Tajikistan to the Badaxšani dambura. The names for parts of the instrument coincide in most cases. Some terms are divergent, however, such as *parda,* instead of *tar,* for string; parda always means "fret" in Afghanistan. Another variant term is *biābun* for the neck, instead of *dasta.* The use of *zil* and *bam* for upper and lower strings is identical on both sides of the border. Also the same is the placing of the three to five sound holes of the lid in the center, under the strings and close to the bridge. A feature of ornament linking all varieties of dambura and dumbrak and connecting them with other instruments of the northern Afghanistan-

Transoxanian area is the widespread use of the bone ornament in the shape of a circle with a dot in the center, cited by Dansker as the most widespread pattern for ornament. He also notes that a special curved axe (*kajkord,* or "crooked knife") is used in instrument making in southern Tajikistan, corresponding to the axe used by Jurai Qul and other Afghan instrument makers (Dansker 1965:249-50).

In comparing the Badaxšani dambura technique with that of another related lute, the Turketsani dambura, one notes some minor differences. One unique practice of the Badaxšani playing style is the use of two or even three fingers on the upstroke, instead of only the index finger, as in Turkestan, to produce repeated or different pitches, often in triplet rhythms. One technique rarely found in Badaxšan but frequent in Turkestan is the use of the middle-finger knock on the lid during the index-finger stroke as a type of accent. The narrowness of the lid of the Badaxšani lute decreases the effectiveness of this particular stroke.

It has been noted that the Badaxšani dambura, though it comes in different sizes and somewhat different shapes, is a distinctive lute found in all areas of the rugged terrain of northeastern Afghanistan. We have seen, further, that the dumbrak of present-day Tajikistan, an instrument nearly identical to the Badaxšani dambura, is widespread only in the mountainous regions, areas which border on Badaxšan and which, historically, were considered part of Badaxšan. It was not until 1895 that a clear line of demarcation was established between Russian and Afghan Badaxšan, so it is safe to assume that the dumbrak and Badaxšani dambura are one and the same instrument, used by the same ethnic group — the so-called mountain Tajiks — on both sides of the present border, and used by that group only.

The Uzbek Dutar

The dutar (Figures 4.10–4.12) is a long-necked, deep-bellied, two-stringed fretted lute — and the first fretted lute of our survey. In Uzbekistan, the dutar is by far the most popular instrument, found in many homes and played by amateurs and celebrated professionals alike for both the folk and classical repertoires. In Afghanistan, the dutar is scarcely to be seen, and one can count the well-known performers of this resonant lute on the fingers of one hand.

The following data are necessarily based on the instruments of one maker, a Turkmen of Andxoi who died around 1953. His are the only Afghan-made Uzbek dutars to be seen today, and there are perhaps only fifteen of these instruments left. His dutars are marked by their finesse of workmanship; it is unfortunate that it is too late to gather information on his method of construction. Table 4.4 gives the dimen-

Fig. 4.11. Uzbek dutar, bottom

Fig. 4.12. Uzbek dutar back

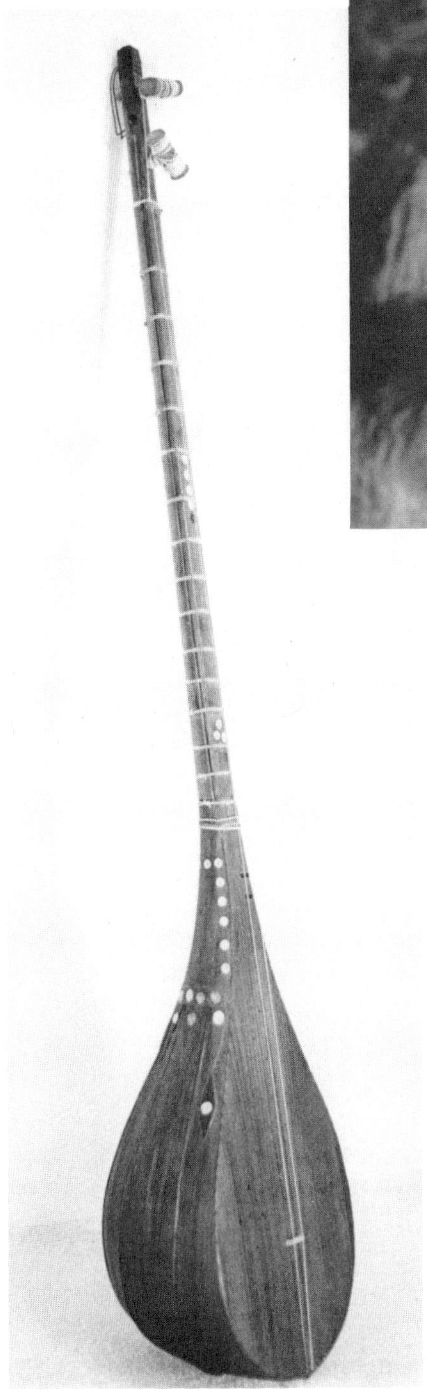

Carol Reck

Fig. 4.10. Uzbek dutar from Andxoi

sions of five Andxoi dutars; the instrument of Figures 4.10–4.12 is number 1 of the table.

Table 4.4 shows that the variations in instrument dimensions noted for other lute types of northern Afghanistan hold equally true for Uzbek dutars, even though the instruments were all built by the same maker. For example, though instrument 4 is by far the largest of the five dutars, its depth is the same as that of number 5, the smallest. Number 2 and 3, quite close in overall length and width, differ markedly in length of neck, an important constructional variable. Even the number of ribs that make up the bellies of the instruments ranges from eight to eleven, a significant variation. Note also that the smallest instrument has three ribs more than the largest.

Andxoi dutars have more constituent parts than any other lutes of northern Afghanistan. On the front, only two parts show, the neck and the lid, but at the back, the construction is more complex. One piece extends from the end of the neck to a ridge some 16 centimeters farther down towards the belly measurements taken from dutar 1); the ridge, 1.7 centimeters wide, borders on the ribs that make up the belly of the dutar. The ribs widen out to form the flare of the belly, then taper down to a joining piece (see Figure 4.11), a thermometer-shaped strip that joins at its upper end with the lid and that contains the slotted fastening point of the strings. Unlike the dambura, the dutar features two separate strings. Like the dambura, the Uzbek dutar of Andxoi includes a prominent sound hole at the center of the back. In the case of instrument 1, this hole has been ornamented with a diamond-shaped segment of wood (Figure 4.12). The ribs of the belly are joined by narrow strips of wood, which are raised above the surface of the ribs. All of the components of the dutar's back are held together by glue.

It is worth noting that the fretting, like the dimensions of the

TABLE 4.4

**Dimensions of Five Andxoi Uzbek Dutars
(In Centimeters)**

Instrument	Overall Length	Length of Neck	Greatest Width	Greatest Depth	Number of Ribs
1	121	71	21.5	20	9
2	118	62	21	19	10
3	117	70	21	17	10
4	125	81	22.5	17	8
5	116	68	20	17	11

instruments, varies from dutar to dutar. Two systems are in use. The
first employs frets placed to produce a chromatic scale over the range
of an octave plus a perfect fourth, while the second, covering the same
range, skips the half-steps between the fourth and fifth and the eighth
and ninth scale degrees. The former system is known as *nimparda,*
or "half-fret," because of the additional tones fixed between whole steps,
and is by far the rarer of the two systems. Additional frets may be
placed on the upper edge of the lid to obtain the fifth and minor sixth
of the second octave. These can be made of small strips of leather,
or other handy material, glued onto the lid. Frets are most commonly
wound from nylon cord, though a given instrument may have both
older gut frets as well as the more modern nylon. The fastening
process is facilitated by a trough at the side of the neck, a feature
to be found in other Near Eastern and Central Asian lutes, such as
the Persian setar and the Uzbek tanbur (not to be confused with the
Afghan tanbur, discussed below).

The Uzbek dutar of Andxoi is the only instrument of Afghanistan
(except for some Turkmen dutars) that is still strung with the wound
silk strings formerly characteristic of most lutes of the area. The silk
is still made in Andxoi at infrequent intervals by Abdul Karim, an
amateur dutarist and producer of silk scarves (for his handiwork, see
Dupaigne 1968). The strings are tuned either to a fourth or to a fifth,
which one Andxoi virtuoso, Ğafur Xan, calls first and second tunings
respectively. A third tuning, in unison, is rarely used; it is called *kuštar*
("paired-string" in Uzbek). Pegs are placed either both frontally,
as in Figure 4.10, or one frontally and one laterally. The latter is the
more common pegging of the dutars of Uzbekistan.

The placement and patterning of the small sound holes of the
Andxoi dutars is similar to that found on Turkestani and Badaxšani
damburas, and approximates the usage of Transoxanian dutar makers
as well. A distinctive feature of the Andxoi instruments is the high
wooden upper bridge. Many Uzbekistani dutars have only the tied-on,
fret-like fastening found on damburas, though some fine instruments of
well-known makers feature the wooden piece of the Andxoi dutars.

Although time has robbed us of the opportunity of discovering the
trade secrets of the Andxoi dutar-maker's art, some of the constructional
features speak for themselves. The maker took exceptional pains to
make the ribs of the belly thin, and to keep the neck fairly slender,
so that the instruments are unusually light for their size and volume.
Like Jurai Qul, the dambura maker of Samangan, the Andxoi master
used a file on the belly across the grain of the wood, but his hand was
considerably lighter in using the tool. There are no visible file marks

across the grain on the lids of Andxoi dutars, and no scrape marks at all on the necks, which are highly polished by use.

A special kind of dutar made at least once by the Andxoi maker is the type that unscrews for greater portability (see Figure 4.13). This instrument is somewhat smaller than some of the other Andxoi dutars, but is made with the same care. The only difference is the insertion of a screw mechanism at the end of the neck. When tightly closed, the dutar shows no sign of this alteration except for a strip of metal appearing at the back of the neck. This type of dutar has its counterpart in Uzbekistan, though there the instrument may have an additional screw that enables it to be broken down into three parts (Avedova 1966:76). The dutar can then be wrapped up in a kerchief and placed in a saddlebag for easy carrying over long distances on horseback.

Instrument 1 of Table 4.4 has the most interesting ornamental design of the five dutars under discussion. The inlay of pearl buttons (see Figures 4.10 and 4.12) is a most original innovation. Buttons are functionally placed on the fingerboard to mark the place of the fifth

Fig. 4.13.
Screw-type Uzbek
dutar from Andxoi

and octave above the open-string pitch. The triangular pattern extending from the ridge toward the top of the belly is a stylistic link between the Andxoi dutar and the Uzbekistani dutar. However, no Andxoi dutars have the elaborate fingerboard ornamentation typical of the finest Transoxanian court instruments, or of the inlay work on older Afghan tanburs.

Most features of Andxoi dutars are shared by the instruments of Uzbekistan. The average length of 1150–1200 millimeters given in the *Atlas* (Vertkov 1963:119) matches the instruments of Table 4.4 quite closely, as do other details of dimension and construction. Nevertheless, there are several differences betwen Andxoi and Transoxanian dutars that imply certain regional preferences. First, it should be noted that many Samarqand dutars I have seen do not feature ribbed construction of the belly, but rather have the one-piece peaked construction typical of the dambura. Second, the fretting of Uzbekistani dutars, as given in the *Atlas* (Vertkov 1963:120), seems a cross between the fully chromatic (nimparda) and the diatonic scaling systems found on Afghan lutes, as the scale is said to be chromatic in the lower register and diatonic in the upper (overall range is identical: one and one-half octaves). Another difference to be noted is the recent substitution of metal strings for silk in Uzbekistan, underscoring the "old-fashioned" nature of Afghan dutar playing.

In terms of basic playing style, there is little difference on the two sides of the border. In right-hand technique, the alternate use of a single-finger stroke and the four- or five-finger stroke remains basic, the only difference lying in the use of the middle finger instead of the forefinger on the dutar as the usual agent on the single-finger stroke. I have seen only one stroke on the Afghan side that I have neither observed nor seen described in Uzbekistan. This is a favorite trick of Ğafur Xan's: he presses the thumb and forefinger of his right hand tightly together to produce a very strongly accented stroke. He uses this technique in pieces featuring variation, as a novel effect.

In left-hand technique, the main departure from dambura style is the use of the thumb to stop the lower string instead of placing one finger across both strings for chords. One reason for this difference may be the dutarist's interest in using the note on the lower string as a drone. If he employs his thumb to hold down the pitch, the index finger is free to move below and above the spot on the string opposite the thumb. Such a device is not necessary in dambura style, since the lower string, if stopped, is employed only for parallel intervals or for solo play and does not hold a stopped drone pitch. The greater freedom of the dutarist's fingers is thus related to the style of the music, in which the Uzbek dutar stands closer to the Turkmen dutar (see below) than to the dambura.

Ğafur Xan distinguishes two kinds of bridges for the dutar, corresponding to two playing styles. A high bridge is said by him to be good for projecting individual notes in a slower tempo, whereas a lower bridge is favorable for the fast-note *reig* style, which he generally prefers. The Andxoi virtuoso is also a strong partisan of the nimparda (fully chromatic) fretting system which he considers to require a more advanced technique on the part of the performer. He derides players who shun the nimparda as weaklings.

The Turkmen Dutar

Like the Uzbek dutar, the Turkmen dutar is hard to find in Afghanistan, is mastered by only a few virtuosi, and represents a tradition that is closely connected to Transoxania. Unlike the Uzbek dutar, the Turkmen lute is found scattered across a wide area of northern Afghanistan and is produced by different artisans in each locale.

Table 4.5 gives the dimensions of dutars from three different communities. The first (Figure 4.14) was made in Qala-i Zal, a large Turkmen settlement northwest of Kunduz near the Oxus; the second (Figure 4.15) was played by a man in Tašqurğan who thought the instrument was made near that town; and the third is from Qizilayaq, an important Turkmen village north of Šiberğan.

From Table 4.5 it can be seen that the variability of dimension noted for other lute types of the North holds equally true for the Turkmen dutar. Particularly striking is the disparity of the proportions between length and width of instruments 1 and 2: the latter is both much longer and far narrower than the former. All three instruments have necks of apricot wood and bellies and lids of mulberry. Instrument 1, shown in Figure 4.14, is by far the most carefully made of the three. Its owner, Axmad-baxši, probably the finest Turkmen musician in Afghanistan, worked with the carpenter in designing and finishing the instrument and is very proud of the result. He would not sell

TABLE 4.5

Dimensions of Selected Turkmen Dutars
(In Centimeters)

Instrument	Overall Length	Greatest Width	Greatest Depth	Number of Frets
1	90	19	10	13
2	97	16.5	9	12
3	91	18	—	14

Fig. 4.14. Axmad-baxši with his Turkmen dutar

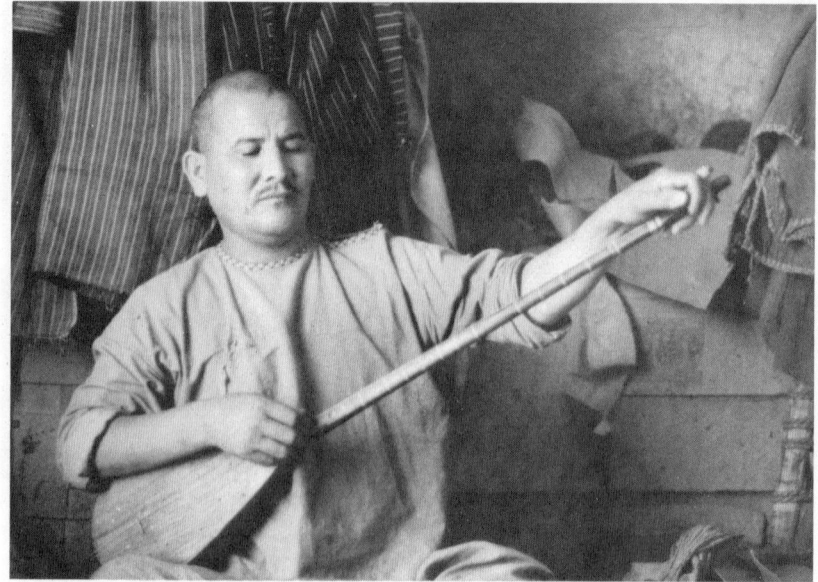

Fig. 4.15. Usta Hassan with his Turkmen dutar

his dutar for any price. Axmad-baxši feels that an instrument will not
come out properly if a musician is not present at the construction.
In this, he is at variance with the dambura makers of Afghanistan,
who cannot themselves play the instruments they make and consult
no one in making them. The most striking constructional feature of
Axmad-baxši's dutar is the raised, wave-like fluting of the belly, which
seems to be his own invention. The other Turkmen dutars under discussion have simple smooth peaked backs like those of Turkestani and
Badaxšani damburas.

Like the Uzbek dutar, the Turkmen lute was traditionally strung
with tightly woven silk cord, and Axmad-baxši continues this practice.
Unlike most Andxoi Uzbek dutars, but like those of Transoxania, the
Turkmen dutar has one peg placed laterally and one on the side.
Axmad-baxši's instrument has silver pegs, which add the final touch
to the overall elegance of his dutar.

The Turkmen dutar of northern Afghanistan is virtually the same
as its counterpart in the Turkmen SSR. It is worthwhile quoting at
length most of the scanty description of the instrument given in Soviet
sources as general background. Below is most of the entry for the
Turkmen dutar in the *Atlas:*

Dutar: a two-stringed instrument, close in construction to the Uzbek and Tajik dutar. Its general length is about 900 mm. In contrast to the Uzbek and Tajik dutars, the Turkmen dutar has smaller dimensions, a hollowed-out body, comparatively shorter neck and metallic, moveable frets with a chromatic scale (except for the farthest, highest pitch) with a range of one and one-half octaves. The strings of the dutar are silk, but in recent years they are often replaced by metal ones; they are tuned in fourths.

During play, the dutar is held in front of oneself in an inclined position; the body of the instrument is at belt level, with the head above the shoulder. The first string is pressed to the frets by the index, middle and ring fingers of the left hand (accomplished musicians also use the little finger), the second by the thumb and ring finger. Right-hand technique is distinguished by a great variety of strokes. Among the most commonly used:

a) striking the strings with the ring, middle and index fingers simultaneously, and in some cases even with the little finger;

b) striking with the index finger back and forth;

c) a sliding stroke up with the nail of the thumb;

d) an up-stroke and a down-stroke of the index finger with a sliding up-stroke of the thumb (for triplets);

e) alternating strokes of the index finger and thumb in fast passages, for grace notes, etc.

f) extracting the sounds of the index finger of the left hand by means of pressing on the string and plucking it simultaneously. (Vertkov 1963:116)

Several comments are in order concerning the information in the *Atlas*. First, it should be noted that the general length of the Turkmenian dutars is roughly the same as that of instruments in northern Afghanistan. The mentioning of a "hollowed-out" body for the Turkmen dutar as a contrast to Uzbek and Tajik instruments perhaps refers to the fact that the belly of the Turkmen instrument is not made of separate ribs, but is composed of one scooped-out chunk of wood. As to the fretting, the use of movable frets holds for instruments in Afghanistan, but the placement of frets varies slightly. Most Afghan Turkmen dutars have a completely chromatic scale without the whole-step placement of the top fret mentioned in the *Atlas*. Some Turkmen lutes of Afghanistan feature a different fretting, namely that of the Uzbek dutar, with whole steps between the fourth and fifth and eighth and ninth scale degrees. The use of metal strings is not at all typical of instruments in Afghanistan, though the practice seems to have almost completely replaced the use of silk strings in Turkmenia, at least among the performers of Radio Ashkhabad. It is worth noting that at the time Beliaev wrote (1928), he found that dutars were strung with silk cord only.

The various strokes described in the *Atlas* are analogous to those used by Turkmen musicians of Afghanistan, and they bespeak the great variety of performance modes open to the Turkmen dutarist. Indeed, accomplished players like Axmad-baxši also employ additional strokes. One of his favorites is a wide, circular motion of the entire right arm, striking the string at the bridge and at the far end of the lid towards the fingerboard. Axmad-baxši feels that virtuosity on the dutar consists of a great variety of strokes, which are used as "ornament" (gul), in his words, offering an important visual dimension to his performance that acts as a counterpart to the diverse vocal and musical effects involved (see the section on Turkmen music in Chapter 3).

Some notes in the classic work on the music of Turkmenia, *Turkmenskaia muzyka* by Beliaev and Uspenskii (1928), offer valuable insights into the lore of the Turkmen dutar. Particularly interesting are the two legends given by Uspenskii's informants about the origin of the instrument:

A close friend of Muhammad's, Hazrat Ali, had a very beautiful horse named Dyul-dyul, for whom he took a groom, Baba-Kambar. This groom made a dutar and played on it so well, that Dyul-dyul began to grow thin. Seeing that the horse was suffering, Hazrat Ali began to worry about it, and, suddenly coming into the stable, discovered Kambar playing on the dutar. Kambar was so frightened by his master that he wanted to smash the dutar on a barrel. But Hazrat Ali stopped him and asked him to tell what sort of thing this was and how he made it. Baba Kambar said that when he made the dutar, it didn't produce any sounds until the devil helped him, after which it began to play. (Beliaev and Uspenskii 1928:89)

This story contains a number of striking elements indicative of the place of music among the Turkmens. The mentioning of Ali and his magic horse relates the story to widespread legends about Ali, a major religious folk hero of northern Afghanistan and Central Asia, and the fact that the sound of the instrument was inspired by the devil points up the negative attitude towards musical instruments and music itself, which continues to have considerable weight among all the peoples of the area. It is also interesting to note that among the Kirghiz, a Central Asian Turkic nomadic people whose music culture is related to that of the Turkmens, the founder of music and inventor of the lute (komuz) is also named Kambar, or Kambar-xan; a major genre of Kirghiz music, the *kambarkan,* is named for this legendary figure.

The second story of the invention of the dutar cited by Uspenskii relates not to the religious world, but to the culture of ancient Greece, which played an important role in the development of Near Eastern music:

Long, long ago lived a wise man, whose name was Eflatun (Plato). In his day there lived a bird Kaknus (phoenix), the feathers of which, when the wings flapped, produced very beautiful music. Eflatun, having studied these sounds, made a dutar and composed music for it, imitating the sound of the feathers of the bird Kaknus. (Beliaev and Uspenskii 1928:89)

Beliaev, commenting on the story, notes that Pythagoras plays a similar role in the legend of the origin of the robab among the people of Khiva, in present-day northwestern Uzbekistan (1928:90). It is also interesting to note that the imitation of bird sounds plays a role even today in the repertoire of various Central Asian lute types. I was not able to record legends similar to those gathered by Uspenskii, since the Turkmens of Afghanistan have forgotten much of the lore of their traditional arts.

Returning to the playing style of northern Afghanistan, it should be observed that left-hand technique plays an important role in dutar performance, because of the nature of the musical style itself (see Chapter 3). Considerable stress is attached to parallel intervals and lower-string drone on various pitches, all of which require great agility of the thumb of the left hand, which covers the lower string. The use of the ring finger for stopping the lower string, mentioned in the *Atlas* as typical of Turkmenistan, does not find currency in Afghanistan. Left-hand pizzicato, however, is in common use among all Turkmen dutarists and is used as a special effect. In general, all deviations from the basic right-hand technique, which consists of the index-finger or the four-finger stroke, and from the basic left-hand technique, using the first three fingers on the top string and the thumb on the lower string, are considered as ornament, and are thus recognized as deviations from a norm of technique.

The Tanbur

The tanbur is the most widespread instrument of the North to be played with a plectrum. It is also the only stringed instrument under discussion that did not originate in the North or in Transoxania.

Of all the stringed instruments in use in the North, the tanbur has perhaps the widest variation in construction. Instruments range in size from quite small to very large. The tanbur in Figures 4.16–4.19 is a medium-sized instrument and is rather old. Generally speaking, size correlates with age: older instruments are smaller, and newer ones are larger, as in the case of the Turkestani dambura.

Size is not the only variable in tanbur construction. Of considerable

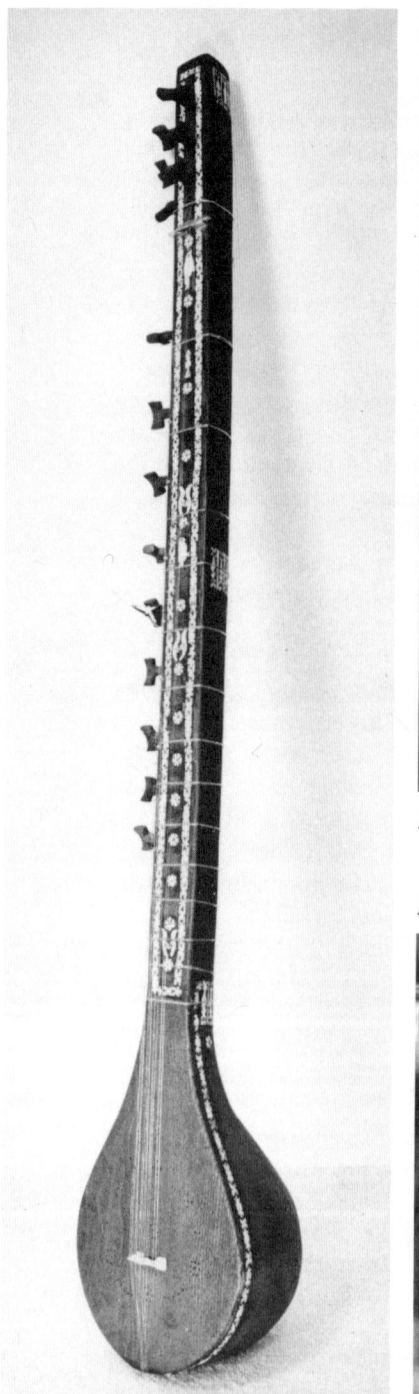

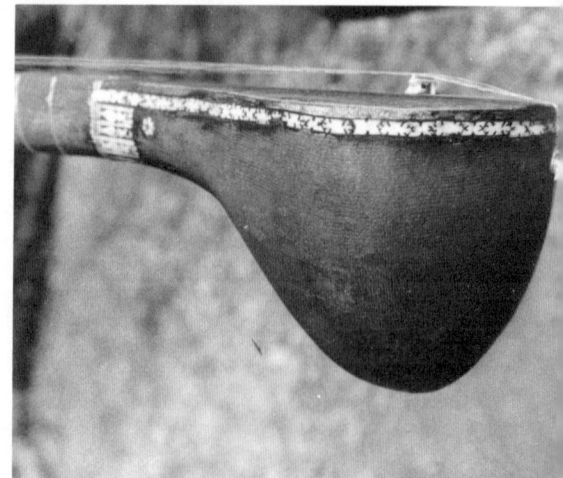

Fig. 4.17. Tanbur lid

Fig. 4.18. Tanbur, side

Carol Reck

Fig. 4.16. Tanbur

Fig. 4.19.
Tanbur neck,
showing bone inlay

interest is the wide range in number of strings and frets. The tanbur pictured is an instrument with six basic strings and eleven sympathetic strings. While the number of basic strings is always six, the number of resonating strings varies from nine to about fifteen. Figure 4.16 shows fourteen frets, but other instruments of the same size may have as many as twenty-one frets, and larger instruments, twenty-three or more. The placement of the movable frets is also unstandardized. The generally accepted tuning is that found on the Uzbek dutar: chromatic, with whole steps between the fourth and fifth and the eighth and ninth scale degrees; however, all-chromatic or simply diatonic tunings are also found. Performers are quite careless about fretting, and when questioned, give no standard response as to what constitutes proper fretting.

Tuning of the strings is also variable. The first two strings are invariably tuned in unison and are usually placed quite close to one another and played together. However, the other strings may be tuned in different ways. The most common tuning consists of pitching the third string a fourth (sometimes a fifth) below the top two (melody) strings, with the fourth and fifth strings tuned in unison with strings one and two. The sixth string may also be grouped with the first five, in which case it is tuned to the pitch of the top strings, or it may be considered as the first of the sympathetic resonating strings, in which case it is pitched a whole step higher than the top strings and begins a scalar tuning pattern carried through all the sympathetic strings; the scale chosen is the scale of the piece to be played. The last, and shortest, of the sympathetic strings may be tuned to the last pitch of the scale referred to, or may be tuned up to the octave of the pitch of the first melody string.

The bridge of the tanbur is constructed to accommodate the pattern of string distribution. The first two strings run through closely spaced slots at a point set off from the rest of the strings. The placement of the remaining strings varies; on some instruments, the third string, while set off from the first two, is placed slightly apart from the fourth and fifth strings. The latter are generally grouped with the sympathetic resonating strings, which run over the bridge at the same level as the other strings. The positioning of the resonating strings in the same plane as the remaining strings makes them accessible to the performer. These small strings are used by tanburists as a coloration, rather than melodically; occasionally a performer will sweep over the resonating strings as an effect.

The targir (upper bridge) at the bottom of the neck of the tanbur is also notched and shaped according to the distribution of strings. As there are invariably six strings pegged at the head of the instrument (three placed laterally and three on the side), the six notches of the targir are usually spaced so that the top two, melodic strings are set apart, as they are at the bridge, while the third string may run at a distance from the fourth, fifth, and sixth.

The holes on the lid of the tanbur usually form patterns of a more complex nature than those found on other lute types of the North. The overall design is usually in a teardrop shape that follows the general curve of the lid (see Figure 4.17). Groups of five holes in an X-shaped pattern are frequently used, as well as the diamond-shaped distribution of four holes that was seen on the dambura (Figure 4.2).

All the strings of the tanbur are always made of metal of equal gauge. When the tanbur is fully tuned, the pressure exerted on the bridge and lid by the combined tension of some twenty strings is considerable. To meet the pressure, bridges are constructed of thick bone, rather than of the usual wood found on other Afghan lutes. In addition, tanbur lids seem thicker than those of damburas. Another precaution frequently taken is the addition of a bone insert at the very end of the lid, where the strings pass over on their way to the fastening post.

Nevertheless, the lids of many tanburs are depressed as a result of the pressure exerted on them.

Overall shape of the tanbur varies considerably. The most common form is that of Figure 4.16: a very long, thick, and wide neck with a short, protuberant belly, somewhat dambura-shaped (see Figure 4.18). However, in recent years the outsized instruments built in Kabul and Mazar-i Šarif seem to be designed in imitation of the North Indian *sitar*. The body flares out sharply at the end of the neck into a definitely gourd-shaped belly like that of the sitar. The basic proportion of neck to belly is the same, however; the neck has simply become thicker, wider, and longer to keep up with the swelling of the belly.

Even among older instruments considerable variation in body shape can be found. One tanbur in my collection has a separate head attached to the neck for the pegbox. The head is set at a slight angle, tilting back from the neck, and is joined by glue to the neck. The instrument is provided with an extra targir of metal wire just at the juncture of head and neck to reinforce the joint and to guide the strings towards the lower targir. The instrument is not a new one, is exceptionally well crafted in general, and probably represents the taste of a particular maker or of the customer who commissioned the instrument. It also features pegs in the shape of a three-leaf clover, in contrast to the flared T-shape most common for tanbur pegs (see Figures 4.16 and 4.19).

The tanbur is held in an upright position, forcing the player to both support the instrument and play the tune with his left hand. He cradles the tanbur against his body but generally does not lean it all the way back at an angle to rest against the shoulder. Instead, he holds it sideways, so that the pegs of the sympathetic strings are against his body and the lid faces to his right. The tanbur is played with a wire plectrum, called *naxun* ("nail") or *mizrab,* similar to that used on the North Indian sitar. The plectrum is fitted onto the forefinger.

The basic stroke is a back-and-forth motion of the forefinger, which may become quite rapid. The right thumb usually hangs free, while the other three fingers often rest on the lid next to the bridge to provide a firm basis for the quick flicking of the index finger. This motion is the extent of tanbur right-hand technique. Left-hand technique is necessarily limited by the awkwardness of the playing position and the extreme length of the neck. On newer, larger tanburs, the distances between frets can be several inches, so that the player spends most of his time swooping from place to place while trying to keep the instrument in an upright position. The fact that there are numerous full-sized pegs for the resonating strings adds yet another limitation to left-hand technique.

Tanburs, like damburas, are made of three pieces — neck, belly, and lid — and the same construction technique is also used for both lute types. Mulberry, the ever-popular wood for lutes, is invariably selected, and the usual hollowing-out process is employed. Tanburs are left unfinished and unpolished, like damburas, and as a result are usually rather heavy and somewhat unwieldy to play. Bone inlay is quite common, especially among older instruments. The ornamental details shown in Figures 4.18 and 4.19 are very typical of tanbur inlay and find wide currency among other wooden items of Afghanistan, such as the wooden-handled pistols and rifles of Khyber Pass fame that fill Kabul's antique shops. Such complex inlay is rarely used nowadays. A connection between the bone inlay of Afghan lutes and that of Transoxanian lutes has already been mentioned in the discussion of the Uzbek dutar. It should be added here that there seems to be no compelling reason to associate such design with Central Asian artisans alone, for similar ornamental detail can be found in Iran and among the Paštuns of Afghanistan as well.

The present-day distribution of the tanbur is somewhat erratic. Its main center of use in the North is Mazar-i Šarif, where there is also an instrument maker whose principal product is the tanbur. The tanbur is found only sporadically in other locales of the North, its use depending upon individual musicians' degree of contact with the instrument and on local taste. Outside of Mazar, the tanbur is most often seen in touring bands with Paštun dancing boys that may visit various towns in the spring and fall. Thus, the tanbur is neither a ubiquitous feature of the music culture of the North, like the dambura, nor the characteristic instrument of a particular group, like the Uzbek and Turkmen dutars, but is rather an intermediate lute type associated with urban music.

The "Pamir Robab"

The "Pamir robab" is an instrument used marginally in the North, in the far reaches of Badaxšan along the Waxan corridor, which borders China at its eastern end and separates the Soviet Union from West Pakistan and Kashmir along its narrow extent (see Map I). I have not personally seen the instrument played, but I was fortunate enough to inspect the specimen brought back by the French Hindu Kush Expedition of 1968 from the village of Sarkan, near Qala-i Panja, in the mid-Waxan. The instrument is shown in Figures 4.20 and 4.21. Sakata (1973:p.c.) has more recently described seeing a Pamir robab at Išmurğ in the Waxan; it had been constructed in the Šuğnan area. Sakata feels that the instrument type perhaps originated in the latter region and adds that there are Pamir robab makers in Časnud, Šeduj, and Rošan.

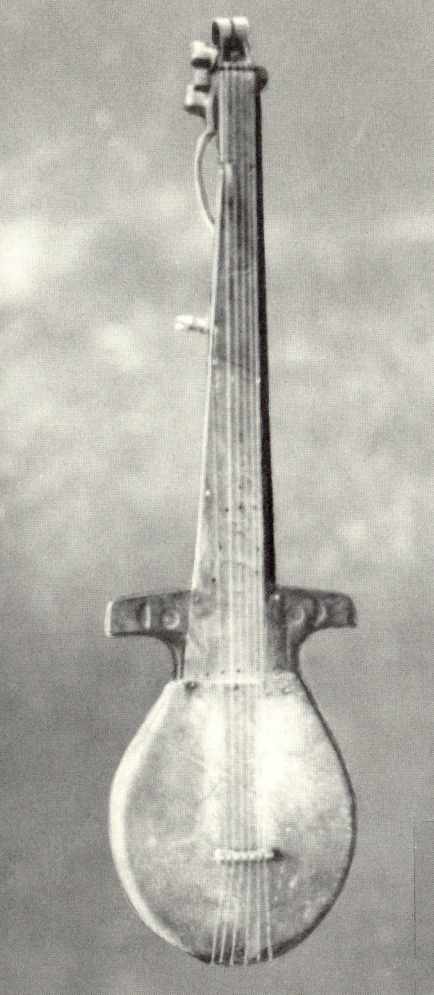

Fig. 4.20. Pamir robab

Fig. 4.21. Pamir robab lid

A similar instrument is pictured in the *Atlas* (Vertkov 1963: Plate 639)
but is unfortunately not described there or in any other Soviet source,
to the best of my knowledge; neither is there a sample of this instrument on display in Dushanbe. I have adopted the Soviet term "Pamir
robab" for the instrument, in the absence of any better term. The
lute's dimensions are given in Table 4.6.

There are six strings on the Pamir robab. The leather covering
on the sound box is quite thick and is fastened with iron nails (see
Figure 4.21). The Pamir robab is played with a wooden plectrum,
which is wedge-shaped and tied to the instrument on a string.

The Tajikistani instrument of the *Atlas* is quite similar in all
respects to that of the Afghan Waxan, but is clearly the product of an
accomplished maker. Both the Soviet and Afghan instruments are
played by mountain Tajiks of the high Pamirs. The Pamir robab
described for both regions is quite similar in appearance to a lute
illustrated in the 1884 notes by Capus on Central Asian music. The
broad neck, bent pegbox, protruding spurs, and thick belly are characteristic, and the instrument was said to be played by the women of
Kašgar (Capus 1884:115).

The Pamir robab is quite close in many respects to another lute
type illustrated in the *Atlas* on the same page. This instrument is called
a "Dulan robab" and features the same bowl-shaped sound box, thick
leather covering fastened with nails, and bent pegbox. There are two
principal differences in stringing between the Dulan and Pamir robabs.
Whereas the latter has six melodic strings, the former has three melodic
plus ten resonating strings. The third string on the Dulan robab is used
as a drone, while the upper two are paired, thus leaving only one effective melody carrier. This suggests that the playing styles on the two
lutes differ as well, since available documentation for the Pamir robab
does not indicate the use of one melody string plus drone. There is also
a difference in the shape of the spur-like extensions, whose lower sides
are finished off at right angles to the neck of the Dulan robab instead of
following a slow curve down to the belly. According to the *Atlas*
(Vertkov 1963:1928), the Dulan robab has an overall length of not

TABLE 4.6

**Dimensions of a "Pamir Robab" from Waxan
(In Centimeters)**

Length	Width of Neck	Width of Belly	Depth of Belly	Circumference of Belly	Width of Each Spur	Length of Pegbox
73	3-9	20	9	33	6.5	13

more than 80–85 centimeters, making it somewhat longer than the Waxan lute. The Dulan robab, like the Pamir lute, is fretless and is played with a wooden plectrum. Beliaev (1933:69) states that according to his informants, the Dulan robab comes from Kašgar, where it is played by the Dulan people.

Until there are further publications on the Soviet side regarding these rare instruments of the Pamirs, and until an extensive, badly needed musical and ethnographic expedition to the Waxan is undertaken, we must remain unenlightened as to the background, playing style, and repertoire of these unusually shaped lutes from the "roof of the world."

FIDDLES

The Ğičak

The most widespread fiddle of the North is the ğičak. Like the dambura, the ğičak has a centralized point of production (the town of Tašqurğan) and has an exceedingly cloudy history.

The ğičak is the most standardized instrument of the North in terms of dimension. All of the instruments I observed employed the same colorful, prefabricated neck-and-spike piece of Tašqurğan. Figure 4.22 shows a typical finished ğičak, while Figure 4.23 presents the basis of the instrument: a single piece of mulberry wood, with a fairly ornate head and pegbox and a straight neck, tapering to an unpainted section to which the performer affixes the tin can of his choice as sound box. A nail is driven into the prepared hole at the base of this spike; a length of twisted wire is tied to the nail to make two strings; a bridge is placed underneath them; and a chunk of rosin is stuck for easy access at the back of the neck where it joins the sound box. This entire process, which costs less than one dollar, takes only a few minutes, and an instrument is created that will last for years. The length of the spike varies little; those I have measured range from 71.5 to 75 centimeters. The size and shape of the tin can are the main variables. Figure 4.22 shows a ğičak that utilizes a five-pound tin of Shahpasand shortening, an Iranian product much in demand in Afghanistan; other instruments may feature round or square motor-oil cans. In general, it seems that a large square resonator provides the best sound quality; smaller or rounded cans tend to produce a more nasal, reedy timbre considered less desirable by performers.

The most striking features of the Tašqurğan ğičak are the carefully constructed details of the head, the deep groove of the pegbox, the extended cylindrical pegs, and the unvarying alternate stripes of green, yellow, red, and black. These colors and woodworking tech-

 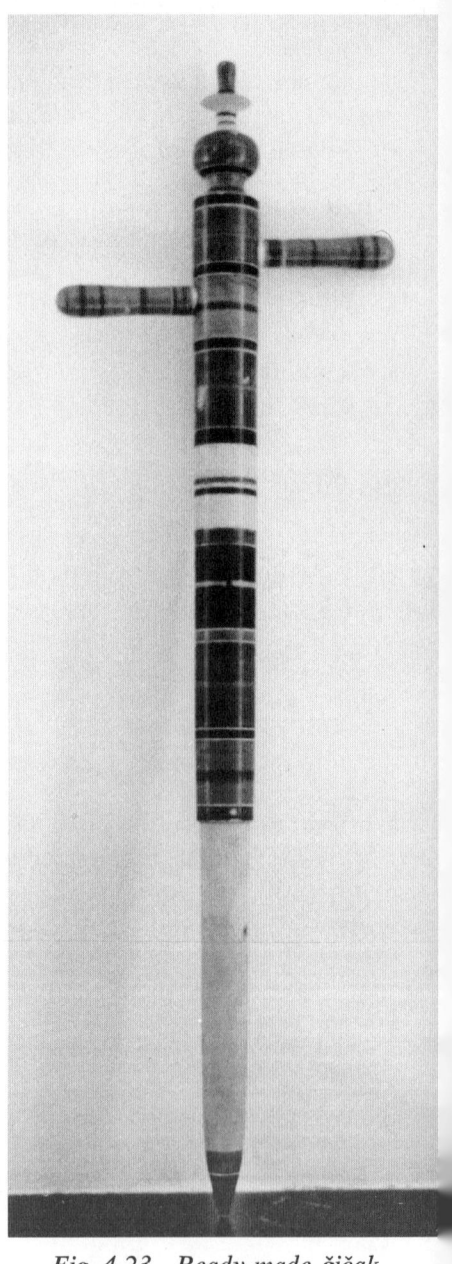

Fig. 4.22. Standard ǧičak

Fig. 4.23. Ready-made ǧičak spike from Tašqurǧan

niques are characteristic of all of the far-famed products of the Tašqurğan *najari* (woodworking) shops, which include such varied items as cradles, tools for woodworking, small three-legged stools, and slingshots.

The bow receives much less attention that the fiddle and is generally made by the performer himself. A stick is simply whittled and horsehair stretched over it; then the hair is fastened to the stick by means of a piece of fabric tightly wound around, tucked under, and perhaps sewn together with thread. The performer supplies the necessary pressure to tighten the hair by pulling the fabric towards himself with the middle, ring, and little fingers and exerting counterpressure with the index finger, placed opposite on the stick. This comfortable hand position is quite effective in properly regulating tension. Nevertheless, the scraping of the bow hair on the metal strings exacts a high price in split hairs, and leads one to suspect that horsehair strings were once in use on the ğičak.

Strings are led high above the fingerboard by a high bridge positioned at the upper end of the south box; the height of the string is often increased by the placing of a broken match at the top of the neck as an upper bridge.

The ğičak is held in a vertical position. When the player sits cross-legged on the floor, the most common resting point of the spike is on the player's foot, usually in the instep or near the ankle. However, if seated in a chair, the performer rests the instrument on his thigh. Most of the time the bow moves across both strings simultaneously, but the player may vary the style and play on a single string or bring out one string above the other by rotating the ğičak slightly on its spike to favor a string.

Right-hand technique involves keeping the wrist loose, making possible a fast, whip-like motion of the bow for special effect. Lefthand technique is quite limited. As in the case of most lutes of the North, the little finger is rarely used, and only comes into play when absolutely necessary for reaching a high pitch. Because of the high position of the strings above the fingerboard, it is difficult to play the instrument beyond the first position. I have never seen a performer reach beyond the range of his little finger, which means the scope of the piece must lie within an octave at most above the open-string pitch; in practice, the range rarely exceeds a fifth or sixth. If a player has to hit a note above this range, he will generally play the pitch an octave lower, on the lower string, instead of trying to reach an uncomfortably high spot on the fingerboard and risk cutting his finger. The placing of the first three fingers across both strings to play parallel fourths is a common practice. The strings are invariably tuned to a fourth.

Recently a new shape for the ğičak has been created by Baba Naim, the gifted Badaxšani musician who helped popularize the ğičak in Turkestan. Formerly a member of the radio orchestra, he is now a steady player at the Afghan Room of the Spinzar Hotel in Kabul and feels a need for expanding the resonance of the ğičak, his principal instrument. His fiddle, and a similar one that I commissioned, are fine examples of the instrument maker's art, and testify to the fact that the old traditions of craftsmanship are not as moribund in Afghanistan as most visitors think. Baba Naim's modern ğičak (Figure 4.24) is in the shape of the traditional Tašqurğan wood-cum-tin-can fiddle; the shape of the head and placement of pegs has been kept, as has the positioning of the bridge. However, it features a skin-covered square wood resonator in place of the metal sound box and set of eight resonating strings to augment the sound production. The main differences between the new and old ğičaks, besides those mentioned, consist in the elimination of the grooved pegbox in favor of an inside track leading the strings to the pegs, the addition of a fixed bone upper bridge, and introduction of a new peg shape to harmonize with the design of the head.

The modern ğičak of Figure 4.24 is the product of several Kabul-area artisans. The bone work is of exceptionally high quality, and the elaborate care lavished on small details, such as the peg tips and the rectangular X-shaped inlay with pearl between the pegs, bespeaks a much more attentive workmanship than is usually found among instrument makers. The wood has also been sanded and polished with unusual care, and even a coat of varnish has been applied to the sound box. The decoration at the back of the neck is done in camel bone, while that on the fingerboard is the traditional sheep bone.

Baba Naim's innovation is not so radical as might appear at first glance. According to H. G. Farmer (1957:445–46), there was a fiddle named the ğičak in classical times in Persia, which had "a larger sound-chest than the Kamancha and had eight sympthetic strings in addition." Moreover, Beliaev (1933:56) notes that in Eichhorn's collection of late nineteenth century Uzbekistani instruments there are two ğičaks with resonating strings.

The present-day distribution of the ğičak, though wide, is somewhat erratic. By and large, it corresponds to that of the dambura. I have seen ğičaks as far southeast as Lağman province, near Jalalabad, and as far northwest as Andxoi. The heartland of the instrument is said to be somewhere in Badaxšan, possibly the Šuğnan area, according to Baba Naim and other informants. In Turkestan, ğičaks are scattered

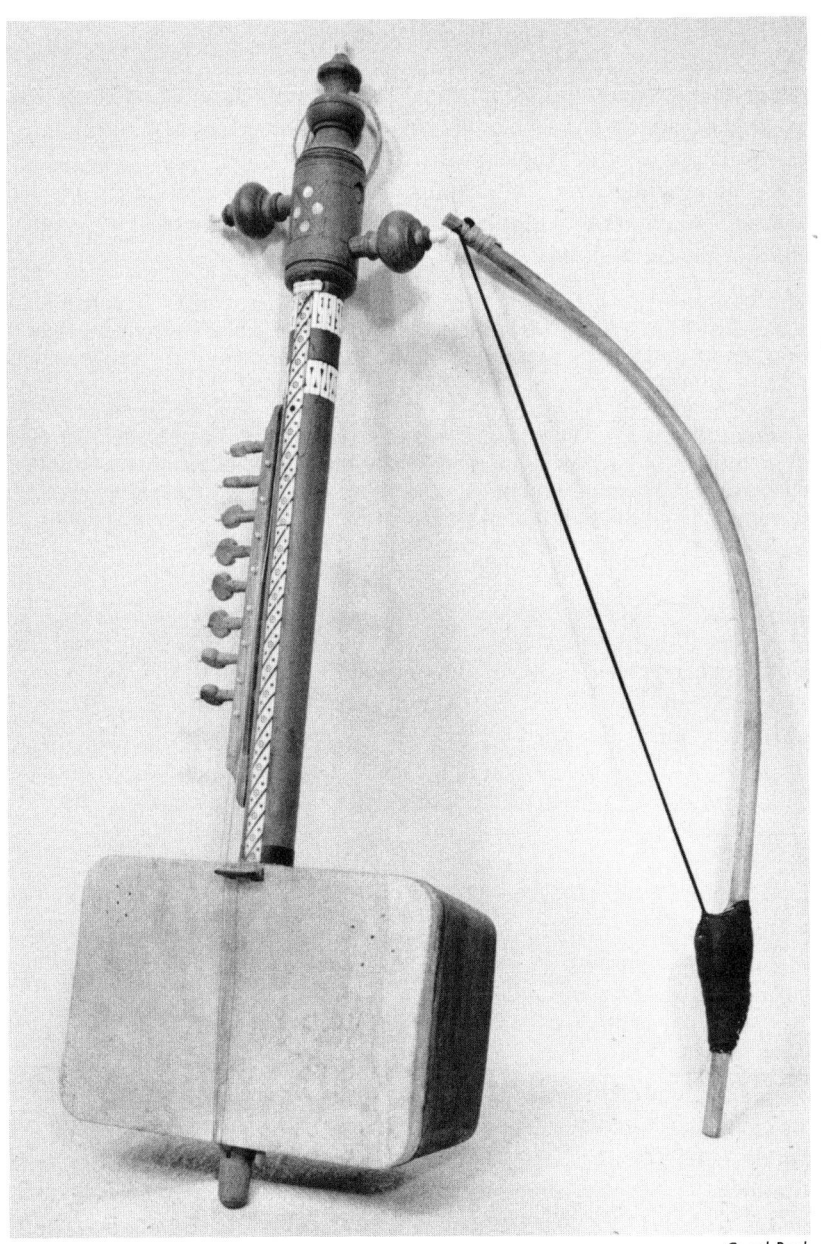

Fig. 4.24. New-style ğičak

rather thinly across the countryside, usually outnumbered by damburas by at least two to one. They are apparently rather popular through the Hazarajat, in central Afghanistan.

Among the *Atlas* entries for Tajikistan, an instrument labeled "ğičak" is remarkably similar to the fiddle of northern Afghanistan. Here is the description:

The two-stringed ğičak has a rather primitive structure. It consists of a wooden pole about 700 millimeters long, one end of which is slightly sharpened and serves as the leg of the instrument, and the other end is widened, serving as a head with two pegs placed in it. On the pole, a tin can (usually a gunpowder can) is placed, filling the function of a resonating body. The strings are of hair, and the instrument is tuned to a fourth. The bow is arched, with black horsehair that is rubbed with rosin. The instrument is held in a vertical position during play. Its sound is weak, with a whining timbre. The two-stringed ğičak is widespread in the mountain regions of Tajikistan, and at the present time is gradually being crowded out by the perfected three- and four-stringed ğičaks. (Vertkov 1963:128)

This description exactly fits the ğičak of Afghanistan, with the single exception of the use of horsehair instead of metal for strings; I have already alluded to the possibility of such a practice in Afghanistan in former times. In addition, Dansker (1965:446) notes that the use of metal strings has recently supplanted horsehair in Tajikistan as well. The three- and four-stringed fiddles mentioned in the *Atlas* are the spiked fiddles of urban Uzbek and Tajiks, which are direct relatives of the Persian and Turkish kamanča. Dansker (1965:446) notes that the two-stringed fiddle is predominantly used even today in the mountainous areas of southern Tajikistan. This location for the two-stringed fiddle is significant, since it is in adjacent Badaxšan that the ğičak has its stronghold in Afghanistan.

The Qobuz

The qobuz (Figures 4.25 and 4.26) is perhaps the rarest of all the stringed instruments of the North. I have documented it in only one locale (the town of K.), where it is associated with a highly unusual tradition: the curing ceremony of the local shaman (baxši). The fiddle pictured is one of three qobuzes I saw in K., all of which were quite similar in construction. The dimensions of the instrument are given in Table 4.7.

These measurements point up the sharp distinctions between the qobuz and all other lute types of the North. For example, the equality of length of neck and head is extraordinary, as in the fact that the head is somewhat deeper than the belly of the instrument. Also strik-

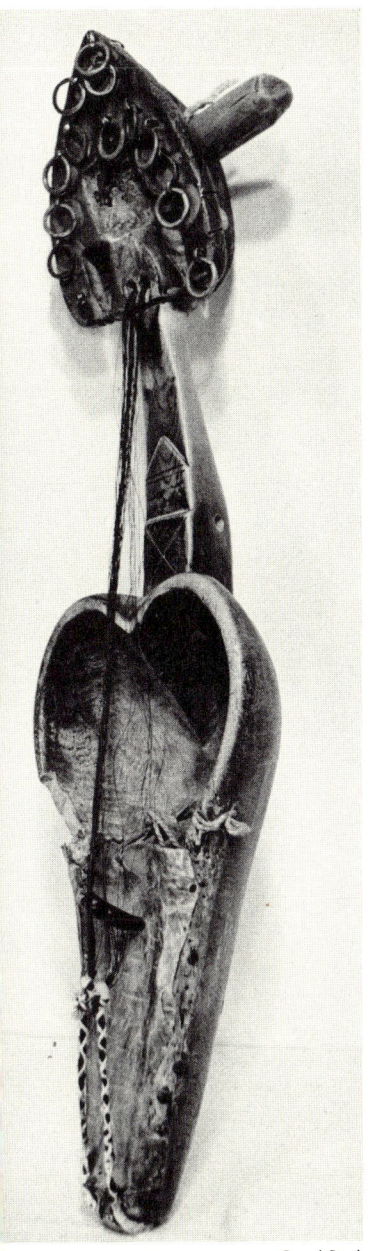

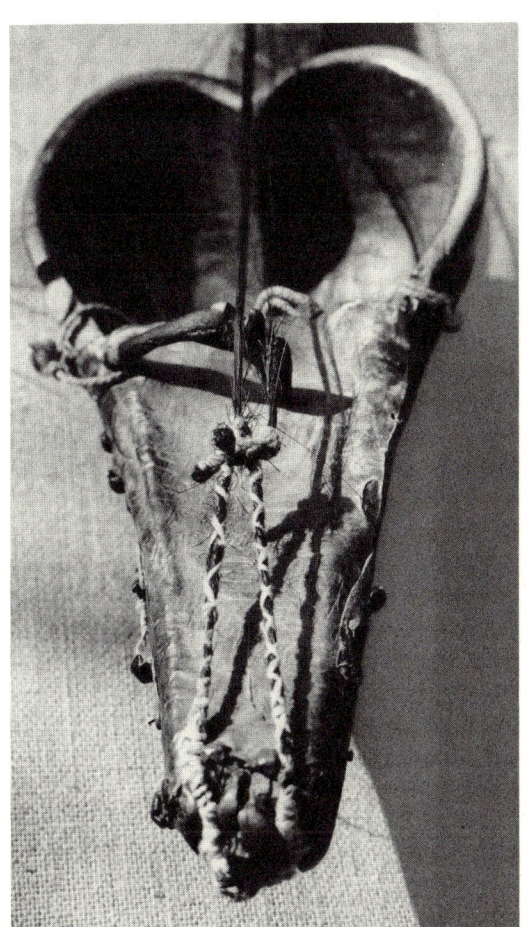

Fig. 4.26. Qobuz soundbox

Fig. 4.25. Qobuz.

TABLE 4.7

Dimensions of a Tašqurğani Qobuz
(In Centimeters)

Overall Length	Length of Head	Length of Neck	Length of Belly	Width of Neck	Depth of Belly	Depth of Head	Height of Bridge
74.5	19	19	36.5	14	7.5	8	4

ing is the great height of the bridge. Other features easily noticeable in Figure 4.25 are the iron rings fastened to the head (used as rattles during the baxši's ceremony) and the rectangular niche between the rings into which a mirror is placed (it is also said to have magical significance).

The qobuz seems less outlandish when compared to an instrument of the Kazakhs of Central Asia called the *qobyz,* described in the *Atlas* in the following way (Vertkov 1963:133):

Kobyz: a two-stringed instrument related to the Kirghiz *kyak.* The body, neck and head are made of one piece of walnut or birch. The body is ladle-shaped and hollowed out; the lower, extended section is closed by a membrane of camel skin, and the upper end is round and open. The neck is comparatively short, arched, without upper limit. The head is flat on the front side, and has projections ["cheeks"] on the back for pegs. The strings are of unwound horsehair (in the form of strands), fastened to a strap of leather below and to pegs above. Under the strings a high bridge is placed, having an almost straight left side and a longer right leg inclined outwards. The strings pass to the head through two round openings in the pegbox . . . the bow is short and arched. The average length of the instrument is 600–700 millimeters.

This account, as well as the photograph accompanying it, tallies precisely with every detail of the Afghan qobuzes and leaves little doubt as to the close ties between the instruments. The only distinctive feature of the qobuz in my collection is the extreme length of its bow (70 centimeters), which is in contrast to the information in the *Atlas.* All other details, including such distinctive features as the oddly shaped bridge, link the qobuz and qobyz closely.

It should also be noted that the qobuz, in one form or another, but under the same name, is played by the Karakalpaks of northwestern Uzbekistan and the Uzbeks of the Surxandarya and Kaškadarya regions just beyond the northern border of Afghanistan. The latter locale is the most probable point of connection between the Afghan specimens and those of Transoxania. Beliaev states that the qobuz was still in use among the Uzbeks of the Ferghana region and even in Buxara at the time of writing (1933:53). His description of the instrument tallies with that in the *Atlas* and with Table 4.7, except for the average length, which is somewhat shorter in Beliaev's version (1933:52).

Unfortunately, all three qobuzes of K. are of considerable age, and no one in the town was able to venture an account of how the instrument came to be there. It was generally felt to be quite archaic, and functions only as the baxši's companion. The only use this performer makes of the fiddle is to keep up a continuous drone on the open strings, thus excluding any possibility of using the repertoire of the qobuz as an aid to confirming its connections.

The qobuz is yet another example of an instrument that relates directly to Central Asian traditions and is in highly restricted use in northern Afghanistan. Its virtual identity with the fiddle of the far-away Kazakhs must remain something of a mystery for the present. It might be added that the Kazakh communities of Afghanistan, while they still use the Kazakh dümbra, do not seem to have brought along any specimens of the qobyz of their homeland.

FLUTES

The Tüidük

The tüidük (Figure 4.27) is the principal Turkmen aerophone, and it is not played by members of any other ethnic group. It is a long, open-ended flute made of six or seven nodes of a local steppe reed. Performers often add a slightly tapered open brass mouthpiece. Table 4.8 gives basic measurements of three tüidüks, all from Andxoi.

While all three flutes have five finger holes on the front and one on the back side, the distances between holes varies considerably from flute to flute. For example, the shortest tüidük, number 3, has distances somewhat greater than number 1, which is a bit longer, and almost as great as number 2, which is considerably longer. This indicates the absence of a standardized "scale" on tüidüks; the playing style leaves considerable latitude in altering pitch to the player.

The extreme length of the tüidük and the rather wide spacing of some of the finger holes make it ncessary for the performer to use the second joints of his fingers to cover the holes; indeed, it is only with considerable effort that even this expedient works. A *tüidükči* rests on his knees while playing the flute (as in Figure 4.27), rather than cross-legged like most instrumentalists, probably to give himself more leeway in handling his instrument. Even so, he must tilt his head to accommodate the length of the flute, and is forced to make a special

Fig. 4.27. Tüidük

effort to raise the bell of the flute when he desires to project the sound further; this is done only in moments of special importance during a piece. The player often sways to the music, describing a circular motion with the flute.

Since the tüidük, like the Turkmen dutar, is virtually indistinguishable from its Turkmenian Turkmen counterpart (called *kargy-tüidük*, a term I have never heard used in Afghanistan), it is again relevant to quote the entry in the *Atlas* (Vertkov 1963:115):

Kargy-tüidük: An open flute made of a large reed (locally called kargy), 750–800 millimeters long. Among Turkmen tüidükchis there is the conviction that the instrument made from a stalk that has seven sections (six joints) will possess the best musical qualities. To make sound production easier, the upper end (head) is sharpened or they put a metal ring on it. Six finger holes are cut into the lower part of the stalk; one of these (the uppermost) is on the reverse side. On the front side, the finger holes are placed in two groups: 3 + 2. The scale of the instrument is diatonic, in the range of a sixth; in performance, it can be increased to two-and-a-half octaves.

During play, the kargy-tüidük is held in front in an inclined position; the tooth (canine) is placed in the upper end of the stalk. The whistling sounds of the kargy-tüidük are accompanied by whistling and

TABLE 4.8

Dimensions of Selected Tüidüks
(In Centimeters)

Instrument	Overall Length	Diameter	Number of Nodes	Distances Between Finger Holes*	Distance From Top Finger Hole to Finger Hole on Back
1	80.3	2	7	6.7, 4.6, 2.4, 2.5	6
2	85	2.5	6	7, 4.8, 2.6, 2.6	7
3	79.5	2	7	7, 4.8, 2.5, 2.5	7

*Measurements are from beginning of one hole to beginning of next hole and proceed from bottom to top.

humming noises that are more audible in the lower register, where the resonance of the instrument is significantly weaker. . . . The finger holes of the front side are covered by the second joints of the straightened fingers. The performer moves the instrument from side to side in time or describes a circular motion; in especially strained moments, the lower end of the instrument is raised above the level of the face. As a rule, it is played in the open air, although the resonance of the instrument is not marked by great strength. . . . The dimensions of *navai* [tüidük pieces] are small, since the difficulty of sound production on the kargy-tüidük leads to quick exhaustion of the musician.

Aside from solo performance, simultaneous performance of two tüidükchis in unison, at which they place themselves opposite one another, is also practiced. Not infrequently, this sort of duet takes on the form of a competition. Under the existing means of playing on the kargy-tüidük, its canal becomes strongly dampened, and the instrument starts to err. For this reason, the performer usually has a whole selection of kargy-tüidüks with him, keeping them in a special leather case.

The kargy-tüidük is primarily a pastoral instrument. In recent years the number of tüidükchis has steadily decreased. The more accomplished players are considered rarities.

This description calls for a number of comments. It can be seen by a glance at Table 4.8 that the average length of tüidüks in Afghanistan is somewhat greater than that given in the *Atlas,* and that the ideal number of reed sections (six) is often exceeded. It is worth noting that in *Turkmenskaia muzyka,* Beliaev gives 83 centimeters as the average length of the instrument. (Beliaev and Uspenskii 1928:96)

The data concerning playing technique and performance style correspond precisely to the data for Afghanistan, although I have never seen a tüidükči raise his flute above the level of his face, and I have not observed that the humming noise of the fundamental pitch, above which the melody is played, decreases markedly in the upper register. It is probably only due to the greater gap in pitch between the fundamental and melody in the upper register that the ear is diverted from the fundamental, making it seem less important. That tüidük pieces are not very long is a fact taken up in more detail in Chapter 3.

Like the other Turkmen instruments (dutar and dili-tüidük), the tüidük is a rare find in northern Afghanistan. Hence, competition as an important basis for performance is a highly unlikely occurrence; there are simply not enough tüidükčis to go around. When the instrument is used today, it is in the hands of a professional musician, or baxši (not to be confused with the shaman of the same title), who plays for special occasions. The reason for the decline of tüidük performance by two players does not seem to lie in Turkmen tribal differentiations. Beliaev (1928:97) states that Uspenskii found the tüidük to be spread mostly in the Merv region, the place of origin of many Afghan Turkmens, and did not see the instrument among the Salyr, Yomud, and Čaudyr tribes. None of these tribes is present in any considerable numbers in Afghanistan, so it seems that the tüidük must have been particularly widespread among the Ersari, who make up the majority of the Turkmens of Afghanistan; its present decline, then, must be due to changes in the cultural milieu. As a final comment on the *Atlas* data, it might be added that I never saw the tüidük used as a pastoral instrument, though Turkmens cite this as a possibility.

Long open-ended, end-blown flutes have a long history in the Near East and Central Asia. Sachs cites the flutes used as early as the Egyptian Old Kingdom (1929:82–83). Today, the tüidük is only one of a great number of open-ended flutes current in the area. To the west, it is closely related to the nai or *mey* of Iran, Turkey, and the Levant; to the east, it shows a certain resemblance to the *sybyzga* of the Kaizakhs and the *čo'or* of the Kirghiz; to the north one finds the Bashkir *kurai,* and to the south the much smaller but similarly constructed nai or tula of the Paštuns and Baluch. Figure 4.28 shows the tüidük of Figure 4.27 placed next to a nai of the Levant and one of Kandahar, in southwestern Afghanistan. Note the similarity in dimension of the Levantine nai (length 74.5 centimeters) and the differences: six finger holes in a 3 + 3 formation instead of five, nine reed sections instead of seven. The nai of Kandahar, only 59.5 centimeters long and with only four finger holes, all on the front, stands in sharp contrast to the other two open-ended flutes pictured, and the rather elaborate carved and painted ornamentation makes this southern flute a much more colorful instrument.

The importance of the tüidük in Turkmen thought is illustrated by the high position the instrument is given in legend. According to Uspenskii's informants, "Adam was made of clay, but had no soul.

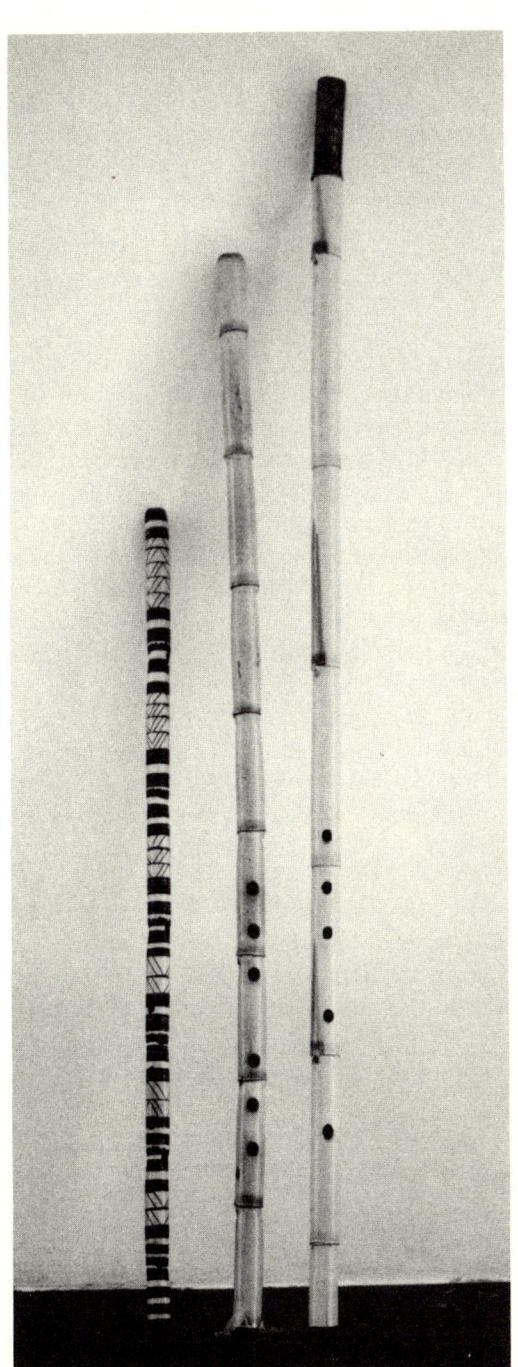

Fig. 4.28. *Tüidük* (right) *with Levantine opened-ended flute* (center) *and Kandahari open-ended flute* (left)

By playing on the tüidük, Israel, Jebiral, and the other angels breathed life into him." Another Turkmen legend gives Alexander the Great the role played by Midas in Western myth, in the story of the barber who mistakenly confides to a reed (in this case the kargy reed) the secret of the king's horns (Beliaev and Uspenskii 1928:95). It is also interesting to note that the hole on the back of the flute is called "the devil's hole" (Beliaev and Uspenskii 1928:95), a term that harks back to the tale of the origin of the dutar cited earlier.

The Badaxšani Recorder

This mellow-sounding flute (see Figure 4.29) is found only in Badaxšan, among the mountain Tajiks. The local name for any sort of flute is tula, or sometimes nai, with little differentiation made for categories of flutes such as block, transverse, etc., except in the case of the metal cross flute known as the *berenji* (probably deriving its name from *berenj,* a type of brass), which stems from Pakistan.

I have seen two types of recorders in Badaxšan: those of a maker from Šuǧnan, and those of an artisan of Yaftāl, near Faizabad. There are probably countless other regional variations of these types. Table 4.9 gives the measurements for a group of Badxašani recorders. Numbers 1–4 are the products of the Šuǧni master, who now lives in Faizabad, while number 5 is a Yaftal model.

I was not able to find out why some recorders have six holes and some five, nor why the Yaftal model has a hole on the back, a feature that is lacking in the flutes of the Šuǧni maker. Performers just didn't feel that it made much difference. Another feature of variation overlooked by players is the difference in basic scales produced by blowing gently on the flute in its lowest register. Such "basic" scales are hardly relevant to the instrument's tone system, both because the lowest register is rarely used and because players do not keep to the pitches provided by the finger holes but produce additional desired tones by lipping. Nor is there any standardization in the placement of fingers on the sound holes; the method shown in Figure 4.29 indicates only the preference of one performer.

An unusual feature of the Šuǧni recorders (Figure 4.29) is the banded decorative pattern encircling most of the surface. The rings are burnt into the wood rather than being incised, a technique that is rather unusual for the area. Sakata (1973:p.c.) has recently discovered the artisan's method: "The article is spun around on a lathe, then a special kind of thorn *(khar)* is lightly touched to it and the friction causes the article to burn (also on yak tail handles, etc.)." The *nai čupāni* ("shepherd's flute") or *tutak* of Tajikistan, as pictured in the *Atlas*

Fig. 4.29.
Šuğni-style
Badaxšani recorder

(Vertkov 1963:125), has similar banding, but it is accomplished by tying on what appear to be strips of gut rather than by treating the wood itself.

It is interesting that the Badaxšani recorder, unlike other members of the local instrumentarium, does not seem to have a direct relative on the Soviet side. The nai čupani, cited above, has a blunt end and does not appear to have an inserted block. These differences, as well as the sharp difference in length (20 centimeters for the nai čupani vs. an average of 30 centimeters for the Badaxšani recorder), set the two flutes apart. However, the fact that the tutak is made of

TABLE 4.9

Dimensions of Five Badaxšani Recorders
(In Centimeters)

Instrument	Overall Length	Minimum to Maximum Circumference	Number of Finger Holes	Distance Between Finger Holes
1	29.5	4-8	5	2, 2.3, 2.3, 2.3
2	30.5	4.5-8	5	2.4, 2.3, 2.3, 2.2
3	32.4	5-9	5	2.5, 2.7, 2.5, 2.5
4	32.5	5-8.5	6	2.2, 2.3, 2.3, 2.3, 2.3
5	29.2	4.7-7.5	6 (one on back)	2.8, 3.0, 2.9, 3.0

two strips of wood glued together length wise (Vertkov 1963:125), like the Yaftal model of the Badaxšani flute, provides some basis for comparison.

The Badaxšani recorder seems to be widely used in its home area. Among a random crowd of perhaps twenty-five men gathered in the Faizabad bazaar to try out my newly acquired instruments, about half a dozen men admitted that they could play the flute, and did so. Considering the shame usually associated with musical ability in Afghanistan, this is a fairly high ratio of positive response. The fact that the flute is made and sold in the town, and played by both townspeople and country folk, is further evidence of its popularity, and it can be assumed that some people out in the hinterland make their own cruder flutes along the same lines. Most townspeople, while they can play the indigenous flute, often prefer the metallic cross flute (berenji) mentioned above, which is imported from Pakistan via Kabul.

It may be worth comparing the Badaxšani recorder with that of Kohistan, the heavily Tajik area just north of Kabul. The latter flute always has six finger holes, and it is a straight cylinder, somewhat longer (39 centimeters) and with a larger diameter than the Badaxšani block flute. It has an invariably diatonic basic scale, unlike the Badaxšani flute. It is also made of much lighter wood, both in density and color, and has no ornamentation at all, beyond two strips of gold paper glued just below the upper sound notch and at the very bottom of the flute. The finger holes are considerably larger in diameter and vary somewhat in size, probably because of the attempt made to regulate the scale.

Thus, the Badaxšani recorder seems to be an indigenous flute that is unique to its home area: it is not found anywhere else, and there are no other flutes either in neighboring Tajikistan or among Afghan Tajiks (such as those of Kohistan) that can be described as close counterparts to the block flute of Badaxšan. A possible exception is a similar block flute (though longer and not tapered) played by Hazaras only in the Bamian area; the scale on the one specimen I have is rather close to Badaxšani tunings, and the piece played by the Hazara who sold me the flute sounded remarkably like a felak.

SINGLE-REED PIPE

The Dili-Tüidük

The dili-tüidük (Figure 4.30) holds the distinction of being the only single-reed pipe in northern Afghanistan today, and probably in all Afghanistan as well. A paired single-reed pipe of the Uzbeks,

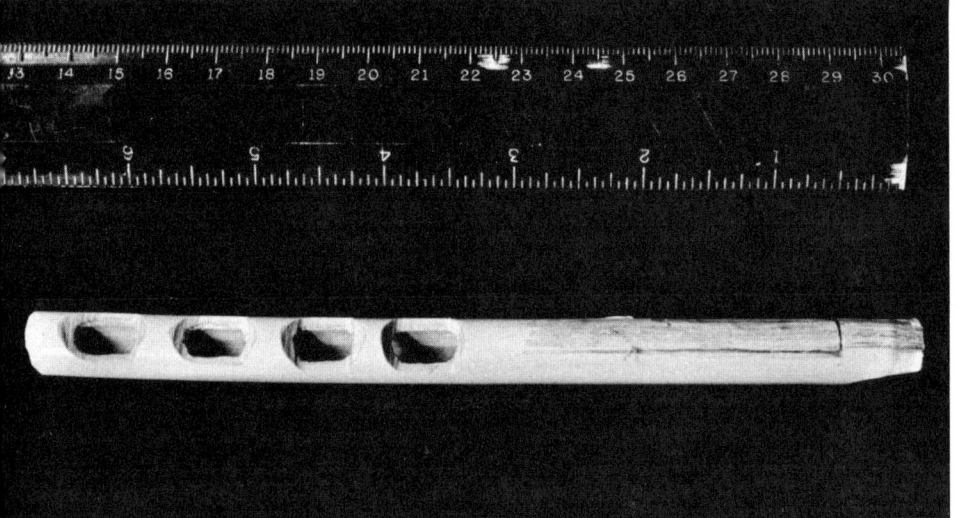

Fig. 4.30. Dili-tüidük

the qošnai, was formerly used in Afghanistan (Çagatay and Sjoberg 1955:108), but seems to have vanished.

The dili-tüidük is a very small instrument (length: 7.5 centimeters), easily carved from a common short steppe reed called *kamšak* and conveniently carried in the pocket. Let us turn once again to the Soviet *Atlas* for a description of the instrument as used in Turkmenistan (Vertkov 1963:115):

Dili-tüidük: the tongue-tüidük (dili = tongue) — made of thin reed, 150–160 millimeters long. In the upper part of the stalk a single reed is cut, and below, 3–4 finger holes are made. The scale of the instrument is diatonic, in the range of a perfect fifth, but performers widen it to two octaves and add necessary chromatically altered tones. This is accomplished by strong blowing, shortening the vibrating part of the reed with the lips, incomplete covering of the holes with the fingers and the placing of the palm at the end-opening.

The sound of the dili-tüidük, according to its coloring, approaches the timbre of the human voice, and for this reason, its most characteristic repertoire consists of songs.

The dili-tüidük, like the kargy-tüidük, is primarily a pastoral instrument, and is gradually going out of use.

The most striking feature of the above description is the estimate of length given, which is exactly twice that of the instrument in Figure 4.30. Perhaps the figures in the *Atlas* are somewhat exaggerated, since Beliaev says of the dili-tüidük that "its measurements do not exceed those of a pencil" (Beliaev and Uspenskii 1928:97), which is much closer to the size of the instrument found on the Afghan side of the border.

It should be noted that the number of finger holes in Afghanistan is usually four, rarely three. In addition, the scale of the instrument in Figure 4.30 is within the range of a perfect fifth, but tends towards a Phrygian rather than a "diatonic" pentachord. The devices listed for changing pitch are in use among the Afghan Turkmens, except for the placing of the palm at the end of the instrument. While the timbre of the dili-tüidük, as stated in the *Atlas,* is somewhat like that of the human voice, in Afghanistan it tends to sound more like the kazoo. In any case, similarity to the human voice is not sufficient reason for explaining the predominance of songs in the instrument's repertoire, a characteristic that typifies all of the aerophones of Afghanistan. Beliaev feels differently about the quality of the dili-tüidük's sound, describing it as "sounding in the higher register like our piccolo" (Beliaev and Uspenskii 1928:97), a phenomenon I have not observed in Afghanistan.

Some features of the dili-tüidük pictured in the *Atlas* (Vertkov 1963: Plate 554) also differentiate it from the pipe of Figure 4.30. The former has dark rings around its finger holes that almost suggest that the holes were burned, whereas the Afghan instrument has clearly had its openings cut quite precisely with a knife. Another distinctive feature of the Turkmenian instrument is the piece of string wrapped around the base of the reed; perhaps this serves to regulate pitch. Dili-tüidüks of Afghanistan need a short piece of thread under, rather than over, the reed to produce proper resonance; indeed the instrument cannot be made to sound without this aid. I have not seen a string tied over the reed, however, and such a practice stifles the sound on the instrument in my collection.

Since paired single-reed pipes are so widespread across much of the Near East, the Caucasus, and Central Asia, one wonders at the absence of joined dili-tüidüks in Afghanistan. An observation of Beliaev's gives some background to this question: "In earlier times the Turkmens had a paired dili-tüidük — the qošo dili tüidük, related to the qošnai of the Uzbeks, but at the present it has gone out of use" (Beliaev and Uspenskii 1928:97). Beliaev gives no indication of why the paired pipe vanished, and we have no way of knowing whether such an instrument was ever in use in Afghanistan.

The immediate neighbor of the dili-tüidük is the Uzbek sibiziq, which Karomatov (1972:63) states is found in "remote areas of the

Republic" and is played mainly by shepherds. His description of the sibiziq tallies closely with that of the dili-tüidük, to which he says the sibiziq is related. In addition, he cites a similar instrument of the Tajiks, the *surnak*, for which unfortunately no information is readily available. Katomatov sees the sibiziq as the ancestor of the qošnai, which looks very much like two dili-tüidüks tied together. I have no data on usage of the sibiziq or the surnak in Afghanistan.

To judge by the data for single-reed pipes given by Sachs (1929: 113–14), the dili-tüidük and sibiziq are somewhat anomalous in structure. First, Sachs notes that most clarinets with more than three finger holes are usually grouped in pairs. Second, he gives an exceedingly wide distribution for clarinets with four finger holes, leaving out the Turkmen area and including the following: Egypt, Russia, Lithuania, Sardinia, parts of Indonesia, and the island of Yap in the Pacific (1929:114). Such a pattern makes it hard to pinpoint the closest relatives of the dili-tüidük and sibiziq. The qošnai does not have the separate mouthpiece (containing the reed) characteristic of most paired pipes of the Near East, and thus stands particularly close to the dili-tüidük and sibiziq, though the greater length (average: 25 centimeters [Vertkov 1963:118]) and number of finger holes (up to seven) make even the qošnai seem considerably removed from the dili-tüidük and sibiziq.

The Turkmen dutar, tüidük, and dili-tüidük make up the basic instrumentarium of the Turkmens of northern Afghanistan. They are also said to play the jew's harp, which is produced in towns with heavy Turkmen concentrations such as Aqča, but I have only seen the instrument played by Uzbeks and Tajiks.

DRUMS

The Zirbaǧali

The zirbaǧali ("under-armpit"), a vase-shaped drum (Figure 4.31), is, along with the dambura and the doira (see below), the most widespread instrument of the North, indeed of all Afghanistan. While it is not an indispensable requisite of musical performance, it is often the boon companion of stringed-instrument players and singers, providing a steady rhythm for the melody. It may be played solo as dance accompaniment, but the doira is generally preferred for such occasions.

Figure 4.31 shows the most common type of zirbaǧali, made of pottery. Other types can be made of wood, and may even be decorated. Wooden drums are by far in the minority but are geographically as well distributed as pottery drums. Wooden drums are considered to be much more valuable, probably because of their greater durability and cost of construction. The latter is probably the reason for the scarcity of wooden zirbağalis, and their greater prestige explains why performers refused to sell them to me. Wooden drums are always made of some hardwood, like apricot.

When the drum is made of pottery, the kind of material used for everyday household items such as pitchers and vases is employed. It is quite crude and fragile. The zirbağali may be glazed or left plain; the instrument in Figure 4.31 is dark green. Goatskin is generally used for the drumhead. It is usually stretched over the instrument and then secured by means of a strip of fabric fastened all the way around the edge of the skin; on the drum in Figure 4.31, the strip is dyed bright red. Only rarely have I seen a zirbağali with the skin laced onto the body, and then only once in the North. Before and sometimes during play, the skin is warmed over a fire to keep the drumhead taut. There seems to be no center of production for the zirbağali in the North; local potters make them on commission, but they are seen for sale in the bazaar only in the Kohistan area north of Kabul, where they are made in the famous pottery center of Istalif. Istalif drums are not exported to the North and are now mainly sold to tourists. Size varies considerably among zirbağalis, but 30 centimeters can be considered an average diameter for the drumhead, and 45 centimeters can be taken as a typical overall length.

True to its name, the zirbağali is usually held under the arm, with its neck resting on the player's thigh as he sits cross-legged on the floor. It is almost always held under the left arm and played with the right hand, but left-handed players can also be found. During play, the left arm may or may not clamp the drum firmly in place. Sometimes no pressure is applied and the drum merely rests along the player's thigh without support. It is never played in an upright position, which would stifle the resonance, but may be placed in a variety of positions. Figure 4.32 shows the zirbağali being rested along the player's instep.

Two sounds form the basic vocabulary of the instrument: a deep tone produced by striking the skin at the center and a less resonant sound produced by hitting the edge. A third type of tone quality can be attained by pressing one finger between the edge and center and varying the tension while striking the center; this produces a kind of swooping tone by changing the basic pitch of the drum.

The thumbs are never used. Quite often the right hand takes a position for striking the center of the skin, while the left is reserved for the tones closer to the edge. Figure 4.32 shows the player just as he has finished the center stroke with his left hand and is about to hit

Fig. 4.31.
Zirbağali

Fig. 4.32. Zirbağali
playing position

the edge with his right hand. In slow play, one hand may play alone. In this case, either all four fingers play at the center, or the three last fingers play at the center while the index finger takes the pitches at the edge of the skin. Sometimes the latter tones are produced by an upward stroke made by the side of the first joint of the index finger. At the center, the stroke may be quite heavy, with an immediate recoil after impact, or if a muffled tone is desired, the hand stops the tone by remaining after impact.

Often when there is a break in his drum pattern, the player raises his right hand after a stroke and performs some gesture related to the dance, such as rotating the wrist gracefully. This is another indication of the close relationship between the zirbağali and the dance, again recalling the close connection in the minds of the audience between musicians and dancers, both of whom occupy the same low status in society.

The zirbağali is not considered to be an instrument that requires specialization on the part of the performer, and it is felt that anyone can play it. Related to this attitude is the lack of a highly developed technique for the drum. No one makes a serious effort to become a virtuoso performer on the zirbağali, and conversely virtuoso performance is not required in the situations in which the instrument is used.

The zirbağali is widespread across all of Afghanistan. I have seen it in Lağman, far to the east, in Kandahar and Girišk in the southwest, in Herat on the western flank of the country, and all across the North, from Maimana to Faizabad. This extensive use of the zirbağali makes it difficult to ascribe the instrument to any particular group or region, as does the fact that vase-shaped drums are found across the entire Near East. Perhaps the most notable feature of the drum's distribution is the fact that it has no relatives in Transoxania, which underlines the western rather than northern roots of the vase-shaped drum found in Afghanistan.

The Doira

The doira (Figure 4.33) is the principal frame drum of the North (and of all Afghanistan) and the main women's instrument. Although men may play the doira as well, it is strongly associated with women, and in particular with women's performance during wedding festivities.

The doira is a rather large tambourine, averaging about 40 centimeters in diameter and with a frame about 6 centimeters deep. Sometimes jingling plates of metal are inserted in slots along the side, as in the Western tambourine, but frequently they are merely nailed to the inside of the frame. Many doiras have no jingles at all. The frame itself

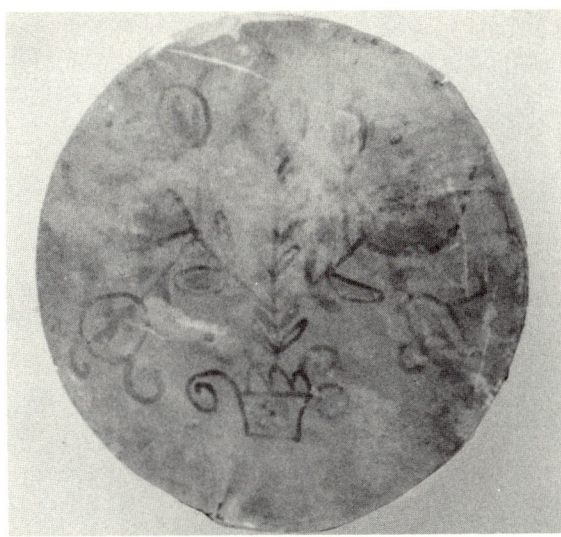

Fig. 4.33.
Doira

is generally made of at least two pieces of wood, roughly joined by a nail. The wood is unfinished and the strips are often not straight. The skin is usually of sheep or goat, but a high-quality drum may have antelope hide. There is rarely any trace of fur on the skin, which is stretched and glued onto the frame. Often the skin becomes slack after a short period of use and must be quite strongly heated to be usable at all. In short, the doira is frequently made with little care for its durability. A further constructional detail is the frequent addition of a crudely painted symmetrical design on the front of the drumhead. The ornamental pattern shown in Figure 4.33 is typical in its floral motif and rough free-hand style. Red and green are the common colors used.

Doiras are almost never sold publicly. The main exception to this rule is the widespread sale of the instrument during Nowruz season at Mazar-i Šarif, when heaps of crude tambourines can be seen around the central square of the great shrine of Ali. While an adequate census has not — and probably never will — indicate the actual spread of the doira, it can be assumed that in towns, nearly every house has a doira to be taken down for festivities.

The playing position of the doira is nearly uniform everywhere in Afghanistan. The instrument is held in the left hand directly in front of the player and is grasped at the center of the bottom arc by the thumb and pressed against the soft part of the palm between thumb and forefinger. The other fingers of the left hand help play on the skin. The right thumb is placed at the three o'clock position, pressing inward to offset the pressure from the left hand and to provide additional support. The other fingers of the right hand play on the skin while the thumb is pivoted from the wrist. Thus, only two fingers are principally occupied in supporting the doira, leaving eight fingers free for playing.

Like the zirbağali, the doira relies mainly on two distinct sounds to build up rhythmic patterns. One is the central, bass sound and the other is the peripheral, treble pitch. Because of the more cramped position of the left hand and the relative freedom of the right hand pivoting on the thumb, it is the latter that reaches out to play the bass tones and the former that supplies the supporting treble pitches. Like the zirbağali, the doira is usually called upon to play only a modest accompanying role, in which all that is necessary is to strongly outline the basic beats of the musical phrase. However, some women take the trouble to develop a more involved technique, which may exceed that usually heard on the zirbağali. The doira, much more than the zirbağali, is absolutely indispensable to the dance, especially among women.

The doira is found in basically the same shape and size across the North and in the rest of the country, and is usually played in the same manner everywhere. However, one distinct usage can be found in the farther reaches of Badaxšan. There the instrument is called a *daf,* a term widespread for many types of drums across the Near East and into India, and it is somewhat larger (diameter: 43 centimeters; depth: 9 centimeters). In addition, it may be rested on the floor for play, with the performer's right hand providing support at the twelve o'clock position.

The term *doira* is common to a number of frame drums of the area, principally in Uzbekistan and Tajikistan. The description of the doira in the *Atlas* (Vertkov 1963:122–23) not only confirms the close ties between tambourines on both sides of the border, but also hints at the greater variety of construction and manner of playing in Transoxania:

Doira: a tambourine with a narrow round wooden frame, on one side of which is stretched a membrane, and on the inside of which metal jingling bells are attached. The frame is bent, with a diameter of about 400 millimeters. The membrane is made of animal skin or stomach, and sometimes of fish skin.

During play the membrane of the doira is heated in the sun or over a fire. A well-stretched skin gives a clean, resonant and strong sound. The doira is held between the thumb and index fingers and is struck by the four fingers of both hands in the center of the skin, close to the periphery and near the frame itself. In the former case, the resulting sound is lower and muffled, in the latter, high and resonant. In addition, players strike with all the fingers together, separately, with a rap of the little finger, etc. At the necessary time the instrument is shaken, producing the jingling sound of the metal rings striking against each other and on the frame. Sometimes, to gain great resonance during solo play on the doira, metal fingernails like thimbles are sometimes worn on the fingers.

In general, the doira has far greater prominence in Uzbekistan and Tajikistan than in Afghanistan. Solo players may even play simultaneously on several instruments and juggle them, performing with great virtuosity. A performance of this sort that I witnessed in Dushanbe (Tajikistan) was truly extraordinary.

Dansker (1965:255–57) reports two shapes of doira for the Karategin and Darwaz regions of Tajikistan: the first is built like the Afghan doira, with jingles nailed to the inside of the frame, while the second is made in the form of a Western tambourine, with slots cut out for the metal rattling plates. The symmetrical, somewhat floral design he gives for the outer surface of the skin is similar to that seen in Figure 4.33.

In rural mountainous Tajikistan, group performance on doiras was formerly practiced. According to informants, there are remnants of this style in present-day Badaxšan, involving several sizes of doira all playing the same rhythmic pattern. Nurjanov reports group performance in the Karategin and Darwaz areas under the name *doirajang* ("doira fight"), in which four or five women participate, but he does not state the degree of rhythmic complexity involved (Nurjanov 1965:138).

The Small Doira

The small doira, a frame drum (Figure 4.34), is a musical toy that is notable for being the only two-headed drum used in the North. In consists of a small (11 centimeters) pair of drumheads fastened to a somewhat larger (19 centimeters) stick that serves as a handle. Figure 4.34 shows the most typical small doira. Extending from both sides of the frame are threads fastened by tacks and wrapped around small pieces of wood that serve as beaters for the drum when it is shaken. The threads run about 8 centimeters long, and the spool-shaped beaters average just under 2 centimeters in length. Players often set the beaters into motion by holding the stick between the palms of both hands and rubbing the palms together. The two skins that form the drumheads overlap, and one layer is glued down over the other. The skins, like those on doiras, are often decorated with red and green natural dyes in geometric designs. The most common is perhaps a cross-shaped pattern that roughly divides the circle of the skin into quadrants; then each quadrant is partially filled with a similar design, such as the cherry-shaped figure of Figure 4.34.

Fig. 4.34. Small doira

The small doira, which does not seem to have a name of its own despite its distinctive structure, is clearly regarded as a children's toy. It appears along with the doira at Nowruz time in Mazar, contributing to the holiday spirit of the occasion. It is rarely seen at other times and places. Large numbers of small doiras are made at Istalif, the potters' town cited above as a center of zirbağali construction, and are sold for a few pennies.

The small doira is a rather provocative instrument in terms of suggesting far-flung points of connection with other music cultures. Sachs (1929:172) has a special subdivision for this type of drum. He calls the instrument a *Klappertrommel* ("knocking drum"), which he defines as "a drum, the skin of which is struck through a jerking motion by small balls hanging on short strings" (1929:172). He gives the areas of distribution as Hither India, Tibet, Mongolia, China, Korea, Japan, Java, and Bali, and he adds that "since the device is given to so many forms of drums . . . this fact speaks against its being of great age" (1929:173). The fact that the small doira has both two heads and a handle confuses the issue somewhat, since the typical small frame drum with a handle "known as the shaman's drum . . . [which is] spread over India, Central and North Asia and the American continent" (Sachs 1940:33) generally has only one head and is struck by a stick or the hand. Thus it is not completely clear what the origin or immediate relatives of the small doira of Afghanistan might be.

IDIOPHONES

The Ğerğerānak

Among the various instruments sold as toys during Nowruz in the North (small doiras, animal-shaped pottery whistles, etc.) is a wooden ratchet (Figure 4.35) called the *ğerğerānak,* an onomatopoetic name. This wooden idiophone measures 17 centimeters long, with an 18 centimeter handle. The eleven-spoked ratchet wheel connected to the handle rotates when the instrument is shaken with a circular motion, pushing the raised slat, which is free at the end near the cog, and making a sharp rapid-fire clacking sound. The wood and the colored streaks of

Fig. 4.35. Ğerğeranak

decoration are quite crude, but the parts fit together well and produce a resonant tone quality, much to the delight of children.

There is little information on ratchets in the Near East or Central Asia. Sachs (1929:227) regards the ratchet as "the most perfected form of the scraper." He adds that "the only non-European ratchets are found — also as children's toys — in Java, Hither India and Mesopotamia," and the illustration he gives of an Indian ratchet (1929:227) corresponds with the instrument of Figure 4.35 quite closely.

The Zang-i Kaftar

The zang-i kaftar ("dove-bell') is a set of small, doughnut-shaped crotals (Figure 4.36) used as a percussive accompaniment for the dambura. Each bell (diameter: 2.5 centimeters) consists of two hollow metal rings fastened together at the inner rims and left slightly open at the outer rims. The sound is produced by tiny metal pellets placed inside as rattles.

The zang-i kaftar (often termed just *zang*) come four to five in a set. They are strung together and donned by the dambura player on his right hand by fastening the string to his wrist, so that one rattle

Carol Reck

Fig. 4.36. Zang-i kaftar

hangs between each of his fingers; thus all of them sound each time he moves his hand for a stroke. Only a small proportion of players, usually well-known professionals, use the zang-i kaftar regularly. Most of the zang sold today are poor-quality Pakistani products brought up from Kabul. Locally made, highly resonant zang are hard to come by and must be obtained from damburačis. I bought my set after lengthy negotions with a jeweler, who had promised to make me brand-new bells. He finally decided it was too much bother and bought them from a local musician, selling them to me for a profit.

The zang-i kaftar is just another example of the attempt musicians make to provide intensive rhythmic support for the tunes they play (indeed, their efforts may sometimes reach the point of making the tune inaudible). Such a practice again confirms the close connection between music and the dance in the North.

The Tal (Zang, Tüsak)

The tal (Figure 4.37), also known as *zang* in Persian and *tüsak* in Uzbek, is a widespread idiophone of the North. It is the constant companion of the Uzbek teahouse singer, which explains its great popu-

Carol Reck

Fig. 4.37. Tal (zang, tüsak)

larity. Its piercing clink is the first evidence of live performance to attract a passerby in the bazaar on a busy market day and lure him into the teahouse for a bit of entertainment.

The tal consists of a small pair of finger cymbals made of brass, with the following average measurements: diameters, 5.5 centimeters; slant from rim to crown, 3.5 centimeters. The cymbals are each equipped with a hole at the peak of the crown for passage of a piece of sturdy string or a short leather thong by which the performer holds the instrument, one cymbal in each hand. He grasps the string with thumb and forefinger and presses the fingers against the crown of the cymbal. The cymbals are usually roughly made, so that the circumference of the rim is not evenly shaped and the slant is not equal from all points of the rim to the crown. The cymbals are also not usually matched exactly for size. Nevertheless, they produce a sharp, ringing tone that is quite effective and even true to pitch.

The tal is usually played by the singers in the conventional teahouse ensemble of dambura player and two singers, perhaps joined by a zirbağali or, less frequently, by a doira player. The singers sit face to face, both striking the tal in time to the beat. The usual playing position has the open faces of the cymbals perpendicular to the floor. In this case, one cymbal, usually the one in the right hand, remains stationary, while the other strikes the first either face-to-face, with the hand quickly removed to avoid damping the tone, or on the rim. In a second playing position, the stationary cymbal is held face-up. The cymbals are never allowed to hang free, but are always tightly controlled by the thumb and forefinger.

The tal is locally made in various towns of Turkestan and is found only in that region of Afghanistan. The existence of three names for the instrument is intriguing, and may help shed light on the origin of the tal. The term *zang,* a Persian word, is clear; it implies any sort of bell in Afghanistan, as in the case of the zang-i kaftar discussed above. The fact that there is a separate Uzbek word, *tüsak,* indicates the Uzbeks' fondness for the finger cymbals. The term *tal* is the most unusual, since it has no clear connection with Afghanistan and seems perhaps related to the Indian term *tal,* meaning a particular rhythmic pattern, as well as referring to certain types of bells (Sachs 1915:19).

Although the *Atlas* and other recent Soviet sources give no information on the spread of finger cymbals in Transoxania, Beliaev (1933:5) quotes August Eichhorn, the pioneer researcher of Central Asian music, who reported (in the 1880s) seeing tal under the name *sagat* in Uzbekistan. Beliaev notes that the term *sagat* is given by Curt Sachs as the Arabic word for castanets, and adds: ". . . under the name of zang it occurs in Persia, Afghanistan and Chinese Turkestan" (1933:6)

Further evidence about the term *zang* in the Persian world is offered by the *Lavignac Encyclopedia of Music* (Huart 1922:3076), which illustrates a pair of small hand cymbals under the name *zeng,* noting that "they are held with the fingers and fulfill the function of castagnets for marking the rhythm of the dance." Sachs remarks that small cymbals are quite ancient, appearing as early as before the turn of the first millennium B.C. on reliefs in Nimrud; he feels that the small cymbals have a Central Asian origin, and he mentions the spread of similar metallophones in Mongolia, China, Siam, Annam, and Burma, as well as in Egypt and Morocco in the Near East (Sachs 1929:149–50).

Thus, it is hard to draw a simple conclusion about the origin of the tal, or zang, or tüsak, of northern Afghanistan, which seems to be only one of a great many small cymbal types found throughout large areas of Asia. The widespread use of the term *tal* along with the Persian *zang* and Uzbek *tüsak* may indicate some recent connection with North India. Such a link would probably relate to the eastern (Mašreqi) sector of Afghanistan, where it is common to find odd bits of terminology picked up from the North Indian music world.

The Čang

The čang or čang ko'uz, or sometimes merely ko'uz in Uzbek, is the jew's harp of northern Afghanistan. Of all of the instruments of the North, the čang is the most widely produced in local market centers for the population of the immediate vicinity. As a result, the shape and size of čangs varies from town to town to the extent that one can identify the place of origin by appearance alone.

Figure 4.38 shows čangs from four northern towns, from west to east (left to right): Andxoi, Aqča, Tašqurǧan, and Faizabad. Table 4.10 summarizes the specimens' basic measurements.

From these data it can be seen that the length of the lamella (bent section) is the most uniform dimension of the instrument. In order to be comfortably played, a tongue of 2 centimeters seems to be the proper length for plucking. Another prerequisite seems to be that the handle of the čang be nearly half of the total length of the instrument (čang 1 is a trifle short), a feature also dictated by comfort of playing. As can be seen in Figure 4.38, the narrow wedge-shaped design of the instrument remains constant despite variation in size.

The most remarkable difference among the four instruments pictured is the elaborate handle of the čang from Aqča. Although the proportion of handle to body is standard, the Aqča model flares out

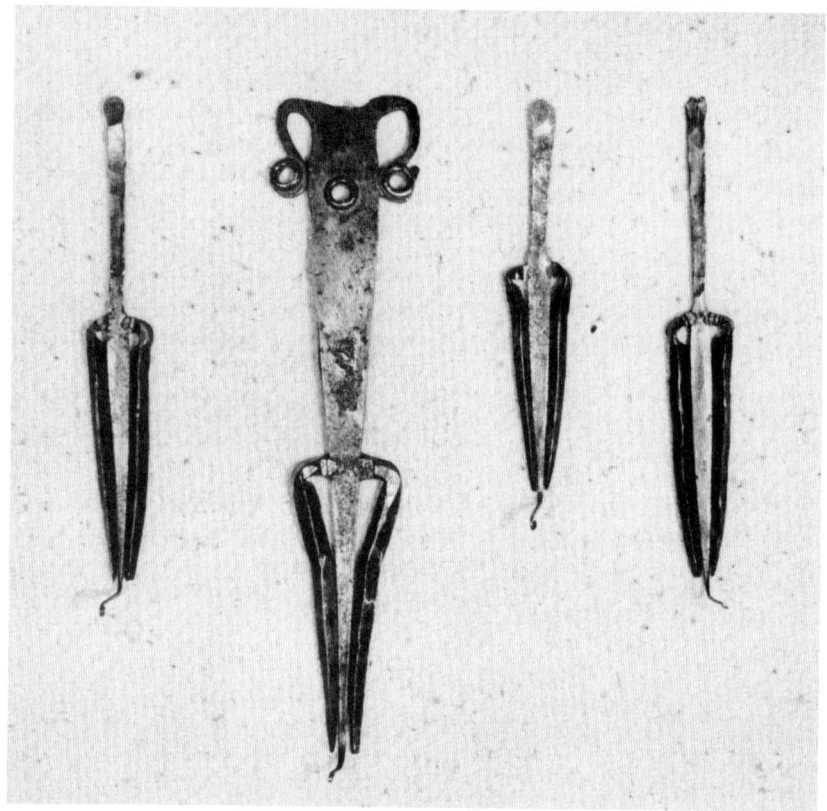

Carol Reck

Fig. 4.38. Čangs from four northern towns (left to right):
Andxoi, Aqča, Tašqurğan, Faizabad

TABLE 4.10

Dimensions of Selected Čangs
(In Centimeters)

Instrument	Place of Origin	Length of Handle	Length of Lamella (Bent Section Only)	Overall Length
1	Andxoi	4.7	1.7	10.5
2	Aqča	8	2	15
3	Tašqurğan	3	2	8
4	Faizabad	5.5	2	11.5

widely towards the top, where an ornamental scroll, resembling the horns of a goat, tops the bulky instrument. Čangs from the town of Saripul, south of Šibergǎn, display the same shape as those from Aqčâ.

Čangs are made in the local bazaar by the ironsmith and are displayed among nails, hooks, and harnesses. They may also be sold in the banjara, or mixed-goods shops. In the North, only the modern towns like Kunduz make no local čangs, but instead import them from Kabul, a practice characteristic of such towns (see Chapter 2).

Figure 4.39 shows the normal playing position of the čang — in this case, a Faizabad specimen. The instrument is braced against the teeth, with the teeth slightly parted to allow motion of the lamella. Movements of the lips make possible some change of pitch. In the case of small instruments, like those of Tašqurgǎn, the instrument is nearly obscured by the performer's hands and lips during play.

The čang, according to all informants, is played mainly by women and children, but I have never seen it played by women and children. The only use of the čang I have witnessed is as an accompanying drone instrument in ensemble performance. A dambura and drum, or dambura and ǧičak, may be joined by a čang, which punctuates every main beat

Fig. 4.39. Playing position for čang

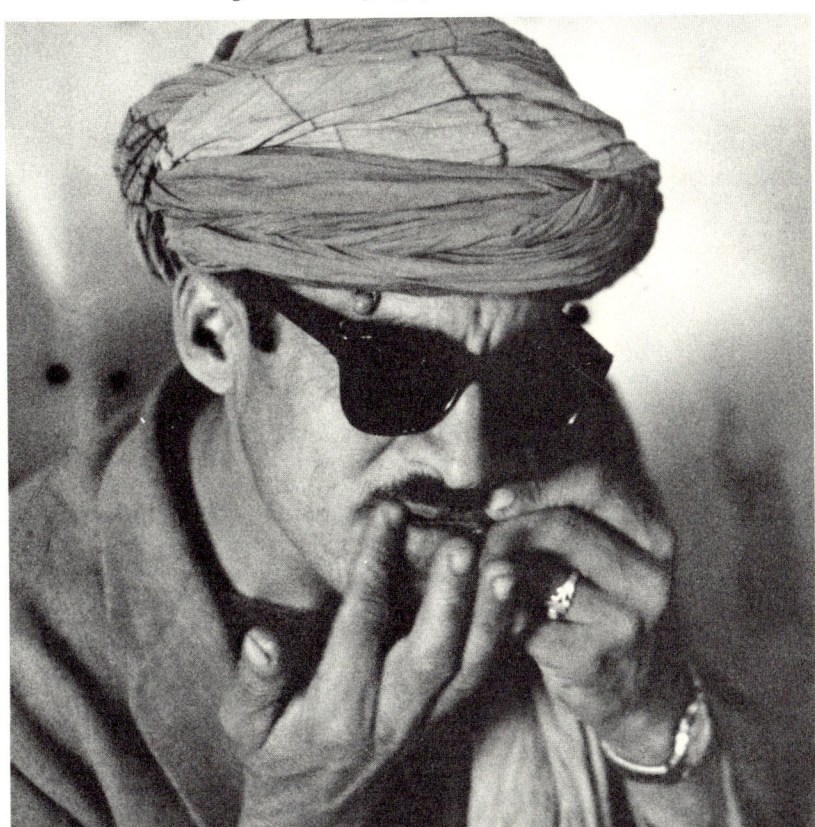

with the same pitch from beginning to end of a piece. Even performers who are esteemed do nothing but provide the drowsy buzz of the čang on the same note throughout.

Čangs are judged by the clarity of their tone. Instruments in which the lamella rubs against the body or which are too small to produce a resonant tone are discarded by players.

The term *čang,* like so many other floating names for instruments in the Near East and Central Asia, does not directly carry over to Uzbekistan, where the instrument of that name is a type of hammered dulcimer related to the Persian santur. In classical Persian verse, the čang was described and pictured as a kind of harp. In Uzbekistan the situation becomes hopelessly complicated by two terms for the jew's harp: *čangkobuz* (pronounced "čangko'uz" by Afghan Uzbeks), in which the Persian word *čang* is coupled with the Turkic *kobuz,* and *temir-čang,* or "iron čang," in which the term *čang* seems ·to take on a more generalized meaning (Vertkov 1963:122). Karomatov (1972:95–101) notes further that a distinction may be made in Uzbekistan between the *temir-čangkobuz* (metal) and the *suiak-čangkobuz* (camel's rib) types of jew's harp. The former is quite similar to the jew's harp of northern Afghanistan, while the latter is not found in Afghanistan. In Kirghizia, where there are both wooden and metal jew's harps (played in virtuoso style), the iron variety is called *temir-komyz (komyz* = *kobuz),* showing *komyz* to be the basic root, since the Kirghiz are beyond the Persian cultural sphere of Central Asia. Full discussion of all of these floating terms is beyond the present study, but just the multiple uses of the term *čang* suffice to show the complexity of the situation. Literally, *čang* means "claw" or "hook" in Persian, and there may be some allusion to the shape of the jew's harp.

Uzbekistani jew's harps, like those across the border, seem largely in the women's domain and are used as accompaniment to certain genres of women's songs. Little of the repertoire has been maintained or transcribed, but judging from the scanty documentation available, Uzbekistani women were able to compose pieces of considerable complexity on the jew's harp, and thus show a link with Kirghiz and Kazakh tradition.

For Tajakistan, Dansker (1965:257) notes that the čang is so closely identified with females that it is often called *čang-i zanāna* ("women's čang"); it is played along with the doira as accompaniment to song and dance on long winter evenings in the women's quarters. He includes a picture of three different shapes for the čang of southern Tajikistan. Of these, one with a long handle comes the closest to the čang of northern Afghanistan but flares out rather more sharply than the Afghan instrument.

The Qairāq

The Qairāq (Figure 4.40) is a set of two matched river stones used as a percussion instrument. It is the only lithophone used in the North and appears to have a highly restricted spread at present. I tracked down only one performer of the qairaq, an older man who had long since given up playing the stones, and convinced him to demonstrate his skill.

His qairaq, which I acquired, is made of the same type of stone used by barbers all across the North as whetstones. They are brownish-grey and measure 12 by 3 centimeters and 12.5 by 3.7 centimeters. During play, the shorter stone, which tapers somewhat, is placed in the right hand between the thumb and forefinger, and the longer stone, somewhat broader, between index finger and middle finger. With a sweep of the left hand, the first joints of the four fingers strike the upper stone against the lower, creating a rapid succession of clicks. Yādgār, the virtuoso qairaq player of Dara-i Zendan (near Samangan), showed great dexterity in manipulating the stones, and would play them on his thigh, forehead, arms, and knee with great speed, provoking great hilarity among the onlookers; he used the qairaq to punctuate a comic ditty he sang without other accompaniment (recorded on Anthology AST 4007). He also used the stones as percussive support

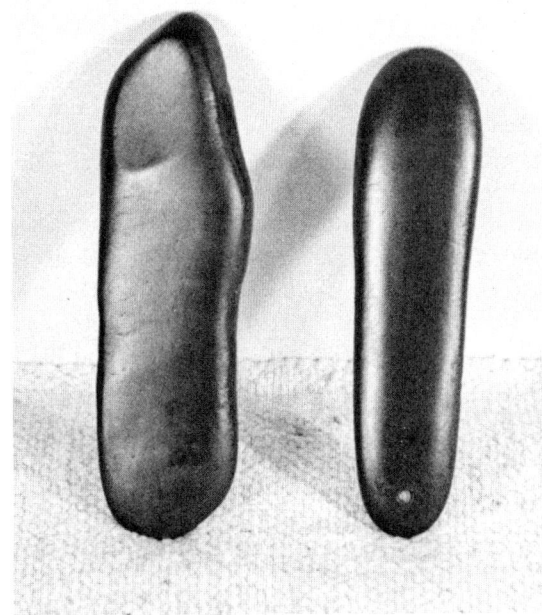

Carol Reck

Fig. 4.40. Qairaq

for a dambura player, but seemed little interested in subordinating his talents for this purpose.

Such an isolated instance of an instrument's occurrence and use would be of little importance, if it were not for the fact that the qairaq is a traditional, widely used instrument of Uzbekistan. Here is part of the entry from the *Atlas* (Vertkov 1963:124):

Qairaq: 120–150 millimeters long and 50–70 millimeters wide . . . they are not specially treated, but found ready-made on the banks of rivers. The performer takes two in each hand and, opening and closing the palms, produces the striking of one plate on the other. Like castanets, the qairaq are used as accompaniment of dance, and different rhythms are struck on them.

From this description we can draw several conclusions. It is clear that the qairaq of Uzbekistan is, on the average, considerably wider than that of Afghanistan, though both types have the same riverine origin and hence lack standardization. The main difference, however, is in use. The Uzbekistani qairaq finds wide currency as a castanet-like companion of the dance, and is held like castanets during play, whereas the Afghan variety is used as percussive accompaniment for song and has a quite different playing position.

Beliaev (1933:4) gives a somewhat broader definition for the term *qairaq* in Uzbekistan:

Qairak: These are four smoothed pebbles, held two in each hand and used to perform rhythmic figures. For this purpose bones, pieces of dry woods, etc., can also be used.

Presumably, the term *qairaq* extends to any sort of castanet-like idiophone, regardless of material of construction. Any sort of hard natural object can be used for this purpose, with little or no treatment necessary to convert it into a musical instrument.

Widespread questioning in Afghanistan yielded little additional information concerning the qairaq. Yadgar himself told me that he learned to play the stones while in India in the 1920s. Since there is such a clear Transoxanian counterpart for the qairaq and no published data on the use of musical stones in India, I find this explanation hard to believe. In addition, the use of what seems to be an Uzbek instrument by a Tajik of a heavily Tajik area only adds to the mystery surrounding the use of the qairaq. Yadgar's great familiarity with the qairaq and his ready coupling of the stones with tunes points to a well-established local style that has fallen into disuse. Without further evidence, we cannot conclusively connect this local style with the qairaq tradition of Uzbekistan.

Glossary of Local Terms

The terms below are defined only in their local context, which may be a variant or extension of meanings given in standard dictionaries of the languages involved. Unless specifically ascribed to a particular language, terms are interethnic and cross-linguistic in usage.

Alaqadari. Smallest unit in the Afghan administrative hierarchy

Armoniā. The harmonium in its Indian form

Bačabāzi. Activity associated with dancing boys

Bāi. A wealthy land and/or livestock owner

Bāijura. An Uzbek secular tale of Afghan Turkestan

Bājaxāna. A municipal police or military band

Baxši. (1) Among Turkmens: honorific title added to the name of a master musician

      (2) In some towns: a shaman (male or female)

      (3) Among Uzbeks of Uzbekistan: a reciter of epic tales

Buniyāt-i Palewān. An interethnic secular tale of Afghan Turkestan

Buzkaši. Afghan and Transoxanian horsemanship contest

Čang (Persian). Jew's harp

Čangkobuz (Uzbekistan). Jew's harp

Čangko'uz (Afghan Uzbek; sometimes merely *ko'uz*). Jew's harp

Cārbaiti. Quatrain song text

Dambura. (1) Long-necked two-stringed fretless lute of Afghan Turkestan

      (2) Similar but smaller lute of Afghan Badaxšan

Damburači. Dambura player

Dili-tüidük. Turkmen single-reed pipe

Doira. Large single-headed frame drum (tambourine)

Dombra, also *dumbura.* Long-necked two-stringed fretless lute of southern Uzbekistan

Dümbra, dömbra. Kazakh long-necked two-stringed fretted lute

Dumbrak. Soviet Tajik name for Badaxšani dambura

Dutar. (1) Large Uzbek long-necked two-stringed fretted lute of Uzbekistan and northern Afghanistan
  (2) Shorter Turkmen lute of same type
  (3) Similar lute-type of Herat and Xorasan (Iran)

Felak. Vocal and instrumental genre of Badaxšan and adjacent regions of Tajikistan

Ġaribi. Lit. poverty; connatation: poor man's work, any work

Ġaribi-šowqi. Music making as part-time or occasional labor

Ġazal. Form of Persian and Uzbek poetry based on couplets; generally urban in provenience

Ġerğeranak. Ratchet; children's toy

Ġičak. (1) Two-stringed fiddle with tin-can resonator of mountain Tajiks, spread to other ethnic groups in Afghanistan
  (2) Four-stringed fiddle with wooden resonator of Uzbekistan and urban Tajiks

Guroğli. Mountain Tajik version of the Turkic Köroğlu epic tale

Ješen. Afghan national holiday, celebrated in late August

Kesp (n.), *kespi* (adj.). Profession, trade, especially manual labor

Komuz. Kirghiz three-stringed fretless lute

Köroğlu. An heroic epic tale widespread among several Turkic peoples

Landai. Paštun folk couplet verse-form

Madā. Religious street singer or street singing

Maqām. Form of classical music of Transoxania, principally of Buxara

Mašreqi. Eastern Afghanistan (Kabul to Khyber Pass)

Mohajer, mohajerin (pl.). Émigré, refugee, usually applied to one who has left the Soviet Union

Nağma. Instrumental tune, usually for dance, of Afghan Turkestan

Nai. Any flute; most often a transverse flute of Pakistani/Indian origin

Na't, na'tiya. Religious song, generally of higher social status than mada

Nowruz. New Year's in the Persian solar calendar (vernal equinox, around March 21)

Qairāq. Stone castanets of Transoxania, rarely found in Afghanistan

Qišlāq. Village

Qobuz. (1) Two-stringed horsehair fiddle of the Kazakhs and Kirghiz
  (2) Fiddle of similar description quite rarely found in certain towns of Turkestan, played only by male shamans

Qošnai. Uzbek paired single-reed aerophone

Robab. (1) Paštun short-necked variably-strung lute, rarely found in northern Afghanistan; called Afghan robab in Tajikistan
  (2) Pamir short-necked six stringed lute of different shape and construction, found only in the Pamir area of Afghanistan and Tajikistan

Samowād. Teahouse (from Russian, "samovar")

Setār. Tajikistani long-necked, fretted multi-stringed lute

Šowq. A hobby or intense preoccupation with a specific type of diversion, including music

Šowqi. (1) A man engrossed by a specific šowq
(2) Specifically, a musician whose vocational or avocational interest in music is not hereditary or occupation-related

Tabla. North Indian paired drum, generally associated with Kabul-Mašreqi music and musicians

Tal. Small finger-cymbals of Turkestan

Tanbur. (1) Long-necked fretted lute, with sympathetic resonating strings, of Afghanistan
(2) Similar lute, without sympathetic resonating strings, of Tajikistan and Uzbekistan

Tüidük. Long Turkmen open end-blown flute

Tüsak (Uzbek). See *tal*

Ustād. (1) A master at any craft or trade; an artisan
(2) One of a small group of Kabul singers associated with court music and with North Indian light classical music

Uzduridan. Turkmen songs specific to one performer

Woleswāli. Medium unit of administration in Afghanistan between alaqadari and province

Xalqi. Turkmen songs of stock rather than individual repertoire with song texts by renowned poets

Zang. See *tal*.

Zang-i kaftar. A group of small round crotals tied on a string and wrapped around a damburači's knuckles to produce accessory jingling during play

Zibājān. An Afghan Uzbek romantic tale

Zirbağali. Single-headed pottery or wooden goblet-shaped drum

Works Cited

Adams, R. McC.
    1969   Conclusion to *Middle Eastern Cities,* ed. I. M. Lapidus. Berkeley and Los Angeles: University of California Press.

Andreev, M. S.
    1953   *Tajiki doliny khuf,* vol. 1. Dushanbe: *Trudy Akademia Nauk Tajikskoi SSR* 7.

Apel, W.
    1961   *Harvard Dictionary of Music.* Cambridge, Mass.: Harvard University Press.

Aslanov, A. B., et al.
    1969   Ethnography of Afghanistan, transl. M. and G. Slobin, in *Afghanistan: Some New Approaches.* Ann Arbor: Center for Near Eastern and North African Studies of the University of Michigan, 11–80.

Avedova, N. A.
    1966   *Iskusstvo oformleniia uzbekskikh muzykal'nykh instrumentov.* Tashkent: Izdatel'stvo khudozhestvennoi literatury.

Babushkin, L. N. (ed.)
    1967   *Uzbekistan.* Moscow: Mysl'.

Barth, F.
    1969   Introduction to *Ethnic Groups and Boundaries,* ed. F. Barth. Boston: Little, Brown and Co., 9–38.
    1969a   Pathan Identity and its Maintenance, in *Ethnic Groups and Boundaries,* ed. F. Barth. Boston: Little, Brown and Co., 117–34.

Bartol 'd, V. V.
    1958   *Turkestan Down to the Mongol Invasion.* 2nd ed. London.

Beliaev, V. M.
    1933   *Muzykal'nye instrumenty uzbekistana.* Moscow: Gosmuziddat.
    1975   *Central Asian Music.* Transl. M. and G. Slobin, ed. M. Slobin. Middletown, Conn.: Wesleyan University Press.

Beliaev, V. M., and Uspenskii, V.
    1928   *Turkmenskaia muzyka.* Moscow: Gosudarstvennoe izdatel'stvo, muzykal'nyi sektor.

Bellew, H.
    1880   *The Races of Afghanistan.* Calcutta: Thacker, Spink & Co.

Berger, M.
1962 *The Arab World Today.* Garden City, N.Y.: Doubleday.
Berry, B.
1967 *Geography of Market Centers and Retail Distribution.* Englewood Cliffs, N. J.: Prentice-Hall.
Bivar, D.
1969 Chapters 1–4 in *Central Asia,* ed. G. Hambly. London: Weidenfeld and Nicolson.
Bregel, Yu.
1959 Etnicheskaia karta iuzhnoi Turkmenii i Khorasana v XVII XVIII vv. *Kratkie soobshchenie instituta etnografii* 31:14-26.
Browne, E. G.
1951 *Literary History of Persia.* Cambridge: University Press.
Bruk, S. I.
1955 Etnicheskii sostav stran perednei azii. *Sovetskaia etnografiia* 2:66–81.
Burnes, A.
1835 Travels into Bokhara. London: John Murray.
Çagatay, B., and Sjoberg, A.
1955 Notes on the Uzbek Culture of Central Asia. *Texas Journal of Science* 7, No. 1:72–112.
Capus, M. G.
1884 La musique chez les Khirgizes et les Sartes de l'Asie Centrale. *Revue d'Ethnographie* 3:97–115.
Centlivres, P.
1970 *Un bazar d'Asie Centrale: forme et organisation du bazar de Tashqurghan (Afghanistan).* Neuchâtel: Faculté des Lettres.
Centlivres, P. and M., and Slobin, M.
1971 A Muslim Shaman of Afghan Turkestan. *Ethnology* 10: 160–73.
Chadwick, N., and Zhirmunsky, V.
1969 *Oral Epics of Central Asia.* Cambridge: University Press.
Chodzko, A.
1842 *Specimens of the Popular Poetry of Persia.* London: Oriental Translation Fund.
Dansker, O.
1965 Muzykal'naia kul'tura tajikov Karategina i Darvaza. *Iskusstvo tajikskogo naroda.* Dushanbe: Donish, 174–264.
Debets, G. F.
1967 Anthropologicheskie issledovaniia v afganistane. *Sovetskaia etnografiia* 4:75–93.

Doerffer, G.
1967 *Türkische Lehnworter in Tadschikischen.* Abhandlungen für die Kunde des Morgenlandes 37:3. Wiesbaden: Deutsche Morgenländische Gesellschaft.

Dupaigne, B.
1968 Aperçus sur quelques techniques afghanes. *Objets et Mondes* 8, No. 1:41–84.

Dupree, L.
1966 *Aq Kupruk: A Town in Northern Afghanistan.* American University Field Service Reports Service (South Asia Series) 10, Nos. 9, 10.

Dupree, N.
1967 *The Road to Balkh.* Kabul: Afghan Tourist Organization.
1971 *An Historical Guide to Afghanistan.* Kabul: Afghan Tourist Organization.

Elphinstone, M.
1839 *An Account of the Kingdom of Caubul.* London: Richard Bentley.

English, P.
1966 *City and Village in Iran.* Madison, Wisc.: University of Wisconsin Press.

Farmer, H. G.
1957 The Music of Islam, in *The New Oxford History of Music,* ed. E. Wellesz, vol. 1. London: Oxford University Press, 421–77.

Ferdinand, K.
1962 Nomad Expansion and Commerce in Central Afghanistan. *Folk* 4:123–59.

Ferrier, J. P.
1860 *Voyages en Perse dans l'Afghanistan, le Beloutchistan et le Turkestan.* Paris: E. Dentu.

Foster, G.
1967 *Tzintzuntzan: Mexican Peasants in a Changing World.* Boston: Little, Brown and Co.

Frye, R. N.
1965 *Bokhara: The Medieval Achievement.* Norman, Okla.: University of Oklahoma Press.

Hahn, H.
1964-65 *Die Stadt Kabul (Afghanistan) und Ihr Umland.* Bonn: F. Dummler's Verlag. Bonner geographischer Abhandlungen 34, 35.

Hambly, G. (ed.)
1969 *Central Asia.* London: Weidenfeld and Nicolson.

Hitti, P.
1963 *History of the Arabs.* 8th ed. London: Macmillan.
Hoerburger, F.
1969 *Volksmusik in Afghanistan.* Regensburg: Gustav Bosse.
Huart, M. Cl.
1922 La Musique Persane, in *Encyclopedie de la Musique,* ed.
A. Lavignac. Paris: Librairie Delagrave.
Hudson, A., and Bacon, E.
1941 Social Control and the Individual in Eastern Hazara Culture, in *Language, Culture, and Personality,* ed. L. Spier
et al. Menasha, Wis.: Sapir Memorial Publication Fund,
239–58.
Izikowitz, K.
1969 Neighbours in Laos, in *Ethnic Groups and Boundaries,* ed.
F. Barth. Boston: Little, Brown and Co., 135–48.
Jarring, G.
1938 *Uzbek Texts from Afghan Turkestan.* Lunds Universitets
Arsskrift N. F. Avd. 1, Bd. 34, Nr. 2. Lund: C. W. K.
Gleerup.
1939 An Uzbek's View of His Native Town and Its Circumstances. *Ethnos* 4, No. 1:73–80.
1939a *On the Distribution of Turk Tribes in Afghanistan.* Lunds
Universitets Arsskrift N. F. Avd. 1, Bd. 35, Nr. 4. Lund:
C. W. Gleerup.
Jung, C.
1971 Some Observations on the Patterns and Processes of Rural-
Urban Migrations to Kabul. The Afghanistan Council of
the Asia Society: *Occasional Paper No. 2.*
Kadyrov, N.
1969 Ritual Folklore of Tajiks of South Uzbekistan. In *Reports
of the 7th International Congress of Anthropological and
Ethnological Sciences,* vol. 6. Moscow: Nauka, 290–96.
Karmysheva, B. Kh.
1960 Etnicheskie i territorial'nye gruppy naseleniia severovos-
tochnoi chasti kashka-dar'inskoi oblasti uzbekskoi SSR.
Kratkie soobschenie instituti etnografii 33:47–59.
1960a Ethnograficheskaia gruppa 'turk' v sostave uzbekov. *Sovetskaia etnografiia* 1:3–22.
1960b Ob uzbekskikh trudovykh kres'tianskikh pesniakh. *Pamiati
Mikhaila Stepanovich Andreeva.* Dushanbe: *Trudy Aka-
demia Nauk Tajikskoi SSR* 120.
1964 K istorii formirovaniia naseleniia iuzhnykh raionov Uzbek-
istana i Tajikistana. Sovetskaia etnografiia 6:95–102.
Karomatov, F.
1962 *Uzbekskaia dombrovaia muzyka.* Tashkent: Gosudarstven-
noe izdatel'stvo khudozhestvennoi literatury.

1972   *Uzbekskaia instrumental'naia muzyka.* Tashkent: Izdatel'-
        stvo literatury i iskusstva im. Gafura Guliama.
1972a   On the Regional Styles of Uzbek Music. *Asian Music* 4,
        no. 1: 48–58.
Karryev, B. A.
1968   *Epicheskie skazaniia o Ker-ogly u tiurko-iazychnykh naro-
        dov.* Moscow: Glavnaia redaktsiia vostochnoi literatury.
Khanikoff, N.
1845   *Bokhara: Its Amir and Its People,* transl. Baron C. de
        Bode. London: James Madden.
Kisliakov, N. A.
1960   Nekotorye materialy po etnografii tajikov verkhovii Kash-
        ka-dar'i. *Pamiati Mikhaila Stepanovich Andreeva.* Dush-
        anbe: *Trudy Akademia Nauk Tajikskoi SSR* 120:77–90.
Kisliakov, N. A., and A. P. Pisarchik
1966   *Tajiki Karategina i Darvaza,* vol. 1. Dushanbe: Donish.
Kushkeki, B.
1926   *Kattagan i Badakhshan,* ed. A. A. Semenov. Tashkent:
        Obshchestvo dlia izucheniia Tajikistana i iranskikh narod-
        nostei za ego predelei.
Lazard, G.
1956   Caractères distinctives de la langue Tadjik. *Bulletin de la
        Société de la Linguistique de Paris* 52:117–86.
Lebedinskii, L. N.
1964   *Bashirkskie narodnye pesni i naigryshi.* Moscow: Muzyka.
LeStrange, G.
1905   *Lands of the Eastern Caliphate.* Cambridge: University
        Press.
Lewis, I. M.
1971   *Ecstatic Religion.* Middlesex, England: Penguin Books.
Listopadov, A. M.
1953   *Pesni donskikh kazakov,* vol. 1. Moscow: Muzgiz.
Lomax, A.
1966   *Folk Song Style and Culture.* American Association for the
        Advancement of Science Publication No. 88. Washington,
        D.C.
Lord, A.
1960   *The Singer of Tales.* Cambridge, Mass.: Harvard University
        Press.
Lubtschansky, J. C. and S.
1969   Record notes for *Afghanistan and Iran,* disques Vogue
        LVLX 191.
Maksimov, S. M.
1964   *Chuvashskie narodnye pesni.* Moscow: Muzyka.
Mamedbekov, D.
1965   *Azerbaijanskie narodnye liricheskie pesni.* Moscow: Mu-
        zyka.

288

Masal'ski, V. I.
1908   *Turkestanskii krai.* Rossiia: Polnoe Geograficheskoi opi-
       saniie nashego otechestva, vol. 19, ed. P. P. Semenov-
       Tian'-Shanskii and V. L. Lamanskii.
Menges, K.
1967   Peoples, Languages and Migrations, in *Central Asia: A
       Century of Russian Rule,* ed. E. Allworth. New York:
       Columbia University Press, 60–91.
1968   *The Turkic Languages and Peoples.* Ural-altaische Biblio-
       thek, vol. 15. Wiesbaden: Harrasowitz.
Mikesell, M. W.
1958   The Role of Tribal Markets in Morocco. *Geographical
       Review* 48:494–511.
Morgenstierne, G.
1938   *Indo-Iranian Frontier Languages.* Vol. 2, *Iranian Pamir
       Languages.* Oslo: H. Aschehoug & Co.
Nemenova, R. L.
1953   Prevaritel'nyi otchet o rabote vo vremia garmskoi etno-
       graficheskoi ekspeditisii 1952g. *Doklady Akademia Nauk
       Tajikskoi SSR* 9:58–64.
Nurjanov, N.
1956   *Tajikskii narodnyi teatr.* Moscow: Izdatel'stvo ANSSSR.
1965   Razvlecheniia i narodnyi teatr tajikov karategina i darvaza,
       in *Iskusstvo tajiksogo naroda.* Dushanbe: Donish, 113–52.
Radloff, W.
1885   *Proben der Volksliteratur der nördlichen türkischen
       Stämme.* St. Petersburg.
Rakhimov, M.
1960   Nekotorye obychai i obriady, sviazannye so skotovodstvom
       u tajikov Karagegina i Darvaza. *Pamiati Mikhaila Stepano-
       vich Andreeva.* Dushanbe: *Trudy Akademia Nauk Tajiks-
       koi SRR* 120:181–87.
Rastorgueva, V. S.
1964   *Opyt sravnitel'nogo izucheniia tajikskikh govorov.* Moscow:
       Nauka.
Rejepov, S.
1966   *Sakhi Jepbarov.* Moscow: Muzyka.
Romanovskaia, E. E.
1959   *Staty i doklady.* Tashkent: Gosudsarstvennoe izdatel'stvo
       khudozhestvennoi literatury.
Sachs, C.
1929   *Geist und Werden der Musikinstrumente.* Berlin: D.
       Reimer.
1940   *The History of Musical Instruments.* New York: Norton.

Sakata, H. L.
1968 *Music of the Hazarajat*. M.A. thesis, University of Washington, Seattle.
1971 Record notes for *Folk Music of Afghanistan*, Lyrichord Records LLST 7230/31.
Samoilovich, L.
1914 Pesni krymskikh tatar pro vtoriu otechestvenniu voinu. *Zhivaia starina* 23:409–20.
Schafer, E. H.
1964 *The Golden Peaches of Samarkand*. Berkeley and Los Angeles: University of California Press.
Schultz, A. V.
1914 *Die Pamirtadschik*. Veröffentlichungen des Oberhessischen Museums und der Gail'schen Sammlungen zu Giessen, 1. Heft. Giessen: Topelmann.
Schurmann, H. F.
1961 *The Mongols of Afghanistan*. The Hague: Mouton.
Schuyler, E.
1877 *Turkistan*. New York: Scribner, Armstrong & Co.
Shpoon, S.
1968 Paxto folklore and the landey. *Afghanistan* 20, No. 4:40–50.
Skinner, G. W.
1964 Marketing and Social Structure in Rural China. *Journal of Asian Studies* 34.
Slobin, M.
1969 *Instrumental Music in Northern Afghanistan*. Ann Arbor: University Microfilms.
1970 Persian Folksong Texts from Afghan Badakhshan. *Iranian Studies* 3, No. 2:91–103.
In Buz-bāzi. A Musical Marionette of Northern Afghanistan.
press *Perspectives on Asian Music* (Asian Music VI, 1–2).
Snesarev, G. P.
1971 K voprosu o proiskhozhdenii prazdnestva sunnat-toi v ego sredneaziatskom variante. *Trudy instituta etnografii* 97: 256–73.
Steingass, F.
1970 *A Comprehensive Persian-English Dictionary* (orig. ed. 1892). Beirut: Librairie du Liban.
Sukhareva, O. A.
1966 *Bukhara XIX-nachalo XXv*. Moscow: Nauka.
Tilavov, B.
1964 *Poetika tajikskikh narodnykh poslovits i pogovorok*. Dushanbe: Donish.

Troitskaia, A. L.
    1971   Nekotorye starinnye obychai, obriady i pover'ia tajikov doliny Verkhnego Zeravshana. *Trudy instituta etnografii* 97:224–55.

Vambery, A.
    1970   *Travels in Central Asia* (orig. ed. 1865). New York: Praeger.

Veksler, S. M.
    1965   *Ocherk istorii uzbekskoi muzykal'noi kul'tury.* Tashkent: Uchitel'.

Vertkov, K., et al.
    1963   *Atlas muzykal'nykh instrumentov narodov SSSR.* Moscow: Gosmuzizdat.

Wood, J.
    1872   *A Journey to the Source of the River Oxus* (1st ed. 1839). London: John Murray.

Yate, C.
    1888   *Northern Afghanistan.* London: William Blackwood & Sons.

Index

General Index

Abdul Nazar, 142
Abdullah Buz-baz, 142, 218
Abdul Mazari, 147, 150, 161
Abdurrahman, 15, 18, 44
Adams, R., 126
Adinabeg, 204-8
Āğā Mohamad, 148
Aimaq (ethnic group), 16, 218
Aimaq, Faizullah, 52, 105, 109, 110, 120
Akbar, 150
Alexander the Great, 71, 256,
Ali, 59, 62, 65, 111, 144, 145, 177, 234, 265
"Alpaqadar tular," 171-3
Amanullah, 34, 45, 50, 63
Ana Durdi, 203
Andreev, M. S., 21, 122
Apel, W., 169
Āq Pišak, 39, 41, 51, 82, 120, 138-9, 141, 169, 180-85
"Aqčai," 180-85
Arabs (of Afghanistan), 7, 16, 44, 66
Aslanov, A. B., 10, 12
"Astā bero," 175-6
Avedova, N. A., 216, 217
Axmad-baxši, 25, 101, 102, 103, 139, 186-99, 230, 232

Bābā Ilbām, 209
Bābā Naim, 57, 88, 91, 164, 178, 205, 246
Bābā Qerān, 41, 42, 142, 143, 168, 169-71
Babur, 73
Babushkin, L. N., 75, 77
"Bāijura," 109, 112-16
"Baiqara," 191
Baluch, 20, 52, 98, 254

Bangeča Tašqurğani, 35, 42, 82, 105, 119, 142, 143, 161, 167, 168, 173-4, 212
Barbers, barber-musicians, 27, 31-3, 35, 48, 49, 50, 52
Barth, F., 1, 2, 60, 89, 90, 91-2
Basmači rebellion, 12
Bāz Gul Badaxši, 40, 42, 120, 143
Beliaev, V. M., 38, 203, 243, 250-51, 278; and Uspenskii, V., 95, 186, 194, 233-5, 253, 254, 256, 260
Bellew, H., 7
Berger, M., 89
Berry, B., 128
Bregel, Yu., 96
Bulbul, 142
"Buniāt-i palewān," 61-4
Burnes, A., 78, 131, 137, 144

Çagatay, B. See Sarafi, B.
Cağatai, incl. Cağatai Uzbeks, Cağatai Tajiks, 11, 77
Canfield, R., 79
Capus, R., 122, 242
Carpet-weaving, 14, 109, 151
Centlivres, P., 9, 31, 32, 40, 82, 84, 85, 125, 127, 128, 133, 134, 137, 143
Chadwick, N. and Zhirmunsky, V., 98, 100, 101, 102, 116
Circumcision celebrations, 29, 119

Dance, 27, 30, 45, 57, 59, 65, 97, 98, 107, 110, 116-20, 122, 139, 145, 161-2, 180-82, 264, 265. See also Dancing boys
Dancing boys, 23, 26, 27, 56, 116-20, 180, 240
Dansker, O., 80, 81, 88, 221-4, 248, 267, 276

[291]

Index of Geographical Terms

Index of Musical Instruments